P9-DWU-478

Adult Learning

Adult Learning
Psychological Research and Applications

Edited by

Michael J. A. Howe

Department of Psychology,
University of Exeter

JOHN WILEY & SONS

Chichester · New York · Brisbane · Toronto

Library of Congress Cataloging in Publication Data:

Main entry under title:

Adult learning.

   Includes indexes.
   1. Adult education.   2. Learning, psychology of.
I. Howe, Michael J. A., 1940–
LC5215.A35   374   76-44226

ISBN 0 471 99458 8

Photosetting by Thomson Press (India) Limited, New Delhi
and printed in Great Britain at The Pitman Press Ltd., Bath, Avon.

CONTRIBUTORS

E. SHEILA HARRI-AUGSTEIN *Deputy Director, Centre for the Study of Human Learning, Brunel University*

DONALD M. BLIGH *Director, Teaching Services Centre, University of Exeter*

PETER BURNHILL *Head, Department of Design, Stafford College of Further Education*

IVOR K. DAVIES *Professor, The Audio-Visual Centre, Indiana University*

JAMES HARTLEY *Senior Lecturer, Department of Psychology, Keele University*

MICHAEL J. A. HOWE *Senior Lecturer, Department of Psychology, University of Exeter*

HARRY KAY *Vice-Chancellor, University of Exeter*

PAUL KLINE *Reader in Psychometrics, Department of Psychology, University of Exeter*

PETER MORRIS *Lecturer, Department of Psychology, University of Lancaster*

JAMES T. REASON *Professor, Department of Psychology, University of Manchester*

J. MIKE SMITH *Lecturer, Department of Management Sciences, University of Manchester Institute of Science and Technology*

v

KENNETH T. STRONGMAN   *Senior Lecturer, Department of Psychology, University of Exeter*

FITZ J. TAYLOR   *Professor and Dean of Education, Bayero University College, Kano, Nigeria*

LAURIE F. THOMAS   *Director, Centre for the Study of Human Learning, Brunel University*

ACKNOWLEDGEMENTS

The Editor gratefully acknowledges the assistance of the following publishers who have granted permission for the reproduction of extracted material quoted in the text. Sources are given in the References section at the end of each chapter.

The American Association for the Advancement of Science
The British Journal of Medical Psychology
The British Psychological Society
Cambridge University Press Limited, London
The Controller of Her Majesty's Stationery Office
Harcourt Brace Jovanovich Inc., New York
Hodder and Stoughton Limited, London

CONTENTS

GENERAL INTRODUCTION

Most of the things people do contain a substantial learned element. Not only are human actions and habits largely the outcome of learning, but thoughts, beliefs, attitudes and prejudices—the worlds which all of us construct for ourselves—are utterly dependent upon man's ability to learn. Human experience is the prerogative of a species which is effectively equipped to learn throughout the course of life.

It is hardly surprising that we should have become interested in the possibility of scientifically investigating learning processes. Although the application of methods and procedures borrowed from established physical sciences to the investigation of mental processes underlying human psychology is a comparatively recent development, intense interest in a variety of psychological phenomena, including human learning, is apparent in the writing of thinkers from all historical periods. Certainly, human learning receives a good deal of attention in that strong tradition of Western philosophy which has roots in the contributions of Plato and Aristotle. Furthermore, there has emerged a more recent branch of the historical tradition in which intellectual curiosity about learning is combined with the explicit desire to make practical contributions to education and training. Such a combination can be seen in the works of J. J. Rousseau, educational innovators including Froebel, and some recent writers, notably John Dewey.

The fact that learning has engaged long-standing interest among philosophers and thinkers and the awareness that it is a matter of daily concern and interest in many aspects of human life have contributed to the general availability of a certain amount of knowledge about learning, at least at a relatively superficial level. Partly for this reason, psychologists introducing experimental methods of investigation have not had to approach the study of human learning as a kind of *terra incognita*—as has been the case for some contemporary scientific enterprises, for example for modern research into cancer. We know a good deal about human learning before embarking upon experimental investigations. When James Mill wanted to make his young son into a man of prodigious intellectual abilities he was able to do so with great success in many respects, despite the absence at that time of any understanding of learning based upon systematic scientific enquiry into the nature of learning processes.

Concern about learning in adults, although no new phenomenon, has become noticeably sharper in recent years. Among the factors contributing to increasing interest are the accelerating need for major vocational changes within an individual's working life, and awareness of the likely necessity for radical alterations in lifestyle as existing forms of energy are found to be rapidly exhaustible. But the existence of pressures for change by no means guarantees that serious efforts will be made to cope with the problems of learning that such changes bring. The major traumas experienced in Britain at the onset of the Industrial Revolution did not evoke a response in the form of a whole-hearted attempt to provide facilities for the kind of education that would equip ordinary people to deal with life in an industrial society until the Education Act of 1870, by which time improved provisions for elementary education were long overdue.

THE SCOPE OF THE BOOK

This book brings together the contributions of a number of psychologists who have been engaged in undertaking or applying research into adult human learning. Learning takes numerous and varied forms, and the topics covered in the present volume are fittingly diverse. For better or worse, researchers enquiring into the differing kinds of learning have proceeded with considerable independence, and whilst most of the scientists investigating human learning clearly share some common methods and approaches, and some assumptions about the way in which learning processes should be conceived, variations and discrepancies between the approaches of individual investigators are large and perhaps more striking. For this reason it is not possible to provide a closely integrated series of separate contributions that satisfactorily 'covers' modern knowledge about adult learning. The field is too broad and too uneven for such coverage to be provided in a collection of articles by leading contributors. The function of relating and integrating elements yielded by researchers who have addressed themselves to a diversity of problems and who have approached their tasks with a range of different guiding principles, theoretical conceptions and rules of procedure could be accomplished more adequately in a single-authored text.

In the present book the procedure has been to ask major contributors to research in each of a number of separate areas within the general field of human learning to write about their area of concern. Broadly speaking, each chapter stands on its own. Through the organization of the book into parts, and through brief introductions to each section, I have attempted to introduce a degree of coherence, if not cohesiveness.

The various chapters have been chosen to give readers concerned about adult learning a clear indication both of the kinds of research activities that have been pursued in recent years and the findings that have emerged. Two particular considerations have influenced the choice of topics. First, I have given some emphasis to areas in which the outcomes of research activities can be regarded as broadly practical, insofar that applications to immediate practical problems of learning encountered in real life can either be made directly or are clearly foreseeable. This emphasis has inevitably led to the exclusion of some research developments which may in the future prove to be of immense value for our attempts to understand more fully how we learn. For instance, among the potentially valuable topics so excluded are a number of modern developments in psycholinguistics and semantic memory. Research currently proceeding in those fields may eventually help us understand how knowledge is represented in human cognitive systems. Thus, in arranging the contents of this book areas of research have been given greater priority if it is apparent that the findings are 'usable' through adding practical knowledge as well as offering the possibility of deepened understanding.

Secondly, I have avoided concentrating on those kinds of learning which are considered 'educational' in the usual sense. Many forms of learning which are given little or no attention in educational institutions have a vital role in adult life. Indeed, many psychologists would claim that a range of phonemena very far removed from the customary concerns of educators, including some types of 'mental illness', are best conceived as instances of social learning, albeit maladaptive. Be that as it may, it is undeniably important to know about learning which normally occurs in everyday life, away from schools and colleges. Hence a number of the chapters in this book examine aspects of learning which usually receive scant regard in establishments undertaking education and training roles. However, it would be absurd to exclude educational problems from a collection of contributions to knowledge of adult learning, and several of the chapters are devoted to educational issues.

The reader will find in this volume a series of chapter-length articles that describe recent research into human learning and its applications to a broad sample of the numerous forms and aspects of learning that are encountered in adult life. He will not find here a comprehensive general overview of research into human learning.

DEFINING LEARNING

We need to be as precise as is possible about our meanings of the term 'learning', but the concept is not easily defined. Undoubtedly, each instance of learning involves some form of modification and, generally speaking, the change can be regarded as helping the learner adapt to circumstances of his life, granted that some learned changes may appear to be inappropriate or restrictive, as in the case of the acquisition of some repetitive forms of behaviour such as ritual handwashing.

If it can be agreed that learning involves change, it remains to be asked, change in what? Can we define learning as changes in behaviour? Learning may certainly involve or bring about behavioural changes, but to state that the change in behaviour *is* the learning brings problems. In addition to the fact that by no means all changes in behaviour constitute evidence for learning, it is quite possible that learning may take place in an individual in the absence of any change in his behaviour. For example, an adult may learn something through watching another person's actions and observing the consequences. The fact that the observer's behaviour does not change at the time clearly cannot be said to prove that no learning has occurred.

Changes in behaviour do often provide admirably clear evidence that something has been learned, but the behavioural change is something done *by* the learner. Behaviour is fleeting and ephemeral by nature; it is undeniably produced by the learner, but it is not part of the learner. It seems most apt to identify learning as being change *in* the learner, granted that the evidence for such learning may customarily take the form of behavioural change.

Pursuing this line does involve problems. In practice, it is not generally possible to obtain objective and reliable identification of learned changes in a person without relying on some kind of behavioural evidence. Indeed, in research on learning in subhuman species there may be no feasible alternative to a complete acceptance of an operational definition by which learning is identified with behavioural change. Trying to acquire proof of learning in the absence of behavioural evidence is rather like attempting to assess the quality of a gramophone record without listening to it. In theory, inspection of the physical structure of a record should be informative, but in effect we find it necessary to use the sounds a record produces when played as the major criterion of quality. The sound is not, however, an identifiable part of the record. Similarly, the behaviour that a learner produces is, strictly speaking, the outcome of learning but not the learning itself. Yet we find it necessary to rely on observations of behaviour, as they may provide the sole convenient indication of what has been learned.

The issue has been clouded by the broader debate about behaviourism, involving questions about the status of behaviour in the science of psychology. Confusion has been caused by the failure to distinguish adequately between the process of learning in individual people and the behaviour which forms a basis for inferences that learning has taken place. The strongly behaviourist tradition in twentieth-century psychology, whereby there is a tendency to regard observable behaviour as the sole permissible data for a science of psychology, has led to conceptualizations from which it is not difficult to appreciate how definitions of the form 'Learning is a change in behaviour ...' have come about. Now that psychology has largely left behind the grosser restricting assumptions of radical behaviourism, there is a clear necessity to make an explicit distinction between characteristics of the individual in whom learning takes place and the changes in behaviour that may illuminate such learning but which in no real sense can be said to *be* human learning.

INDIVIDUAL DIFFERENCES

Individuals differ enormously in their ability to learn. In fact, differences between individuals in the skills and capacities they possess are often so striking and apparently fundamental in nature that it is easy to forget that most elements of such capacities actually do have to be acquired through learning, there being no real short cuts. Thus, when we discover that Sir Richard Burton had a good knowledge of around 40 languages, including dialects, we might be forgiven for assuming that the processes of foreign-language acquisition must have been in some respects fundamentally different for Burton than for the rest of us. Yet the fact of the matter is that each one of those languages had to be carefully acquired through lengthy and arduous sessions on Burton's part. Separate languages do have aspects in common, and there are some acquired skills that have broad applicability to the acquisition of languages in general, but there are no magical formulae. In reading Burton's accounts of the manner in which he went about learning each new language we are struck by the absence of unusual or exotic methods. He undoubtedly showed unusual energy and determination, and he frequently and regularly devoted large amounts of time to systematic and repetitive practice and drills, but there was nothing unique about his techniques and learning strategies. He quite simply applied more time, more energy, more determination and more concentrated effort to acquiring foreign languages than most of us would be able or willing to do. Sir Richard Burton was highly methodical, but not in any particularly unusual way.

Could it be that Burton's superior ability to learn languages depended on hereditary factors? It is quite possible that this was so, but we must nevertheless appreciate the fact that one individual's being hereditarily better equipped than another for acquiring certain abilities does not bypass the need for learning. To acquire a foreign language, roughly the same things have to be learned, whoever is doing the learning. Furthermore, the knowledge that hereditary factors may underlie differences in human capacities does not in itself explain how the hereditary processes exert their influence. To return to Burton, it is conceivable that he may have possessed a superior learning ability that was directly based upon hereditary factors. Alternatively (or perhaps additionally), hereditary influences might have been involved in a combination of those aspects of Burton's personality and temperament that affected his action. Some of the dynamic factors contributing to his great powers of determination or to his unusually high motivation to learn foreign languages may have rested upon a genetic component.

Although systematic differences between people in a range of learned abilities are easy to demonstrate, the investigation of individual differences in learning is beset with serious difficulties. A major problem is that only rarely is it possible to equate differences in the observed capacities with any simple learning process. A variety of additional factors contribute to measured performance in most learning situations. For instance, motivational influences, attentional variables, listening and reading ability, perseverance, fatigue, and, perhaps most important, previous learning may each contribute to determining level of performance on tasks ostensibly designed to assess ability to learn. Thus the superior performance of one individual over another on a task purporting to assess learning ability may be due in part to a difference in the availability of prerequisite skills which affect ease of learning in the new task, or to any of a number of other factors.

What is needed is a test which measures new learning alone, is not influenced by what the individual has learned previously, and permits adequate control of the additional variables customarily found to influence performance. To devise such a task is extremely difficult, if not impossible. The circumstances in which psychologists come closest to meeting these requirements involve simple forms of classical conditioning. Comparisons of classical conditioning by groups of individuals appearing to differ considerably in ability to learn, such as 'normal' and 'mentally retarded' groups under conditions allowing close control of extraneous variables, have generally yielded no major differences in rate of conditioning. Failure to find differences in classical conditioning certainly does not amount to proof that no individual differences in basic learning processes exist, and there may well be such differences, although it has not yet proved possible to locate them.

Conceivably, analysis at a physiological level may lead to the detection of process differences underlying inter-individual variability in ability to learn. E. L. Thorndike suggested in the 1930's that learning capacity may be related to the number of neural connections available for the formation of new associations, and there has been no shortage of alternative explanations in which ease of learning is regarded as being related to aspects of nerve impulse transmission along neural networks. However, plausible though accounts of this kind may appear, firm evidence has yet to be obtained concerning the possible contribution of such processes to individual variability in learning.

As the contents of the following chapters demonstrate, some marked changes can be detected in approaches to human learning within the past few decades. There are no attempts to produce grand all-inclusive theories of learning comparable in breadth to those advanced during the early part of this century. Significantly, however, recent years have witnessed widespread acceptance of the view that it is both necessary and scientifically acceptable to give attention to hypothesized mental processes underlying human activities. This has encouraged awareness that the adult human learner is a highly active and relatively autonomous being who makes plans and decisions, who organizes his experience, and is very far from being the passive recipient of environmental influences that earlier ideologies tended to suggest. The activities of an independent and largely selfregulating species cannot be simple to predict or easy to understand and control, but there is some reassurance to be gained from the knowledge that the human learner studied in contemporary psychology begins to bear a decent resemblance to the genuine human individual in all his complexity, rather than being a highly simplified and distorted conception of man as a a mere automaton.

For convenience, the book is divided into three parts. The chapters in Part One concern kinds of learning that occur in the day-to-day lives of people in all civilized societies. Part Two covers varieties of learning that contribute to the acquisition of knowledge. Learning in these forms normally involves reading, and is always dependent upon language and verbal skills. The chapters in the third section, Part Three, consider some of the special circumstances and the special problems necessitating learning and change that life in modern societies presents. In general, these final chapters deal with research into the acquisition of learned abilities which are markedly different from any needed by the human species until comparatively recently.

MICHAEL HOWE
University of Exeter

PART ONE

HUMAN LEARNING IN ADULT LIFE

INTRODUCTION TO PART ONE

Part One contains five chapters, each of which is concerned with the acquisition of abilities or attributes that influence individuals in many aspects of human life. Harry Kay, in Chapter 1, Learning and Society, considers in detail a number of ways in which the evolution and the continued existence of man have depended upon his advanced and specialized learning abilities. Kay suggests that the coming of civilization has increased the demands upon man to adapt and change himself, and that the accelerating rate of change encountered in contemporary societies may press human adaptive capacities to their limits. In a closely reasoned series of arguments he shows that extensive knowledge about the characteristics of man as a learner is essential if we are to deal with the increasing and changing needs for continuous learning that today's world imposes.

Chapter 2, Skill and Error in Everyday Life, by James Reason, describes human motor abilities and habits, the things we actually do. Reason discusses the nature of skilled behaviour in man, noting that common everyday activities often require highly complex and coordinated sequences of organized parts, and he examines ways of describing and analysing such activities. He shows that automatic skilled actions which are undertaken largely without awareness generally only become automatic following a lengthy period of learning, during which deliberate verbal and perceptual control may be necessary. Reason develops a model for skilled performance which, as he demonstrates, makes it possible to understand and to classify a number of the errors that are encountered in skilled performance and in the 'absent-minded' mistakes of daily life.

Whereas Reason's chapter examines the acquisition of habits and abilities in which physical movement is crucial, Kenneth Strongman in the following chapter, Learning Social Skills (Chapter 3), considers abilities underlying social behaviour and social interaction. As Strongman points out, social interaction, in addition to being dependent upon learning, does itself constitute a kind of experience to the participants which may produce change in the individuals concerned. Socialization occurs in adults as well as children, and the high frequency of social incompetence in adults, and of circumstances where maladaptive social learning contributes to inadequacy or to inability

3

to cope with essential aspects of personal life, indicate that many individuals, lacking appropriate social skills and social habits, are in need of further adult socialization. The chapter considers alternative conceptions of socialization and the contributions of learning to a number of its facets. It discusses the acquisition of roles, conceptions of the 'self', attitudes and social judgments, as well as the behaviours adopted when people interact with others. The learning which enters into social skills also helps determine the personality of the individual, and Chapter 4 by Paul Kline examines Personality and Learning. Kline gives a detailed description of one approach to personality as it affects and is influenced by adult learning. This approach, developed by R. B. Cattell, relies heavily upon factor analysis, by means of which a large number of traits are shown to contribute to personality. The interdependence of personality variables and learning is illustrated in Cattel's 'structured learning theory', which considers learned changes from the viewpoint of measurable structures of ability, temperament and motivation. Individual change and personal development are related to the integration of mature personality, since they involve change in the combinations of resources used in reacting to new situations.

Part One is completed by Chapter 5, Learning to Learn: The Personal Construction and Exchange of Meaning, by Laurie Thomas and Sheila Harri-Augstein. In this highly individual account the authors indicate some dissatisfaction with the limits to the kinds of scientific activity accepted by most psychologists who attempt the experimental investigations of learning. This chapter emphasizes the highly personal nature of human learning, a characteristic that follows inevitably from the personal elements in the meanings and the experience which give birth to learning. The authors consider the ideas of Carl Rogers and George Kelly, and they develop an analysis of learning based upon 'learning conversations', an approach which gives full justice to the importance of the interaction and give-and-take between the learner and the source from which his knowledge is acquired.

1

LEARNING AND SOCIETY

Harry Kay

As we watch people going about their daily lives, talking to each other, reading a newspaper, greeting a friend, we forget that all these actions are examples of learning. If man, as in some science fiction fantasy, suddenly lost his ability to learn, whilst retaining what he already knew, his life on this earth would collapse as his cities and communications ground to a halt. We take learning for granted; it seems to be a part of our life, as much as breathing and eating. But, in fact, learning is very different and we should not allow its ubiquity to hide its uniqueness to the biological kingdom. Long ago, in the early stages of biological time, learning became necessary as creatures developed that were no longer fixed in one location and were able to move around under their own resources. The greater the freedom, the more dependent they became on learning, and in humans learning contributes to a vast range of actions and responses. That is not to say man learns at a uniform rate throughout life, or that at any one time in life he is equally adept at learning different tasks. Indeed, the reverse is the case. Learning abilities change with age and experience, and for much the same reason an individual may learn some material easily enough whilst finding other subjects beyond his ability.

BIOLOGICAL AND CULTURAL EVOLUTION

In this chapter, where we shall consider the implications for adult learning of a child being brought up in today's world, we shall first focus upon the problem from two different standpoints, namely, man's biological inheritance and the characteristics of today's world that distinguish it from previous ages.

Man's biological history stretches across an immensity of time, spanning the last 50,000 years and contrasting with the much shorter span of recorded history. Nevertheless, against the aeons of geological time, say, 4,600 million years, and the vast record of biological time, say, 2,500 million years, both are comparatively short periods. It is revealing for us to position man's life in this vast context of time, since it is only during the past 200 years that he has begun to see his own relationship to the world he inhabits and the species which live upon it. Man was around for a long time before he found out that his own earth was not the centre of the universe. It was even longer before he discovered his own kinship to other species, and the many and profound implications of this latter discovery have not yet been widely understood.

The timespan for cultural change is very short in relation to the massive scale of geological and biological evolution. From about 10,000 BC, with the beginning of agriculture and a settled community existence, cultural change has been accelerating in a way altogether different from other phenomena in the biological world. In the space of a few thousand years man began to live in very different homes and developed different habits and customs from those of his ancestors. However closely he was related to other species, his culture changed his way of life to such an extent that his outward connections with them were quickly hidden.

Throughout history there have been many instances where new ideas and technical developments have transformed man's way of life, as in Greek and Roman times and in the Renaissance. Natural phenomena, too, have led to fundamental changes, as when famine or nature's catastrophes have caused whole populations to migrate and adopt new ways of life. Yet over the last two centuries there has been an astonishing acceleration in the pace of cultural evolution, so much so that the peoples of the developed world now work and play in a completely different environment from that of former civilizations. This has come about as technological development has redrawn the everyday routines of life; it could do so because technology provided the machine-power to mould the natural world into new forms. Often this has taken place with insufficient attention being paid to the consequences of the changes, as when new highways have been literally carved through nature's and man's environment. The jet aeroplane has woven its way across the skies, and television and radio have gained access to any location from anywhere on this world or from its satellites. Electronics have shaped our lives and computers have given shape to future predictions, at the same time keeping our personal records as they oversee the nation's bookkeeping. Medicine has turned to electronics for spare-part surgery and to pharmacy for antibiotics and tranquillizing drugs. Such examples can be multiplied endlessly, from the professions to the house-wife, or from the farm to the factory.

Urbanization

These developments have done more than change the old order in its physical form. They have contributed to bringing about a radical change in the social and psychological order of society. As an indicator, let us consider the size of communities. Although man had lived in cities for 5,500 years, their size and number grew very slowly over the centuries. It is estimated that as late as 1800 only 3 per cent of the earth's population lived in towns of over 5,000 population (Trewartha, 1969). The movement towards urbanization started in the nineteenth century and was sufficiently evident for A. F. Weber (1899) to write, 'The most remarkable social phenomenon of the present century is the concentration of people in cities'. Yet by today's standards the movement had only just begun; no country would have been regarded as predominantly urbanized before 1850, and by 1900 only Great Britain would have been so described (Davis, 1965). The movement towards urbanization has accelerated rapidly in this century, as can be judged if we take as an index of urbanization the proportion of the population living in cities over 100,000. On that scale between 1850 and 1950 the index changed much more rapidly than from 1800 to 1850, but even so the rate of change from 1950 to 1960 was twice that of the preceding 50 years (Davis, 1965). We are saying that for the first time in man's history the majority of the citizens in industrialized countries have become city dwellers. As an indication we may note that between 1900 and 1960 the number of people living in cities over 100,000 increased from 75 to 525 million.

But within these populations further changes were taking place. Man left his home on the land to take up different work in the industrial city, only to find that such work was to change more in this century than had his agricultural work during the whole of its history. An industrialized country like the United States has seen its white-collar workers (professional and technical workers, managers, clerical and sales workers) increase from 16.6 per cent in 1900 to 46.1 per cent in 1967; correspondingly, its manual workers, including craftsmen, decreased in the same period from 71.4 per cent to 38.9 per cent. Within that group, farm labour reduced from 23.6 per cent to 2.1 per cent (Bendix, 1971). This increase in what Galbraith has called 'the techno-structure'—the shift out of agriculture, away from unskilled labour towards technical and maintenance work, with a corresponding increase in clerical and kindred jobs—has contributed to an astonishing increase in industrial productivity and a corresponding rise in general educational standards. Throughout the industrialized world there was a demand for better education and more of it. The results were spectacular. For example, amongst the 17 age group in the United States high-school students rose from 6.4 per cent in 1900 to 76.2 per cent in 1967. Furthermore, in the period 1946 to 1967 the number of students in higher education increased more than threefold to over 6 million, and there were similar rates of increase in other industrial countries.

Rapidity of Change

The increases to which we have drawn attention are typical hallmarks of today's world and they contribute to one of its most quoted characteristics, rapidity of change. Such a change is widespread and penetrating, influencing the structure and thinking of whole societies. And the world is now so organized that what someone thinks today may be communicated tomorrow to anyone in any remote corner of the world. It follows that society now requires its citizens to learn very different skills from those of previous ages. It expects them to know what was literally unknown in former times; its requires them to travel by different systems, to use different equipments, wear different materials and respond to a whole range of new items that have become commonplace. We may well ask if any meaningful generalizations can be made about these activities. Certainly, as we distinguish the features of man's work we see that there has been a change of emphasis. Man has ceased to be the labour force contributing the muscle-power and the energy that society requires. Nowadays efficient machines can be built to generate far more power than man himself could ever produce. The labour-force role that man has held for centuries, resulting in so much slavery and bondage, is obsolete in many parts of the world. In nearly all his work roles he is acting as the controller of energy. As he sits on the farm tractor, in the cab of the long-distance lorry, the cabin of the super-sized tanker or the box of the rolling plant of the steel mill, he is *directing* the use of power. He brings into play a carefully designed programme which will enable him to control a sequence of operations, achieving the desired end result.

Much the same applies to his other occupations. Man at all levels in his society has become the manipulator of symbolic material. He uses written material far more frequently and in ever-increasingly complex situations. He plays with machines such as computers, desk calculators, electric type-writers, and he translates their output quickly and distantly over a communication network that spans the world. The game becomes ever more abstract. Long ago, man invented money as a form of exchange of goods; now, instead of money, he transacts his business in the form of credit cards, loan systems, cheques and similar facilities.

SOCIETY'S DEMANDS UPON LEARNING

We may say then that man has created a society where the reward systems are more and more distant, where written communications are increasingly used to convey his instructions in circumstances and with equipment that are both sophisticated and remote. In other that his interacting society can survive, he has to construct ever more subtle legislation to control its activities and more sophisticated organizations to ensure its enforcement. Thus, we witness an insatiable demand for lawyers and accountants, whilst numbers in professions such as medicine are limited only by the cost of training and employment. It is also characteristic that one profession employs the skills and knowledge of another. Medicine, for instance, calls upon a range of sciences, from bio-chemistry and pharmacy to physics and engineering. Many jobs have become more sophisticated, whilst a host of new ones have been created. In particular, the support services, involving social security, welfare and assistance for children and the elderly, have multiplied.

A marked effect of the changes in communications and occupations is for man to spend more and more of his time moving paper around. And as the volume of paperwork has increased so has the complexity of the communications. Any student of income tax instructions or social security legislation will appreciate that for most readers we have reached the limits of comprehension.

Psychologists and educators have made efforts to simplify different forms of messages; for example, they have compared instructions restricted to verbal material with similar information where diagrams were added and the whole presented in the form of a logical tree. This diagrammatic form of presentation is found to be more easily comprehended. We require much more research of this kind, since present society relies at so many stages upon using written information.

In a complex society it is a *sine qua non* for everyone to be familiar with the basic codes we use. Those who cannot read and write are seriously handicapped and society has begun to recognize the sin of illiteracy. But it is far more than that. Society is now demanding a higher and higher level from its readers and the ability to handle documentary material of increasingly complex character. It requires us to teach a greater range of subjects and to a greater depth of subject-matter. It is essential that our schools take young adults to a standard that makes this possible and, above all, avoid giving pupils a permanent antipathy to learning. This is not to impugn the school system, a solution that is far too easy and which fails to recognize that learning is often a searching and unhappy process for many individuals. Learning quickly reveals the limitations of the pupil and, understandably, many in the past have left education with a hatred of it and all that went with it. Today, this could be fatal. No-one can be sure where his present or his next job will take him and what new skills it will require. To this extent, we all have to be prepared to relearn or even to start learning a subject.

This, then, is the kind of world which new adults now enter. It has been identified as a world of communication systems, in which time and space no longer hold their familiar values. We can, literally, watch events taking place on the other side of the world, indeed, on the other side of the moon. The 'narrowness of presented time and place' was fixed for early biological life, anchored as it was to one location and responding only to the immediate stimulus. Gradually the animal kingdom extended the two frontiers, until finally man achieved his most far-reaching of evolutionary changes, firstly by developing a symbolic language and then discovering a means of storing it outside himself. The written record gave him permanent storage and transmission. It is the achievement of today's technology to have extended present time and space to hitherto unimaginable limits and also to have given us accurate and permanent records in both visual and auditory forms. It is in this kind of world that our young adult grows up, and whether he uses technology to play pop music or Mahler, to fill in bingo forms or meterological charts, he has much to learn that was not available to his forefathers.

MODELS OF LEARNING

We have been making the case that man's learning has changed his way of life. We might expect, then, that our understanding of learning—how it happens, what factors influence its progress, why some individuals are more efficient than others—would be comprehensive if not complete. Here is something that is fundamental to life on our planet, so surely we may expect man to have devoted corresponding energies to unravelling its mysteries.

But, as so often, the facts are very different. By the middle of the nineteenth century man knew no more about how he learned than in Greek or Roman times. In spite of all the efforts that he then began to make in the field of education, it was based on no new theory of learning. Much of the schooling of the day was both brutish and ill-directed and rested on the twin pillars of discipline and repetition. It was characteristic of that confident era that the strengths of those pillars were not questioned.

During the last hundred years the position has certainly improved. Research has attempted at many biological levels to examine the process of learning and indeed it might be expected that after such a sustained effort more progress would have been evident. Why has progress been so slow? It seems that the basic problem has always lain in the inadequacy of the proposed models. When the researcher tried to understand how human learning took place by finding analogous systems he was forced into the discovery of the obvious, namely, that there were none outside the biological world of his investigations. The phenomenon was common enough in the natural world but non-existent outside. Hence, if the researcher were examining at the molecular level how the plasticity of the nervous system was modified as a result of learning, there were no analogous models in man's world to simulate this action. His thinking had to start *ab initio*. It is only in the last few decades with an increasing understanding of the properties of matter, as in solid-state physics, that constructive analogies have been possible at the molecular level of enquiry.

Again, at a more general level of investigation, when the researcher examined the conditions and variables which influenced learning there was no analogous system upon which he could draw outside biology. None of his own creations, in spite of sophisticated developments in the engineer's world of feedback and cybernetics, gave insight into how man himself learned. The position seemed to change suddenly with new data storage systems, and particularly with the advent of the computer, that could manipulate and retrieve data according to instructions. Without doubt the computer has done much to illuminate man's own learning, and not least by establishing how different the two systems are. Man does not store in the same way as a computer, his address procedure for locating stored material is more varied and complex, whilst his retrieval of data has to cover a much wider range of conditions and is less predictable. But after the computer at least we knew what man's learning was not, and this negative contribution had the positive effect of spurring on research to examine the differences in greater detail. It has been one of the successes of recent research to identify some of these detailed characteristics of learning.

Appearances can be Deceptive

In order that we may appreciate the general complexity of the problem, let us take a familiar example of learned behaviour and observe how misleading it would be if we were to base conclusions on what *seems* to be happening. A young man is driving a car in a crowded street. He has the car radio switched on, he is conducting a conversation with his passenger, he responds appropriately to a series of traffic lights and pedestrians, whilst at the same time he notices a close friend and waves to him. If now we were to make a statistical assessment of the amount of information to which our driver was apparently responding, we might rashly conclude that he was so successful because he possesses an enormous channel capacity for handling information. It appears as we watch him responding appropriately that no matter how much information is presented, his perceptual analysing system can cope with it. Again, as we consider our everyday world and the complexity of its scenes, we might draw a similar conclusion, namely, that man's perceptual system can process enormous quantities of information at any one time and analyse them into meaningful messages.

We should, of course, be completely wrong in that conclusion. Man has only a limited capacity for dealing with information from his outside world. He is able to cope with its complexity only because he has learned its salient features and is in fact predicting or anticipating events. When events do not occur according to his predictions, as in the classic accident situation, he is quite unable to cope. It may be a truism, but every accident is a result of there being too much information for the limited channel capacity of the human system; too many events happen in too short a time for an individual to cope with them.

Many experiments have measured this channel capacity and it comes as something of a shock to find that it is very small indeed, only a few bits of information. But our present interests lie not so much in the exact measure of that limited channel capacity (a matter which is examined by James Reason in Chapter 2) as in the broad characteristics of human learning. We know the system itself depends primarily upon a huge data store with a variety of ways of gaining access to it and retrieving data from it. However, such a statement makes human learning sound all too simple, ignoring the subtle characteristics that are unique to it and making no reference to the yet unsolved neurophysiological mechanisms that are its constituent parts. Let us consider the efficiency of the strategies that are adopted to make it possible for man to live in his everyday world of movement and change, as in the car-driving example. Often a person will be bombarded with stimulation of high complexity and yet is able to respond appropriately to such situations. We have then to ask the question, what is it that we have to learn in order to live in our world of high-speed, simultaneously occurring events? Very simply, what exactly do we learn?

What do we Learn?

We are considering a feature that is common to learning both in the animal and in man's world. Organisms are exposed to events, and the resulting behaviour reveals that they have learned their frequency and their consequences.

They will learn to distinguish between those happenings which do not affect them and those that do. Sheep in their field respond differently to a loud noise followed by no harmful effect, such as a passing train, than they do to the lesser noise of the bark of a dog, heralding the possible invasion of their territory.

We are saying then that organisms learn the probabilities of events, and in the case of human learning we may illustrate this briefly a different stages. Man's receptor system, covering all his different sense modalities, is sensitive to a wide range of stimulation, whilst within certain modalities he has ingeniously extended that range by developing a highly successful symbolic code. Hence, at any one time, he may be confronted with a display where the information is way beyond his capacity to assimilate, yet his experience enables him to cope. He may have only a few moments to see the scene in front of him, but because it is familiar to him, he quickly categorizes items and selects those that are relevant to his requirements. Of course, this has its dangers. Since it is based upon knowledge of probabilities, man's perception will generally be correct; but insofar as he sees the world he expects to be there, he is creating the world around him, and there will be some occasions where he is strikingly wrong. Examples of this occur in the social situation, where events are less predictable and where the time-scale for any one item—say, a few words of speech—may be brief. It has often been pointed out that to listen to the comments of playgoers leaving the theatre is to form the impression that each has been witnessing a different performance.

In man's world of variety and change, an individual has to find some measure of regularity—what is constant in his surroundings. He has to cope with serial events, as in common speech, where the time intervals may be very short and the sequence all-important. The normal rules of grammar make it possible to predict the order of the likely parts of speech that will occur in a sentence and therefore, fortunately, it is not necessary to listen to every word a speaker utters or read every word in a sentence. In a familiar visual scene, we can quickly scan and verify that everything is as expected, and this will apply to crossing a busy traffic crossroads or sitting at our own dining-table.

Where does this leave us in trying to understand the broader features of learning? We are clearly examining a very different kind of system from that designed by man in the field of computers or cybernetics. When man designs a system it is exact and limited in the sense that it will carry out the specific operation for which it has been programmed; if it is to give priority to selecting items under one category rather than another, it will do precisely that. It will never change that priority until new instructions are given to it. Human learning does not display such a simple ordering and recovery of material. Basic operations may be stable enough but we expect considerable flexibility in handling complex data. For example, in an everyday case of visual recognition, we may ask whether we are looking at the same person whom we met for the first time a few hours previously? Then she was wearing a tee-shirt and jeans, with her hair over her shoulders; now she is apparently an older person, with hair tied tightly round her head and dressed in long evening clothes. Yet we say confidently that it is the same person. The outward and visible signs which are constant, though they may be few, are judged more important than the many signs which have changed, and we have no difficulty in 'recognizing' (learning to see) the same person. This may be a common enough example of human learning and recognition, but it requires an advanced, sophisticated system if we are to reproduce anything like it with present electronic equipment. It will be noticed that we have now introduced into our answer to the question "What do we learn?" a component relating to the contextual events associated with an incident. Not only does an individual categorize items, but he is able to select from an almost infinite sample of possible events those few which he expects to be related to the incident. He does not search through an endless file of possible items, but scrutinizes the few that are related to the context as he conceptualizes it.

This is a characteristic of human learning. On the one hand, it is concerned with single items, for example, names of familiar abstractions such as the days of the week, numbers, etc. These become the tools of learning. But they are all manipulated within a much bigger context, and one that may change rapidly from time to time. Numbers, for instance, may be used to score a golf or football match, to add a wage sheet, measure a person's age, and so on. Once the item is learnt, it may be retained in its original context but the chances are that it will eventually be used in a context unknown to the learner at the time of his original learning of the item. For example, he may follow a particular route because he wishes to go to a designated place, or he learns a person's name because he intends to address its owner. But as the size of the learned context grows during the course of daily life, the situation becomes more complex. In the above examples, the individual follows a route which he has never seen before, because he is able to fit the street map into some schema of the geography of the city; or he recalls a name which he never intended to learn because he has related it to other names of similar sound, shape and size.

MAN'S EARLY LEARNING

Man's extraordinary facility to store items and then retrieve them from a vast complex of materials does not come about quickly. We have been slow to appreciate what a large proportion of man's lifespan is devoted to learning and perfecting the basic skills of life. Man's childhood is more prolonged and is more dependent upon adult care than that of other primates. There are obvious anatomical reasons for this. The human brain at birth, though over 10 per cent of body weight, is only about one-quarter of its adult size, reached at 18 years; this contrasts markedly with, say, the rhesus monkey and gibbon, which complete their brain growth in six months. It has been argued that human infancy with its more malleable dependency is a prolongation of the foetal period of the earlier primates (Bruner, 1972). Certainly, that long infancy is followed by a long childhood in which the outstanding feature is the gradual learning of innumerable skills. Complex routines, from the construction of grammatical sentences to the coordination of actions—kicking or throwing a ball—are practised again and again, until by adult life the pattern has been so learned that we think of it as a habit. We have only to listen to the way an 18-year-old talks or watch the way he walks to observe the influence of society upon him and the extent to which he has established responses which are very much part of himself.

There are two other features pertinent to our discussion, and here again both emphasize the difference between man's learning and any computer system. In the human case we are not examining a unitary mechanism which controls the whole of an individual's ability to learn. We accept that the same person will have widely varying abilities, showing exceptional skill at football perhaps, but failing lamentably at Greek. And this is not because one skill is necessarily more complex than the other: indeed, if we think in terms of possible models which might be devised to learn, say, Greek and football, it is not necessarily easier to design the football-learning machine than the Greek. We have to accept that in the young adult we will find examples of well practised and advanced forms of learning, side by side with examples of elementary and often inefficient learning. This is certainly not determined solely by intellectual ability. Some brilliant minds have apparently been incapable of learning simple, coordinated actions that would have been invaluable to them.

Attitudes and Prejudices

It would be idle to pretend that we have an explanation for this variability within the same individual. We can draw comparisons with the same computer using efficient and inefficient programmes to retrieve items, but the analogy is misleading in that in the human example the programme or strategy is part of the process of learning. That is to say, an individual learns not only a particular item such as a name or concept but many of its associated attributes. He learns about its context—its spatial whereabouts, its temporal recurrences, its related events—and, often more important, he learns a host of affective associations with the item. In this way there are established attitudes, predilections, prejudices towards items and classes of material. Sometimes the individual is only too well aware of his attitudes, and at other times he is not. But either way they become an important constituent of the programmes which an individual uses in learning and remembering.

Without entering the controversies of learning theory, we can say with confidence that by the age of 18 the adult has not only established many of his patterns of learning but that these are bound up with his individual personality. It is this link between the cognitive and affective elements that contributes to making the process so permanent. An adult, faced with a new situation, quickly establishes what he likes and dislikes. When called upon to learn material he will show his interest in some events and his indifference to others. As we examine these attitudes, we observe that long before adulthood they have become part and parcel of the individual's learning.

We begin now to appreciate the enormous influence which society will exert on the learning ability of young people. Those subjects and skills which are highly regarded by society, and particularly by young people, will have a considerable advantage. The processes involved are more subtle and have profounder implications than those changes of fashion whereby the music-making teenagers of one generation are rejected whilst similar groups become the guitar-playing pop-idols of another. We are really discussing a way of thought that permeates the whole values and ethos of a society and to which every new member has to react. Nowhere is its influence more pervading than on the gradual change in the accepted vocabulary of each generation. There are no written rules declaring which words are 'in' and 'out', but the rigidity of the guidelines drawn up by usage and custom could not be stricter.

In considering how the young react to the contemporary scene there is an obvious but often forgotten point. Each younger age group deducts one year from the perspective through which the surrounding world is viewed. From the safe distance of 50 years today's problems may seem in focus, but the long-distance viewpoint is not within the teenager's experience. Hence the present makes a much greater impact upon him than upon an older adult. He seems so much closer to it, and from a psychological standpoint he is indeed much closer—a lifetime's experience does not get in the way. At the same time, because his own emotions are so much a part of his learning the teenager may be just as much a victim of his own prejudices as his elders, except that his attitudes are less fixed in him and more open to the possibility of being changed.

LEARNING HABITS

This balance between what is likely to be permanent in an individual's life and what may still undergo change with further experience is crucial to the young adult's learning. In his famous chapter on Habit, James (1890) saw the professional mannerisms settling in the young man of 25 and, as he put it, 'by the age of thirty, the character has set like plaster and will never soften again'. Today we may be less sure than James that at 30 'it is best that he should not escape', and we do not doubt that for young adults new courses of action are possible and new subjects may be learned, provided there is no built-in resistance to them. As this is so important let us consider an example, whilst bearing in mind that in all studies of learning we cannot scrutinize the process directly by entering the private world of the individual, and we can only infer how he conceives items and his attitudes towards them by his responses and general behaviour.

Suppose we ask a group of young adults to learn how to solve a statistical problem. We receive a variety of responses: some give answers quickly and correctly, some hesitate and some hardly appear to be involved in the question. These are expressions of the different attitudes we find to such a subject and, as we noted, we have to accept that they have already become very much a part of each individual's learning. One person apparently finds it difficult to learn about statistical concepts and expresses himself as bored with the subject. Closer examination reveals that the subject presents a real threat to the individual's concept of himself; he does not wish to enter into the very difficult exercise of trying to learn statistics because he is not sure that he has the necessary ability, and he does not want to demonstrate that incompetence. If learning is to be successful in such circumstances, the learner needs to receive the encouragement gained through experiencing some achievement in that area. Teaching him a new approach or explaining a concept from a different standpoint may make this possible. Again, motivation can be improved by establishing the relevance of the material to the individual's own needs. As long as he can maintain the attitude that he has no need to learn this material because it has not bearing upon his work, he can and will justify his indifference, however illogical it may be. By establishing the relevance to his own interest, the individual may be persuaded to participate.

This is the kind of world we face in the young adult. In its overt expression youth often appears to reflect confidence, certainty and even rigidity, but behind the behaviour is a complex and vulnerable individual, uncertain how to answer many challenges of life. So many unknowns surround the young. As life continues, a person will push aside too many subjects as being outside the range of his capabilities and often give them a derogatory tag to minimize the personal loss. But, especially in the relatively young, few unlearnt areas of knowledge ought to be out of the individual's range, as long as they are communicated with some appreciation of the difficulties and anxieties they may arouse in each learner. This is especially important in today's society, in which established subjects and professions have to keep extending their boundaries and where new disciplines are being established. Today's message comes over loud and clear that the indivisibility of knowledge should be emphasized more than ever. Young people need to be well aware that the frontiers of knowledge as between subjects are continuously being redrawn.

AN OVERVIEW OF THE PROBLEMS

Let us now sum up the argument presented in this chapter about learning and society. We began by attempting to see the lifespan of our species—say, 50,000 years—against the aeons of time during which geological and biological systems have evolved. The nub of the argument is that evolutionary freedom always demanded learning, the primate level requiring an increasing capacity. Cultural evolution has now quickened the pace of biology and in our century this has accelerated beyond that of any former developments. Today, man has changed his role and become primarily a director of energy and a manipulator of symbolic material.

We then considered how man is equipped to learn. He has a brain which will store immense quantities of information, but at any one time he can receive only a very limited amount. Hence man increases his interaction with his environment by learning the probabilities of events; he sees what he is expecting to see, responding quickly to those items which he regards as meaningful and significant, whilst ignoring or failing to select much of the data presented to him. In view of this style of learning it is perhaps not surprising that man's period of learning during infancy and childhood is much longer than that of the other primates. Even before the beginnings of speech, during the first 12 months of life, this pace is comparatively slow; thereafter it takes on a new dimension of complexity as man learns to speak and begins to handle more and more abstract concepts.

We have put forward one accepted view of the psychology of learning—and to use such a phrase is to invite someone to deny it—in which an individual receives information by an active, selective process. Within such a view common features may underlie a variety of skills, such as recognizing a patterned display, solving a problem or learning a new concept. In these situations the learner examines and often transforms the information with which he is presented. But the facility with which he handles the data depends on the practice he has had with related materials. The following chapters will give some indication of what we now know about the many specific stages of the process, its assimilation, retention and retrieval, the individual idiosyncracies which can be built into it. But here our concern is limited to the more general problem and how it is influenced by the kind of society which has evolved.

We have indicated that two main features of that society—and they are closely related—are the extent to which it is now using highly developed, coded material and the rapid rate of change throughout all communities. More and more of our population are required to learn to a higher level of performance the symbolic skills of our society. There are few precedents in recorded history for such extensive use of symbolic material at all social levels, and the demands which this entails upon learning are equally un-precedented. The pivotal question which follows is whether man can sustain this rate of progress which he has initiated.

There is some evidence for believing that the answers to the two questions—the extent and the rate of change—may differ. Much learning requires the individual to sustain effort and attention over long periods of time, but provided the exposure to material is conducted in a systematic, progressive way there is no doubt that man is capable of learning materials that are both complex and arduous. He is rarely handicapped by any limitations on what he can store mentally, and his ability to invent and to continue using the varied language systems of the world shows the range of symbolic material to which he can adjust. But there are some limits to the mature man's adaptability. It is one thing to learn Chinese when growing up in China and quite another to start learning it as an adult who has previously learned only English. It is unfortunate that the rate of change within society too often seems to result in demands being made upon its members which can be as exacting in their way as the example of the adult being made to learn Chinese. An individual may have learned, say, a branch of science only to find it becomes bypassed by new advances. Innovations have often revolutionized a technology overnight, facing a dozen related professions with the need to master new equipment and procedures. Situations of this kind impose an enormous learning premium upon those professions which are responsible for either passing on the new knowledge, as in the case of lecturers or teachers, or for making direct use of it, as is demanded of doctors, architects or industrial researchers. Such professions generally attract individuals with highly developed learning skills, at least within their own subjects, who can probably cope well enough with the problems. But the pattern of change runs through the rest of society. When industry alters a manufacturing process it affects both the workers who make the product and the many consumers who use it. Both may encounter situations that require difficult relearning.

AN AGE OF CONTRADICTORY EXPECTATIONS

I shall end with one further comment upon the curious challenge of our present world. We have noticed how by the time man reaches adult age he has acquired both a vast store of interrelated information and a whole complex of attitudes and prejudices relating thereto. In this way society influences the motivations of its new adults. A striking example has occurred over the last few decades as we have witnessed a transformation in the lifestyles and the work habits of our populations in the developed countries. Concomitant with ever-changing jobs has been an increasing share in national wealth as living standards have materially improved. The expectation has gradually taken root that material wealth will go on increasing and that everyone is entitled to his share.

But as the twentieth century enters its last quarter, it becomes apparent that early impressions were based on only partial information. Certainly technology can create its new environment, but only at a cost in resources which we now know to be limited. We in the rich countries will live at the standards we are projecting only by taking more than our share of the world's resources. Hence the unexpected paradox that the gap between the rich and the poor nations keeps widening. Within its ever-shrinking frontiers our present world juxtaposes the rich and the poor, the fed and the unfed, the developed and the undeveloped. The world's population grows apace, accentuating the difference between the educated and the uneducated, between the technological and the non-technological societies.

In considering the social aspects of the problem, some people have asked whether we shall ever have sufficient resources to satisfy our demands. Is it in our nature to say 'Enough'? This point underlies a second and more profound paradox of this age, that expectations have risen faster than achievements, in spite of the enormous technological advances of the last decades. Alan Bullock sees ours as 'a Promethean Age', reminiscent of Prometheus stealing fire from Heaven for man and being punished by the Gods for his 'gift'. Man has learned to live in an affluent society and in a way that would have astonished his ancestors. But his expressed needs and demands have not lessened, nor does he seem satisfied with his standards. As the contrasts grow ever sharper, an age of contradictions has come into being. Not only do the rich of the world contrast too sharply with its poor, but within any one section of society we have come to recognize conflicting standards as our hallmark. It was the young who made this apparent when large numbers of them rejected the standards of their prosperous society and stood out for a less materialist way of life. It may be argued that it was easy enough for them to make such a gesture, having so little to lose; nevertheless it is indicative of the contradictions within our society and of the direction it could take if newer minds were brought to bear on such problems.

REFERENCES

Bendix, R. (1971). 'Man, Freedom and the Future', in Alan Bullock (Ed.), *The Twentieth Century*, Thames and Hudson, London.
Bruner, J. S. (1972). *The Relevance of Education*, Allen & Unwin, London.
Davis, K. (1965). 'The Urbanization of the Human Population', *Scientific American*, **213**, 40.
James, W. (1890). *The Principles of Psychology*, Holt, New York.
Trewartha, G. T. (1969). *A Geography of Population: World Patterns*, Wiley, New York.
Weber, A. F. (1899). *The Growth of Cities in the Nineteenth Century*, Macmillan, New York.

2

SKILL AND ERROR IN EVERYDAY LIFE

James T. Reason

THE NATURE OF SKILL

Judging from even the most acceptable of psychological definitions, it is remarkably difficult to capture the essence of skilled performance in words. Consider the following statement by Fitts (1964); 'Spatial–temporal patterning, the interplay of receptor–effector–feedback processes, and such characteristics as timing, anticipation and the graded response are thus seen as identifying characteristics of skill' (p. 245). Few would quarrel with the notions contained in this description, but taken as a whole it conveys little or nothing of the adverbial quality of skill, the practised ease of execution and fluidity of movement that are immediately apparent on watching the actions of a highly skilled performer. Bartlett (1958) came close to the heart of the problem when he stated that skilled actions form a *series*, not simply a succession of events. Skilled behaviour is continuous and holistic in its organization. Words, on the other hand, are discrete, and no matter how carefully chosen, they impose categories and discontinuities where none exist in the phenomenon being described.

This widespread problem of description in psychology has recently been discussed by Spence (1973). He distinguished between *analog* and *digital* modes of representing behaviour. Analog representations are achieved without the use of numbers; thus, what is continuous in nature can be described continuously by, say, a fluctuating line on a moving chart, or by any other means where there is roughly a one-to-one correspondence between the event and its representation. But because of the many limitations of this mode of description, our cultural bias is towards the use of digital representations, that is towards the use of numerical and verbal descriptions. And this, he argued, leaves us unprepared for the fact that in a number of situations, of which skilled performance is one, the use of a digital mode introduces rather than eliminates error. 'We intuitively believe that putting a number on something adds precision; nothing in our experience would lead us to believe that precision may be greater when the number is omitted. It is not just that the number is

21

inadequate .... It is more serious; by fixing on a number, we are forcing a continuous space–time event into a procrustean bed that may disguise its true properties and cause all kinds of future mischief' (Spence, 1973, p. 481).

Let us consider what is involved in the acquisition of a complex skill. Since, as Polanyi (1958) pointed out, 'the aim of a skilful performance is achieved by the observance of a set of rules which are not known as such to the person following them' (p. 49), the traditional way of passing on a skill is through the master–apprentice model in which the teaching is effected more by example than by words—or, in Spence's terms, more by an analog than by a digital means. Even the most articulate tennis coach, for example, is likely to find it impossible to express verbally all the complex actions involved in, say, making a service. Instead, he invites the student to observe and copy his actions. Only when the student has internalized his own analog of the required actions does he approach a truly skilled level of performance, for it is only then that he possesses a standard of comparison from which to gauge whether a particular movement 'feels right' or not.

We see the reverse side of this coin when we ask a skilled performer to attend to specific actions in a complex sequence. More often than not, bringing 'focal awareness' to bear on component actions disturbs their smooth flow and may even destroy their coordinated quality altogether. As Freud (1922) remarked, '. . . many acts are most successfully carried out when they are not the objects of particularly concentrated attention, and that mistakes may occur just on occasions when one is most eager to be accurate . . .' (p. 28). Here, it is the adoption of a digital or partitioning mode of experience rather than an analog one which causes the error.

Must we then resign ourselves to accepting that a continuous process like skilled performance will always defy adequate description in a digital mode such as words? Not altogether, Spence maintained. Some forms of literature come very close to communicating the realities of behaviour as we experience them in life. One reason for this, he suggested, is that these novelists are not concerned with measurement nor even with explanation, but with making the reader *sense* the fictional scene. And they achieve this by highlighting the inconsistencies, the paradoxes and the minutiae that are likely to be glossed over by the behavioural scientist in his search for unifying and explanatory principles.

Some support for this view can be found in the following extract from Arnold Bennett's *Clayhanger* in which he describes more eloquently than any psychological text the gulf that separates the beginner from the skilled performer:

'The next morning, in the printing office, Edwin came upon Big James giving a lesson in composing to the younger apprentice, who in theory had "learned his cases". Big James held the composing stick in his great left hand, like a matchbox, and with his great right thumb and index picked letter after letter from the case, very slowly in order to display the movement, and dropped them into the stick. In his mild, resonant tones he explained that each letter must be picked up unfalteringly in a particular way, so that it should drop face upward into the stick without any intermediate manipulation. And he explained also that the left hand must be held so that the right hand would have to travel to and fro as little as possible. He was revealing the basic mysteries of his craft, and was happy, making the while the broad series of stock pleasantries which have probably been current in composing rooms since printing was invented. Then he was silent, working more and more quickly, till his right hand could scarcely be followed in its twinklings, and the face of the apprentice duly spread in marvel. When the line was finished he drew out the rule, clapped it down on the top of the last row of letters, and gave the composing stick to the apprentice to essay.

The apprentice began to compose with his feet, his shoulders, his mouth, his eyebrows—with all his body except his hands, which never the less travelled spaciously far and wide.

"It's not in seven years, nor in seventy, as you'll learn, young son of a gun!" said Big James.

And, having unsettled the youth to his foundations with a bland thwack across the head, he resumed the composing stick and began again the exposition of the unique smooth movement which is the root of rapid typesetting.'

(Bennett, 1910, p. 114)
Reproduced by permission of Mrs Dorothy Cheston Benett.

If literature such as this mimics life more closely than the analytic descriptions of the scientist, what—in the absence of the actual scene before our eyes— can we learn about the nature of skilled performance from this passage? And how does this relate to the body of psychological knowledge that has grown up over the past 80 years with regard to the organization of skilled sensory–motor behaviour and the basic limitations of the human operator?

Let us focus first upon the ways in which Big James's actions differ from those of his apprentice, because if the nature of skill is to be understood at all then the answers must lie in the differences that exist between the skilled and the unskilled performer and in the various transitional stages that intervene. The printer's task is essentially one of processing information: in this case, to translate lines of manuscript into appropriately spaced lines of type. Neither Big James nor his apprentice have an infinite capacity for processing information; both can only do so much in a given time. These limits are innate, imposed by the nature of their receptors and effectors, and by the structure of their nervous systems. The most obvious difference between them, however, is that Big James—by virtue of his smooth timing and economy of movement—can achieve so much more than the apprentice in a given period of time, and more accurately as well. This suggests that Big James has in some way succeeded in restructuring the flow of information through his nervous system so that its handling capacity is maximized—or, to put it another way, so that its limitations are minimized. The question is: how? It is certain that if Big James were available to be questioned, he would be unable to tell us— at least directly—in the same way that words failed him when it came to explaining anything more than the component actions of the task to his apprentice. Quite simply, the 'twinklings' of his hands have no adequate verbal equivalent.

But suppose we could question him: would he give us any due as to the mechanisms underlying his high level of performance? Suppose we asked him what went through his mind while he composed. The chances are that much of what he reported would have little to do with the job in hand. But, if pressed, he might perhaps mention that he was thinking of a tricky piece of layout some lines further down, or if he could finish the job by tea-time. We need not pursue this speculation further: the point to be made is that Big James would certainly *not* be thinking of where his left hand was in relation to his right, or where a particular letter was located in the case. In sharp contrast, however, it is just these details that are likely to be uppermost in the mind of the apprentice. For him, the immediate demands upon conscious attention are very great. Not only does he have to concentrate on individual movements so that he can *see* what his hands are doing, but it is also likely that he will be struggling to recall Big James's instructions—the plan of action—so that he can *talk* himself through step by step.

The apprentice, therefore, relies heavily upon visual feedback to guide his actions, while Big James 'feels' his way through them at a barely conscious level of awareness. Big James, if he gives it any thought at all, is considering the overall strategy of the job; the apprentice, however, is preoccupied with immediate tactical matters. Like all adults, even young ones, he has brought to the task of composing a whole range of previously acquired skills. Even such an unpromising apprentice as this is likely to be quite capable of carrying out the component actions individually. But what he lacks at this stage is the capacity to organize and coordinate these separate actions into a smooth and effective sequence. Because he has not yet entirely assimilated the overall plan, he needs words to covertly guide his actions—with all the discontinuity that this entails. This is what Adams (1969; 1971) has termed the *verbal–motor stage* of skill acquisition. From what has been said earlier, it need hardly be stressed that verbal control does not persist in the later stages of skill acquisition. As Adams (1971) put it: 'It would be silly to postulate a theory where *all* motor behaviour is under verbal control because words are crude when compared to the fineness of motor movements. The fingers of a concert violinist are not under verbal control, but they probably were in the beginning when he first started with his teacher' (p. 115).

With continued practice, the need for covert verbal control and the close visual monitoring of actions diminishes as the trainee creates his own internalized and largely proprioceptive analog of the complete piece of behaviour he is trying to achieve. The responses lose their laborious quality and become more and more automatic, seemingly occurring with little or no direct attention on the performer's part. William James (1890), as ever, expressed it with elegant simplicity: 'Habit diminishes the conscious attention with which our acts are performed'. The importance of automatization is that it liberates the performer's focal attention from the immediate present, and allows him to consider future actions. In short, this process brings with it that most distinctive feature of the skilled operator, the appearance of having 'all the time in the world'.

Skills, like armies, are hierarchically organized: only when the general is confident of the capabilities of his subordinate commanders and their units can he give his full attention to planning the dispositions of the army as a whole, and so it is with skilled performance. This was clearly demonstrated by Bryan and Harter (1899) in their classical study of trainee telegraphers. Mastery of the telegraphic language, they argued, involved mastering successive levels in the hierarchy of language units. 'In the first days one is forced to attend to letters. In the first months one is forced to attend to words. If the learner essays a freedom for which he is unfit, suddenly a letter or word which is unfamiliar explodes in his ears and leaves him wrecked. He has no useful freedom for higher language units which he has not earned by making the lower ones automatic .... Only when all the necessary habits, high and low, have become automatic, does one rise into the freedom and speed of the expert.' (Bryan and Harter, 1899, p. 357)

MACHINE MODELS FOR MAN

A perusal of the skills literature over the past 80 years might well leave the reader with the pardonable impression that most modern theorizing merely involves a reexamination of the issues raised by the early pioneers, particularly Woodworth (1899), James (1890), Watson (1907) and Lashley (1917), but stated now in the form of metaphors and models made possible by technological advances outside psychology, especially in the fairly recent development of complex machines for performing control, communication and computing operations. Certainly, the early skills researchers were concerned with many of the major theoretical issues of the present day: the role of sensory feedback, the hierarchical organization of skilled behaviour, and the centralist–peripheralist debate (now often called the inflow–outflow issue). And it is often the case that essentially similar ideas are nowadays couched in a mechanistic rather than a humanistic language. Before we examine the theoretical issues themselves, it would be helpful to trace the origins of these machine models for man.

To a large extent, the impetus for these developments came from Second World War pressures to understand the behaviour of the skilled operator in complex weapon systems. Scientists and technologists were constantly striving to improve existing weapon systems, and the need to assess the results of their efforts by evaluating the *man-machine system* as a whole, rather than by considering the man and the machine separately, brought psychologists into close contact with the thought and methods of other disciplines, notably those of the engineering sciences. Partly because it eased the communication problem, and partly because a rapidly developing technology made the exercise increasingly meaningful, psychologists began to consider the human operator in terms similar to those used by engineers to describe the function of their machines. Three 'machine models' for the human operator were found to be particularly useful in stimulating research and in providing a conceptual framework for organizing human performance data.

The advent of complex communication systems and the related development of *information theory* (Shannon and Weaver, 1949) provided the means for analysing the human operator as an *information-processing system*: that is, one that receives, stores, collates and emits information in a way that shares many important features with sophisticated telecommunication networks. An important advantage of this approach was that it provided a more meaningful model for skilled performance than the simple stimulus–response notions that had emerged from animal-learning studies.

Although self-regulating machines had been in use long before the Second World War, it was only during this period that sophisticated *servomechanisms* or feedback-control systems (such as the autopilot, for example) came into widespread use. The idea of using servomechanisms as a model for the human operator was proposed by Craik (1948) and later elaborated by Hick and Bates (1950), a development that represented a considerable growing-point in our understanding of complex sensory–motor performance. In 1948, Norbert Wiener proposed that a separate discipline—*cybernetics*—should concern itself with the study of self-regulation in both physical and biological systems. The central concept was that of feedback, and although this notion had a long history within psychology (see Woodworth's (1899) 'polyphase motor units'), it was only within the framework of cybernetics that it achieved any degree of precision or quantification. The role of feedback in skilled performance is still under debate (see Keele, 1973), but certainly in the initial stages its function is to provide information about the extent to which our actions depart from our intentions, or the degree of error. In many important respects, the human operator, like the self-regulating machine, is error-actuated. That is, if everything is running according to plan there is no modification of action, because the system is so organized that information conveying the absence of error tends to be largely disregarded.

The third and most important model for skilled behaviour has been provided by the development of stored-program, data-processing systems such as the digital computer. As Newell *et al.* (1958) pointed out: 'The real importance of the digital computer for the theory of higher mental processes lies not merely in allowing us to realise such processes "in the metal" and outside the brain, but in providing us with a much profounder idea than we have hitherto had of the characteristics a mechanism must possess if it is to carry out complex information-processing tasks' (p. 163).

Digital computers are governed in their operation by *programs*, or sequences of instructions. Parts of these programs, like the actions of a driver or a pilot, may be repeated many times over in one operation, and these relatively invariant sequences of instructions are termed *subroutines*. Subroutines are under the control of higher-level instructions termed *executive* programs which define the overall plan of action and call into play the various subordinate routines at appropriate points within the data-processing operation. Like human skill, therefore, computer programs can be organized in a hierarchical fashion, and it is this feature together with their considerable adaptive potential that makes them such attractive analogies for complex performance in man (see Miller *et al.*, 1960).

Having set the scene, let us now look briefly at some of the more influential of the theoretical ideas presently existing in the field of skills research.

KEY THEORETICAL CONCEPTS IN SKILLS RESEARCH

1. The Single-channel Hypothesis

Over the past 30 years or so, a number of mainly British investigators have sought to define and measure the limits of man's capacity as an information-processing system. As was shown in the previous chapters, the form of such limitations has wide implications for human learning. In this work, they have focused to a large extent upon the input aspects of human performance, placing special emphasis upon such issues as the selection of sensory inputs, their short-term storage and whether or not information is processed serially along a single channel or in parallel along multiple channels. An important outcome of this research has been the formulation of the *single-channel hypothesis*. This states that the human operator can be meaningfully regarded as a single-channel communication system whose capacity for receiving, storing, processing and acting upon information is limited. This means, in effect, that a person performing a sensory–motor task has one central communication channel linking input and output functions through which each 'bit' or meaningfully organized 'chunk' of information has to be cleared before other signals are dealt with.

The experimental evidence for the single-channel hypothesis (see Welford, 1968; Allport *et al.*, 1972) has been drawn from many sources: from the inability of human subjects to take in more than one piece of information at a time (Cherry, 1953; Broadbent, 1958; Neisser, 1969); from choice reaction time and psychological refractory period studies (Hick, 1952; Hyman, 1953; Brown, 1960; Vince, 1948; Davis, 1956; Smith, 1967); from measures of the speed of continuous performance and from investigations of mental load (Craik, 1948; Welford, 1968). Many of these studies have in common the fact that they demanded from the subjects simultaneous attention to two closely similar tasks. The general conclusion from this work is that as signals become less regular and predictable (and so convey more information), the subject's ability to process concurrently signals from two sources becomes increasingly degraded.

Although there exists an impressive body of evidence to indicate that the single-channel hypothesis holds for many situations, more recent findings have challenged its universal applicability. Moray (1967) argued that the results of a number of studies involving either highly practised subjects or tasks in which there was a high degree of input–output compatibility do not fit the notion of a many-to-one convergence of inputs upon a single, limited-capacity channel. Instead these findings show that '... there is no narrow throat, no point at which parallel messages *must* be held up as we see in un-practised subjects and incompatible situations' (Moray, 1967, p. 87). Moray suggested an alternative model of the human operator '... which envisages not a limited capacity channel in the sense of a transmission line, but a limited capacity *central processor* whose organisation can be flexibly altered by internal self-programming' (p. 85).

Allport *et al.* (1972) argued that subjects' inability to pay simultaneous atten-tion to two closely similar tasks derived not so much from the limited capacity of the single central processor, but more simply from the difficulty of confusing two similar but unrelated messages. They predicted that where the concurrent tasks were highly dissimilar, this problem would not arise and the two tasks could be carried out simultaneously without too much error in either. In two experiments, they found that people could attend to and repeat back continuous speech at the same time as taking in complex, unrelated visual scenes, or when sight-reading piano music. In both cases, performance with divided attention was very good, and with sight-reading it was as good as with undivided attention. They concluded that these results were incompatible with the single-channel hypothesis, and instead proposed a 'multi-channel' hypo-thesis in which a number of independent, special-purpose computers (processors and stores) operate in parallel. However, they did concede that the brain may, in certain circumstances, exhibit 'single-channel' operation; but they denied that this mode of operation was obligatory.

Another finding which clearly favours a 'multiple-channel' rather than a 'single-channel' interpretation was obtained recently by Shaffer (1975). He studied the performance of one remarkably skilled typist who could copy-type visually presented material equally well (at a rate of about 100 words per minute) with or without a second task involving 'shadowing' auditorially presented material. What is surprising about these results is that both tasks involved verbal material, albeit employing different sensory modes. She was less successful when she had to shadow visually presented material, and when she was required to audio-type while reciting. Here, the same modality had to serve two different functions.

Legge and Barber (1976), in a review of the evidence for the single-channel hypothesis, summed up its present status as follows: 'The progress of the single channel hypothesis has been like that of an old drunk lurching his way home, every minute in danger of falling flat on his face but ever finding a conveniently placed lamp-post, passer-by or whatever for support .... It remains to be seen whether he will fail to get home one evening, or whether he will be retired first' (p. 108). Legge and Barber predict that he will be replaced by a 'team of whizz-kids one of whom will be delegated the old man's job', or, more precisely, 'by a collection of subordinate special-purpose parallel channels'. However, there are still many who would maintain that there is plenty of mileage in the old man yet.

2. TOTE Units, Executive Programs and Subroutines

George Miller, Eugene Galanter and Karl Pribram in their influential book *Plans and the Structure of Behaviour* (1960) proposed a now famous alternative to the S–R reflex as the basic unit of behavioural analysis. They called it the TOTE unit, where TOTE is an acronym for 'Test–Operate–Test–Exit'. The 'test' phase of the cycle checks for any incongruity between the actual and desired state of affairs. If an incongruity is detected, the 'operate' phase is set into action. Then a further test is made. If the incongruity still exists, the 'operate' phase is again activated—and so on until the 'test' phase detects no mismatch, whereupon the cycle is ended. Another important feature of the TOTE unit is that the 'operate' phase can be expanded hierarchically to incorporate any number of subordinate TOTE units.

As a unit of behavioural analysis, the TOTE concept has a number of distinct advantages over the S–R reflex—which held sway for many decades in experimental psychology. First, the *test* notion implies that we have a clear image of the desired outcome against which to check our progress. This means that behaviour is oriented towards the attainment of some future goal rather than being determined solely by immediate or past stimulus events. A major weakness of the S–R approach was, as Luria (1973) put it, that 'it . . . closed its eyes to those forms of behaviour which are controlled, not by the past, but by the *future*, which are constructed as the putting into effect of intentions, plans or programmes, and which, as it can easily be seen, constitute the greater part of all specifically human forms of activity' (p. 246). Second, the provision of feedback loops which shift control from the 'operate' to the 'test' phases, and back again, means that the behaviour so described is highly flexible and adaptive. In the familiar hammering example, used by Miller *et al.* (1960), the objective of the nail being flush with the wood is achieved irrespective of the amount or style of hammering involved. Such an idea is very much in accord with the high degree of variability observed in human actions. To quote Luria (1973) once more: 'It is a most important fact that the invariant motor task is fulfilled not by a constant, fixed set, but by a varying set of movements which, however, lead to the constant, invariant effect' (p. 248).

Another way of conceptualizing human performance, and one that is equivalent in all essentials to the TOTE analysis, is in terms of the *executive programs* and *subroutines* mentioned previously. Executive programs are identical to plans. That is, they define the goal to be achieved, specify the tests and control the sequence of subroutines. In writing a computer program, it is usual to make all subroutines end by transferring control to the executive program, which then orders what to do next. In complex programs, subroutines will call in subordinate subroutines, and so on. However, as Neisser (1967) pointed out, 'the regress of control is not infinite: there is a "highest" or executive routine which is not used by anything else' (p. 296).

In human performance terms, subroutines are analogous to oft-repeated pattern of efferent command signals governing habitual sequences of actions, which demand little or no conscious involvement. But subroutines do not arrive ready made. Each is a 'has been' executive program. The simple act of tying a tie, for example, initially required a conscious plan to govern the nature and order of the individual actions. But with continued practice, it becomes a largely automatic subroutine in the overall plan of dressing. With increasing skill, therefore, each repeated set of actions comes to be relegated to a lower, more automatic level of control in the hierarchy. This gradual down-grading of control with practice provides us with a way of resolving an apparent paradox: the fact that the actions of the highly skilled operator make compara-tively small demands upon his supposedly limited capacity. The key to this resolution is to make the assumption that only executive programs occupy time in the central processor (loosely identified with consciousness). The corollary to this is that when, at any particular moment in the execution of a sensory–motor task, control resides within an automatic subroutine, the central processor is temporarily free to occupy itself with other plans. We shall pursue the implications of this further when we come on to consider so-called 'absent-minded' errors. But for the moment, let us consider the task of learning to drive.

In the very early stages of driving, the learner finds that each movement re-quires continuous conscious control in order to achieve even a partially success-ful outcome. Put in computer language, we can say that each gear change, each turn of the steering wheel, each glance in the mirror, each depression of the brake or clutch pedals, initially required a separate executive program, and each of these compete for the limited capacity of the central processor. The subroutines governed by these many executive programs are the basic skills acquired earlier in life—skills like pushing, pulling, holding and the general ability to coordinate our hand and foot movements. With further practice, the executive programs controlling gear-changing, steering, braking and the like themselves become semi-automated or even wholly automated subroutines. Some take longer to establish than others. Braking, for example, becomes a subroutine long before the many different actions involved in gear-changing become automatic. As the learner driver becomes more and more proficient, so there are fewer and fewer executive programs to occupy central processing time. As Ellingstadt et al. (1970) showed in a study involving real cars and static car simulators, there comes a stage in learning to drive where the learner-driver can subsume all of his actions under two separate executive programs, one relating to speed control and the other to direction control. But while he can perform each one of these subtasks well enough by themselves, he is not yet able to coordinate them under the control of one superordinate executive program. This only occurs in the later stages of skill acquisition.

Thus, the process of learning to drive—and other similarly complex sensory–motor tasks—is characterized by a gradual decrease in the total number of executive programs as they become 'demoted' to the status of automatic subroutines. As this occurs, so the demands on the limited capacity of the central processor slacken off. Finally, of course, the act of driving becomes very largely automated, and the driver is left with 'spare mental capacity'— a concept that has been explored systematically by Brown (1962; 1965a, b).

3. Open-loop and Closed-loop Control Systems

One way of regarding the changes underlying the acquisition of a skill, particularly those relating to the decline in the importance of visual feedback, has been to propose that they reflect a transition from a continuous *closed-loop* mode of control to a condition where control is intermittently *open-loop*; that is, one not actuated by feedback. Keele (1973) has described this transition as follows: 'Early in practice, individual movements may be made, the outcome analysed by the visual system, a correction initiated, feedback analysed again, and so on. Such a skill is said to be under closed-loop control, reflecting the circular relationship between feedback and movement. But gradually, the skill may shift to the open-loop mode, in which movements, at least for some short period, may be autonomous of visual feedback' (p. 118).

Some support for this notion comes from a study by Pew (1966) in which subjects were required to keep a moving spot of light centred on a line using two keys. Performance records taken from the early stages of practice showed that the pattern of correction movements was slow, irregular and of a kind that allowed large errors to build up. In this phase of learning, movements appeared to be wholly under visual control. But after some weeks of practice, the style of responding changed quite dramatically for some subjects. Now they exhibited a rapid and regular pattern of responding in which there was a gradual drift away from the target line which was corrected periodically by a single move-ments of fairly wide excursion. Pew termed this open-loop control because the small regular movements did not appear to be under visual control. Vision was only used occasionally to bring these movements back to the target line.

If skilled movements are not constantly under closed-loop visual control as these results and everyday observations suggest, we are left with at least two alternatives to consider: either that the movements are under proprioceptive feedback control as James (1890) suggested in his *response changing hypothesis;* or that movements are controlled by a motor program independently of peri-pheral feedback, as Lashley (1917) originally suggested. This is the periphera-list–centralist debate that was touched upon earlier.

More recent evidence directed at answering some of the questions raised by this issue has come up with rather equivocal answers. On the one hand, studies like that of Fleishman and Rich (1963), investigating the roles of kinaesthesis and spatial orientation in learning a two-handed coordination task, have led to the conclusion that kinaesthesis plays an increasingly important function as a skill becomes more proficient. On the other hand, there are studies like that of Taub and Berman (1968), using surgical de-afferentation techniques with monkeys, which suggest that kinaesthetic feedback is not essential for skills such as walking, climbing and picking up raisins. Some further data from human subjects in whom kinaesthetic feedback was temporarily blocked by cutting off the blood supply to the forearm and hand with a pressure-cuff lead to the same conclusion: namely, that certain well-practised movements do not necessarily require feedback for their successful execution.

These findings have contributed in recent years to the appearance of a number of theories involving the notion of a *motor program*. Basic to this notion is the idea that movement patterns must be represented certainly in the brain, or perhaps the spinal cord, and that these control skilled movements in the absence of visual, kinaesthetic or auditory feedback. A motor program, therefore, is a sequence of centrally stored commands that is organized prior to the actual execution of the movements. As Lashley (1917) described it, these commands were stored on something like a gramophone record, which once begun could set off the appropriate actions without the need for further modifications from sensory feedback.

Most contemporary theorists favour the notion of a motor program that has the ability to detect error in the motor output, without the use of peripheral feedback, by means of an internal feedback loop (see Adams, 1971; Laszlo and Bairstow, 1971). These are closed-loop models of a motor program. Keele (1968), however, has proposed an entirely open-loop version of a motor program in which the only corrections possible are those that arise *between* movements from knowledge of results. Once initiated, the motor program cannot be modified to take account of small changes that occur during the response, although it is likely that gross changes will cause the operator to revert to a closed-loop mode of control. The evidence for these two types of motor program has recently been reviewed by Gundry (1975).

A COMPOSITE MODEL OF SKILLED PERFORMANCE

A composite model of skilled behaviour is presented below which attempts to summarize and bring together in a parsimonious and logically consistent fashion the various theoretical notions discussed in the previous section. The model consists of a number of information-handling functions linked by communication channels and feedback loops so as to mimic as far as possible certain important aspects of human performance, including the occurrence of the commonplace slips and lapses known generally as absent-minded errors—or, as they will be termed here, '*actions-not-as-planned*'.

Although such a composite model runs the risk of trampling roughshod over the finer shades of theoretical difference, and also of conveying greater 'closure' than the data warrant, it may help the reader to impose some kind

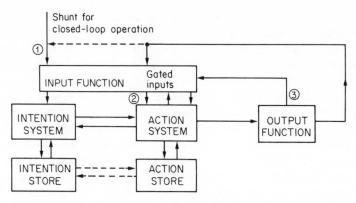

Figure 2.1 Flow diagram showing the basic components of the composite-skill model. The ringed numbers refer to communication channels discussed in the text

of order on an otherwise rather confused and sometimes contradictory set of findings and theories—particularly since the model seeks to emphasize the areas of agreement rather than the points of conflict. The basic components of the model and their interrelationships are shown in Figure 2.1.

The two principal components are the intention system (IS) and the action system (AS). The IS is concerned with formulating plans, initiating the actions necessary to execute them and testing their progress and outcome. Very crudely, we can suggest that the activities of the IS at any one point in time are evident in the current contents of consciousness. In addition, we can assume that these activities are highly verbal, and that the limited capacity of this system is reflected in the fact that only one plan or intention can be maximally activated (within this system) at any one time, though other plans may be more weakly activated (see Shallice, 1972). It is this feature, in particular, that makes the total system vulnerable to error, especially to 'actions-not-as-planned'.

Whereas the IS is the chief executive of the total model, the AS is best regarded as its operations branch. Like the motor programming unit in Laszlo and Bairstow's (1971) theory, the role of the AS is primarily that of structuring well-practised sequences of motor commands. That is, it assembles the sub-routines called for by the executive program received from the IS, and then deals with their moment-to-moment control and intermediate testing.

Linked *via* a two-way channel to the IS is the intention store (I-Store), which contains a variety of previously established executive programs or sets of instructions defining the nature and sequence of their component sub-routines. Similarly linked to the AS is the action store (A-Store), which can hold a great number of subroutines in varying degrees of consolidation.

The two remaining components are the input function (IF) and the output function (OF). Signals originating from independent events in the outside world (channel 1) or as extrinsic (channel 2) and intrinsic (channel 3) feedback are transmitted by the IF to the intention and action systems as indicated in

Figure 2.1. Passage of information through the IF to the AS is *via* selective 'gates' which can be preset to admit certain classes of signal at the expense or even exclusion of other classes. The output function contains the various effector mechanisms necessary to execute the commands of the intention and action systems.

The dashed arrows in Figure 2.1, one extending the external feedback loop so that it enters directly into the IS and others joining the two stores, signify closed-loop operation. When these are in use, control of output functions resides primarily with the IS on a moment-to-moment basis and the motor programming function of the AS is largely bypassed. In this way, the model can function in an entirely closed-loop mode, as in the early stages of skill acquisition, or it can switch between the closed-loop and open-loop modes, as in a well-practised task. We can illustrate these two modes of control with some examples.

Consider the case of getting from bed to the breakfast-table on, say, a Monday morning. First the familiar sequence: the alarm clock rings (incidentally, this external stimulus is not essential; the IS could initiate the actions without it), the IF communicates this to the IS, the IS evaluates the signal by reference to the I-Store and formulates a plan of action—'get out of bed, get washed and shaved, get dressed in the appropriate clothes for a Monday morning, and get down to the breakfast-table by such-and-such a time'. The I-Store is searched for an appropriate executive program. On being found, it is retrieved and the details transmitted to the AS. The AS assembles the individual subroutines of the required action sequence from the A-Store, after which three things occur at more or less the same time. (1) The AS signals back to the IS that the program is complete and can run automatically with only occasional IS test phases (the lower-order tests will be carried out by the AS). This allows the IS to drop the current program into a readily accessible part of the I-Store and to start on a new plan. Like Nature, the IS abhors a vacuum and is always active in working up new plans or reviewing old ones—at least during waking hours; what happens during sleep is more problematic. In selecting the next plan to work on, the IS has two constraints: it should not actually deal with (as opposed to hold in store) more than one major plan at a time; second, new plans should not involve the same subroutines as the ongoing program (that is, the one currently being monitored largely by the AS). (2) The AS sets the 'gates' of the input function so that only intermittent signals are allowed through. (3) The AS signals the OF to set in train the various effector mechanisms involved in the planned set of actions.

During the course of these actions, intermediate tests are performed by the IS. To a large extent, the rigour with which these tests are carried out depends upon the nature and urgency of other plans competing for IS processing time. If these competing plans are ones that can be rapidly dealt with (e.g. 'Shall I carry an umbrella today?', or 'Do I fancy a boiled egg for breakfast?'), then there will be plenty of 'lulls' into which the IS can slot the necessary tests for the 'getting-up' program. But if the IS is occupied with some absorbing or difficult plan, then these tests can either be omitted or carried out inadequately. When the final criterion is met (i.e. the 'exit' rule for the plan)—being washed and shaved, being correctly dressed and being seated in front of a plate of cereal—the IS returns the 'bed-to-breakfast' program to the I-Store, and gets to work on another set of plans.

These events show how the model could operate on a well-established sequence of events in a predominantly open-loop mode. But consider what might happen if, instead of being aroused normally by the alarm clock, our sleeper was awakened by thick smoke coming under the door of the bedroom. Under these circumstances, it is highly unlikely that an appropriate executive program for evacuating the family to safety would be held in store. Consequently, the IS would have to switch to a predominantly closed-loop mode, either welding together existing programs and subroutines, or else devising entirely new sequences of actions. And this would involve heavy reliance upon verbal plan formulation with continuous checking on actions through visual feedback, just as it does for any trainee in the early stages of skill acquisition.

AN ANALYSIS OF EVERYDAY SLIPS AND LAPSES

Another function of the model which is of practical significance is that it offers us a means of both classifying and conceptualizing the various ways in which skilled performance can go wrong. Earlier, we used the getting-up routine as an illustration of how the skill model works when things run smoothly; now let us examine the same procedure as it might be performed by someone who was prone to 'absent-minded' mistakes—that is, actions that do not run according to plan. As we know from personal experience, absent-minded slips seem to occur most frequently when we are carrying out some habitual or largely automatic sequence of actions while, at the same time, we are preoccupied with some engaging but unrelated mental activity. These conditions could easily be met (and frequently are) during the bed-to-breakfast routine.

Suppose, for example, the intention system failed to specify that it was Monday morning. The action system would have no problem in putting together the washing, shaving and underclothes subroutines of the executive program. But when it came to selecting the appropriate outer clothes, the AS would have to rely upon past experience—or, more specifically, upon the habit strengths of the various stored subroutines dealing with outer clothes. It is probable that the most recently used subroutine would be selected. In such a case, instead of putting on the proper shirt, tie and suit, our absent-minded man might select the Sunday-morning routine and dress himself in sweater and jeans. This, then, would be a *selection failure* in which an inappropriate action sequence gets substituted for the intended one. These errors frequently occur when the correct and incorrect actions share an initially common sequence of instructions, as in the dressing example just cited, or when we intend to drive to A but 'wake up' to find ourselves *en route* to B (usually a well-driven path).

On reaching the bathroom, he could fail to distinguish between similar tubes containing toothpaste and shaving cream, and so find himself cleaning his teeth with shaving cream or lathering his face with toothpaste. This would be an example of a *discrimination failure* in which the stimulus is incorrectly identified, usually because it is very similar to one that is expected during the course of a well-established sequence of actions, and triggers an inappropriate response (although one that is usually appropriate for the wrongly classified input). The more practised the actions, the coarser will be the setting of the input function 'gates', and the more likely it is that similar inputs will be confused; or so the model would predict.

On returning to the bedroom, he could open a drawer to select a handkerchief, and then forget what it was that he was seeking. Who has not experienced the 'what-have-I-come-here-for?' phenomenon on entering a room or a shop, or upon staring at the contents of a cupboard or drawer? This represents one form of *storage failure*, and in this case the fault would appear to originate in the I-store. Notice that the model makes separate provision for both the forgetting of intentions and the forgetting of actions. Thus, another form of storage failure involves the forgetting or incorrect recall of preceding actions—as when we lose our place in the sequence or mislay objects we have recently set down. And there are yet other forms of storage failure, as we shall see shortly.

Finally, our absent-minded man could exit the dressing routine too early and leave the bedroom, or even the house, without his tie or jacket. Alternatively, there is the reverse situation, described by William James (1890), in which the 'stop-rule' is disobeyed and the sequence continues beyond its intended termination: 'Very absent-minded persons in going to their bedroom to dress for dinner have been known to take off one garment after another and finally get into bed, merely because that was the habitual issue of the first few movements when performed at a later hour' (p. 115). Both of these represent breakdowns in the verification process, and are termed *test failures*.

In a recent study (Reason, 1976), an attempt was made to collect a corpus of absent-minded errors, much as Meringer and other psycholinguists have done slips of the tongue (see Fromkin, 1973). Thirty-five volunteers (23 women and 12 men) kept a diary of the occasions in which their actions deviated from their intentions over a two-week period. For each of these lapses, the diarists were asked to note down the time of day, their intended action, the nature of the error and the circumstances of its occurrence.

The diaries produced a total of 433 incidents, an average of just over 12 per person for the fortnight, with a range from 0 to 36 incidents (SD = 7.54). There were no statistically significant effect due to age or sex. Women, on average, made slightly more errors—12.5 as opposed to 10.9 for men—although this may simply have reflected their greater conscientiousness in reporting. There was a tendency, although again not significant, for errors to occur more frequently at three periods of the day: between 8 and 12 in the morning, between 4 and 6 in the afternoon, and a smaller 'peak' between 8 and 10 in the evening. Over 20 per cent of all the men's slips occurred between 8 and 10 in the morning; whereas, for women, the morning 'peak' was somewhat later, falling between 10 and 12 o'clock.

Before trying to classify these lapses, it was first necessary to establish where they fitted into the broader spectrum of human error in general. As Singleton (1973) has pointed out, a search for the meaning of the term 'error' yields only synonyms—'fault', 'mistake', 'defect', and the like—not a true definition. But it seemed reasonable to assume that 'an error is a planned action that fails to achieve its desired consequences', and this without the intervention of some chance or unforeseeable agency. Logically, we can fail to achieve the desired outcome of our actions in at least two ways: when the actions go as planned, but the plan is inadequate; or when the plan is satisfactory, but the actions do not go as planned. On the face of it, absent-minded slips and lapses fall into the second category rather than the first, hence the

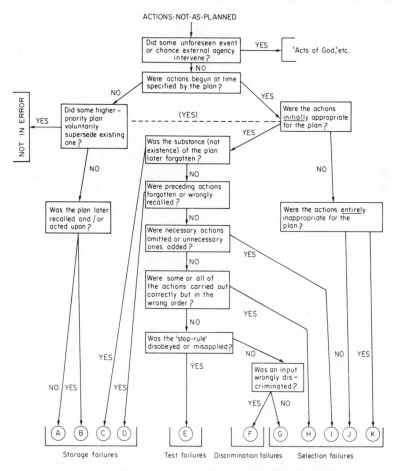

Figure 2.2 Algorithm for classifying actions-not-as-planned

cumbersome but more apt term 'action-not-as-planned' was used to describe the focus of the enquiry.

Using the diary material to guide its construction, an algorithm for classifying the actions-not-as-planned was devised. This is shown in Figure 2.2. The reason for producing it in this form was to make the logic explicit so that, in theory, its reliability could be checked by having other judges apply it to the same data, although in practice this has not yet been done. The classificatory scheme yielded 11 categories of error, which could be further grouped into the four types of failure discussed earlier. Actual examples of these categories together with a percentage indication of their relative frequency of occurrence are given in Table 2.1.

Not surprisingly, forgetting or storage failures of one kind or another represented the most common class of error (41.4 per cent), with selection failures (37.2 per cent) a close second. Nearly 5 per cent of the incidents were unclassifiable according to the scheme shown in Figure 2.2. These included such things as waking to find cigarette ends in the bedside ashtray with no recollection of having smoked them, and various non-actions such as having trouble in putting a name to a familiar face. There was little or no relationship between the type of error and time of day, but there was a marked tendency (falling just short of the 5 per cent level of significance) for women to have proportionately more selection and discrimination failures, while men tended to have relatively more storage and test failures.

Inspection of Table 2.1 reveals that some of the underlying mechanisms of failure are difficult to establish. Branching errors (category G in Figure 2.2), for example, have been included among the selection failures. But it could equally well be argued that errors such as these can arise because the choice point is incorrectly discriminated, or because the original plan is temporarily lost from store, or even because there was a failure in the testing procedure. Nevertheless, these data provide some support for the failure categories derived from the model. Although the precise allocation of certain errors is questionable, most of them can be encompassed within the four types of failure:storage, discrimination, selection and test.

These everyday examples of actions-not-as-planned usually have trivial, even amusing consequences. But when the same types of error occur on the flight-deck of an aircraft, for instance, their effects can be catastrophic. The details of a number of aircraft accidents (taken from the Accident Investigation Branch reports, HMSO) involving some determinable pilot error are given in Table 2.2. Examination of the contributing factors indicates that, taken by themselves, these pilot errors are hardly distinguishable from our everyday slips and lapses. Their disastrous consequences would appear to stem not so much from the erroneous action as from the unforgiving environment in which it was committed. It follows, therefore, that a closer study of our commonplace errors may provide a valuable insight into the nature of accidents in general. To quote Freud (1922) on the subject: 'In scientific work it is more profitable to take up whatever lies before one whenever a path towards its exploration present itself. And then, if one carries it through thoroughly, without prejudice or pre-conceptions, one may, with good fortune and by

Table 2.1. Examples and Relative Frequencies (Given as Percentages in Parentheses) of the Categories of Actions-not-as-planned Derived from Figure 2.1

Presumed type of failure	Category	Examples and percentages
Storage	A	*Undetectable errors*—both the original intention and the failure to execute it are forgotten. (0)
Storage	B	*Forgetting items in the plan*—part of the plan is temporarily lost but later recalled. Example: forgetting to post a letter during a shopping expedition. (22.4)
Storage	C	*Forgetting the plan*—where the existence of the plan is not forgotten, indeed its actions are usually under way, but its substance cannot be recalled. Example: 'Went, over to open the drawer, but forgot what I wanted'. (6.5)
Storage	D	*Forgetting preceding actions*—preceding actions are either forgotten or incorrectly recalled. Often results in losing one's place in the plan. Example: boiling a second kettle of water after the tea has already been made. Another common variant is forgetting where articles were put down. (12.5)
Test	E	*Verifications errors*—where a planned sequence is terminated too early or is continued beyond its intended conclusion. Example: getting into bath with clothes still on. (6.0)
Discrimination	F	*Classification errors*—input wrongly identified, often leading to actions appropriate for erroneous classification but not for ongoing plan. Example: taking out one's own front-door key on approaching a friend's house. (10.9)
Selection	G	*Branching errors*—where two different outcomes have initial actions in common, but the actions proceed towards the unintended outcome. Example on passing through back porch on the way to his car, one subject put on the clothes and wellington boots that are kept there for gardening. (14.3)
Selection	H	*Misordering errors*—the correct actions are executed, but in the wrong order. Example: while filling a bucket with water, subject replaced the lid before turning off the tap. (6.0)
Selection	I	*Insertions and omissions*—when unwanted actions are added, or necessary actions omitted. Example: turning on a light when leaving a room in daylight; filling electric kettle, switching on socket, but failing to insert plug. (12.5)
Selection	J	*Corrected errors*—where a sequence of actions initially deviates from plan, but is later corrected. Example: starting to look for a jar of coffee in a cupboard and then realizing it is kept in pantry. (1.2)
Selection	K	*Total errors*—where all actions are inappropriate for plan. Example: trying to light an electric fire with a box of matches. (3.2)

virtue of the inter-relationship linking each thing to every other (hence, also, the small to the great), find, even in the course of such humble labour, a road to the study of the great problems' (p. 21).

What have we learned from this preliminary study of our everyday errors? The results of the diary study tell us little that is new or surprising; indeed,

Table 2.2. Pilot Error Resembling Absent-minded Behaviour

Aircraft type; place and date of accident	Type of accident	Casual factors and presumed* category of failure
Dove; London Airport, 22 June 1955	Crash following power failure	Pilot shut down port instead of starboard engine in which a fault had developed (selection failure)
Viscount; Blackbushe Airport, 20 Jan. 1956	Crash shortly after take-off on training flight	Training Capt. operated No. 3 high-pressure cock lever instead of No. 4 when simulating a failure of No. 4 engine. Resulted in loss of all power in starboard engines on take-off (selection failure)
Viscount; Tarbolton, 28 March 1958	Aircraft flew into high ground	Capt. misread altimeter: read 4500 ft as 14500 ft and perpetuated the 10000 ft error until aircraft crashed 5 min later (discrimination failure)
Varsity; Gloucester, 27 March 1963	Crashed during asymmetric approach exercises with port propeller feathered	Pilot selected starboard engine IDLE/CUT-OFF switch to CUT-OFF instead of the port engine switch to RUN position when attempting to restart port engine (selection failure)
Britannia; Ljubljana, 1 September 1966	Crashed short of runway	Capt. did not set altimeter to local barometric pressure as instructed by Air Traffic Control. Error overlooked in check procedure (storage? and test failure)
Piper Apache; Hamble, 10 January 1967	Port engine failed to respond when overshooting from simulated single engine approach	Instructor probably omitted to return mixture control of port engine to FULL RICH ON when prop. was unfeathered during approach (storage failure)
HS 125; Luton Airport, 23 December 1967	Crash following practice engine failure after take-off	Following closure of thrust lever to simulate engine failure, other engine was inadvertently shut down (selection failure)
Boeing and VC10; over Surrey, 11 November 1969	Air miss	Capt. of Boeing failed to reset altimeter at transition altitude (storage? and test failure)
BAC One-Eleven; Italy, 14 Jan. 1969	Crash immediately after take-off	After failure in No. 2 engine, crew closed throttle of No. 1 engine in error. Failed to notice their mistake and also were not aware that No. 2 engine had been reduced in thrust after an inadvertent displacement of throttle control (selection and test? failure)

*It must be emphasized that these are speculative categories of failure.

the surprise would be if they had, since we have all been making similar observations for most of our lives. But they do suggest at least two general conclusions, and point to some further lines of research.

First, it seems that actions-not-as-planned are a particular hazard for the skilled performer. That is, the errors described in Table 2.1 appear to be a feature of well-practised or habitual tasks in which the component actions are run off fairly automatically with only intermittent conscious checking. In other words, they seem to be a particular characteristic of the 'open-loop' mode of operation. If our limited-capacity central processor is not engaged in the moment-to-moment control of all our actions, then it is likely to be occupied with something other than the job in hand for a good deal of the time. With this dual activity comes the risk of mutual interference. So, built into the fabric of skilled performance, we have a prescription for errors of in attention and forgetting. But, as we have already mentioned, attending too closely to the individual actions of a skilled task is likely to be even more disruptive. Thus, to achieve an error-free performance when we have reached a certain level of proficiency, it is necessary to strike a very delicate balance between attending too closely or not enough to the ongoing activity. What is remarkable, then, is not that we make errors, but that we make them so comparatively rarely.

The second conclusion is that actions-not-as-planned are hardly ever purely random events. This is not necessarily to suggest, as Freud (1914; 1922) did, that they are prompted by some unconscious wish or need. Rather that absent-minded actions bear some meaningful relationship either to the existing plan and its subordinate network of associated actions, or to some past, future or coexistent plan and its subroutines. The implication is that these errors are to some extent lawful and predictable. Certainly, the psycholinguists have established some general laws for slips of the tongue, errors that are very similar to those considered here (see Fromkin, 1973). The fact that 95 per cent of the 433 behavioural slips netted in the diary study were reduced without too much abuse to some 10 observable categories indicates that 'laws of absent-mindedness', albeit tentative and probabilistic, are not beyond the bounds of possibility. At least, if established, they would be open to empirical testing—which is more than can be said for Freud's theory of unconscious motivation.

One line of research presently being pursued is the investigation of 'programmable errors'. That is, errors that have such a high probability of occurrence given the right circumstances that the investigator can create them at will in his subjects. A good example of such an error is the children's question-and-answer game cited by Kimble and Perlmuter (1970):

'Q.　What do we call the tree grows from acorns?
A.　Oak.
Q.　What do we call a funny story?
A.　Joke.

Q. The sound made by a frog?
A. Croak.
Q. What is another word for cape?
A. Cloak.
Q. What do we call the white of an egg?
A. Yolk (sic!)'

There appear to be two powerful error-inducing factors operating together to trigger the incorrect response 'yolk'. The preceding questions establish a strong *image set*: that is, an expectation that the answer will rhyme with 'oak'. In addition, there are the widely differing strengths of the *associative bonds* between the key word 'egg' and its possible responses. The correct answer, 'albumin', is likely to have a much weaker bonding than 'yolk'. The combined effect of the image set and the associative bond is almost irresistible: the victim is primed to select the incorrect response with the stronger bond by his tendency to retrieve words from store on the basis of their sound rather than their meaning (see Brown and McNeill, 1966). An error as predictable as this 'oak–yolk' effect gives us an opportunity to study systematically, the consequences of manipulating its circumstances. It also raises other questions: will the same combination of factors produce errors in non-verbal tasks? For example, can we make an individual strike the wrong response key by biasing the direction of his responses to right or left (equivalent to establishing an image set) and also the strengths of association (the bond) between the keys and their respective signals?

Of necessity, accident researchers are primarily concerned with the reduction of human error. But there is a strong case for arguing that we are likely to learn more about the mechanics of error if we deliberately set out to create them rather than eliminate them. This approach is in accord with the recommendations of Hughlings Jackson and Lashley (1951), who suggested that we can learn a great deal about cognitive functioning by studying its transitory malfunctions, and by working 'backwards' into the system from its output rather than forward by its input. Research in the rapidly expanding field of psycholinguistics has demonstrated that speech errors can provide many insights into the underlying structure of language. The theme developed in the latter part of this chapter is that a closer study of actions-not-as-planned will tell us more about the underlying organization of complex motor skills, and thus provide us with a theoretical base from which to limit the occurrence of these errors in unforgiving situations.

REFERENCES

Adams, J. A. (1969). 'Acquisition of motor responses', in M. H. Marx (Ed.), *Learning Processes*, Macmillan, Toronto.

Adams, J. A. (1971). 'A closed-loop theory of motor learning', *Journal of Motor Behaviour*, **3**, 111.

Allport, A., Antonis, B., and Reynolds, P. (1972). 'On the division of attention: a disproof of the single channel hypothesis', *Quart. J. exp. Psychol.*, **24**, 225.

Bartlett, F. C. (1958). *Thinking: An Experimental and Social Study*, Allen & Unwin, London.

Bennett, A. (1910). *Clayhanger*, Penguin, Harmondsworth.

Broadbent, D. E. (1958). *Perception and Communication*, Pergamon, London.

Brown, I. D. (1960). 'Many messages from few sources', *Ergonomics*, **3**, 159.

Brown, I. D. (1962). 'Measuring the "spare mental capacity" of car drivers by a subsidiary auditory task', *Ergonomics*, **5**, 247.

Brown, I. D. (1965a). 'A comparison of two subsidiary tasks used to measure fatigue in car drivers', *Ergonomics*, **8**, 467.

Brown, I. D. (1965b). 'Effect of a car radio on driving in traffic', *Ergonomics*, **8**, 475.

Brown, R. W. and McNeill, D. (1966). 'The "tip of the tongue" phenomena', *Journal of Verbal Learning and Verbal Behaviour*, **5**, 325.

Bryan, W. L., and Harter, N. (1899). 'Studies on the telegraphic language: The acquisition of a hierarchy of habits', *Psychol. Rev.*, **6**, 345.

Cherry, C. (1953). 'Some experiments on the reception of speech with one and with two ears', *Journal of the Acoustical Society of America*, **25**, 975.

Craik, K. (1948). 'Theory of the human operator in control systems', *Brit. J. Psychol.* **38**, 56.

Davis, R. (1956). 'The limits of the "psychological refractory period"', *Quart. J. exp. Psychol.*, **8**, 24.

Ellingstadt, U. S., Hagen, R. E., and Kimball, K. A. (1970). *An Investigation of the Acquisition of Driving Skill*, Technical Report No. 11, Dept. of Psychology, University of S. Dakota, Vermillion, S. Dakota.

Fitts, P. M. (1964). 'Perceptual motor skill learning', in A. W. Melton (Ed.), *Categories of Human Learning*, Academic Press, New York.

Fleishman, E. A., and Rich, S. (1963). 'Role of kinesthetic and spatial–visual abilities in perceptual motor learning', *J. exp. Psychol.*, **66**, 6.

Freud, S. (1914). *Psychopathology of Everyday Life*, Benn, London.

Freud, S. (1922). *Introductory Lectures on Psycho-Analysis*, Allen & Unwin, London.

Fromkin, V. A. (1973). *Speech Errors as Linguistic Evidence*, Mouton, The Hague.

Gundry, J. (1975). Unpublished Ph.D. thesis, University of Reading.

Hick, W. E. (1952). 'On the rate of gain of information', *Quart. J. exp. Psychol.*, **4**, 11.

Hick, W. E. and Bates, J. A. V. (1950). 'The human operator of control mechanism', *Permanent Records of Research and Development*, No. 17,204 Ministry of Supply, HMSO, London.

Hyman, R. (1953). 'Stimulus information as a determinant of reaction time', *J. exp. Psychol.*, **45**, 188.

James, W. (1890). *The Principles of Psychology*, Vol. 1, Holt, New York (reprinted by Dover, 1950).

Keele, S. W. (1968). 'Movement control in skilled motor performance', *Psychol. Bull.*, **70**, 387.

Keele, S. W. (1973). *Attention and Human Performance*, Goodyear, California.

Kimble, G. A., and Parlmuter, L. C. (1970). 'The problem of volition', *Psychol. Rev.*, **77**, 361.

Lashley, K. S. (1917). 'The accuracy of movement in the absence of excitation from the moving organ', *Amer. J. Physiol.*, **43**, 169.

Lashley, K. S. (1951). 'The problem of serial order in behaviour', in L. A. Jeffress (Ed.), *Cerebral Mechanisms in Behaviour: The Hixon Symposium*, Wiley, New York.

Laszlo, J. I., and Bairstow, P. J. (1971). 'The compression block technique: A note on procedure', *Journal of Motor Behaviour*, **3**, 313.

Legge, D., and Barber, P. L. (1976). *Information and Skill*, Methuen, London.

Luria, A. R. (1973). *The Working Brain: An Introduction to Neuropsychology*, Penguin, Harmondsworth.

44

Miller, G. A., Galanter, E., and Pribram, K. H. (1960). *Plans and the Structure of Behaviour*, Holt, Rinehart & Winston, New York.

Moray, N. (1967). 'Where is capacity limited? A survey and a model', *Acta Psychol.*, **27**, 84.

Neisser, U. (1967). *Cognitive Psychology*, Appleton-Century-Crofts, New York.

Neisser, U. (1969). Proceedings of XIX International Congress of Psychology, London.

Newell, A., Shaw, J. C., and Simon, H. A. (1958). 'Elements of a theory of human problem solving', *Psychol. Rev.*, **65**, 151.

Pew, R. W. (1966). 'Acquisition of hierarchical control over the temporal acquisition of a skill', *J. exp. Psychol.*, **71**, 764.

Polanyi, M. (1958). *Personal Knowledge*, Routledge & Kegan Paul, London.

Reason, J. T. (1976). 'Actions not as planned. A study of absent-minded behaviour, *New Society* (in press).

Shaffer, L. H. (1975). 'Multiple attention in continuous verbal tasks', in P. M. A. Rabbit and S. Dornic (Eds.), *Attention and Performance*, V, Academic Press, London.

Shallice, T. (1972). 'Dual functions of consciousness', *Psychol. Rev.*, **5**, 383.

Shannon, C. E., and Weaver, W. (1949). *The Mathematical Theory of Communication*, University of Illinois Press, Urbana.

Singleton, W. T. (1973). 'Theoretical approaches to human error', *Ergonomics*, **16**, 727.

Smith, M. C. (1967). 'Theories of the psychological refractory period', *Psychol. Bull.*, **67**, 202.

Spence, D. P. (1973). 'Analog and digital descriptions of behaviour', *American Psychologist*, **28**, 479.

Taub, E., and Berman, A. J. (1968). 'Movement and learning in the absence of sensory feedback', in S. J. Freedman (Ed.), *The Neuropsychology of Spatially Oriented Behaviour*, Dorsey, Homewood, Illinois.

Vince, M. A. (1948). 'Intermittency of control movements and the psychological refractory period', *Brit. J. Psychol.*, **38**, 149.

Watson, J. B. (1907). 'Kinaesthetic and organic sensations: Their role in the reactions of the white rat to the maze', *Psychol. Rev. Monogr. Suppl.*, Whole No. 33.

Welford, A. T. (1968). *Fundamentals of Skill*, Methuen, London.

Wiener, N. (1948). *Cybernetics*, Wiley, New York.

Woodworth, R. S. (1899). 'The accuracy of voluntary movement', *Psychol. Rev. Monogr. Suppl.*, Whole No. 13.

3

LEARNING SOCIAL SKILLS

Kenneth T. Strongman

It seems reasonable to say that one cannot interact socially without being changed in some way by the experience. The change might be small, it might occur unconsciously, but it will be there. This is rather like the forensic scientist's point that one leaves physical traces of oneself on whatever environment one moves in. One is changed socially by any encounter, and one's actions change others. Social interaction must therefore involve learning, in adults as well as more obviously in children.

To take another vantage point for a moment, a brief look around shows quite clearly that many adults are socially incompetent. They upset and embarrass their associates, they say the wrong things in interviews and fail to get jobs, they strike others as untrustworthy because their direction of gaze is 'shifty', and so on. To explore one example in a little more detail, think of the consternation which is caused by the person who, as part of his discourse in a crowded social gathering, cuts across other conversations by penetratingly mentioning the name of someone who is engrossed at the other side of the room. There is no way of responding to, or ignoring this without ruining the tempo of most of the surrounding interactions. Those who behave in such ways *seem* to have learned but little socially. Yet, of course, they must have learned a great deal, and in fact, research and everyday experiences show that they are capable of learning far more and of becoming more socially competent (competence naturally being defined by the particular society or culture).

A viewpoint commonly found in texts of social psychology is that social interaction is one area of behaviour in which everyone shows steady, if in some cases slow, improvement throughout adult life. Many capacities reach their peaks in the late teens or early twenties and thereafter slide gently downhill. This is not the case with social propensities, or so the texts lead us to believe. Again, this seems to be a reasonable, and a comforting point. But it is difficult to document. It is easy to accept that adults learn new social skills and refine those they already have, but how do they do so? what do they learn? where? and when? and what makes them learn? Answers to these questions are difficult to provide and sometimes even more difficult to accept.

It is self-evident that human social behaviour is extraordinarily complex, arguably even more so than individual behaviour. It has many facets, each of which has received separate study, much of this study never mentioning the word learning. And yet by its very nature, any change in an individual's social behaviour involves learning, be it analysed cognitively or behaviourally. So, the idea that adults learn social skills gives a *frame of reference*, a *viewpoint*, from which to study social behaviour. Some social psychologists have adopted this viewpoint and it has led them to empirical investigations of social learning and to the development of social learning theory. It is with representative examples of this research and theory that the remainder of this chapter will be concerned. However, it should be borne in mind throughout that this look at social psychology will inevitably be biased. Although learning is accepted in studies of children's social behaviour (socialization *must* involve learning), it is not so integrally recognized at the adult level.

SOCIALIZATION

There have been vast amounts of research and theory into the socialization of the child, such work usually emphasizing traditional aspects of learning plus the somewhat thorny matter of identification—thorny, since it is still unresolved whether or not identification itself can be accounted for by learning theory. Texts are vague about where the socialization process ends. If it is regarded as a matter of turning a socially ignorant and incompetent child into a socially adequate adult, the reason for this vagueness is obvious: what is social adequacy or maturity? This is a question to which there can be no definite answer; social interaction is a relative matter and involves constant change. Socialization does not simply end, even though it might slow down.

Argyle (1964) suggests three all-embracing ways in which adult socialization continues. The first, and most obvious to a learning theorist, is that of instrumental learning, *via* the usual rewards and punishments. The conditioning of verbal behaviour and the changes brought about by behaviour therapy provide the most straightforward examples.

The second route to adult social learning, and one which is doubtless obvious to the cognitive theorist, is *via* cognition or higher mental processes. Here, interest is centred on social learning through changes in the perception and interpretation of social events. As will be seen below, examples of such learning come from analyses of attitude change, persuasion and psychotherapy. Changes can also take place in self-perception, easily brought about for example by wearing formal rather than informal clothes or by adopting different roles to fit various social circumstances.

Finally, there is social learning through what Argyle terms emotional arousal. He characterizes this as involving sudden changes in behaviour, intense emotional arousal, and taking place under extreme social pressure. Examples would come from brainwashing, indoctrination and, less obviously, some aspects of formal education.

An example which embodies these various types of learning (which in real life would probably be inseparable) is given by a person who is starting a new occupation. Not only does he learn the techniques of the job, but also the social behaviour and attitudes which society considers to be appropriate to the occupation. Consider a teacher, for example. In his new role, he is partially cut off from the rest of society and caught up in a somewhat cloistered environment. He rapidly learns what to do and to say, and when. He will probably change his self-perception a little, perhaps by starting to wear clothes somewhat different from those he wore as a student. He might start to imitate the social behaviours of some teacher whom he particularly admires. He will pick up new ways of talking, and new manners of expression. In sum, through complex learning processes, his identity will undergo some change.

This example shows the rather arbitrary distinctions which were made in the analysis above. In practice, any adult social learning contains elements of reward and punishment, perceptual change and emotional involvement. Again, this highlights the point that adult social learning is a matter of looking at social behaviour from a particular perspective. Most of social behaviour can be seen as learning if this particular orientation is taken.

LEARNING ROLES

To some extent the order in which one discusses the various aspects of adult social learning is arbitrary. As good a place as any to begin is with social roles. At various times in adult life, each of us has to learn new roles. For example, the social behaviour expected of an accountant is different from that expected from the same person reading accountancy at university. The social behaviour expected of parents is different from that expected of childless couples. Retirement brings with it an enforced learning of new roles, at a time when learning is especially difficult.

One of the most cogent analyses of role-learning is made by Secord and Backman (1974), to whom the interested reader should refer for a fuller exposition than is given here. They distinguish between the content and process sides of role-learning. To deal with the *content* first, when acquiring a new role, a person has quickly to pick up the norms of behaviour which go with it. He has to learn to share the attitudes (or some of them at least) of his role partners. If he does not, then he will not gain acceptance as a creature in that role. So, in general, for example, the teacher has to share attitudes with his fellow teachers rather than with his pupils, and, to gain acceptance, the retired person has to take on (however unwillingly) some of the attitudes of other retired persons. Not only does this refer to the attitudes themselves, but also to the emotional reactions that typically go with them. For example, a trainee doctor who becomes red in the face and apparently panics at an emergency will not easily be accepted in his role. Doctors are supposed to remain calm.

Further, on the content side, new roles require the learning of new skills; not merely the skills of the job or position but also the attendant social skills, such as dealing with new partners who share the role. Take the example of someone who is attending a university for the first time as a student. Clearly, he must acquire the necessary academic skills, but he also has to learn how to cope with his fellow students, persons who have probably come from many areas of society and who are thrust together in a group which has little in the way of external constraint or responsibility. The strain can be considerable, and not surprisingly, a great deal of social learning occurs as the student adjusts himself to this somewhat unusual role.

Finally, under the heading of the content part of role-learning, Secord and Backman make mention of identity. The person in a new role has to learn a perfect conception of himself in the role. A young man qualifies as a barrister; apart from learning the attitudes and behaviour expected from him in chambers and in court, he must gain a picture of himself as he would like to be within a few years—an ideal that he can work towards. Probably, he does this by emulating the characteristics of some successful barrister whom he admires, much as the child emulates the admired adult.

As the term implies, the *process* side of role-learning is concerned with the actual way in which the learning occurs. It does not happen simply by an old-stager teaching the young blood what is expected of him, although doubtless this is a part of it. It comes about through an active process of practice, problem-solving and studying the attitudes of those already in the role. Perhaps the best way of understanding this process is through a consideration of the factors which might enhance or impede it.

Broadly, there are two levels of influence on the learning of new social roles—those which stem from the social system and those which arise from the specific situations in which the learning has to occur. The obvious influence from the social system is that of rewards and costs. What will it be worth to the person to adopt his new role, and what will it cost him? Will the financial gain of a new job outweigh the possible loss in personal integrity? The theme of social rewards and costs will be returned to later.

Other influences on role-learning from the social system are less obvious but no less important. For example, a clearly defined social role is more easily learned than one which is less well defined. It is easier to learn the social role of a plumber, for instance, than it is to learn that of a social worker. Another source of influence is the similarity between a new role and an old. Role-learning is a continuous process, and if a new role is similar to or at least compatible with an old one then it will be more easily acquired. For example, it would be easier for a civil servant to learn the social role of a business administrator than it would be for him to learn that of a sailor.

This leads to the more general point that much of role-learning depends on what has been learned, or partly learned, beforehand. Each of us lives out roles in fantasy. For example, if person A works alongside person B, who is his superior, A will probably find it is a fairly simple matter to adopt the new role if he is promoted to B's job; more so than would an outsider. He has had a chance to see the role being applied and has probably fantasized about it.

Finally, from the social system comes the influence of what is termed the pervasiveness of the role. If a role is broad, covering many aspects of life and behaviour, then it will be learned slowly. The more circumscribed it is the more quickly it can be learned. It would (or should) take many years to learn the complex social roles of a politician, and perhaps only weeks to learn those of an assembly-line worker.

The other major source of influence on role-learning is the situation in which it occurs. Some groups and institutions bear this point in mind actively and are constructed to bring about the most effective learning in their members. This is particularly the case where fairly extreme changes have to be wrought, p.o.w. camps, indoctrination programmes and the armed forces providing good examples.

Such institutions or programmes usually work on two fronts. First, they desocialize, that is, they rapidly exorcise any previous roles their members might have played. They achieve this mainly by isolating the person from his previous sources of reward and punishment; they cut him off from the society he has known. Think for example of the few weeks of 'basic' training the army recruit has to undergo, when he is allowed out of the camp rarely, if at all.

Second, they build the person up again in the new way; they resocialize him. Usually, this is done by bombarding him with a massive number of demands, so that most of his waking life is filled with learning his new role. Again, the armed forces provide good examples. But more surprising perhaps is that this is how some postgraduate schools in North American universities go about their indoctrination. The student is put under such pressure of work that he cannot possibly get it all done. To do well, he must think of nothing other than his work.

Often this resocialization process emphasizes interaction only with members of the new group, helped along by ritual and ceremony. The prospective member is given a status lower than the low, whilst the existing member has enormous status. All of which promotes envy, which is thought to act as a motivator in learning the new roles. The person may even have to go through primitive ordeals such as hazing in American military academies or fagging in British public schools.

Perhaps enough has been said about role-learning for the general points to be made. Adults learn new roles all the time, both in fantasy and reality. Such learning can be broken down into its content—what is learned, and the processes of learning themselves and the influences on them. As with all adult social learning, role-learning is a continuous process.

PROPAGANDA, EDUCATION AND PERSUASION

As well as learning new roles, adults also learn much in the broader social context of education. Other chapters in this book deal more precisely with higher education, so the purpose of this section is to look at some of the links between education and propaganda, and to explore the ways in which it is possible to persuade people to change their viewpoints. For a fuller account of the ideas which follow the reader is directed to Aronson (1972) and Zimbardo and Ebbeson (1969).

Advertisements on hoardings and on the screen are obvious attempts to sell by persuasion, often with chicanery. Could the same be said of literature and film, for example, where the characters and situations are often crudely stereotyped and two-dimensional? What about attempts by pop-stars and politicians to project images? Does such behaviour fall under the same heading? And more extremely, consider formal education. Is the teaching which goes on in universities, colleges and centres of adult education so very different from advertisements and image-projection? It has its built-in prejudices and over-simplifications, often without the instructor being aware of them.

It is possible to regard any attempt to change people by persuasion, that is, to make them learn something new, as either education or propaganda. One's viewpoint on this depends on more basic values. This apart, the general point is that it is possible to persuade people, adults, not just children, into new beliefs and new ways of behaving. Persuasion works, we learn from it; but how?

According to the analyses made by Aronson and Zimbardo there are three significant factors which help to determine persuasability: the characteristics of the message itself, where it comes from, and the person(s) to whom it is directed.

To deal first with the nature of the communication, this has at least four important aspects.

(1) A message designed to persuade someone can be couched in *emotional or logical* language. In general, it has been found to be more effective if it is mainly emotional, although of course it is sometimes difficult to distinguish between the emotional and the logical (e.g. Leventhal, 1970). Also, what has become known as the 'fear–fact' sequence is effective. The procedure is to make the person one is trying to change fearful or anxious, and then show him how the desired attitudes or behaviours will reduce the fear.

(2) In presenting a persuasive argument, one can present *both sides* of it or merely *one side*. The effectiveness of these alternatives depends on the audience. An intelligent person is more likely to be persuaded by a two-sided argument, whereas a less intelligent person is more easily persuaded by a one-sided argument. In the former case, the person will perhaps feel that no attempt is being made to con him, and in the latter, the person will probably not know of the alternative argument anyway.

(3) Next is the matter of the *order* in which information is presented. Is it better to present the most important item first or last? The answer here is that it depends on the circumstances. It is best to present the important item first if there is no time gap between this and the other information and the audience does not have to make a decision for some days. On the other hand, it is best to present the important information last if there is a time gap between items and a decision has to be made straight away by the audience (e.g. Miller and Campbell, 1959).

(4) Finally, how *extreme* should the message be? If the persons being persuaded are already extreme in their views, what is the best way for the persuader to act? The evidence here is less clear. Some investigators find that a moderate amount of discrepancy between the communicator and the audience leads to the maximum change or learning. Others find that the larger the discrepancies the more the change in attitudes or behaviour. Aronson (1972) argues that it depends on the source of the communication. If its source is highly credible, then the information can be strongly discrepant from the views of the recipients and still be effective. If the source has low credibility, highly discrepant views will not be persuasive.

This leads on nicely to the general question of the source of a persuasive communication. *Credibility* is of prime importance. Information from a high-status source such as *The Times*, a medical journal, a leading sportsman, etc., is more likely to persuade than the same information from a low-status source such as *The Mirror*, a pulp magazine or an unknown athlete (e.g. Hovland and Weiss, 1951). Of course, this credibility factor depends somewhat upon the audience. Harold Wilson, for example, although obviously of high status, is not equally credible to everyone.

Linked to the credibility of the source of information is its *trustworthiness*. This can be manipulated in a number of ways. For example, a person in an attractive occupation will appear more trustworthy and hence be more effective in changing behaviour than will someone from a less attractive job (e.g. Walster and Festinger, 1962). An athlete will sell more cornflakes than a nutritionist. Or apparent trustworthiness can be increased by seemingly arguing against self-interest. For example, if I wish to persuade someone of something and begin by saying that universities are vastly overrated places, he is more likely to find me trustworthy. I must be honest if I am saying such things.

Finally, there are features of the audience which help to determine how much they learn or are changed by social persuasion. In general, women are more easily persuasible than men, and he who feels inadequate is more easily persuasible than the person of high self-esteem. Also, if a person comes to the communication in a content, well-fed, relaxed state he will be more receptive.

These then are some of the main research findings concerning persuasive communications. Doubtless, when they are all combined, they provide a means of social learning; they bring about changes in attitudes and behaviour. If a lecturer is of high status, is credible and trustworthy, if he takes into account his particular audience, weighs his words in the right balance between the emotional and the logical, presents his information in the appropriate order and with the right amount of discrepancy between himself and his listeners, then he will be persuasive. His audience will have learned something; they will have been manipulated, socially persuaded.

But there are still several qualifications to this already well-qualified summary. For example, a person whose basic beliefs have been made a little shaky by what has been said to him becomes less likely to continue listening and looking. Instead he is likely to spend his time distorting the arguments or creating other arguments to avoid making basic changes to his beliefs. Unless a person's time is so occupied that there is no opportunity for other thoughts, his fundamental and important beliefs are difficult to change with direct communication. Using the principles which come from what is described above, it is easy enough to change a person's opinions. Attitudes which are firmly grounded in an emotional base are far more resistant.

It may be that the work and ideas which have been briefly reviewed in this section seem only remotely connected to social learning in adults. As ever with this topic, it is a matter of orientation. Variously viewed, the notions described above can be seen as the learning of new beliefs or ideas through social influence or persuasion; or, on the other hand, the manipulation or education of people to new ways of thinking.

JUDGMENTS

Via a discussion of how adults learn to make judgments of themselves and others, this section will accept straightforwardly that any social interaction involves reward and punishment, praise and blame and positive and negative feedback for each of the interactants. It has been suggested by some social psychologists that it is through the process of social learning and feedback that we gradually form opinions about ourselves. Again, this must be seen as a never-ending and constantly changing process.

Hill (1968) makes a cogent appraisal of what he terms evaluative reinforcement. He suggests that the probability of some social responses increases through interaction. Stimuli *might* acquire evaluative meaning in a number of ways. First, they might be associated with a primary drive such as pain. Second, some words, glances or bodily movements might be aversive to the receiver since they arouse anxiety. The person made anxious in this way could well evaluate himself negatively.

Although Hill discusses other ways in which stimuli might gain evaluative meaning, there is little point in pursuing them here, since they have no good supporting evidence. In spite of this lack of experimental support, it is clear that evaluative reinforcers do spring from interaction. For example, if someone is consistently evaluated as 'creative' or 'hard' or 'warm' by those around him, he will almost inevitably gain this as a self-impression and begin to judge his own actions accordingly. Thus he will learn a whole new range of verbal and non-verbal social behaviours which are consistent with his self-impression.

The general point here is that the 'self' is a social product. Through an incessant stream of discriminative training and verbal behaviour, the individual learns his own strengths and weaknesses, at least as they are seen by others. Often this learning can lead to gross changes in behaviour. Naturally, much will depend on the social situation. Behaviour which is negatively evaluated in one situation may be approved in another. After a good goal, to cheer is appropriate; after a good sermon, it is not. So, through social judgments the individual learns about himself, and he also learns to adapt to a variety of social situations.

There has been an extensive series of investigations concerning the way in which adults make judgments of others. Here, there is space to discuss only one or two aspects of this complex process. For instance, the order in which a person gains information about someone else will influence the impressions he forms of him, that is, will influence what he learns about him. Luchins (1957) found that, in general, first impressions are more important than those gained subsequently. However, this affect disappears when the person is *made* to take account of later information rather than to ignore it.

There has also been a reasonable amount of work on interpersonal attraction, in which the guiding principle has been that people interact to the extent that reciprocal rewards result; that is, to the extent that they each get something from the interaction. The major work has been carried out by Byrne (e.g. 1961). In one study he found that subjects who had been led to believe that certain other persons had responded to questionnaires in ways similar to their own evaluated these persons more positively. These and similar results led Byrne to express his law of attraction, which has received much empirical support. It is a law which well expresses one aspect of adult social learning, namely, attraction towards a person is a positive linear function of the proportion of positive reinforcements received from him (Byrne and Nelson, 1965).

GROUPS

There have been few attempts within traditional social psychology to analyse group processes from a social learning viewpoint. However, it is self-evident that membership of a new social group must lead to the acquisition of fresh or altered social skills. Such work as has been conducted on groups from a learning orientation has dwelt mainly on conditions which promote mutual liking amongst group members. It has rested on the assumption that the greater the mutual liking then the more cohesive will be the group.

Clearly, the influence of social reinforcement in a group is a complex matter. For example, if person A is reinforced by the group through being promoted to a higher position or status, this may well act as a punishment to person B. Homans (1961), whose social learning theory will be discussed later, makes the most penetrating analysis of group reinforcement. He concentrates on what he terms *rewards*, that is, whatever is received in a social exchange, and *costs*, that is, whatever is given up in an exchange, including any risks that the individual might have to take. It should be pointed out, however, that within the intricacies of ongoing interaction, rewards and costs might be very difficult to identify in the individual case. The motivations which lie behind group membership are frequently not what they would seem at face value.

Homans makes many reinforcement analyses of group processes, but the most central is based on the following assumptions. Behaviour which A emits in response to B is *valuable* to B, and the more valuable A's behaviour is held to be, the greater he is esteemed. Then, the more valuable the behaviour of group members generally to the group, the more cohesive the group will be. It is easy to see how the members of a group learn new social behaviours through this type of mechanism, and research has shown that rewards do affect interpersonal attraction and increase group cohesiveness (Lott and Lott, 1965).

One way in which group cohesiveness seems to be affected by learning is through conformity. Conformity can be regarded as instrumental behaviour which is maintained by reinforcement (through the satisfactions of various needs or the attainment of various goals). Alternatively, conformity to group ways can be viewed as a deserved reward which promotes social exchanges between group members or as a sort of payment in advance for rewards which might be received in the future. So, it is reasonable to regard people as learning to conform to the mores of their groups either through reinforcement which might come from the behaviour itself, or through anticipated rewards (such as promotion), or through mutual attraction.

It is perhaps worth mentioning a particularly unfortunate outcome of adults learning to conform to social customs. It appears, at least to the eyes of Aronson (1972), to lead to the shattering type of obedience to authority described by Milgram (1974) and the surprising findings on the uninvolved bystander by, for example, Darley and Latane (1968). By now, Milgram's work is too well known to discuss here, but brief mention of the bystander work might be instructive. The sort of experiment this was based on was to stage an accident to a woman whilst subjects were completing questionnaires. When subjects were working alone, 70 per cent of them offered to help the woman, but when they were in pairs, the proportion dropped to 20 per cent. It seems that people learn to view non-intervention as an act of conformity. Hence, paradoxically, if you are seen to be in trouble by many persons you are less likely to receive help than if your problem is seen by only one. Of course, there are exceptions to this. Help will be given in a crowded and enclosed environment, such as a train, or when the onlookers are face-to-face with the victim. But these are both situations from which there is no escape. The general point that we *learn* to become uninvolved is disturbing.

TRAINING SOCIAL SKILLS

So far in this chapter discussion has centred on some representative examples of ways in which adults learn new social behaviour as part of their normal social interaction. The ideas on which these examples are based are reinforced by turning the coin over and asking whether it is possible to train people to achieve better levels of social competence. It is possible to teach a 40-year-old to drive a car or to improve his driving. Is it similarly possible to teach him to improve his social skills? Argyle (1969), who has done much work in this area, makes one of the few systematic analyses of this to be found in the psychological literature. This section presents a resume of some of his findings and ideas.

Argyle bases his analysis on a division of social competence into four aspects, each of which he suggests could be trained. There is what he refers to as *motivation*, by which he means a person's enduring personality characteristics such as propensity to be extraverted or dominant, anxious or overly submissive. He feels that such qualities can be changed by training. Next, there is *perception*. It should be possible to teach adults to be more aware of the nuances of their interactions, to make them more socially sensitive. Third, there are *responses*, this being the obvious category. It should be possible to manipulate a person's social responses so that they be more effective; for example, to change a generally punishing person into one who is more rewarding to others. Finally, Argyle mentions the possibility of changing the way in which a person *presents* himself to the world, and of altering the degree of self-confidence he feels in this. It remains to see how such training can be done.

(1) *Everyday learning.* As has already been seen, the most common way in which adults learn new social responses is as a part of their everyday lives. Most people engage in enormous numbers of social interactions, they are very repetitious, they are given little feedback and even less training, but they still improve. They must be learning something. Argyle suggests that an important factor in this type of learning is feedback, although this argument is made largely on the basis that feedback is known to be important in all other types of learning. The problem is that feedback is rarely given in a direct way for social behaviour. It is difficult to tell a person that he would get on better with others if he looked at them more often, or stood further away, or used a quieter tone of voice. Somehow this is too personal, and anyway he might not even be aware that his interactions are not all that they might be. It is acceptable to comment on a person's work, but more difficult to criticize his social style in doing it.

Argyle develops a comparison with the learning of motor skills by suggesting that new social skills *must* be acquired through trial and error and feedback, even though exactly how is unknown. Is it through the usual processes of reward and punishment, or imitation, or both? Also, it is probable that small units of social skills are learned continually and then later integrated into larger units. Certainly, this occurs with the acquisition of motor skills such as driving or typing. There are obvious advantages to the everyday learning of social skills, and undoubtedly adults do learn them in this way, but it is a very haphazard process on which more research needs to be done.

(2) *Formal learning.* There have been many attempts to teach social skills by lecture, discussion and film. It is certain that knowledge and even understanding can be conveyed in these ways (particularly if the principles of persuasion are borne in mind). But there has been little or no research into the general effectiveness of such methods in actually helping people to learn new skills. From such research as there is, Argyle concludes that these formal methods of instruction *can* affect social skills, but only when they are supported by other social influences.

In a similar way, a fair commercial success has been made from teaching social skills and techniques through the written word and self-instruction. This has been so since the days of the books on gentlemanly etiquette. In spite of the popularity of such self-instructional methods, there is no information at all about their effectiveness. As well as the obvious difficulties involved in making any assessments, any methods of this sort must inevitably have to cope with (at least) two major problems. Often they will be concerned with teaching nonverbal social skills using solely verbal material, and also they cannot insist on practice at the skills themselves.

(3) *Role-playing.* Some of the determinants of the acquisition of new social roles have been discussed earlier. In recent years, knowledge gained in this area has been put to practical use in the training of people for jobs such as interviewing, teaching, supervising and selling. The procedure followed usually takes a fairly standard form. First, a list of problems is made up which bear on those which the person will probably have to face in his job. Then social incidents are devised with these problems as their ingredients. The person is put into these mock situations and asked to play various roles. For example, the prospective interviewer might be faced with interviewing an actor who has been instructed to look at him too much, or is too extravert, or too taciturn. Whatever the outcome of such simulation exercises, they must rest on the assumption that the instructor knows what social skills are required for a particular job and also knows what situations can best draw them out. This assumption is by no means always well founded.

In more detail, the procedure usually involves the following steps: (i) a lecture, film or discussion about the relevant social skills, (ii) roleplaying, and (iii) a feedback session, often with videotaped recordings. Argyle is reasonably well convinced that such methods are effective in producing social learning, although he admits that research is scanty. Once again, he suggests that any learning that does occur is through trial and error plus feedback, although of course it is difficult to separate the effects of feedback from those of reward and punishment. But Argyle argues that social role-playing exercises lead to increased social awareness and sensitivity, particularly when there is strong negative feedback. (In an artificial situation designed for the purpose it becomes permissible to make social criticism.) Apart from these speculations needing empirical verification, the obvious difficulties with role-playing are that trainees often believe it to be stupid and feel self-conscious, and that it needs application from the classroom to real life.

(4) *T-(training) groups.* T-groups provide the most widely used, voguish and *possibly* the most successful ways of encouraging social learning in adults. They are the nearest that I shall come in this chapter to discussing psychotherapy and behaviour therapy, which although beyond the scope of this book obviously bring about modifications to adult social behaviour. Much has been written about the form and efficacy of T-groups and only a very broad outline will be given here. The reader who wishes to pursue the matter further is referred to Argyle (1969), Aronson (1972), Bradford *et al.* (1964), Schein and Bennis (1965) and Stock (1964).

The goals of T-groups are to bring about increased social sensitivity to the emotional reactions of oneself and others, and to things interpersonal in general, to develop clearer self-perception, to improve awareness of how others see oneself, to learn to be simultaneously democratic and accepting and yet independent, to produce more effective work, and to learn how to learn socially. Grand aims, but are they realized and how is the attempt made?

The working of T-groups follows a number of general principles. The first is that the members are to learn from one another by communication. If, in everyday life, a person behaves in a particular way, those around him evaluate this and ascribe motives and reasons to his behaviour. This process is explored far more openly and in more detail in T-groups. All that is discussed is the here-and-now, whatever is going on at the time. The members of the group are completely open about what is happening without necessarily revealing their more enduring hopes and fears. All the openness is in the present, with no pressure to make public anything the person prefers to keep close.

Throughout all meetings the emphasis is on feedback. Group members are given *immediate* insights into whatever they say or do. This gives them new information to accept or reject or use as they think fit. Naturally, the persons involved need some training in how to give feedback. It has to be done carefully, since, as most people know, too much openness can hurt. This problem is circumvented by carefully exploring *feelings*. If A calls B a hypocrite the why's and wherefore's are discussed. Feedback about feelings is easier to accept than feedback given as a judgment. It is easier to accept the statement, 'I feel you are a hypocrite', than it is to accept, 'You are a hypocrite'. If honestly given, an expression of feeling is a fact which says something about the expresser as well as he to whom it is directed. Judgment is conjecture which sounds unpleasantly like fact. Linked to this; the members of T-groups also try to work out one another's intentions. Something which sounded hurtful might not have been meant.

This is perhaps enough to give an idea of the aims and workings of T-groups. In the present context, the important question is how effective are they? Many research studies have been carried out which bear on this question, but they are difficult to evaluate. How, for example, is it possible to separate the effects of the group interactions from those of simply being closed in a country house for a weekend, as one would be in many T-groups? It is difficult, if not impossible, to make comparisons with the proper control groups.

Some generalizations can be made. For example, experience in a T-group does tend to lead to increased attention to things interpersonal, although without necessarily producing an improvement in social perception other than self-perception. Human relationships do *seem* to be improved, as is effectiveness at work. On the other hand, a situation as intense as the T-group carries dangers with it. Some people simply cannot cope with the extreme, self-conscious feedback and analyses of feelings: they crack and are made generally worse socially by the experience.

One survey (Stock, 1964) suggests that persons who benefit most from a

T-group are those who enter the group with an unsure self-image, some internal social conflicts and not too much anxiety. Be this as it may, Argyle's (1969) summary of T-group effectiveness is still pertinent. He describes them as having laudable, far-reaching goals, being of some benefit to 30–40 per cent of members and of positive harm to others, and as not providing good evidence that they teach much in the way of social competence. Certainly, T-group members are often changed by their experiences, they learn something socially, but this is by no means necessarily anything which makes them more socially skilful.

SOCIAL LEARNING THEORY

A few experimental and social psychologists have long been aware that the study of adult social learning is but one perspective to take in investigating interactional phenomena. But they have thought this perspective important enough to develop it into a set of theories which have come to be termed social learning theories. To conclude the substantive part of this chapter, I shall discuss some of the more significant of these theories. For a more detailed account the reader should see McLaughlin (1971).

Miller and Dollard (1941; Dollard and Miller, 1950) made the first systematic application of Hullian learning theory to social behaviour. The key concepts in their theory were as follows. *Drive*: which can be innate or acquired, although in adult social behaviour it is normally acquired, being based for example on fear, money or approval; they suggested that any stimulus can become a drive if it is powerful enough. *Cues*: any strong stimulus can have a cue function which will determine when and where the person will respond and what responses he makes. *Response*: which is learned most easily if it is followed by *rewards*.

The nub of Miller and Dollard's earlier argument was that much of social learning is promoted by the secondary drive of anxiety, and the secondary reward of relief (from anxiety) which may reduce the drive. So, a person learns a new social response (to speak less, for example) to reduce or avoid the anxiety caused by embarrassment, and is reinforced in this by the relief of no longer being anxious. Miller and Dollard also emphasized the importance of anticipatory rewards, so laying the foundations for the more cognitive social learning theories which were to follow. Later (Dollard and Miller, 1950), they 'liberalized' notions of S–R psychology to include higher mental processes in general, as long as these could be shown to function as stimuli and responses.

Mowrer's (1950; 1960) theory was sufficiently similar to that of Miller and Dollard not to describe in any detail. He moved away even further from the strictly S–R theory of Hull and definitely led others to put forward theories of social learning which combined the traditional learning approach with cognitive involvement. Both *Rotter* (1954) and *Thibaut and Kelley* (1959) constructed such theories. A resume of Rotter's theory will give the general flavour of this approach.

Like Hull, Rotter saw behaviour as a function of both learning and motivation, but unlike Hull, he viewed these two processes as controlled by cognitive variables. Rotter's three basic concepts derived directly from traditional learning theory. They were: (1) behaviour potential, which, like reaction potential, is the potentiality of behaviour occurring in a given situation in relation to reinforcement; (2) expectancy, which is the probability held by a person that particular reinforcement will occur following his behaviour in particular situations: clearly a cognitive factor; (3) reinforcement value, which is the degree of preference for a particular reinforcement given that all are equally available.

The remainder of Rotter's theory was made up of less well-defined terms which apply more specifically to social learning. (1) Need potential: that is, functionally related behaviours which lead to some reinforcement, identification with an authority figure, for example. (2) Need value: that is, the preference value a person has for a set of functionally related reinforcers. (3) Freedom of movement: that is, the mean expectancy that a set of related behaviours will lead to functionally related reinforcements. (4) Psychological situation: that is, the meaningful environment of the person. Clearly, these concepts are all based very much on the past history of the individual, and their heavily mentalistic flavour means that they carry enormous measurement problems.

The Skinnerian approach to learning has not produced much in the way of social learning theory. The exception is *Homan's* (1961) theory of social exchange. His theory is best summarized by mentioning its main variables and formal propositions. The two central variables are: (1) value, which is a function of the degree of reinforcement and punishment which comes from a unit of activity. This reflects preferences which are themselves determined by a person's past history. And (2) quantity, which refers to the number of units of activity which are emitted within a given time.

Homans' five propositions are as follows. (1) If a past stimulus situation has led to a reward for some social activity, then the more similar to it is the present stimulus situation the more likely is the person to emit the same activity. (2) The more often A's activity rewards B's activity, the more often B will emit the activity. (3) The more valuable is a unit of B's activity to A, the more often A will emit activity which will lead to it. (4) The more often A has recently received rewarding activity from B, the less valuable it is to him. (5) The more disadvantageous to a person is his realization of distributive justice, the angrier he becomes.

Underpinning all of Homans' ideas is the law of effect. He believes that a person learns socially for profit, that is, on the basis of an evaluation of profits against costs. Notice that *evaluation* is mentioned. So, even though Homans is from the strictly behavioural Skinnerian school, he emphasizes the cognitive factor of expectations about rewards and costs for social learning.

All that can be concluded about social learning theories in general is that they have not yet been put to good empirical test. There are not many such theories and those which do exist are fairly tentative. Psychologists are worried about extrapolating from animal research on learning to human social behaviour. Clearly, more research is needed on human behaviour which is learned in social situations.

CONCLUSIONS

The aim of this chapter has been to give a representative overview of some of the psychological ideas and research on the learning of social behaviour by adults. Because this area depends so much on the viewpoint that is taken of social behaviour, it unfortunately leads to extremes. On the one hand, from the most casual observation it is reasonable to make the general statement that adults learn new social responses constantly. Adult social skills are under a process of virtually continuous modification. On the other hand, a glance at almost any current textbook of social psychology will show little reference to social learning. The main areas of social psychology, such as group processes, attitudes, dyadic interaction, and so on, tend to be dealt with as discrete topics each with its own tradition of research and theory.

In one sense it is possible to say that any aspect of adult social behaviour involves learning. If this statement is accepted, then the problem is to choose for consideration those areas in which the emphasis on learning is more obvious. These areas are represented in this chapter and the general approach is endorsed by the past 30 years of attempts to create theories of social learning. It is beyond doubt that adults learn social skills and indeed can be trained to improve their social competence. It is equally clear that far more research is needed before more definitive statements can be made about the determinants of social learning and prescriptions made for the confident training of social skills.

REFERENCES

Argyle, M. (1964). *Psychology and Social Problems*, Methuen, London.

Argyle, M. (1969). *Social Interaction*, Methuen, London.

Aronson, E. (1972). *The Social Animal*, McGraw-Hill, New York.

Bradford, L. P., Gibb, J. F., and Benne, K. D. (1964). *T-group Therapy and Laboratory Method*, Wiley, New York.

Byrne, D. (1961). 'Interpersonal attraction and attitude similarity', *Journal of Abnormal and Social Psychology*, **62**, 713.

Byrne, D., and Nelson, D. (1965). 'Attraction as a linear function of proportion of positive reinforcements', *Journal of Personality and Social Psychology*, **2**, 884.

Darley, J., and Latane, B. (1968). 'Bystander intervention in emergencies: diffusion of responsibility', *Journal of Personality and Social Psychology*, **8**, 377.

Dollard, J., and Miller, N. E. (1950). *Personality and Psychotherapy*, McGraw-Hill, New York.

Hill, W. F. (1968). 'Sources of evaluative reinforcement', *Psychological Bulletin*, **69**, 132.

Homans, G. C. (1961). *Social Behaviour: Its Elementary Forms*. Harcourt, Brace & World, New York.

Hovland, C., and Weiss, W. (1951). 'The influence of source credibility on communication effectiveness', *Public Opinion Quarterly*, **15**, 635.

Leventhal, H. (1970). 'Findings and theory in the study of fear communication', in L. Berkowitz (Ed.), *Advances in Experimental social Psychology*, Vol. 5, Academic Press, New York.

Lott, A. J., and Lott, B. E. (1965). 'Group cohesiveness as interpersonal attraction: A review of relationships with antecedent and consequent variables', *Psychological Bulletin*, **64**, 259.

Luchins, A. S. (1957). 'Experimental attempts to minimize the impact of first impressions', in C. I. Hovland *et al.* (Eds.), *The Order of Presentation in Persuasion*, Yale University Press, New Haven.

McLaughlin, B. (1971). *Learning and Social Behaviour*, Free Press, New York; Collier-Macmillan, London.

Milgram, S. (1974). *Obedience to Authority*, Harper & Row, New York.

Miller, N., and Campbell, D. (1959). 'Recency and primacy in persuasion as a function of the timing of speeches and measurements', *Journal of Abnormal and Social Psychology*, **59**, 1.

Miller, N. E., and Dollard, J. (1941). *Social Learning and Imitation*, Yale University Press, New Haven.

Mowrer, O. H. (1950). *Learning Theory and Personality Dynamics*, Ronald Press, New York.

Mowrer, O. H. (1960). *Learning Theory and the Symbolic Processes*, Wiley, New York.

Rotter, J. (1954). *Social Learning and Clinical Psychology*, Prentice-Hall, New Jersey.

Schein, E. H., and Bennis, W. G. (1965). *Personal Learning and Organisational Change through Group Methods*, Wiley, New York.

Secord, P. F., and Backman, C. W. (1974). *Social Psychology*, 2nd ed., McGraw-Hill, New York.

Stock, D. (1964). A survey of research on T-groups. In L. P. Bradford, J. R. Gibb and K. D. Benne (Ed.), *T-Group Theory and Laboratory Method*. Wiley, New York.

Thibaut, J. W., and Kelley, H. H. (1959). *The Social Psychology of Groups*, Wiley, New York.

Walster, E., and Festinger, L. (1962). 'The effectiveness of "overheard" persuasive communications', *Journal of Abnormal and Social Psychology*, **65**, 395.

Zimbardo, P., and Ebbeson, E. (1969). *Influencing Attitudes and Changing Behaviour*, Addison-Wesley, Massachusetts.

4

PERSONALITY AND LEARNING

Paul Kline

INTRODUCTION

A precise definition of personality has (as Allport pointed out in 1937) eluded psychologists, and ultimately each of the many varieties is bound up with its implicit assumptions. In this chapter we shall take up a psychometric position: personality will be considered in terms of traits, temperamental and dynamic traits.

Within this framework, however, we can be precise. Temperamental traits are concerned with *how* a person does what he does, his general style and tempo. Dynamic traits on the other hand are concerned with *why* a person does what he does, a field which until recently has been the preserve of psychiatry. In what follows, therefore, we shall examine the influence of the two types of traits upon adult learning. Intuitively (poor though intuitions have been shown to be throughout the history of psychology), we should expect this influence to be considerable. We would not expect a circus ringmaster to excel at learning ancient Suffic poetry. Conversely, the Persian scholar would lay his head poorly indeed within the lion's mouth.

TEMPERAMENTAL TRAITS

The trait approach to personality is dogged by two intertwined questions: (1) how many temperamental traits are there or what are the most important of them? and (2) how can we measure them? Since there is now more than 40 years of empirical research directed at these points, in this chapter all we can do is summarize the most recent position, although at the outset readers must be aware that this is a field of considerable contention, often over highly technical research procedures. Thus any summary could be felt to be unjust, by some at least. Nevertheless, from the chaos of findings from research by Burt (1937), Eysenck (1970), Guilford (1959), Edwards (1959), Comrey (1970) and Cattell (1973), to name only the most distinguished of the workers, some order can be drawn.

In the field of temperament, two recent publications (Cattell, 1973; Cattell and Kline, in press) have demonstrated that much of the disparity in the results stems from methodological problems, the most important being concerned with technically faulty factor analyses. The significance of this claim resides in the fact that almost all workers agree that factor analysis is the best method for the study of personality traits. Thus before we can appreciate the technical resolutions of the different results, we must briefly set out the rationale for using factor analysis at all in the study of personality.

Rationale for Using Factor Analysis

The trait analysis of personality is extremely broad in scope. Indeed, Cattell (1957) has argued that it embraces the totality of behaviour, i.e. all overt and covert responses. This means that personality research must involve a very large number of variables. This in turn means that multivariate methods, as distinct from univariate or bivariate, are necessary.

In fact, there is a wide variety of multivariate techniques, multiple correlation, canonical analysis, discriminant function and latent class analysis for example, of which factor analysis is simply one. However, factor analysis has been the favoured technique because it is ideal for elucidating the two problems inherent in the trait approach to personality.

A factor may be regarded as a construct operationally defined by its factor loadings (i.e. by the correlations of the variables salient to the factor) and accounting mathematically for the correlations between the variables. An example will make this clear. We might be interested in the question of why children who were good at one school subject were usually good at most of the others. A factor analysis of correlations between school subjects might well reveal that they could be accounted for by two constructs (factors) or dimensions: verbal ability and numerical ability. These factors would be operationally defined by their loadings on Latin, Greek and French, and geometry, algebra and physics, respectively. They would not, therefore, be vague verbal concepts and they would account for the variance and convariance in the original scores. Thus we could argue that performance in school depended upon an individual's position on these two dimensions—an economical, parsimonious account. Two factors are therefore important, in this example, in school performance. Historically, work of this sort pursued by Spearman, Burt and Thurstone has led to the development of a rich picture of human abilities which has enabled psychologists to select personnel with high efficiency for certain specific jobs (see Ghiselli, 1966).

The factor analysis of abilities especially as applied to intelligence has become well known. However, it is less often realized that the same methods have been applied in the personality area, perhaps because there is really no consensus of opinion, as we indicated earlier, concerning the results. Nevertheless, our example should indicate clearly why factor analysis has been the chosen method for the investigation of personality traits. Here we have an apparently limitless number of variables, dominance, outrageousness, anger, fury, aggression, timidity, shyness, naivety, wilfulness, strength of character, ... there is no need to go on. The factorial analysis of the correlations between these traits should reveal what are the important dimensions. We could then concentrate our research efforts on these and when we know the dimensions measurement becomes relatively simple. This is the rationale for the use of factor analysis in the study of temperamental traits.

Objections to Factor Analysis

If our argument is valid, the obvious question arises as to why the factor analysis of personality has not been more widely adopted and is but one of the many approaches, as evidenced by even a cursory glance at Hall and Lindzey (1957) or Sarason (1972). The answer to this lies in certain problems inherent in the statistical nature of factors, problems which have led many psychologists to demean factorial findings: Mischel (1968) would be a good example. Two main objections to factor analysis are listed by its opponents. First, they argue, there is an infinity of possible solutions to any factor analysis—analysis—each mathematically equivalent. To trust any one solution, therefore, is foolhardy. Associated with the first objection is the claim that any factorial interpretation must be subjective. The second objection is that even though the results are untrustworthy, the factors obtained are only what were inserted in the original data. Clearly, if we are to claim the factorial results in personality as being of substantive value, as we do in this chapter, these objections must be answered.

Refutation of the Objections

Both the objections can be answered. To begin with the second, it is demonstrably untrue. As Eysenck (1967b) has shown, if the symptoms of tuberculosis were inserted into a factor analysis together with those of other diseases, a general factor loading on the TB symptoms would emerge. This factor would represent the effect of the causative organism, and would demonstrate clearly a syndrome of covarying symptoms. This factor is not 'what was put in' but is a genuinely new construct. Of course, in the study of abilities, for example, if we have no measures of numerical ability no numerical factor can emerge. However, this is a trival point analogous to an objection to the experimental technique that if $\times$ is not studied we shall never know its effects. In practice this objection can be answered by ensuring, as far as possible, that the universe of variables is properly sampled.

The first objection is more serious. However, if factors are regarded as constructs which account for observations or correlations too numerous to encompass as they stand, then all solutions are not equal other than mathematically. By invoking the principle of parsimony we can see that the simplest solution is best. Hence we are set right back to the work of Thurstone (1947), who devoted so much thought and labour to the attainment of simple structure in factor analysis—briefly defined as factors with a few high loadings and all the other loadings zero. However, there has been a great development in the techniques of factor analysis, especially those aimed at obtaining simple structure and further demonstrating that it has been obtained. These, however, fully discussed in Cattell (1973) and Cattell and Kline (in press), are outside the scope of this chapter. Nevertheless, it can be said that simple structure solutions are preferred (because parsimonious and hence more meaningful) and can be reliably obtained. This, therefore, answers the objections of the infinity of solutions. As to the subjectivity of interpretation, this remains always the case. Nevertheless, prolonged study of factors, as has been the case with g in the field of abilities and extraversion for example, usually by nonmultivariate methods, has made interpretation reasonably confident.

These two answers to the objections to factor analysis now lead us on to the resolution of the disparate results of the factor analysis of temperament suggested by Cattell (1973)—namely, that many of the differences can be attributed to technical flaws, especially in the rotational procedures, which, therefore, lead to the failure to reach simple structure. In addition, of course, this refutation shows that factor analysis is the ideal technique for the study of personality.

Technical Flaws

Cattell (1973) has argued that there are eight technical requirements for proper factor analyses and that where these are infringed we get results which depart from simple structure and are not replicable. These requirements are set out below:

1. Strategic choice of variables
2. Proper sampling of subjects
3. Objective tests for the number of factors to be rotated
4. Iteration of communalities
5. Maximizing of simple structure in oblique rotation
6. Significance test for simple structure
7. Invariance of primary factor pattern in different researches
8. Invariance of higher-order factors in different researches

A few comments on these will show their importance in resolving the disparate findings.

Proper sampling of variables we have mentioned. Cattell, with his concept of the personality sphere (Cattell, 1957), has come as close as can be expected to delineating and hence to sampling the gamut of personality traits. There should be adequate sampling of subjects. Homogeneity of variance restricts correlations and thus obliterates factors. An extreme example would be to attempt to isolate high-level reasoning factors among an ESN or SSN group. More relevant to our chapter is the relatedness (Eysenck and Eysenck,

1968) of the P or Psychoticism factor in questionnaire data, a factor which is of small variance among normal adults.

Testing the number of significant factors from the principal components for rotation is also important. Various devices have been used, such as rotating factors with latent roots greater than unity (Kaiser, 1958), while the scree test (Cattell, 1966b) seems highly effective. Nevertheless, there is no doubting the importance of rotating the correct number of factors. Underfactoring leads to second-order factors appearing at the first order, while overfactoring makes simple structure difficult to obtain.

The iteration of communalities is a technical statistical point which has been shown (Cattell, 1973) to lead to better simple structure, the stated aim of the fifth requirement. This is best brought about by oblique rotation, for only in rare instances would it be likely in the multivariate situation that factors would not be oblique (i.e. correlated). This means that all factorial studies where principal components are not related or where orthogonal (i.e. uncorrelated) rotations have been carried out are highly unlikely to have obtained simple structure. However, not all oblique rotations are equally good, and Cattell (1966a; 1973) has convincingly demonstrated that topological programmes such as Maxplane and Rotoplot which maximize the hyperplane count (in effect the low loadings) are superior to analytic solutions such as promax.

The last three points are almost self-evident. To ensure that simple structure has been reached it is sensible to apply a significance test (although few researchers take the trouble). Bargmann's (1953) test is well suited for this. Finally, since it is important that all results are replicable, attempts should be made to match the results across researches. Ideally, different variables and populations could also be used. Again statistical techniques are available to test the accuracy of matching factor patterns.

As Cattell (1973) points out, when the researches where all these requirements are met are considered together, the apparent disparity of findings disappears. In other words, the disparities are due to technical flaws in execution. Furthermore, where the data have been reworked to these higher technical standards we also find that there is a good agreement among results.

Resolution of Results: The 23 Temperamental Traits

For a full discussion of this highly complex issue readers must turn to Cattell (1973) or Cattell and Kline (in press). What we shall do is to indicate how the infringement of some of these requirements has led to problematical results and then set out the 23 temperamental first-order traits upon which the technically adequate researches are agreed.

Eysenck's factorial solution to the number of personality traits (e.g. Eysenck, 1967a) postulates three orthogonal factors: extraversion, neuroticism and the more restricted psychoticism. However, examination of Eysenck's work reveals two serious flaws—underfactoring and failure to reach simple structure.

The underfactoring has led, as Cattell (1973) has shown, to the appearance of second-order factors at the first order. This alone has prevented the attainment of simple structure.

Guilford's factors (Guilford, 1959) are different from those of Cattell because an orthogonal solution has been chosen. When, however, they are rotated to the oblique position, as in the work of Cattell and Gibbons (1968), it is clear that they map out the same factorial space. The work of Comrey (1970) is vitiated by subjective rotational procedures and his habit of parcelling items up before analysis so that any factors are in reality second-order.

Mention should be made of Eysenck and Eysenck's (1969) combined study of the Cattell, Guilford and Eysenck scales, which purports to show that the primary factors of Cattell especially, but to some extent also of Guilford, are not sufficiently robust to be useful, but that the extraversion and neuroticism factors are reliably replicable. However, against the requirements of adequate factor analysis which we have discussed previously this study contains flaws. First there was poor sampling of variables, since there were far fewer items the Guilford and Cattell scales than for the Eysenck scales. There were no checks on the number of factors rotated, although 20 factors should not lead to underfactoring. Unities rather than communalities were put in the diagonal, and no check was made on the hyperplane count so that the adequacy of the promax rotation is unknown. All these flaws, albeit not gross, would lead to weak first-order factors. These, however, are the crux of the work in that both Guilford's and Cattell's factors are of this kind. For all these reasons this investigation must be treated with some caution.

Since, therefore, we can see how technical flaws have vitiated many of the researches which give results contradictory among themselves and with the work of Cattell and his colleagues at Illinois, we shall now set out the temperamental traits which have emerged from the technically adequate researches.

Before considering these factors readers should remember that they have all emerged from L data, ratings of real-life behaviour, and/or Q data, based on questionnaires. The original research from which the majority of the factors emerged was highly comprehensive in that ratings were made of traits themselves based upon a dictionary search of all behaviour-descriptive terms. This procedure ensured as far as possible that the whole universe of personality variables (the personality sphere) was covered. In addition, the psychological meanings of most of these factors have been extensively investigated, in more than 350 books and articles by Cattell and colleagues alone. All this work cannot be summarized here and readers must be referred to Cattell and Kline (in press).

Table 4.1 sets out the first 16 factors which have been regularly found in studies of adults with questionnaires. The missing letters refer to factors isolated in ratings (L factors) which failed to emerge in these questionnaire data. The Q factors, on the other hand, indicate that these factors were not found in ratings of behaviour. These titles and descriptions are taken from the latest edition of the 16 P.F. test (Cattell *et al.*, 1970).

Table 4.1. First 16 Temperamental Traits (Cattell's)

Source–trait index	Low-score description	High-score description
A	Sizia Reserved, detached, critical, aloof, stiff	Affectia Outgoing, warmhearted, easygoing, participating
B	Low intelligence Dull	High intelligence Bright
C	Lower ego strength At mercy of feelings, emotionally less stable, easily upset, changeable	Higher ego strength Emotionally stable, mature, faces reality, calm
E	Submissiveness Humble, mild, easily led, docile, accommodating	Dominance Assertive, aggressive, competitive, stubborn
F	Desurgency Sober, taciturn, serious	Surgency Happy-go-lucky, gay, enthusiastic
G	Weaker supergo strength Expedient, disregards rules	Stronger supergo strength Conscientious, persistent, moralistic, staid
H	Threctia Shy, timid, threat-sensitive	Parmia Venturesome, uninhibited, socially bold
I	Harria Tough-minded, self-reliant, realistic	Premsia Tender-minded, sensitive, clinging, overprotected
L	Alaxia Trusting, accepting conditions	Protension Suspicious, hard to fool
M	Praxernia Practical, 'down-to-earth' concerns	Autia Imaginative, bohemian, absent-minded
N	Artlessness Forthright, unpretentious, genuine, but socially clumsy	Shrewdness Astute, polished, socially aware
O	Untroubled adequacy Self-assured, placid, secure, complacent, serene	Guilt proneness Apprehensive, self-reproaching, insecure, worrying, troubled
Q_1	Conservativism of temperament Conservative, respecting traditional ideas	Radicalism Experimenting, liberal, free-thinking
Q_2	Group adherence Group-dependent, a 'joiner' and sound follower	Self-sufficiency Self-sufficient, resourceful, prefers own decisions
Q_3	Low self-sentiment integration Undisciplined self-conflict, lax, follows own urges, careless of social rules	High strength of self-sentiment Controlled, exacting will power, socially precise, compulsive, following self-image
Q_4	Low ergic tension Relaxed, tranquil, torpid, unfrustrated, composed	High ergic tension Tense, frustrated, driven, overwrought

Some of the missing factors have appeared in research with adolescents and children, and recently further studies with adults with new items and more refined analyses have revealed the seven missing factors (Cattell, 1973). These, for obvious reasons, have not been as extensively investigated as the previous 16, so that their definition is indicated by a typical item rather than a brief description. The seven missing factors are set out in Table 4.2. It should be stressed that there are temperamental traits among normal adults.

Here are the 23 temperamental factors, source, traits, which emerge from the factorial analysis of personality where the researches have been adequately

Table 4.2. Seven Missing Temperamental Traits

D:	Insecure excitability		
	I bubble over with ideas of things I want to do next		
	(a) Always	(b) Often	(c) Practically never
	The people I want never seem very interested in me		
	(a) True	(b) Uncertain	(c) False
J:	Coasthenia *vs* zeppia		
	I enjoy getting a group together and leading them into some activity		
	(a) True	(b) Uncertain	(c) False
	People tell me I'm		
	(a) Apt to be noisy	(b) In between	(c) Quiet and hard to understand
K:	Mature socialization *vs* boorishness		
	I prefer plays that are		
	(a) Exciting	(b) In between	(c) On socially important themes
	If I take up a new activity I like		
	(a) To learn as I go along	(b) In between	(c) To read a book on it by an expert
P:	Sanguine casulness		
	I rarely let my mind stray into fantasies and make-believe		
	(a) True	(b) Uncertain	(c) False
	I most enjoy talking with my friends about		
	(a) Local events	(b) In between	(c) Great artists and pictures
Q_5:	Group dedication with sensed inadequacy		
	I like a project into which I can throw all my energies		
	(a) Yes	(b) Perhaps	(c) No
	In a situation which puts sudden demands on me I feel		
	(a) No good	(b) In between	(c) Confident of handling it
Q_6:	Social panache		
	I am good at inventing a clever justification when I appear in the wrong		
	(a) Yes	(b) Perhaps	(c) No
	I have never been called a dashing and daring person		
	(a) True	(b) Uncertain	(c) False
Q_7:	Explicit self-expression		
	I am not concerned to express my ideas at public meetings		
	(a) True	(b) Uncertain	(c) False
	In many undertakings I am in I don't seem to get a definite idea of what to do next		
	(a) Yes	(b) Perhaps	(c) No

Table 4.3. Second-order Factors of Temperament

Second-order factors	Description in terms of primary factors
1. Exvia–invia	Sociable (A), surgent (F), adventurous (H), dependent (Q_2)—i.e. extraversion
2. Anxiety	Weak ego strength (C −), timid (H −), suspicious (L), guilt-prone (0), low self-resentment (Q_3), tense (Q_4)
3. Corteria	Unsociable (A −), insensitive (I −) and shrewd (N)
4. Independence	Surgent (F), dominant (E), adventurous (H), suspicious, unconcerned (M)
5. Discreetness	Shrewdness (N), sociable (A)
6. Prodigal subjectivity	Unconcerned (M), radical (Q_1)
7. Intelligence	Intelligence (E)
8. Good upbringing	Superego (C), submissive (E −), desurgent (F), self-sentiment (Q_3)

carried out. These factors, Cattell and his colleagues agree, underlie much of the variance of personality. However, these are oblique first-order factors. It is, of course, possible to factorize the correlations between these factors—thus producing second-order factors. When this is done there is considerable agreement among almost all investigators in that extraversion and neuroticism are found to be the two largest factors. It is noteworthy that technical shortcomings contribute more to error at the first than second order. The main second-order factors among normals are set out in Table 4.3.

These eight factors are based on 14 carefully matched studies, although it must be stressed that the seven missing factors were not included in these analyses.

These are the important temperamental traits as they have emerged from L and Q data, studies using ratings and personality questionnaires. Before we leave these temperamental traits and turn to the dynamic factors, we must briefly mention the temperamental factors that have emerged from objective tests (T data).

Temperamental Factors from Objective Tests

An objective test is defined by Cattell as a test which can be objectively scored and the purport of which must be hidden from the subject. It therefore avoids the problems inherent in questionnaires of deliberate or unconscious distortions. Since by definition objective tests have no face validity (if they did, subjects would be able to see through them), it is difficult to demonstrate that validity. Thus there is far less agreement among factorists of personality concerning the interpretation of objective test factors. Indeed, in the Compendium of objective tests (Cattell and Warburton, 1967), although more than 200 are described, evidence for validity is lacking for many of them. For this chapter it must suffice to set out in Table 4.4 the main T factors as they have emerged from the only two laboratories (those of Cattell and Eysenck) which

Table 4.4. The Largest Objective Test Factors of Known Validity

U.1.16	Assertive ego; competitive striving for excellence
U.1.17	General inhibition
U.1.18	Hypomanic tendency
U.1.19	Independence
U.1.20	Herd conformity
U.1.21	Exuberance
U.1.22	Cortical alertness
U.1.23	Capacity to mobilize *vs* aggression
U.1.24	Anxiety
U.1.25	Realism
U.1.26–31	Not clearly identified
U.1.32	Exvia (extraversion)

have attempted to develop them, potentially the most efficient personality tests of all.

Relation of T Factors with Q Factors

The first thing to strike the reader is that the first-order T factors resemble to some extent the second-order Q factors. Thus the two largest second-order Q factors, exvia and anxiety, are both found in these objective test factors. Similarly, U.1.22 aligns with Q_3 and U.1.19 with Q_4. However, it cannot be a general principle that T factors are equivalent to second-order Q factors, because far more of the former have been found. Nevertheless, this overlap eventually supports the view that Q and T are highly similar.

However, Cattell (in press) presents an interesting argument that T factors measure *the interactions* of the first orders which produce second orders— *spiral action theory*. The example of exvia will clarify this point. High A drives exviants to seek company, thus increasing their social skills (N). This social success tends to produce dominance (E), while H (thick-skinned) is inevitably increased by all the social processes. A similar process can be seen in the case of anxiety. Spiral action theory, therefore, suggests that objective test factors may be measuring an interaction of traits.

So far we have seen the rationale for conceiving of personality in terms of certain temperamental traits which have been isolated in factorial studies. An individual's behaviour is seen as a function of his scores on these traits, but not on those alone. We must now turn to the dynamic aspect of personality, from the how to the why of behaviour. Then we shall be in a position to see how adult learning is a function of temperament and motivation.

MOTIVATIONAL TRAITS

The factorial analysis of motivation has proved considerably more daunting to factor analysts than the field of temperament. Indeed, Cattell would appear to be the lone worker in this area. Much of this work is described in Cattell

(1957), Cattell and Child (1975) and Cattell and Kline (in press), where an attempt is made to link the findings to clinical and intuitive motivational theories. Readers must consult these references for detailed arguments. Here we shall briefly present the theoretical background to the work and set out the main motivational traits.

Cattell and Child (1975) see motivation as reflected in attitudes. Attitudes are to be understood not as verbal statements but as: 'In these circumstances (stimulus), I (organism), want (interest, need), so much (of a certain intensity), to do this (specific goal response), with that (relevant object)'. This is the model which underlies the factor analyses of attitudes of as wide a variety as possible to reveal dynamic traits. The tests used in these investigations are of the objective test variety and a battery of them for the measurement of motivation is now freely available—the Motivational Analysis Test (MAT). We must stress that this work on motivation is not so highly validated by experimental results as are the majority of temperamental factors.

Obviously there are two aspects to the dynamics of personality. First there arises the question of what are the major human drives or propensities. This in the past has proved a hotbed of controversy. McDougall (1932) proposed 15 propensities and a large number of sentiments. Murray (1938) also enumerated a large number of needs, while Freud (1940) in his final phase proposed only two drives, Eros and Thanatos, although previously for Freud (1933) sex and aggression were paramount. Some ethologists, notably Lorenz (1956), regard aggression as an important human drive. The other aspect of motivation is strength of drives, which would appear to be an important variable.

The factorial studies of motivation have supplied answers to both these questions. Table 4.5 sets out the strength of motivation factors and Table 4.6 sets out the most important drives.

Second-order factors
1. Integrated :   loading on beta and gamma
2. Unintegrated: loading on alpha, delta and epsilon

It will be noted that the existence of the seven factors of interest strength makes the sociological study of interest by questionnaire or interview naive, most of the variance in such responses being taken up by beta. In addition, the components of the total score will considerably affect the quality of interest

Table 4.5. Strength of Motivation Factors

1. Alpha:	autism, believing one's desires are true and practicable	the 3 largest and best understood factors
2. Beta:	realized integrated interest	
3. Gamma:	this factor has an 'I ought' quality about it	
4. Delta:	a physiological factor	
5. Epsilon:	a factor related to conflict	
6. Zeta	these are recent and have not	
7. Eta	yet been identified	

Table 4.6. Ergs and Sentiments

Main ergs		Chief sentiments (in MAT)	
Fear	Parental	Self-assertion	Sport and games
Sex	protectiveness	Religious sentiment	Self-sentiment
Gregariousness	Curiosity	Career sentiment	
Hunger	Pugnacity		
Narcissism	Acquisitiveness		

(see Cattell and Kline (in press) or Kline (1975) for a full discussion of this point).

An erg is defined by Cattell (1957), as 'an innate reactive tendency the behaviours of which are directed towards and cease at a particular consummatory goal activity'. Sentiments, on the other hand, are defined by Cattell and Child (1975) as 'dynamic structures visible as common reaction patterns to persons, objects or social institutions and upon which all people seem to have some degree of endowment'. Ergs resemble biological drives, sentiments are culturally moulded.

These are the main variables of personality, temperament and dynamics, main in the sense of accounting for the most variance, a definition in contradistinction to the intuitive methods of most clinical theorists. The remainder of the chapter, now that we have been able to define operationally what we mean by personality and to justify this definition, will be taken up with the relation of these variables to learning.

MOODS AND STATES

Before we can begin this task one further set of results must be briefly mentioned: the work on moods and states. A trait is regarded as relatively stable, the central tendency of a variable for an individual, while a mood or state is transient, fluctuating over time. A frequent objection of subjects attempting to complete personality questionnaires on temperamental traits is that they cannot properly complete the items. Sometimes, they argue, they are talkative and sociable, at other times not, depending on their mood. This objection turns out to have some force since, as Cattell (1973) and Cattell and Kline (in press) show, most trait factors have corresponding state factors. Indeed, in the study of anxiety (Cattell and Scheier, 1961) this distinction between state and trait anxiety is of the utmost importance.

The reason that there is relatively little known about moods and states lies in the fact that normal R factor analysis cannot logically discriminate between traits and states, although most investigations have relied on this technique. What is needed is P factor analysis, where the changes within one individual are factored—a procedure which already has considerable subject-sampling problems—or R technique, where *the changes* in scores between testing sessions are factored. A combination of these methods, chain technique, could be employed, although there is little research up to this date using it.

A full discussion of the problems with all these methods is contained in Cattell and Kline (in press). This is beyond the needs of this chapter, where we shall simply indicate the results.

In fact, 10 states have been found of which the most important are anxiety, exvia, alertness, independence and psychoticism. It should be noted that the first four states are parallel with the first four second-order temperamental factors. When T tests are used further states of stress fatigue, arousal and regression have been identified.

These moods or states are equally determiners of behaviour along with temperamental and dynamic traits. In some instances moods can be perhaps the most important, as for example when a tired driver responds aggressively and differently from normal. In any understanding of behaviour, therefore, these transient states need to be taken into account.

STRUCTURED LEARNING THEORY

All these variables of personality have been tied in with learning by Cattell (1976) by means of *structured learning theory*. This we must now describe.

Structured learning theory differs from learning conceived of as operant and classical conditioning first in that learning changes are defined not in terms of specific behaviours alone but in terms of describable and measurable ability, temperament and motivation structures, i.e. the factors we have discussed in the preceding sections, although we have omitted the ability structures (such as fluid and crystallized intelligence) as falling outside the purview of this chapter. Thus structured learning theory is able to embrace not only learning in the narrow educational sense but in the broadest sense, where the whole development of character and personality is seen.

It also differs from the conventional theories of learning in that these complex changes affecting the growth of an individual are not held to be changes in trait elements as such. They are conceptualized as changes in the combinations of resources used in our reactions to any situation. In other words, they affect the way we integrate our personality.

In fact, this is a three-vector learning theory.

(1) *The trait vector*. This reflects the changes in traits: (abilities), temperamental and motivational factors. For example, when a young man learns how an officer has to behave, there will be (along with other changes) changes in the trait vector: factor A sociability, C ego strength, N naivety, would be likely factors to be changed.

(2) *The bearing vector*. This reflects the change in the bearing of traits upon the action. As we learn, so the combination of our capacities that *bears* on any action will change. A good example taken from Cattell and Kline (in press) can be seen in egg-collecting. For a boy this hobby may be sustained by the opportunities it gives for tree-climbing (factor H adventurousness). However, when our subject learns about eggs the hobby may be sustained by

biological interests. The career erg self-sentiment (the great embryologist), the mating erg (a successful biological scholar is more attractive than the less successful) and the temperamental factors associated with invia (being alone in the country) will all be involved. The bearing vector reflects changes of this kind.

(3) *The situation or involvement vector*. This reflects changes in the emotive meaning of a situation. The fact that a beautiful girl has a different effect on a man if he is out with mother or alone exemplifies the situation vector.

All learning in structured learning theory is to be described in terms of changes in these three vectors. At once the implication of personality and motivation factors in learning becomes obvious, especially with reference to the trait and bearing vectors. It means that learning is a three-dimensional process. In measurement, therefore, we must take account of all dimensions. It implies that all individual states and traits are involved in learning and are themselves affected by learning. The extent of the involvement already varies with what has been learned. Thus to learn that a number 18 bus goes to Clapham probably affects few traits and those mostly ones of ability rather than personality or motivation, unless the situation vector is important. If, however, this is the case, as for example when a girl-friend lives in Clapham, there may be more fundamental changes. To learn how to attract women, or men, clearly has considerable affects on all vectors, and the ease of acquiring such techniques is influenced by one's position on these dimensions.

It should not escape the mathematically inclined reader that the term vector has important implications. It is possible to develop equations in matrix algebra using these vectors to predict some learning performance and this has been done by Cattell and Child (1975), although the mathematics are complex. This finally allows structured learning theory to define with great precision the changes taking place through given types of experience. In nonmathematical terms such learning can be illustrated by the *Adjustment Process Analysis chart*, where we see how an erg may be gratified in various ways and what the outcomes of the various methods are.

This APA chart is a verbal and visual example of changes in the three vectors that can be accurately measured, utilizing the factors which we have discussed in the earlier sections of this chapter.

Structured Learning Theory and Reinforcement

This theory does not only bear on the nature of learning itself—changes in three dimensions. In addition, it is highly relevant to reinforcement. Now it is not useful to argue that some behaviour has occurred because it has been reinforced unless we also know what this reinforcement is. This seems to us (e.g. Kline, 1972) the Achilles heel of the operant approach to human (as distinct from animal) learning, because it is by no means certain what does or does not constitute a reinforcer in any individual case.

Structured learning theory, on the other hand, can specify what reinforcement

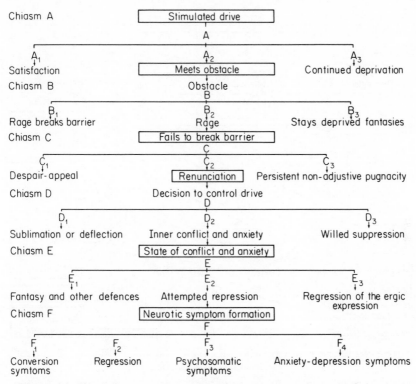

Figure 4.1 The Adjustment Process Analysis chart. From Cattell and Child (1975, p. 60)

is. Hull (1943) regarded drive reduction as the crucial reinforcer. However, it should be noted that he refers to drive in the abstract. It either posits that there is only one human drive or it implies that all drives behave equally in learning and remembering. However, there is no evidence that this is the case, and Cattell and Kline (in press) cite evidence that conditioned responses learned under hunger extinguish more quickly than those learned under fear. In the section 'Motivational Traits' we were able to set out the major drives so far discovered—ergs and sentiments—and consequently in Hullian terms we would argue that reinforcement consists in ergic tension reduction overall, the difference in ergic tension before and after learning. The psychological implications can be seen by briefly examining a typical *dynamic lattice*

There are several points to be made about this dynamic lattice. First, such a lattice could be constructed for each individual, while a common lattice for a group might also be made by averaging a set of results. Our example shows how various behaviours have the effect of satisfying ergic tensions although there may be no obvious connection between the two. Churchgoing subsumes the ergs of self-submission, appeal and self-esteem. Each sentiment structure gives satisfaction to several ergs and each erg is expressed through several sentiments.

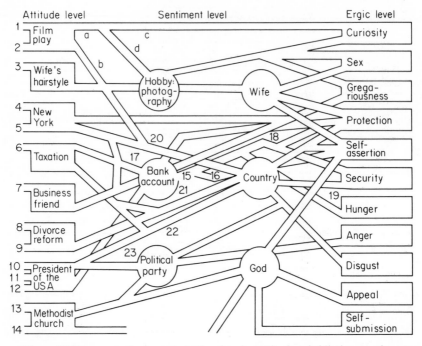

Figure 4.2 Fragment of a dynamic lattice showing attitude subsidiation, sentiment structure and ergic goals

However, this dynamic lattice is unqualified and hence vague. Structured learning theory is able to express such tension reduction reinforcement in precise terms, i.e. in reductions in scores on the ergic tension measures, and thus changes in the trait vector especially but also in the other vectors. Thus reinforcement can be almost operationally defined in terms of ergic tension reduction.

To return from the abstract to the particular case, such a concept of reinforcement helps us understand why we feel that we can learn best those topics in which we are interested. We have previously shown (Kline, 1975) that we feel interest when we are ergically involved with something. An obvious example which is nevertheless apposite is the nymphomaniac. Her high sex erg means that she is 'interested' in men. Vocational education may be good for adolescents because ergs and sentiments such as career, mating and spouse are all likely to be affected by such learning. On arguments such as this, however, it is questionable who would learn Greek grammar or matrix algebra. Nevertheless, for able children such subjects may allow expression of the self-assertion and self-sentiment.

Integration learning

As we have seen, structured learning theory can account for reinforcement in terms of ergic tension reduction—changes in ergic tension before and after learning. This affects the trait vector and the bearing vector. The situational vector plays its part, reflecting previous experience. We should not imagine, in this formulation, that motivational factors only are involved. To a large extent how we effectively release ergic tension depends upon our temperamental traits and states. So far, however, this formulation leaves unanswered one difficult question: how do we maximize this tension reduction? This is achieved by what Cattell (1965) refers to as *integration learning*.

As we can see from the dynamic lattice in Figure 4.2, each action may allow expression of more than one erg. Sometimes, however, conflict may occur when the expression of one ergic goal means the frustration of another, or even more ergic satisfactions. An obvious example is seen with students who, as finals approach, deny for the sake of study all other ergic expressions. Such delayed satisfaction or gratification is clearly important in all civilized society (in psychoanalytic terms a sign of maturity, ego, reality-based, activity). Infants usually demand immediate ergic satisfaction. Adults have learned, in most situations, to achieve maximal ergic satisfaction over a time period. This is known as integration learning. To name a phenomenon is not, however (except in sociology), to understand it. How then does integration learning come about?

From the evidence summarized by Cattell and Kline (in press), two motivational factors play a vital part in this process—supergo and selfsentiment. Superego in the MAT, as in psychoanalytic theory, is concerned with shame and guilt and has its origins in early family experience, especially the relationships of a child with his caretakers, usually, of course, his parents. This superego factor acts as a restraint on the ergic expression of sex and pugnacity in our society (except perhaps at pop festivals and footballs matches). By such inhibition it leads to greater ergic satisfaction in the end. However, only in certain neurotic groups is the superego the main instrument of integration learning.

Among normals the self-sentiment is the most important. We modify our behaviour in the light of our self-respect and reputations. The officer and gentleman of the British tradition, the $K\alpha\lambda os$ $K''\alpha\gamma\alpha\theta os$ of Greek education, for example, were high on self-sentiment. Thus, in McDougall's phrase, the self-sentiment is the master sentiment, for it is the instrument for the satisfaction of other ergs. If the self is destroyed, physically or otherwise, no ergic satisfaction can be obtained.

The Dynamic Calculus

Among normal adults in our society (although infants are forgiven) we expect that ergic satisfaction will be controlled by the combined influence of these two factors, superego and the self-sentiment. Now implicit in this control are some quantitative assumptions: that individual ergic satisfaction can be summated; that to satisfy one erg is not necessarily the same, in ergic satisfaction, as to satisfy another. However, this implicit quantification has been made explicit in the dynamic calculus, which again involves matrix algebra and is explicated in more detail in Cattell and Child (1975).

That these complex variables can be mathematically represented turns upon the fact that self-sentiment and superego to which we refer, although indeed similar to their counterparts in psychoanalytic theory and in the work of McDougall, are factor-analytically derived constructs with reliable tests—the MAT. In the dynamic calculus the emotional quality of an attitude (say to blacks) and the combination of ergs involved in it can be expressed by the *direction* of a vector. The length of the vector indicates its strength. Where several attitudes contribute to some overall position, as in authoritarianism, characterized by xenophobia, anti-semitism and anti-intellectualism, vector summation can quantify the data. Similarly, the dynamic calculus enables an ergic investment vector to be calculated, indicating the quality and quantity of ergic satisfaction for an individual in a given sentiment.

Our discussion of reinforcement has involved so far the reduction of ergic tension, the motivational factors accounting for why we respond as we do. However, the temperamental traits are also implicated inasmuch as these determine the way we respond. Acute readers will have noticed that our two most important dynamic factors, superego and self-sentiment, are also found as temperamental traits, largely because of their pervasive influence on behaviour. However, in the integration of behaviour, the maximizing of ergic expression, one temperamental factor—C ego strength—is highly important. This factor is our way of handling the drives and conflicts illustrated in the dynamic lattice. The person high on C can make reality-based demands and act reliably in difficulties. It is characteristically low in neurotics, and it is interesting to note in the light of this theoretical framework that emotional difficulties are so frequently associated with learning problems. A low factor C disables people from maximizing efficiently their ergic tension reduction and from integrating behaviour, so that reality-based learning—involving delayed gratification—cannot occur.

The theoretical discussion of structured learning theory indicates clearly how personality is implicated in learning, not vaguely as in clinical trials, but operationally defined in terms of personality, mood and motivational factors. All these together with ability traits can go into the tri-vector equations of the theory.

An Alternative View

This, of course, is not the only theory that attempts to tie factor-analytic personality variables into learning. Eysenck (1967a) has linked one of his personality factors, extraversion, to conditionability. Extraverts are harder to condition than introverts, and their conditioned responses extinguish more quickly than do those of introverts. Since, in this theory, our behaviour is learned (conditioned), this view has many ramifications. Criminals tend to be extraverted (they have failed to learn the mores of society) and certain kinds of neurotics (dysthymics) would be expected to be introverted, others (hysterics) extraverted. Since extraversion is a function of the arousability of the central nervous system, we would expect (and find) differential learning performance in tedious tasks among introverts and extraverts.

There are several objections to this theory, which appears too simple to be useful. First, it assumes that conditionability is a unitary trait which has not been demonstrated. If one response in an individual is easy to condition, are all responses? Secondly, it deals with only one of the second-order factors, while, as we saw, there are in technically satisfactory studies at least five second-order factors. Furthermore, it takes no account of state or motivational factors. In the main it is concerned with classical rather than operant conditioning, which is a limiting factor in its applicability. Finally, as Gale (1973) has shown, the very notion of arousability is somewhat dubious. For all these reasons, the more comprehensive structured learning theory is to be preferred.

Conclusions: Practical Applications and Value of the Theory

With the development of factored personality tests there have been a large number of virtually atheoretical studies of personality and academic performance among adults, in many different cultures. In America the stable introvert is superior, while in Great Britain we find that the stable introvert is best in the arts, the mildly neurotic introvert in the sciences (Entwistle, 1972). However, the fact is that these correlations are small and much of the variance is still unaccounted for. Interestingly enough, the present writer has found similar results in Ghana and Uganda (Kline, 1966; Honess and Kline, 1974), cultures very different from the West, and the findings have been replicated in India, Japan and with Chinese students (Cattell, 1973).

Cattell and Butcher (1968), working with children, obtained a multiple correlation of ability, personality and motivational variables and academic success of around 0.7, i.e. about the half the variance was accounted for. Conceding that the reliability of all tests was imperfect, it can be argued that this is a very powerful prediction. The motivational factors alone, as with the personality factors, produced small but significant correlations. There is no reason to expect that results with adults would be inferior. The fact that the multiple correlation was higher than the ability, personality or motivational correlations on their own indicates clearly that each of the groups of variables is contributing something different to the overall result.

As Entwistle's (1972) review of the work relating academic performance to personality indicates, the main finding is that correlations with the separate factors are small but significant, so small that practical selection would be hardly improved. While classroom interaction studies might enable us to see what it was that brought about these correlations, structured learning theory enables us to put them into a theoretical framework. We can see how the individual correlations could be small, because in addition to the trait vector (of which personality is but a part) there is the influence of the bearing and situational vectors. The expectation of high correlations assumes a one-vector theory of learning.

Studies of special groups where we know that there was unusual keenness (such as the special language courses in the army) and of groups matched for the necessary ability traits for their subjects could quickly reveal some of the secrets of the dynamic lattice. What is highly interesting is the nature of the ergic tension reduction of scholarly work. Such investigations constitute, in effect, the quantitative study of sublimation!

Another area where structured learning theory can help us to group the facts is the field of occupational success. Here the correlations between temperament and success, and to some extent motivation, have been computed for a number of occupations in America (see the handbook to 16 P.F. test, Cattell *et al.*, 1970), although much of the work so far has concerned itself with differences between occupational groups. Similarly, the study of the symptomology of neurotic and psychotic groups (accepting the claim that these are maladaptive learned behaviours) and the changes in these over psychotherapy together with the requisite personality and motivation scores can help us to unravel quantitatively rather than intuitively the complex dynamic lattice of the mentally sick. In other words, in both these fields structured learning theory *could* enable us to see the reinforcement behind occupational satisfaction and success and mental illness.

In fairness to other theories which have signally failed in this task, we must add a note of caution. This research remains to be done. Nevertheless, there seems little doubt that structured learning theory sets out how and to what extent personality is involved in learning. For the first time in psychology factor analysis has given us the instruments for the quantification of what has previously been the preserve of clinical intuition. As researchers in personality and learning, we are now in a position to re-echo some famous words: 'Give us the tools and we'll do the job'.

REFERENCES

Allport, G. W. (1937). *Personality: A Psychological Interpretation*, Holt, Rinehart & Winston, New York.

Bargmann, R. (1953). The statistical significance of simple structure in factor analysis. Frankfurt Mun. Hochschule Fuer Internationale Raedagogesche Forchung.

Burt, C. (1937). 'The analysis of temperament', *British Journal of Medical Psychology*, **17**, 158.

Cattell, R. B. (1957). *Personality and Motivation Structure and Measurement*, World Book Co., Yonkers.

Cattell, R. B. (1965). *The Scientific Analysis of Behaviour*, Penguin, Harmondsworth.

Cattell, R. B. (1966a) (Ed.) *Handbook of Multivariate Experimental Psychology*, Rand McNally, Chicago.

Cattell, R. B. (1966b). 'The scree test for the number of factors', *Multivariate Behavioural Research*, **1**, 140.

Cattell, R. B. (1973). *Personality and Mood by Questionnaire*, Josey Bass, San Francisco.

Cattell, R. B. (1976). *Personality and Learning Theory*. In preparation.

Cattell, R. B. 'Source trait structure seen in laboratory measurement: T data, in press.

Cattell, R. B., and Butcher, H. J. (1968). *The Prediction of Achievement and Creativity*, Bobbs Merrill, New York.

Cattell, R. B., and Child, D. (1975). *Motivation and Dynamic Structure*, Holt, Rinehart & Winston, London.

Cattell, R. B., and Gibbons, B. D. (1968). 'Personality factor, structure of the combined Guilford and Cattell personality questionnaires, *Journal of Personality and Social Psychology*, **9**, 107.

Cattell, R. B., and Kline, P. *The Scientific Analysis of Personality and Motivation*, Academic Press, London, in press.

Cattell, R. B., and Scheier, I. H. (1961). *The Meaning and Measurement of Neuroticism and Anxiety*, Ronald Press, New York.

Cattell, R. B., and Warburton, F. W. (1967). *Objective Personality and Motivation Tests*, University of Illinois Press, Urbana.

Comrey, A. L. (1970). *The Comrey Personality Scales*, Educational and Industrial Testing Service, San Diego.

Edwards, A. L. (1959). *The Edwards Personal Preference Schedule* (Revised), Psychological Corporation, New York.

Entwistle, N. J. (1972). 'Personality and academic attainment', *British Journal of Educational Psychology*, **42**, 137.

Eysenck, H. J. (1967a). *The Biological Basis of Personality*, Thomas, Springfield.

Eysenck, H. J. (1967b). *The Logical Basis of Factor Analysis*, in D. N. Jackson and S. Messick (Eds.), *Problems in Human Assessment*, McGraw-Hill, New York, Ch. 20.

Eysenck, H. J. (1970). *The Structure of Human Personality*, 3rd edn., Methuen, London.

Eysenck, H. J., and Eysenck, S. B. G. (1968). 'A factorial study of psychoticism as a dimension of personality', *Multivariate Behaviour Research*, All Clinical Special Issue, 15.

Eysenck, H. J., and Eysenck, S. G. B. (1969). *Personality Structure and Measurement*, Routledge & Kegan Paul, London.

Freud, S. (1933). *New Introductory Lectures*, Hogarth Press and the Institute of Psychoanalysis, London.

Freud, S. (1940). *Outline of Psychoanalysis*, Hogarth Press and the Institute for Psychoanalysis, London.

Gale, A. M. (1973). 'Individual differences: studies in extraversion and the EEG', in P. Kline (Ed.), *New Approaches in Psychological Measurement*, Wiley, London.

Ghiselli, E. E. (1966). *The Validity of Occupational Aptitude Tests*, Wiley, New York.

Guilford, J. P. (1959). *Personality*, McGraw-Hill, New York.

Hall, C. S., and Lindzey, G. (1957). *Theories of Personality*, Wiley, New York.

Honess, T., and Kline, P., (1974). 'Extraversion, neuroticism and academic performance in Uganda', *British Journal of Educational Psychology*, **44**.

Hull, C. L. (1943). *Principles of Behaviour*, Appleton-Century-Crofts, New York.

Jackson, D. N., and Messick, S. (1967) (Eds.). *Problems in Human Assessment*, McGraw-Hill, New York.

Kaiser, H. F. (1958). 'The varimax criterion for analytic rotation in factor analysis', *Psychometritix*, **23**, 187.

Kline, P. (1966). 'Extraversion, neuroticism and academic performance among Ghanaian university students', *British Journal of Educational Psychology*, **36**, 93.

Kline, P. (1972). *Fact and Fantasy in Freudian Theory*, Methuen, London.

Kline, P. (1973) (Ed.). *New Approaches in Psychological Measurement*, Wiley, London.

Kline, P. (1975). *Psychology of Vocational Guidance*, Batsford, London.

Lorenz, K. (1966). *On Aggression*, Methuen, London.

McDougall, W. (1932). *Energies of Men*, Methuen, London.

Mischel, W. (1968). *Personality Assessment*, Wiley, New York.

Murray, H. A. (1938). *Explorations in Personality*, Oxford University Press, New York.

Sarason, I. G. (1972). Personality: an Objective Approach (Second Edition) Wiley, London.

Thurstone, L. L. (1947). *Multiple Factor Analyses: A Development and Expansion of the Vectors of the Mind*, University of Chicago Press, Chicago.

5

LEARNING TO LEARN: THE PERSONAL CONSTRUCTION AND EXCHANGE OF MEANING

Laurie F. Thomas and E. Sheila Harri-Augstein

1. A PERSONAL CONSTRUCT APPROACH TO LEARNING TO LEARN

Living is an opportunity for learning; but how each person uses it depends upon what they bring to each event and what they make of each experience. It is the meaning attributed to each event, not the event itself, which influences a person's reaction to it. Experimental psychologists constructing their theories in the meaning-isolated laboratory have largely ignored this simple truth. People do not necessarily learn from experience; only from reviewing the the meanings which they attribute to it. The source of a person's attitudes is their personal knowledge and past experience evaluated within a personal system of beliefs and values. These combine with their individual strategies, tactics and skills as they negotiate personally viable meanings onto their environment.

Clinical psychologists acknowledge personal meaning as a source of man's actions. Carl Rogers, for example, has used the philosophy and practices of his non-directive counselling to formulate a person-centred approach to learning. He believes in the concept of a 'natural' and continuing process of personal growth. This is often distorted, stunted or halted in modern society by the development of non-viable meanings which disrupt or contort a person's relationships with himself and his environment. This belief leads Rogers to concentrate upon identifying and providing the conditions within which these disabling contortions can be released and 'natural' growth can re-commence. Whilst Rogers pays little attention to how meaning is constructed, his understanding of the conditions within which personal changes can take place is highly relevant. Towards the end of this chapter the idea of a learning conversation is outlined. One necessary function of such conversations is to offer the personal support which facilitates significant personal change.

85

Another clinician, George Kelly, viewed learning as a largely positive construction. The essence of his beliefs can be expressed in the phrase 'Man makes man'. Man and woman are continually reinventing themselves and their alternative futures. They are prisoners only of their own lack of effective imagination. This view led to the invention of the theory of personal constructs, which focuses on how personal meanings are generated. The authors of this chapter have used this approach as a starting point for reconsidering the nature of human learning processes.

Learning might be defined as:

'The construction and exchange of personally relevant and viable meanings'.

Kelly's theory proposes that each organism operates through a system of personal constructs. In the human being these are bipolar differentiations revealed by the similarities and differences which the person conceives and perceives in his or her inner and outer world. The constructs are hierarchically organized as a system within which meaning is created, stored and attributed. This process of modelling experience into more or less viable meanings enables the person to anticipate events.

Kelly's 'Man as Scientist' suggests that people live by developing personal theories about everything in their experience. These theories are the basis of all action and are tested, improved, revised, validated or discarded in the light of the ongoing perceived consequences. This validation process can be more or less adequate, both in terms of its short-term and long-term power of anticipation and in the range of experience to which it is applied. Inadequate modelling leads to inappropriate anticipations and can be regarded as the source of what Rogers views as disruptions of 'natural' growth. More adequate modelling enables men and women to cope, to achieve competences and to live creatively. The process of modelling establishes relationships between the emotional world of the person and the meanings he is achieving in the outside world.

Competences, from talking to juggling, from mathematical thinking to painting, and from social skill to yoga, all derive from this capacity to create meanings which viably model ourselves in our environments. Kelly developed the repertory grid as a technique for use in therapy. It was designed to help a person to exhibit and review his or her system of personal constructs. It can be developed and extended for use in many learning situations.

Learning is itself an inference from behaviour and/or experience. The psychological position of the observer (i.e. teacher, student, parent, child, experimenter or subject) will influence the nature of the learning he will infer.

A teacher-orientated approach to learning to learn has offered various programmes for encouraging the acquisition of what other people judge to be good study habits. Such 'cookbook' methods are often discarded by the learner as irrelevant or inadequate. The authors of this chapter have carried out a series of studies concerned to develop a learner-centred approach to learning to learn. This derives much from the approaches of both Carl Rogers and George Kelly. In these studies awareness of one's own processes in learning is taken as a prerequisite for learning to learn. What is effective for one person may not work for another. What satisfies one person may he totally unsatis-factory to another.

This implies that the conditions in which a person can be encouraged to learn to learn must be conversational, in the sense that the learner has to assume joint responsibility with the tutor for bringing his or her own learning processes under review. Together, they learn to negotiate the purposes of learning from the learner's personal needs, to develop more effective strategies and tactics in learning and to review the criteria by which they would judge 'effectiveness of the enterprise'. As the learner moves into greater self-organization, he takes more of the tutor's activities into himself. He becomes his own tutor and the learning conversation continues within his head.

In the final section of this chapter an outline is offered of the process for conducting a learning conversation. This uses specific tools and procedures, including a modified form of the repertory grid, as part of a highly organized but sensitive process of control, encouragement, guidance and interchange. A learning conversation is not just inspired chit-chat. Each dialogue within the conversation serves a specific purpose and the whole process is rigorously conceived. Its rigour arises from different assumptions than those of the traditional norm-based methodology.

2. THE REPERTORY GRID

(a) Elicitation

The repertory grid is a procedure whereby a person can be encouraged to exhibit part of his system of personal constructs. The content of the grid is determined during the elicitation conversation. It will be as significant or as trivial as the quality of the interaction between elicitor and subject. For an effective elicitation to take place, both must participate fully in the conversa-tional process. This aspect of repertory grid technique has often been under-emphasized.

Before any content is entered into the grid the purpose of the exercise has to be negotiated. In this context, the grid should be seen as contributing to the solution of a learning problem experienced by the subject. The nature of this problem is explored and an understanding of it shared. This under-standing forms the basis for guiding, controlling and selecting, during the latter part of the elicitation conversation.

This shared understanding of a problem provides the criteria for deciding what the elements should be. For example, a person who is experiencing diffi-culties in writing might decide that the problem arises in his or her conflicting ideas and feelings about what constituted 'good' writing. The usefulness of the grid might depend upon identifying a series of pieces of personally signi-ficant writing. These would form the elements to be constructed. The elicitor's task is to conduct the conversation so that personally meaningful items emerge. Usually these are contributed by the participating subject, but on occasions 'offered items' may open up the whole discussion. The decision about 'when to elicit' and 'when to offer' and how to regulate and mix this process is part of the conversational skill. The aim of the element elicitation is to decide upon a complete set of elements which form a representative sample of the items of central concern to the subject. The elicitor should remain sensitive to this requirement, and if subsequent discussion leads to a shift in emphasis, elements can be discarded and added to reflect this.

Studies carried out by the authors illustrate the range of topics which can be explored.

(1) Trainee teachers each named 15 'children I have taught' elements in a grid which explored the system of personal meanings which they brought to interacting with children in the classroom.

(2) Industrial inspectors used 'windscreen-wiper blades' as elements in a grid to explore the meanings which each assigned to the terms 'acceptable' and 'defective' in this difficult area of subjective judgment. (The grid is potentially a very good technique for exploring many issues in which individual perception and judgment play a part.)

(3) Undergraduate social science students used statistical concepts such as 'risk', 'chance', 'probability', 'frequency', 'significance', 'mean', etc., to explore how their personal meanings differed from those of their statistics lecturer.

(4) Industrial trainers used 'training situations' such as 'on the job', 'lecture', 'project', 'film', 'discussion', as elements in grids used to explore the assumptions they brought to the designing of a course.

(5) Art students used pieces of sculpture as the elements in grids for exploring the artistic and aesthetic meanings which contributed to their own work.

(6) 'A'-level students at technical college used 'significant events in my life from which I have learned' as elements for exploring the personal meanings surrounding the word 'learning'.

The range of items that can be used as elements in a grid is limited only by the ingenuity of the users. 'Musical recordings', 'essays', 'relationships', 'physical concepts', 'poems', 'jobs' and 'offences' have all been used.

The 'learning grid' will be used to illustrate how the complete grid procedure is carried through. The main phases of the conversation are:

(a) negotiating the purpose,
(b) eliciting and agreeing the elements,
(c) eliciting the constructs,
(d) assigning elements to position on the constructs.

The elicitation of this grid is reported colloquially and in an abbreviated form to demonstrate the 'conversational' atmosphere. More formal reporting might give a false impression of a predetermined verbal procedure rather than the systematic but flexible pursuit of relevant and significant meaning. Harry S attended three 'A'-level courses full-time at a technical college. As participating subject, he was encouraged to talk about the problems which he experienced in learning. It became clear that for him personally relevant learning mostly took place outside formal educational institutions. Together with a number of his peers, he decided that 'Events from which, in retrospect, I seem to have learned' would form the elements in his grid.

Before any elements were elicited the purpose was discussed in more detail. It became clear that Harry was having difficulties with his course and wanted to leave college, but his parents objected. He had no clear alternative which attracted him sufficiently to deliberately flout their views. The elements were negotiated to span academic and other areas of learning.

As the discussion proceeded notes were made and these were used jointly by the elicitor and Harry to decide on a representative set of elements. Some 60 events were mentioned, of which 18 seemed to define the problem area. Only nine are used here to illustrate the technique.

Three of Harry's elements were:

E1 Near death in a dinghy
E2 A highly condensed history course with an enthusiastic young teacher
E3 A trip to Finland.

The remaining six are shown in the grid (Figure 5.1).

Harry wrote each element on a separate card. He was offered three cards at a time and asked to 'think and feel' about them, concentrating on the total impact of each event rather than any specific aspect of it. He was then asked:

'Which two are most alike, and which one differs from the other two?'

Harry differentiated

E2 History course
E3 Finland

from

E1 dinghy.

When asked to describe what was similar about the two he said that E2 and E3 were 'relaxed', whilst E1 was 'tense'. 'relaxed' v 'tense' is one of Harry's personal constructs by which he attributes meaning to significant learning events. Harry was asked to elaborate exactly what he meant by relaxed and tense. The conversation continued. Each of the remaining elements was assigned either to the 'pair' as relaxed or to the 'single' element as tense. The ticks and crosses on the grid record these assignings.

Three more cards were offered and another construct (i.e. a pair and a single-ton) was identified. The two poles were described. The conversation goes on to explore whether the constructs being elicited are those most relevant to the problem. This is a sensitive process. Any discrimination which reveals itself should be recorded, but seemingly trivial constructs should be discussed to reveal their true significance.

As the elicitation proceeds, the choice of 'triads' (i.e. the sets of three elements from which a construct emerges) can be varied. Generally, the triads should be 'controlled random selections' from the complete set of elements. Each element should occur as frequently as any other and no pair of elements should occur in more than one triad until all pairs have appeared. However, the purpose in eliciting the grid is more important than arid statistical purity. If the conversationalists (subject and elicitor) identify some area to be explored in greater

Element	Individual activity, looking after myself, self-reliance / Group activity	External events (no control) impinging on emotions / Emotion internally generated, controlled	Spontaneous activity / Considered activity	Tense / Relaxed	Intellectual freakout / Great use of intellect	Grudge against someone / No grudge
Enduring educational system to obtain ambition in electronics	√	×	×	○	×	×
Technical college gave me surprising freedom	×	√	×	×	√	×
Musical outlook broadened by Deep Purple	√	×	√	×	×	×
Short eyesight made me give up playing football for a team	○	√	×	√	○	√
Interest in electronics inspired by father	√	×	√	×	×	×
Near death in a dinghy	√	√	√	√	√	√
Learning to avoid trouble when in early teens	○	○	○	√	×	√
A month visit to Finland	√	○	√	×	√	×
Highly condensed history course by enthusiastic teacher	×	×	×	×	○	×

Figure 5.1 Raw grid

depth, the choice of triad elements can reflect this. On occasions elements can be added to or eliminated to keep the grid focused on conversationally central issues. The keynote is psychological centrality and significance. The elicitation conversation continues until it becomes clear that it has exhausted the source of meanings which the subject can attribute to the problem situation.

The participants can control the elicitation conversation to focus attention on different types of construct. At one stage or for one purpose it may become important to explore feelings, whereas at another stage or for another purpose perceptual discriminations may seem more central to the issue. Abstract constructs, emotional constructs and descriptive constructs all have their uses.

The elicitation conversation is analogous to a participative interview in which the grid procedures serve to articulate issues which might otherwise remain unrevealed.

(b) The Meaning in the Grid

The process of conversationally eliciting a grid is in itself a learning experience, both for the elicitor and the subject. When successful, it raises awareness of the underlying processes whereby thoughts and feelings combine to give meaning to events. But there is a peculiar sense in which the real learning is not exhibited in the content of the grid. It is this which has made it suspect as a formal psychological procedure, and yet this very property enhances its value as a tool for encouraging people to learn to learn. The exercise is awareness-raising. Much of the process goes on in the less articulated layers of consciousness out of which the elements and constructs emerge and back into which the relations which are revealed must again redissolve. It is this experience of learning at two levels simultaneously which constitutes the process of learning to learn. It must be experienced to be appreciated, and is similar to the experience of the occasional tutorial argument or discussion in which the participants feel something significant has happened. The conversational grid procedure helps to enhance both the quality and frequency of such experience.

It is not only the individual elements and constructs which have significance for learning. It is the relations between them which embody the raw material to learn to learn. The whole pattern of relationships in the grid is itself simultaneously both an articulated property of the responses and a fluctuating shadow of the more important processes which underlie it.

The raw grid is difficult to interpret. The process of focusing the grid can be used to display the relations more explicitly. Focusing can be carried out by a computer and the results fed back at a later session, but this loses some of the immediacy of the experience.

Visual focusing of the grid can become an integral part of a learning conversation. The subject's participation in the act of discovering the relations involves him or her more totally in the process of constructing meaning.

Focusing consists of putting like with like. The easiest method is to start by cutting up a copy of the raw grid into vertical columns, each of which represents the responses to one element. The strips are compared one with another and those which are most alike are placed side by side. This process is continued until a new linear order of elements has been decided. This maximizes the similarities between adjacent elements. This partially 'focused grid' is again copied and cut into horizontal strips containing the responses for all the elements on any one construct. The similarities are again identified. (Extreme differences are also important since the construct is bipolar and the poles and responses can be reversed with no loss of meaning.) The constructs are sorted and if necessary reversed and rewritten to reveal the maximum amount of agreement between the rows.

This two-way resorting of the elements and the constructs is the process of focusing the grid. Harry's grid is focused in Figure 5.2.

The focused grid points to relationships which exist in the subject's system of meanings but it does not fully capture all the subtleties there. Sensitive conversation which uses the patterns in the focused grid as a take-off point for exploration of the patterns in the mind can significantly contribute to the provocation of personally valued learning.

In this sense, the elicitation and focusing conversations are learning conversations in which the subject becomes aware of the processes which are being facilitated. These grid conversations can be viewed as a paradigm of the process of learning to learn.

3. LEARNING: AN INFERENCE FROM BEHAVIOUR AND EXPERIENCE

Learning is not self-evident. It must be inferred, either from behaviour or experience. Preferably, it is inferred participatively from both. The observer of behaviour sees things which the learner cannot, but only the learner has access to his own experience. Yet the drawing of inferences implies the existence of a position or criteria against which the adequacy of the learning can be assessed. The teacher will often value changes in the responses of the learner which the learner himself does not.

The learner almost certainly values changes in both his experience and his actions which the teacher thinks of less highly.

Thus, for the authors the construct:

As viewed by the teacher

v

As viewed by the learner

is an important differentiation to be made in thinking and feeling about learning.

The point of view of the teacher (or of the experimenter in psychological learning experiments) pervades the literature on learning. It also colours the thoughts and feelings of most individuals who have been through school, college or university. Most of the supposed theories of learning are solely concerned with the conditions under which teacher-defined learning takes place and methods for enhancing the purposes of the teacher. They are thus

Element	Individual activity, looking after myself, self-reliance — Group activity	Spontaneous activity — Considered activity	Tense — Relaxed	Grudge against someone — No grudge	External events (no control) impinging on emotions — Emotion internally generated, controlled	Intellectual freakout — Great use of intellect
Near death in a dinghy	✓	✓	✓	✓	✓	✓
Short eyesight made me give up playing football for a team	○	×	✓	✓	✓	○
Learning how to avoid trouble when in early teens	○	○	✓	✓	○	×
Enduring educational system to obtain ambition in electronics	✓	×	○	×	×	×
Interest in electronics inspired by father	✓	✓	×	×	×	×
Musical outlook broadened by Deep Purple	✓	✓	×	×	×	×
A month visit to Finland	✓	✓	×	×	○	✓
Technical college gave me surprising freedom	×	×	×	×	✓	✓
Highly condensed history course by enthusiastic teacher	×	×	×	×	×	○

Figure 5.2 Focussed grid

theories of teaching. It is only when the purposes of the learner are used as a basis for assessing what learning has taken place that an approach can be made to understanding the individual processes of learning. Earlier it was suggested that learner-defined learning could be viewed as: 'The construction and exchange of personally significant meaning'. In its ignoring of behavioural activity, this can only be a partial definition, but it pinpoints the centre of attention in this article.

The construction of meaning may not be totally intentional. Many retrospectively valued changes take place unplanned by either an outside agency or the learner himself.

Thus another important dimension for construing learning is:

As assessed against the original purpose (if any)

v

As assessed retrospectively.

Harry S at the end of his grid conversation commented upon how surprised he was by some of the implications of what he was now thinking and feeling. Only six weeks later was the able to discuss the outcomes in a reflective and evaluative manner.

Thus, if learning is an inference, 'who' makes the inference and against 'what' criteria will greatly influence how the process of learning (and learning to learn) is understood. The two-by-two category system yielded by our two constructs serves as a useful device for clarifying thinking on this topic.

	Original purpose	Retrospective assessment
Teacher's view	Teacher original (TO)	Teacher retrospective (TR)
Learner's view	Learner original (LO)	Learner retrospective (LR)

Most learning in education falls into the TO-category. The teacher sets the purpose of the exercise and the learning is measured by reference to what he set out to teach.

Most personally valued learning falls into category LR. The learner recognizes after the event that something significant has happened. Then and only then does the learner set about evaluating what has happened.

It is this twofold difference between institutionally valued learning and personally valued learning which has bedevilled any attempt to enhance our capacities for learning to learn.

4. PHENOMENOLOGICAL WORLDS

There are many adult-to-adult situations in which a client is dependent on the knowledge of an expert. The process of understanding called for from the client in these circumstances approximates to type TO learning. A patient consulting a doctor, a client consulting a solicitor, a builder consulting an architect, a manager calling in a computer expert, a client using an industrial designer, an old-age pensioner attempting to obtain advice from social security, are all partially dependent upon their ability to understand what is offered in the expert's terms. Problems arise when the personal construct system of the expert differs considerably from that of the client. For example, most patients want to be able to relate their own thoughts and feelings about their aches and pains to what their general practitioner has to tell them. But in these trying circumstances understanding is difficult, and many doctors avoid even attempting it. The expert can be helped in his explanations if he can see the terms in which the client is construing the problem area. Skilled discussion may reveal this, but quite often it does not and the negotiation of meaning gradually peters out in an atmosphere of mutual misunderstanding and distrust. The quality of learning type TO is also enhanced when the client understands the terms in which the expert is talking. Either way, if the expert can be enabled to achieve his purposes of explanation and the client understands what is being said, then learning has taken place. But usually the difficulty is not solely one of terminology. The words have been specially chosen and developed to express a whole approach to the construing of the subject-matter. The expert thinks and feels differently from the client.

The repertory grid can be used to embody the meanings of the expert. Each of the elements is operationally defined by its position on the constructs. Each of the constructs is operationally defined by the way it differentiates the elements.

For example, if an architect were to place each of his own designs within his own system of personal constructs, clients might find it easier to understand the terms in which he was thinking. If their requirements did not seem to be represented, the range of elements could be expanded to include other designs. The ordinary processes of negotiation may appear to follow such a path, but explicit grids usually disclose thoughts and feelings that do not often appear in free-flowing professional conversation. Thus, learning type TO can be enhanced by using grids. But the expert may feel the need to understand the client in the client's terms. Or the client, understanding the expert better, can more easily make his own purpose explicit. In this manner, type LO learning can be increased. Industrial design sometimes follows this pattern, but more often the client is frustrated by his inability to express his needs in terms that the designer can translate into action. The grid used conversationally is one aid to enhancing type LO learning. The learner is enabled to express his needs in the expert's terms.

The situations in which either the expert (T) or the client (L) fully understand their purpose prior to the negotiating event are, however, perhaps the least interesting. In the more creative exchanges the purpose arises out of the negotiation. Thus, types TR and LR learning can occur in expert/client negotiations. Often the occurence of such creative encounters seems to be a product of chance or happenstance. Negotiating with the aid of grids increases the probability of creative outcomes.

For example, the industrial designer may work with a client to arrive at a product which neither had conceived prior to the event. Commissioned work in art and music can at best also be the result of such encounters. In this situation the expert is usually given the final decision and the process may perhaps best be seen as type TR learning. However, the client contribution can be crucial.

The education situation ideally offers the paradigm of type LR learning. The ideal result of tutoring is that the learner is enabled to pursue his own purposes more effectively because the expert has entered into a more complete understanding of his world and his needs within it.

5. COGNITIVE REFLECTION: GRID-AIDED CONVERSATIONS WITH ONESELF

Within a learner-centred personal construing approach to learning, type TO becomes irrelevant, except as a short-term exercise. Effective long-term learning is not achieved if the learner indiscriminately takes on someone else's meanings. Type LR learning enables the learner to explore an area of personally important understandings without initially having committed himself to any clear-cut ideas about what would constitute a successful outcome. This process of exploration has three aspects.

1. The revision, elaboration and extension of one's own personal construct system.

2. The close regarding of others' systems of construing to compare and contrast them with one's own. The consequent interaction or review should lead to the digestion and incorporation of whatever one values.

3. Eventually processes 1 and 2 stabilize to produce a new pattern of personal meanings. Out of this emerges the retrospective definition of purpose.

In the next section procedures for the exchange of meanings are developed. Here, procedures are offered which facilitate the process of becoming aware of one's own system of meaning, exploring it, expanding it, differentiating it. This enables it to become more flexible and amenable to growth.

The learner starts with an area of interest and some feelings of need within it. If he or she is familiar with the processes which were outlined in section 2, the grid can sometimes be self-elicited. This process has the great advantage of being totally private. Personal meanings can be examined without fear of censure or ridicule. But sometimes a person is not able to tap his own resources alone and the techniques for developing a learning conversation with another (section 7) can be recruited.

When elicited alone the grid forms an excellent vehicle for articulating a conversation with oneself. The elicitation systematizes and displays the less disciplined ideas and feelings which the learner finds elusive whilst they remain unexpressed inside him. The grid can thus be seen as a mirror in which some of one's thoughts and feelings can be reflected.

The process of focusing the grid (section 2b) becomes part of the active striving after meaning. No one pattern reflects all the relationships implicit in one's responses. The grid and the focusing procedure should be treated as a hand-mirror, to be tilted and rotated to reflect the many different aspects that can be explored.

Thus, a mathematics student used the grid to explore his understanding of mathematical problem-solving. Examination questions were used as the original elements, but as the elicitation proceeded the grid was focused and certain elements and constructs were discarded whilst new ones were introduced. This led the student into new insights of how he solved or avoided problems.

Eliciting and focusing the grid offers unique opportunities for learning to learn. Used to create conversations with oneself, it is both a method for achieving personally relevant changes and a paradigm of how this can be done more informally.

Six 'grid games' are outlined as examples of this self-conversational technique.

1. *Elaboration.* When a grid is focused, clusters of elements and constructs emerge. If each cluster is split by introducing new constructs to differentiate between similar elements and new elements to split constructs, the meaning represented is elaborated. It is easy to pursue this exercise trivially introducing simple descriptive constructs, and even this can sometimes prove illuminating, but the trick is to really concentrate on producing centrally important ideas.

2. *Extending the range of convenience.* An exercise in divergent thinking is to look for elements and constructs which would form into additional clusters to those already in the grid. The degree of the extension can be varied, offering an exercise in systematic extrapolation. This is achieved by defining the responses in the grid which would fit an as yet unimagined construct/or element and then articulating it.

3. *Superordination.* Another approach to the focused grid is to look for unifying concepts, which adequately subsume a whole cluster of elements or constructs. Three new elements can now be added and three new constructs can be elicited. Refocusing the extended grid will reveal which clusters continue and which dissolve. One can then explore what this means for one's unifying concepts.

4. *Cross-grids.* If two grids A and B containing different but related sets of elements are combined, all the A elements can be placed on the B constructs and all the B elements on the A constructs. Examples of this exercise would be to relate a grid on members of the family with a grid on peers or colleagues; or a grid on books with a grid on reasons for reading; or a grid on artists with a grid on paintings. The exercise of making oneself use familiar constructs on unfamiliar elements is in itself mind-expanding. The combined grid can be focused to reveal how the 'different' elements and constructs cluster with each other.

5. *Types of construct.* A procedure similar to that in (4) can be used to explore how different types or levels of construing relate one to another. A grid on art objects can be elicited using only perceptual/descriptive constructs.

Then the same elements can be used to elicit feelings about the art objects. When the two grids are combined much material for thought and feeling emerges.

6. *Non-verbal construing*. An interesting perceptual exercise is to collect together a set of objects that are important to oneself. One can now take any three and identify the two that are most alike; but one must not name the similarity, even silently in one's head. Next, one can sort the rest of the objects onto operationally defined poles. The exercise can be continued with new triads. The usual result is a greatly heightened awareness of visual and/or tactile phenomena.

Grid exercises of this kind can be invented *ad infinitum*. Each should be chosen or developed to achieve specific mental or/and emotional awareness. At best, they become part of a battery of techniques for learning to learn. They enhance one's ability to carry on systematic developmental conversations with oneself.

Most adults are unable to converse effectively with themselves. Their thoughts and feelings rapidly consolidate into the old self-perpetuating patterns. Techniques for exhibiting, exploring and systematically changing personal meanings can go some way towards freeing us from our own internal bonds. But on their own, these are often not enough. It has been necessary to extend these techniques to go beyond one's own understandings into those of another.

6. THE EXCHANGE OF PERSONAL MEANINGS

The amount that any one person can learn from his own first-hand experience is limited. Each of us cannot unaided reinvent the cumulative understandings of the human race. The rate at which recorded and published knowledge has expanded has led many parts of education to define their task as the re-creation of well-established knowledge and skills in each new individual learner. The type TO point of view sees any individual pursuit of understanding as misguided if it does not rapidly align on the teacher-valued dogmas. This too often produces the related phenomena of the learners who are taken over by the subject-matter and those who massively reject it. Both are the prisoners of their inability to take meaning apart and evaluate it and rebuild it in personally acceptable forms.

Effective processes of learning (type LR) consist of the creative search for personally viable meanings within an informed context of established knowledge and the reported experiences of others. But one has to learn that to understand a position does not necessitate finally agreeing with it, and that initial disagreement need not be a harrier to understanding. Disabled by their education, many people remain unskilled conversationalists. They are not able to enter creatively into the world of another, nor to exhibit their own so that others may enter in.

The exchange of meaning can take many forms. People can share experiences and then explore the meanings which those experiences have for them. Encounter groups are based on this process. So is the shared maintenance of a motor-cycle.

People can have different experiences and yet seek through words and other means to find the common links. They can share feelings or ideas and can extend and test these out in arguments and discussion. People can also record their thoughts and feelings in artifacts: art objects, machines, technologies, books and buildings. Others can seek to extract meanings from these artifacts. Gradually, shared meanings emerge. They become part of the life of the group that has created them. Slang, technical language, literature and pop music illustrate this. But unreviewed, the shared meanings of yesterday become the dogmas of tomorrow. Public meaning loses its personal relevance.

The various forms of exchange grids articulate components of the conversational process. Each contributes to helping the learner to renegotiate his meanings with other members of the human race.

Entering the World of Another

The grid displays some sample of a person's phenomenological world. Personal meaning lies in the pattern of relationships which exists between the elements and the constructs. Thus, the ability to reproduce this pattern of responses for oneself is a prerequisite for entering the phenomenological world of another.

Method A—One-way Exchange

A grid is elicited from person X. The constructs and elements are copied onto an empty grid form and person Y is invited to fill in the ticks and crosses as he feels person X would have done. The distribution of similarities and differences between this grid and the original pinpoints the areas of understanding and misunderstanding.

Method B—Two-way Exchange

Two people agree on a set of elements and each then elicits an independent grid. The responses (ticks and crosses) are not revealed but the constructs are discussed. The constructs are then pooled and each independently produces a completely new set of responses. Each grid is then focused and the clusterings are compared and contrasted.

Method C—Validated Exchange

This method is similar to method B, but before commencing the participants agree two matching sets of elements. Method B is then carried out and the similarities and differences are discussed. The procedure is then repeated on the matched set of elements and changes in position are noted.

Variations on those techniques allow the difference between understanding and agreement to be explored. If method A is employed, understanding is revealed. If methods B/C are used, agreement is revealed. Careful combinations of these techniques allow a wide range of mutual explanation to develop. Often the problems of communication arise from a second-order effect. One person X thinks that another person Y thinks he thinks differently about him than he actually does. Thus X thinks Y thinks that X thinks grids can be used to articulate understanding and misunderstanding and these higher-order levels.

Three possible outcomes of this exploration can be summarized as:

I. Give-over: 'I understand you but you cannot really mean it.'

II. Compromise: 'I understand you and you seem to understand me, we differ, now what shall we do.'

III. Creative encounter: 'I understand you, you understand me and we differ. Let us see if we can throw our meanings into the melting pot and create something that really achieves it all.'

Negotiation with Established Knowledge

An expert or group of experts can be thought to represent an area of established knowledge. They can define the area in a set of elements. They can agree the established constructs and place the elements accordingly. An individual wishing to interact with such a grid must accept it on its terms.

Method A

The elements can be used as the basis for a personal grid and the experts and the personal constructs can be pooled and focused. The relationships which emerge show how the public knowledge maps into the private space.

Method B

The elements and constructs can be accepted and all that remains is the assigning of elements to constructs. Comparison with the master grid reveals similarities and differences.

The Creation of Shared Meanings

People can cooperate in producing a grid. Elements can be explored and negotiated. the exchange methods described earlier can contribute to the process.

Constructs from shared grids can be extracted, discussed and refined. They can then be operationally defined by the group in the assigning of elements to them. Again, exchange techniques can facilitate this negotiation.

Once a group grid has been established, individuals can define their own positions as deviations from it. Deviations can take the form of additional private constructs, additional privately relevant elements and variations in the assigning of elements to constructs.

Once these methods for exchanging and negotiating meaning become familiar, an infinite variety of procedures begin to be invented to serve individually important aspects of the process of learning to learn.

7. LEARNING CONVERSATION: THE ACHIEVEMENT OF SELF-ORGANIZED CHANGE

In this chapter learning has been viewed as the act by which personally viable meanings are constructed and exchanged. Reading, writing, listening and talking can each be viewed as skills by which such learning is achieved. These skills are themselves learned although they are seldom explicitly taught. A variety of psychological tools have been developed to negotiate this process of learning to learn in each area of skill. The focused grid is one such tool. It has been specifically designed to elicit and display a system of personal meaning. As has been shown, it can be used to extend a person's range of meaning and to exchange meanings with others. Used conversationally as outlined in this chapter, it demonstrates the paradigm of learning to learn. The early stages of a learning conversation involve an apprentice and a master; but for conversation to occur, there must be a small area in which they meet as equals. Gradually, as the apprentice develops, this area of equality expands. As he becomes more self-organized, some of the conversation disappears into the learner's head. He becomes his own tutor. If he is to continue to develop, the conversation does not stop. The part of the conversation which goes on in his head remains available to awareness, and the external conversation becomes concerned with more complex issues and learning organized over longer periods of time.

It is unfortunate that conversation within one person's head tends to die away into non-consciousness unless renewed. In the absence of this conversation learning ceases, and the learning processes become habitual and eventually approximate to Colin Wilson's robot. External conversation can reestablish contact with the robot but this process is difficult, hence the need for specialized 'awareness-raising' tools.

A learning conversation is designed to achieve effective review and development of these deeply embedded habitual skills. This requires three parallel dialogues. Together these reflect the learner's cognitive processes back to him, support him through painful periods of change and encourage him to develop stable referents which anchor his judgment of the quality of his assessment.

The three dialogues can be described as:
(a) commentary on the learning process;
(b) personal support of the learner's reflection; and
(c) referents for evaluating learning competence.

The 'commentary on process' dialogue is concerned with raising the learner's awareness of his own processes. It requires consideration of a number of phases:

1. the negotiation of needs into learning purposes;
2. the development of effective learning strategies and tactics;
3. the evaluation of learning outcomes; and
4. a continuing review of this whole process.

Any effective dialogue requires a specialist language in which awareness can be articulated into consciousness. Tools for exhibiting the processes of learning (of which the repertory grid is one) contribute to the development of this language.

The second dialogue, which is necessarily interwoven with the first, deals with the emotional context of learning. The earlier discussion of Carl Rogers' ideas indicates one approach to the freeing and regulating of emotion. But there are other more directive techniques which can be used to help people over difficult periods. The language of personal support is only partly verbal. Gesture, expression and posture contribute to the communication, in which there is a mutual testing out of beliefs and intentions. Gradually a supportive relationship is built up. Teachers/tutors differ in their ability to generate this dialogue of personal support and much teaching founders when it is not developed.

The third dialogue is about the quality of learning. It is designed to help the learner to articulate the dimensions of quality as he or she personally evaluates. This process is partly reliant upon self-assessment, using subjective criteria, and partly upon the identification of referents in the outside world. Such referents can take the form either of significant other people with whom the learner compares himself, or groups such as professional or peer groups. This dialogue, about quality and referents can easily degenerate into a dogmatic system of rules. For the dialogue to remain active, a language is required in which to articulate the developing dimensions of quality and the ways in which these relate to the referent in the learner's world.

Each of these three dialogues can become internalized, but people differ in the ease with which they can sustain each of them. Effective internalization of the complete learning conversation produces the self-organized learner and the fully functioning man or woman. Such people learn from experience and continue to learn through life. Frozen internal conversations disable us as learners, and it is only when the external conversation is reestablished that the frozen processes can be revived. Living then becomes an ongoing opportunity for learning.

PART TWO

THE ACQUISITION OF KNOWLEDGE

INTRODUCTION TO PART TWO

The four chapters in Part Two consider ways in which people acquire knowledge. Human knowledge is highly dependent upon language, and verbal habits and verbal skills, acquired largely during childhood, form an essential base for adult learning. Chapter 6, by Fitz Taylor, is entitled Acquiring Knowledge from Prose and Continuous Discourse. Taylor provides a broad survey, with emphasis upon the very considerable amount of research in this area that has been undertaken in recent years. Ausubel's modern contributions to the old transfer-of-training issue are discussed, and Taylor introduces a model of prose communication which takes into account the learner's knowledge and aptitude as well as factors associated with the method of presentation. The juxtaposition of characteristics of the material and attributes of the learner receives emphasis, and information about both of these is used to arrive at an index of learning difficulty that has considerable predictive value. The chapter includes discussion of a number of additional determinants of learning difficulty in prose materials, including organizational factors, grammaticality and semantic aspects.

Taylor's attention to the role of the individual learner in the acquisition of knowledge is reiterated in Chapter 7, Practical Strategies for Human Learning and Remembering, by Peter Morris. Morris examines the effects of a variety of things that individuals do as they attempt to learn: their active strategies and procedures, and the ways in which they deal with incoming information. Individual learners are by no means passive as they encounter knowledge they wish to learn; on the contrary, they code, organize, categorize, scan, retrieve and, broadly speaking, become engaged in a wide variety of highly active behaviours. Morris is mainly concerned with those strategies that are undertaken deliberately, with the learner's awareness. Clearly, many coding actions are carried out automatically, without awareness, although, as in the case of the motor skills described by James Reason in Chapter 2, many verbal activities which in maturity take place automatically and unconsciously have initially to be undertaken deliberately and consciously. Morris's chapter includes a systematic survey of those mnemonic techniques that have been found to be effective, and he relates their success to the coding and organizational activities involved in them.

Chapter 8, Learning and the Acquisition of Knowledge by Students: Some Experimental Investigations, by the Editor, takes an alternative approach. Rather than surveying research findings and theory, it attempts to give an indication of the manner in which research progresses, to achieve increased understanding of the processes by which people acquire knowledge. One conclusion, supporting a principle discussed earlier by Fitz Taylor in Chapter 6, is that it is the combined characteristics of the learner and attributes of the material which exert effects upon learning that cannot be discovered by examining either of them in isolation.

James Hartley and Ivor Davies have contributed Programmed Learning and Educational Technology, which forms Chapter 9, the final element of Part Two. Hartley and Davies describe early and more recent approaches making use of programmed learning, and they briefly survey research into the effectiveness of the alternative methods available. They examine some broader methods which have been influenced by early programmed learning techniques but which are less constrained, and they give an interesting account of recent developments based upon computer-assisted instruction.

6

ACQUIRING KNOWLEDGE FROM PROSE AND CONTINUOUS DISCOURSE

Fitz J. Taylor

NEW DIRECTIONS IN RESEARCH

Within the last two decades, psychological research on learning has undergone a major change in direction and emphasis. Interest in the study of psycholinguistics, free recall, cognitive structure, cognitive style and learning strategies has led to a concept of an active learner busily working upon incoming material (Di Vesta, 1974). He scans it; he searches for cues and meaning (Chomsky, 1965). He decodes the material, associating it to information present before him (Adams and Montague, 1967), and draws heavily upon his past knowledge (Bransford *et al.*, 1972). He forms mental pictures to aid recall (Palermo, 1970; Paivio, 1971). He uses the total context to get understanding or deep structures (Fodor *et al.*, 1974). He organizes and structures the new material to fit in with the way he likes to structure his own knowledge (Franks and Bransford, 1972). The learner is indeed a hive of cognitive activities; some he is aware of, others remain tacit and automatic (Polanyi, 1966).

The old notion of learning and retention as a faithful reproduction of reality and events (Ebbinghaus, 1885) has given way to the equally old notion of learning and retention as a generative, transforming, modifying and creative search after meaning (Bartlett, 1932). The desire to map the path of pure new learning unadulaterated by past associations and meaning led to Ebbinghaus's invention of nonsense material. The use of nonsense syllables makes it possible to control meaning and limit the influence of past learning. Now we know that the learner injects his own meaning into nonsense syllables. More important, we know that any learning material which masks the influence of past knowledge, requiring recall in exactly the form in which it was first learned, offers evidence of a rare and unusual type of learning; a type more reminiscent of the laboratory than real life. So the current emphasis has shifted. It has shifted to prose and continuous discourse as learning material and also to a greater readiness to make inferences from research data.

AN ADVANCE ORGANIZER

This chapter reviews the work done on continuous discourse as a means of imparting information to the learner. It starts with a general model of one-way communication such as lectures, speech, radio and television broadcasts. Three main components of this model determine learning outcome. The first is the learner's *initial level of knowledge* on the topic in question, i.e. his cognitive structure. The second is his *special aptitude* in the relevant field, i.e. all accumulated contributors and inhibitors to acquisition. The third is the *method of communication*, i.e. the organization, the extent of internal and external connectedness (Greeno, 1972), the strategy of presentation which provides or fails to provide advance organizers on which to hinge subsequent details of information (Ausubel, 1963), the amount of elaboration of new concepts and principles, its pace, the complexity of language, appropriateness of media and the extent of correspondence between communication technique and cognitive style. Next, the chapter reviews those factors which have been shown by recent research to influence each component in turn.

This overview of what is treated in the chapter provides an advance organizer of the material. Advance organizers are information introduced before the learning material which gives the learner some perspective of the more detailed material to come and provides the 'intellectual scaffolding' on which he hangs the new details (Ausubel and Robinson, 1969). Good organizers are formulated in terms familiar to the learner. They are of necessity at a higher level of abstraction, generality and inclusiveness than the learning material itself (Ausubel, 1963).

Organizers can take the form of an introductory summary. They may equally well be the specification of the objectives the material is expected to achieve. Both are useful to the learner. The best organizers, however, are the substantive concepts and principles which have the widest explanatory powers in a discipline. According to Di Vesta (1974), behavioural objectives by being too specific may lead to undue emphasis on details without sufficient grasp of general principles. This can lead to regurgitation of isolated facts.

Ausubel and Robinson reviewed research on the effective use of advance organizers. One study compared the relative effects of (i) an historical organizer which related a brief history of the subject, (ii) a comparative organizer which contrasted the learning topic with another well-known topic, and (iii) an organizer which summarized the learning material. The last gave the best results, particularly so for learners low in verbal and analytic skills and those with large knowledge gaps, having no previous acquaintance with the subject. The comparative organizer was useful to learners with relatively small knowledge gaps. This concept has received some attention in psychological research dealing with the effect of preparatory set in learning. More recently, Bransford and Johnson (1972) have given a dramatic illustration of how prior knowledge of what a discourse is about can change the learning experience from one of incomprehension and failure to one of ease and assimilation. Not long ago

I repeated a modified version of this study in one of our laboratory sessions. You may be interested to try it yourself.

Read the passage below once through.

This is neither an art nor a science but an acquired skill. Many are deterred by lack of confidence, and those who consult the literature on the subject are further put off by directions which make it appear necessary to passess considerable knowledge, skill and speed. In fact it is quite simple. All that is needed is the right equipment and some practice. An inadequate tool will result in too much pressure, and quite possibly in personal injury. An adequate tool, on the other hand, may be lightly used and is always under control. Those who are keen will obtain the best equipment and take care to keep it in prime condition. In preparing your tool, remember that a very fine taper is required, and therefore the angle should be no greater than 15°. You can test the angle this way. If the front rests on a flat surface and the back on the thumb, which is in turn touching the flat surface, then the angle will be correct. When using the tool, draw it back and forth in long light motions. Never try to push it without this action, or the result will be jagged. Try to maintain the same angle all the way through, and keep a constant thickness, if this is possible. Across or away from yourself is best. With a little practice you will be able to attempt it successfully before your family and friends and this does add greatly to the sense of occasion.

(1) Rate the passage you have just read.

Very   1   2   3   4   5   6   7   Very
incomprehensible   comprehensible

(2) Write down all the ideas you can recall without looking at the passage.

Like Bransford and Johnson, we found that many subjects failed to guess the main theme and consequently their recall and understanding were poor. When the theme was given in advance, both comprehension and retention were twice as high. The theme of the passage you have just read is carving a joint.

The learner's intention at the time of learning is another potent factor influencing comprehension and retention of continuous discourse (Belbin, 1956; Taylor, 1966; Longstreth, 1970). According to Mace (1961), a learner remembers at least 25 per cent more from a lecture if, during the lecture, he sets himself the conscious task of reporting it to a friend.

THE MODEL

Arising from research into information overload from continuous discourse (Taylor, 1972), a model of one-way communication was proposed. In essence, it defines a way of measuring information at a cognitive level, as a composite

110

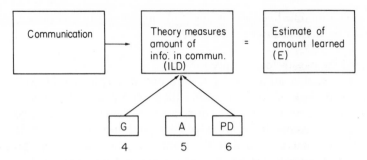

Figure 6.1 Model illustrating the way the learning outcome from a communication may be predicted (Taylor, 1974). G = gap in initial knowledge; A = aptitude; PD = presentation difficulty

concept which takes into account the learner's present knowledge, his aptitude in the field and any difficulty associated with the method of communication These three variables are used to quantify the level of information contained in the discourse. The unit of quantification is ILD, which stands for index of learning difficulty.

A constant relationship was found between amount of information as indicated by this model, i.e. the ILD scores, and an estimate of the amount learned. The stability of this relationship enables prediction of learning outcome once the level of information or ILD is calculated. Alternatively, it permits prediction of the level of information a message should contain in order to produce a predetermined level of learning. A graphical representation of the relationship is given in Figure 6.1.

The figure implies that a communication can be measured in theoretical units (ILD) which give the amount of information it contains. Thus box 1 of the figure is numerically encoded into box 2. ILD is itself a resultant of three factors, G, A and PD, illustrated in boxes 4, 5 and 6, respectively. Further, ILD is a reliable index of learning outcome, having a stable and reliable relationship with E, the estimate of amount learned. ILD is also a valid measure of learning since E is itself a valid measure of what Tulving (1972) calls semantic memory as distinct from episodic memory.

On the basis of the relationship between E and the amount of information, it is possible to fix E and any two other factors and deduce the fourth. The model therefore provides three degrees of freedom. When E, G and A are fixed beforehand, for example, the presentation difficulty can be predicted. Similarly, when E, G and PD are predetermined, then A can be calculated. The relationship between ILD and E is constant from individual to individual irrespective of the contents of communication. Figure 6.2 shows this relationship.

A second relationship, equally important, is that between the perceived level of presentation difficulty (PD) and the objective factors associated with the learning event. Factors isolated by research so far are the amount of elaboration the message contains, the style of language, the number of 'signposts'

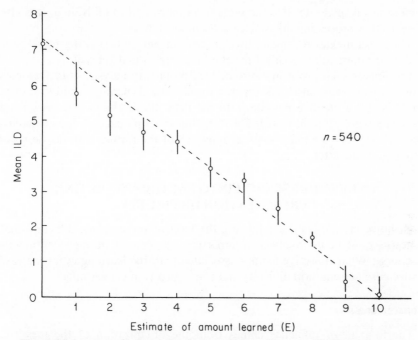

Figure 6.2 Amount of information in a continuous discourse (ILD) as a function of amount of learning (E). (Taylor, 1972. Reproduced by permission of Elsevier Scientific Publishing Company)

or major clustering foci, the degree of discriminability between these signposts and the general organization of content.

On the basis of this second relationship, tables have been drawn up showing how presentation difficulty can be manipulated to achieve the required level of learning (Taylor, 1972).

THE EMPIRICAL CONCEPTUAL ANALYSIS TECHNIQUE

The theoretical model underlying this approach is a concept of man as a multivariate processing organism with invariate processing laws. Thus it is possible to ask him to combine a number of incoming stimuli and produce a single uniform reaction to them. In formulating his reaction the individual puts together a number of different basic dimensions and arrives at a single but composite reaction.

The reaction will vary from individual to individual. The basic dimensions which each combines are the same. A similar process underlies the work of Osgood *et al.* (1957) on the measurement of connotative meaning.

Differences between individuals are attributable to the varying degrees of emphasis each places on one or more of the underlying dimensions. From the data already gathered, one can say that the process used to combine these dimensions is invariate. It is the same from individual to individual. It is also obvious that processing takes place without awareness.

The experimental technique used in tensing out and isolating these basic underlying dimensions is called the empirical conceptual analysis.

Previously, such problems were tackled by factor analysis, as/in Osgood's work, already mentioned. The repertory grid method (Bannister and Fransella, 1971) is still a creative newcomer to the field. Its flexibility and breadth of application are yet to be tested. The technique of empirical conceptual analysis (ECA) combines the mathematical approach of the former with the personal probing of the latter.

CURRENT RESEARCH INTO FACTORS AFFECTING PRESENTATION DIFFICULTY

It is, however, the task of adjusting the level of presentation difficulty that concerns most of us involved in imparting information through continuous discourse. What objective factors associated with the learning event increase or decrease presentation difficulty and consequently affect learning?

Connectedness

The first major influence comes from the organization of the message. Greeno (1972) offers an analysis of cognitive structure with an Ausubelian flavour. He distinguishes internal from external 'connectedness'. Internal connectedness refers to the stability, clarity, strength and complexity of the interrelationship between items within the cognitive structure. External connectedness is the clarity and stability of the relationship between the learning material and other areas of knowledge. A parallel analysis is appropriate for the material in continuous discourse.

Internal 'connectedness' of continuous discourse is affected by the general organization of content: the word order, including grammatical and semantic considerations; the number of 'signposts' or major clustering foci; the degree of discriminability between these signposts; the complexity of the language used. The amount of elaboration, i.e. number of ideas per unit sentence, does not appreciably affect the difficulty of the discourse.

External 'connectedness', on the other hand, is influenced by the degree of correspondence achieved between the internal organization of the discourse and the cognitive structure of the learner. Maximum comprehension and ease of learning are obtained when there is adequate match between the complexity of the message and the complexity of cognitive structure.

Organization of Content

The more organized the discourse, the better it will be understood. The learner is constantly striving after meaning (Bartlett, 1932). The structure of the discourse should facilitate this striving.

The German philosopher Johann Herbart stated this position over two centuries ago (Travers, 1973). Like Ausubel after him, Herbart saw the organization of the content of a message as one of the prerequisites of retention. Recent research, particularly that using the free-recall technique, has added substance to Herbart's speculation.

Bousfield's (1953) often quoted study shows how learners presented with disorganized material impose their own organization onto it. He instructed subjects to recall as many words as they could from a list of 60. The list was randomly arranged but the words were chosen from four distinct categories: animals, names, vegetables and professions. The results indicated that the subjects reclustered the words under the original categories despite the random sequence in which they were presented. This arrangement made more sense to the learner and corresponded more to his own cognitive arrangement. From the many variations (e.g. Cohen, 1963; Tulving, 1962) and added refinements (see Puff, 1970) to this study, one may conclude that learners organize their material and that organization facilitates learning and retention.

Coleman's (1962) illustration of the effort after meaning is even more vivid. He took a passage of connected prose from a book and scrambled the order of the words like this:

'about was good-looking way and treating made of that a him the quiet youngster nice he manners a them girls wild go with'.

Coleman gave this nonsense material to a subject who studied it and tried to reproduce it verbatim. The reproduced passage was given to another subject, and so on through 16 subjects. The sixteenth subject gave this version:

'he was a youngster nice quiet with manners good-looking and a way of treating them that made the girls go wild about him'.

This study is, of course, a modified version of Bartlett's classic experiment.

Learners strive after meaning, and the organization of the discourse can either facilitate or hinder this striving. The more the organization of content approximates to normally spoken language, the easier the communication (Miller and Selfridge, 1950). Both speed and accuracy of recall improve as the content of continuous discourse gets closer to normal English (Johnson, 1966). As the organization of the content improves, learners understand more, learn more and remember more (Deese, 1961).

Good internal organization offers a coherent underlying plan or scheme. The plan should be easily apparent or, better still, revealed. It should be easy to label. It should blend in with the learner's cognitive structure and style.

George Miller (1956) reports Smith's demonstration of the way on underlying plan can be used to facilitate learning and retention. Smith tried to recall sequences of binary digits, zeros and ones, after one presentation. The average subject can manage between 5 to 9 digits after hearing a series once. Smith gave himself intensive training and mastered the underlying coding plan of binary number, i.e.

$000 = 0$	$100 = 4$	$1000 = 8$
$001 = 1$	$101 = 5$	$1001 = 9$
$010 = 2$	$110 = 6$	$1010 = 10$
$011 = 3$	$111 = 7$	

He was then able to recall 40 binary digits at one attempt (Miller, p. 94).

Similarly, faced with a sequential verbal task, the learner needs a plan for organizing the material into manageable chunks. He is then able to recall the material by retrieving a few information-rich items from his plan. Recalling is a reconstructive process. The learner employs rules acquired during learning to decode his plan for specific details. His ability to retrieve information from continuous discourse depends on his ability to organize the information according to same plan (Tulving, 1962). The better his plan, the better his storage (Lachman and Tuttle, 1965). Communicators, on the other hand, can increase their efficiency by providing a clear and well-organized plan to begin with. Several practical hints come from the studies of Frase (1969; 1968a, b), Frase and Silbiger (1970) and Rothkopf and Johnson (1971).

There is evidence too that plans which are readily described in words are more effective (Stefan, 1970). When subjects were asked to recall a series which was easily coded into words, they recalled it successfully (Glanzer and Clark, 1963). But when the series required a lengthy verbal description, recall was less successful. The most difficult series to recall is a random one which by definition requires as much information to describe it and store it as it itself contains (Chaitin, 1975). A random series cannot be reduced to an underlying plan. The point, therefore, is that a well-organized content displays a plan which simplifies the message. This is what Sir Frederick Bartlett meant when he said that we rarely attempt to remember material in full, details and all; we schematize what is given to us. This is also what David Ausubel means when he says that new ideas and information can be efficiently learned and retained only to the extent that more inclusive and appropriately relevant concepts are already available in cognitive structure to serve a subsuming role or to furnish ideational anchorage.

Grammaticality and Semantics

The order in which words are arranged in continuous discourse also adds to the effectiveness of internal connectedness. Continuous discourse requires the chaining together of a sequence of sentences to convey ideas which themselves are grouped around main points. The main points are in turn clustered to present a unified theme. The sentences used can be real or quasi. The syntactical and grammatical arrangements of words in sentences are intended to facilitate comprehension (Johnson, 1968). Consider the example 'The dog bit the man'. A rearrangement of these same words 'The man bit the dog' gives a different meaning. The recipient of a communication employs a number

of word-order cues to arrive at the speaker's meaning (Katz and Fodor, 1963).
Grammatical cues resolve ambiguity, as in the examples:
Is that fair? or Is that the fair? Semantic cues clarify sentences:

The *page* handed the sword to his knight.
This *page* explains why the page handed the sword
to his knight.
They are cooking plums.
They are hunting dogs.

Words can be combined for greater clarify and effect. Osgood *et al.* (1957)
demonstrated by use of the semantic differential scales that adjectives tend to
receive greater emphasis than nouns when both are combined. When Howe
(1963) examined the influence of adverbs on adjectives, the effect appeared so
great that he concluded that adverbs function as multipliers of intensity of
meaning. In general, to say that something is slightly X, whether X is favourable
or unfavourable, will reduce the effect of the adjective X by half. The adverbs
'extremely' and 'very' multiply the meaning of the adjective by 1.5, thereby
increasing its effect by half as much again. For example, slightly clear is half as
clear as just clear, and very clear is one and a half times clearer. Is that clear
or slightly clear?

The influence of adverbs on clarity of meaning seems to be a regular research
finding. Other grammatical influences on presentation difficulty include the
effect of different linguistic transformations (Clifton and Odom, 1966). Learners
grasp affirmative more easily than negative statements. They understand the
active voice more readily than the passive. Equally, a declarative sentence is
more easily understood than an interrogative.

Abstract nouns make continuous discourse harder to understand. They can,
in most cases, be replaced by verbs. For example, 'Great emphasis must be
placed on the importance of consultation of the attached plates in attempting
the identification of a particular species', which can be rendered, 'We must
emphasize how important it is to consult the attached plates when you are
attempting to identify a particular species'. The use of personal pronouns
facilitates the transformation from abstract nouns to verbs. Coleman (1971),
p. 167), for example, feels that must of the abstractness in scientific writing
can be attributed to the traditional avoidance of the words 'I' and 'we'. Verbs,
on the other hand, increase the ease of presentation. A high proportion of
verbs makes understanding easier. However, a difficult passage is not made
easier by merely adding more verbs without taking into account the length
of sentences or the frequency of occurrence of the verbs. A useful strategy,
as already indicated, is to change abstract nouns into verbs. By this means the
communicator gains the double advantage of increasing the number of verbs
and reducing the number of abstract nouns. Educational psychologists who
insist on properly defined behavioural objectives usually make precisely this
transformation. They exchange nouns like appreciation, understanding and

knowledge for infinitives like to differentiate, to identify and to write (Mager, 1962). Comprehension decreases as adjectives increase, but pronouns, on the contrary, make the message easier. Miller (1951) found that communications with more pronouns were easier to understand, and attributed that fact to the personal interest they stimulated. Apart from such psychological factors, however, other and more powerful linguistic variables may well be involved. Lastly, prepositions decrease comprehension. The more prepositions, the harder the communication.

These findings are broad generalizations derived from correlational studies and should be applied cautiously and intelligently. Until more rigorous and controlled experimental studies are designed, these are all we have. The many obvious interactions between different grammatical classes of words and the more complex measures of language like kernel sentences, idea units, degree of emboddedness, etc., are still to be experimentally investigated.

Main Points and Clustering Foci

The number of 'signposts', or major clustering foci, offers another valuable means of reducing the presentation difficulty of continuous discourse. This concept has been given many names. The BBC newscasters, for example, refer to them as 'main points'; 'Here are the main points again'. Ausubel (1968) calls them 'subsumers'. Tulving (1966) regards them as higher-order categories. If one analyses any piece of continuous discourse, a lecture, speech, broadcast, written prose, it should be possible to identify a main theme or topic. In the case of a book, this should be its title. It should be further possible to break down the topic into a few basic points which summarize the way the topic is treated. Books reflect these in the chapter headings. They are the signposts or clustering foci of continuous discourse.

Ease of learning and recall is related to the number of clustering foci. This issue arose early in the study of free recall. Mathews (1954) investigated the effect of number of categories and found that when the total number of items which made up a list was held constant, recall was an increasing function of the number of categories used. Dallet (1964), using a 12-item list, found that recall improved as the number of categories used increased from one to four. Over four, recall got worse. Taylor (1972), however, found that recall was better for continuous discourse with more than four clustering foci.

Progressive Differentiation

The way in which clustering foci are interrelated and organized affects presentation difficulty. Ausubel (1963) advocated the use of the principle of progressive differentiation in organizing and programming continuous discourse. Clustering foci are arranged in an hierarchical series in descending order of inclusiveness, the first being more general and inclusive than the second. Each focus in turn becomes more and more detailed than the one before and is, in a sense, included in it.

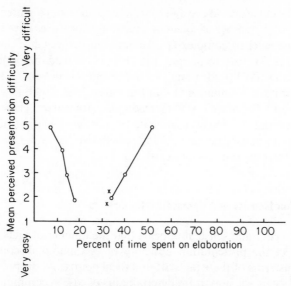

Figure 6.3 A pronounced V-function is found when the amount of time spent elaborating old concepts is plotted against perceived presentation difficulty. The points written as X's are obtained from two radio programmes

Elaboration and Redundancy

The effective communicator elaborates his discourse. He identifies the novel and more difficult concepts. He gives examples. He rephrases his exposition and provides repetition. The relationship between amount of elaboration and presentation difficulty is given in Figure 6.3.

When the amount of elaboration is low, the presentation is considered difficult. As elaboration increases, the discourse gets easier for the subject. Up to 30 per cent elaboration reduces presentation difficulty. When the amount of elaboration exceeds 30 per cent, the presentation gets more difficult.

A more general statement of this effect would be that redundancy improves ease of comprehension. This point has received ample experimental support (Miller *et al.*, 1951). Taylor's (1953) study using the 'cloze' technique also illustrated how messages with a high level of redundancy convey their meaning more successfully than those low in redundancy.

Language Level

The level of language employed in a discourse strongly affects presentation difficulty. Simpler sentences are easier to understand. There is some indication that the complexity of language influences comprehension even more than the inherent complexity of the points being made (Coleman, 1971). The two major variables which influence language level are the familiarity of words used and the length of sentences. More familiar words and short sentences increase comprehension. A number of so-called readability measures have been proposed to scale the level of complexity of connected prose. Chief amongst these are Taylor's (1953) cloze technique, Flesch's (1948) readability index, Morris and Halverson's (1938) idea-analysis technique, Dale and Chall's (1948) readability formula, Gunning's (1952) fog index, McLaughlin's (1969) smog-grading test and Coleman's (1971) readability formulae. These indices are highly intercorrelated. However, in spite of more systematic studies into the scaling of continuous discourse (King, 1960; Miller and Coleman, 1967; Coleman, 1971), only crude scales exist.

Communication Density and Semantic Memory

Contrary to common sense, it appears that the number of facts per sentence does not affect the presentation difficulty of continuous discourse (Taylor, 1972). The clustering of these facts around focal points and the proper sequencing of these foci are the important determinants of ease in communication.

The distinction between episodic and semantic memory (Tulving, 1972) throws some light on this point. Episodic memory deals with discrete and isolated events. Detailed facts, concrete events and experiences are recalled without any relation to general principles or concepts. Semantic memory, on the other hand, is recall of meaningful information. It is recall at the conceptual integrated level. Memory of detailed facts and events is coded in a more general and conceptual form. One recalls underlying principles. Information stored in semantic memory is retrieved in a form essentially different from the form in which it was first learned. True assessment of semantic memory cannot be made from word-perfect reproduction of information. It is done by attention to the overall grasp of the main conceptual points and underlying meaning of the material.

It is clear that in continuous discourse we are more concerned with semantic memory than with episodic memory. Failure to appreciate this fundamental distinction has led to the formulation of unrealistic objectives for single-exposure discourse like lectures, lessons, radio and TV programmes. Their objectives must be to increase information in semantic memory and not to impart many detailed episodic facts and events. To make the teaching of these details the principal objective of the single-exposure discourse would constitute a futile attempt to usurp the functions of books, private reading or revision from notes. The assimilation of such details is normally a post-lecture event. Confusion about the role of the spoken discourse is also responsible for same of the contradictory findings of attempts to evaluate the lecture. A simple look at some measuring techniques reveals attempts to assess episodic learning outcome from a semantic learning tool. A recent ingenious series of experiments by Bransford and Franks (1971) illustrates how in real-life situations learners store information from continuous discourse in a different form from that in which it is presented. The learner extracts meaning, combines and integrates sentences to form more complex ideas. The form of recall reveals more about the learner's cognitive structure than about the exact wording of the continuous discourse. Words are chunked into sentences, sentences into units of ideas and separate ideas into more complex semantic units. The final complexity of the units will depend on the nature of the learner's cognitive structure.

Correspondence with Cognitive Structure

Comprehension is impaired when continuous discourse is presented in a form which differs markedly from the cognitive structure of the learner. The aim is to minimize the difference in organization between the message and the learner's structure. Communication can be aided by use of relevant previously learned ideas as a basis for subsuming and incorporating new semantic information. New learning depends on how past learning is organized. Only recently has there been a scientific look at the way new knowledge from continuous discourse is processed and integrated with past knowledge (Bransford *et al.*, 1972).

ET ALIA

In reducing this large and growing area of research to chapter size it has been necessary to select and omit. In particular, the many specific and general strategies the learner uses to increase his learning efficiency have not been mentioned. These include mediating processes, imagery (Kjeldergaard, 1968; Paivio, 1971), retrieval plans (Bower, 1970) and a group of activities now known as 'mathemagenic behaviours'. This name, which comes from the Greek *Mathema*, meaning 'that which is learned', and *gineisthos*, meaning 'to be born', was introduced by Rothkopf in the early sixties (see Rothkopf, 1968; 1970; 1971). It has since gained acceptance in the literature as 'activities that give birth to learning'. A number of studies have addressed themselves to the question of how best to encourage mathemagenic behaviour in the learner, for example taking notes (Howe, 1974; 1975; and Chapter 8 in the present volume), asking general and specific questions before, during and after a discourse (Frase, 1969; Rothkopf, 1970; 1971), pacing the delivery (Sticht, 1971) and the use of audiovisual aids (Glaser and Cooley, 1973; Levie and Dickie, 1973). The omission of these topics by no means implies a lower order of importance, and for those interested in these areas the references given provide appropriate points of entry into the literature.

SUMMARY

With the current interest in language, free recall, cognitive structure and information processing, more attention is being paid to the learning of meaningful material. The study of continuous discourse in the form of lectures, lessons, speeches, radio and television broadcasts offers a richer source of information about the learner's role in the acquisition of knowledge than has been possible with meaningless material. The chapter has surveyed current developments in the field.

An overview of what is to be covered, when presented in advance of the actual discourse, acts as an advance organizer, providing the 'intellectual scaffolding' on which the learner hangs the new details he acquires. Such scaffolding is more abstract, more general and more inclusive than the discourse which follows. The best organizers are the substantive key concepts of any given discipline, and these have proved easier to identify in the physical sciences than in the social sciences.

Other types of organizers are introductary summaries and behavioural objectives. Functional models may also serve same as useful advance organizers.

A functional model of one-way communication is described. It defines a way of measuring information at a cognitive level, as a composite concept which takes into account the learner's present knowledge, his aptitude in the field and the level of presentation difficulty. The factors which have been recently shown to affect the level of presentation difficulty of continuous discourse are discussed.

Current developments are summarized under the following headings.

Connectedness, which deals with internal and external stability and clarity.

Organization of content, which deals with studies on categorizing, decoding and labelling.

Grammaticality and Semantics, under which is reviewed work showing the influence of these factors on comprehension of continuous discourse.

Main points and clustering foci. This refers to the number of main points contained in a given discourse and the sequencing of them. This global organization of a discourse is an important determinant of learning.

Progressive differentiation is Ausubel's principle for programming the main sections of a discourse to obtain maximum effect.

Elaboration and redundancy. A number of studies have shown that both amount of elaboration and redundancy are functions of comprehension.

Language level is another strong influence on learning from continuous discourse. There is, however, some difficulty in adequately assessing this variable. The main measures of language readability are given.

Communication density contrary to popular opinion, the number of facts per unit sentence does not appreciably influence the comprehension of a discourse. Tulving's distinction between episodic and semantic memory appears to help explain this finding.

Correspondence with cognitive structure. The closer the match between the structure of the discourse and the learner's cognitive structure, the more effective the communication. Here Bransford and Franks' series of experiments helps to clarify the way the learner structures and integrates his material.

REFERENCES

Adams, J. A., and Montague, W. E. (1967). 'Retroactive inhibition and natural language mediations', *Journal of Verbal Learning and Verbal Behaviour*, **6**, 528.

Ausubel, D. P. (1963). *The Psychology of Meaningful Verbal Learning; An Introduction to School Learning*, Grune & Stratton, New York.

Ausubel, D. P. (1968). *Educational Psychology; A Cognitive View*, Holt, Rinehart & Winston, New York.

Ausubel, D. P., and Robinson, F. G. (1969). *School Learning; An Introduction to Educational Psychology*, Holt, Rinehart & Winston, New York.

Bannister, D., and Fransella, F. (1971). *Inquiring Man, The Theory of Personal Constructs*, Penguin, Harmondsworth.

Bartlett, F. C. (1932). *Remembering, A Study in Experimental and Social Psychology*, Cambridge, University Press.

Belbin, E. (1956). 'The effects of propaganda on recall, recognition and behaviours', *British Journal of Psychology*, **47**, 163.

Bousfield, W. A. (1953). 'The occurrence of clustering in recall of randomly assigned associates', *Journal of General Psychology*, **49**, 229.

Bower, G. H. (1970). 'Analysis of a mnemonic device', *American Scientist*, **58**, 496.

Bransford, J. D., Barclay, J. R., and Franks, J. J. (1972). 'Sentence memory; a constructive versus interpretive approach', *Cognitive Psychology*, **3**, 193.

Bransford, J. D., and Franks, J. J. (1971). 'The abstraction of linguistic ideas', *Cognitive Psychology*, **2**, 331.

Bransford, J. D., and Johnson, M. K. (1972). 'Conceptual prerequisites for understanding; some investigations of comprehension and recall', *Journal of Verbal Learning and Verbal Behavior*, **11**, 717.

Chaitin, G. J. (1975). 'Randomness and mathematical proof', *Scientific American*, **232**, 47.

Chomsky, N. (1965). *Aspects of the Theory of Syntax*, M.I.T. Press, Cambridge, Mass.

Clifton, C., and Odom, P. (1966). 'Similarity relations among certain English sentence constructions', *Psychological Monographs*, **80**, No. 613.

Cohen, B. H. (1963). 'Recall of categorized word lists', *Journal of Experimental Psychology*, **66**, 227.

Coleman, E. B. (1962). 'Sequential interference demonstrated by serial reconstruction', *Journal of Experimental Psychology*, **64**, 46.

Coleman, E. B. (1971). 'Developing a technology of written instruction; some determiners of the complexity of prose', in E. Z. Rothkopf and P. E. Johnson (Eds.), *Verbal Learning Research and the Technology of Written Instruction*, Teachers College Press, Columbia.

Dale, E., and Chall, J. S. (1948). 'A formula for predicting readability', *Educational Research Bulletin*, **27**, 11–20, 37.

Dallet, K. M. (1964). 'Number of categories and category information in free recall', *Journal of Experimental Psychology*, **68**, 1.

Deese, J. (1961). 'From the isolated unit to connected discourse', in C. N. Cofer (Ed.), *Verbal Learning and Verbal Behavior*, McGraw-Hill, New York.

Di Vesta, F. (1974). *Language, Learning and Cognitive Processes*, Brooks/Cole, Monterey, California.

Ebbinghaus, H. (1885). *Uber das Gedachtnis: Untersuchungen zus experimentellen Psychologie*, Duncker & Humblot, Leipzig.

Flesch, R. F. (1948). 'A new readability yardstick', *Journal of Applied Psychology*, **32**, 221.

Fodor, J. A., Bever, T. G., and Garrett, M. F. (1974). *The Psychology of Language*, McGraw-Hill, New York.

Franks, J. J., and Bransford, J. D. (1972). 'The acquisition of abstract ideas', *Journal of Verbal Learning and Verbal Behavior*, **11**, 311.

Frase, L. T. (1968). 'Some data concerning the mathemagenic hypothesis', *American Educational Research Journal*, **5**, 181.

122

Frase, L. T. (1968b). 'Questions as aids to reading; some research and theory', *American Educational Research Journal*, **5**, 319.

Frase, L. T. (1969). 'Paragraph organization of written materials; the influence of conceptual clustering upon the level and organization of recall', *Journal of Educational Psychology*, **60**, 394.

Frase, L. T., and Silbiger, F. (1970). 'Some adaptive consequences of searching for information in a text', *American Educational Research Journal*, **7**, 553.

Glanzer, M., and Clark, W. H. (1963). 'Accuracy of perceptual recall; an analysis of organization, *Journal of Verbal Learning and Verbal Behavior*, **1**, 289.

Glaser, R., and Cooley, W. W. (1973). 'Instrumentation for teaching and instructional management', in R. M. W. Travers (Ed.), *Second Handbook of Research on Teaching*, Rand McNally, Chicago.

Greeno, J. G. (1972). 'On the acquisition of a simple cognitive structure', in E. Tulving and W. Donaldson (Eds.), *Organization of Memory*, Academic Press, New York.

Gunning, R. (1952). *The Technique of Clear Writing*, McGraw-Hill, New York.

Howe, E. S. (1963). 'Probabilistic adverbial qualifications of adjectives', *Journal of verbal Learning and verbal Behavior*, **1**, 225.

Howe, M. J. A. (1974). 'The utility of taking notes as an aid to learning', *Educational Research*, **16**, 222.

Howe, M. J. A. (1975). 'Taking notes and human learning', *Bulletin of the British Psychological Society*, **28**, 158.

Johnson, N. F. (1966). 'The influence of associations between elements of structured verbal responses', *Journal of Verbal Learning and Verbal Behavior*, **5**, 369.

Johnson, N. F. (1968). 'Sequential verbal behavior, in T. R. Dixon and D. L. Horton (Eds.), *Verbal Behavior and General Behavior Theory*, Prentice-Hall, Englewood Cliffs, N. J.

Katz, J. J., and Fodor, J. A. (1963). 'The structure of a semantic theory', *Language*, **39**, 170.

King, D. J. (1960). 'On the accuracy of written recall; a scaling and factor analytic study, *Psychological Record*, **10**, 113.

Kjeldergaard, P. M. (1968). 'Transfer and mediation in verbal learning', in T. R. Dixon and D. L. Horton (Eds.), *Verbal Behavior and General Behavior Theory*, Prentice-Hall, Englewood Cliffs, N. J.

Lachman, R., and Tuttle, A. (1965). 'Approximations to English and short-term memory; construction or storage', *Journal of Experimental Psychology*, **70**, 386.

Levie, W. H., and Dickie, K. E. (1973). The analysis and application of media', in R. M. W. Travers (Ed.), *Second Handbook of Research on Teaching*, Rand McNally, Chicago.

Longstreth, L. E. (1970). 'Tests of the law of effect using open and closed tasks', *Journal of Experimental Psychology*, **84**, 53.

Mace, C. A. (1961). *The Psychology of Study*, Penguin, Harmondsworth.

Mager, R. F. (1962). *Preparing Instructional Objectives*, Fearon, Palo Alto.

Mathews, R. (1954). 'Recall as a function of the number of classificatory categories', *Journal of Experimental Psychology*, **47**, 241.

McLaughlin, H. (1969). 'Smog grading—a new readability formula, *Journal of Reading* **22**, 639.

Miller, G. A. (1951). *Language and Communication*, McGraw-Hill, New York.

Miller, G. A. (1956). 'The magical number seven, plus or minus two; some limits on our capacity for processing information', *Psychological Review*, **63**, 81.

Miller, G. A., and Coleman, E. B. (1967). 'A set of 36 passages calibrated for comprehensibility', *Journal of Verbal Learning and Verbal Behavior*, **6**, 851.

Miller, G. A., Heise, G. A., and Lichter, W. (1951). 'The intelligibility of speech as a function of the context of the test materials, *Journal of Experimental Psychology*, **41**, 329.

Miller, G. A., and Selfridge, J. A. (1950). 'Verbal context and recall of meaningful material', *American Journal of Psychology*, **63**, 176.

Morris, E. C., and Halverson, D. (1938). 'Idea Analysis Technique', Unpublished thesis, Columbia University.

Osgood, C. E., Suci, G. J., and Tannenbaum, P. H. (1957). *The Measurement of Meaning*, University of Illinois Press, Urbana.

Paivio, A. (1971). 'Imagery and language', in S. J. Segal (Ed.), *Imagery; Current Cognitive Approaches*, Academic Press, New York.

Palermo, D. S. (1970). 'Imagery in children's learning: discussion', *Psychological Bulletin*, **73**, 415.

Polanyi, M. (1966). *The Tacit Dimension*, Doubleday, Gardes City, N. Y.

Puff, C. R. (1970). 'Role of clustering in free recall', *Journal of Experimental Psychology*, **86**, 384.

Rothkopf, E. Z. (1963). 'Some conjectures about inspection behavior in learning from written sentences and the response mode problem in programmed self-instruction', *Journal of Programmed Instruction*, **2**, 31.

Rothkopf, E. Z. (1970). 'The concept of mathemagenic activities', *Review of Educational Research*, **40**, 325.

Rothkopf, E. Z. (1971). 'Experiments on mathemagenic behavior and the technology of written instruction', in E. Z. Rothkopf and P. E. Johnson (Eds.), *Verbal Learning Research and the Technology of Written Instruction*, Teachers College Press, Columbia.

Rothkopf, E. Z., and Johnson, P. E. (Eds.) (1971). *Verbal Learning Research and the Technology of Written Instruction*, Teachers College Press, Columbia.

Stefan, S. (1970). 'Phonemic recording of digital information', *Journal of Experimental Psychology*, **86**, 398.

Sticht, T. G. (1971). 'Failure to increase learning, using the time saved by the time compression of speech, *Journal of Educational Psychology*, **62**, 55.

Taylor, F. J. (1966). 'The effect of learning instruction on motor and verbal responses in recall', *British Journal of Psychology*, **57**, 291.

Taylor, F. J. (1972). 'Adjusting the amount and level of information to one's audience', *Instructional Science*, **1**, 211.

Taylor, F. J. (1974). 'A-V technology and education, a theory of evaluation', *University Vision*, **11**, 24.

Taylor, W. L. (1953). '"Cloze procedure"; a new tool for measuring readability', *Journalism Quarterly*, **30**, 415.

Travers, R. M. W. (1973). *Educational Psychology; A Scientific Foundation for Educational Practice*, Macmillan, New York.

Tulving, E. (1962). 'Subjective organization in free recall of "unrelated" words', *Psychological Review*, **69**, 344.

Tulving, E. (1966). 'Subjective organization and effects of repetition in multi-trial free-recall learning', *Journal of Verbal Learning and Verbal Behavior*, **5**, 193.

Tulving, E. (1972). 'Episodic and semantic memory', in E. Tulving and W. Donaldson (Eds.), *Organization of Memory*, Academic Press, New York.

7

PRACTICAL STRATEGIES FOR HUMAN LEARNING AND REMEMBERING

Peter Morris

Early in his book *How to Develop a Super Power Memory*, Harry Lorayne tells his readers that after studying his systems they should be able to remember a 50-digit number after looking at it only once! They will also be able to memorize the order of a shuffled pack of cards after hearing them called just once and remember a shopping list of 50 items. Few individuals who have not trained themselves in one of the classical memory systems would even attempt such feats. Yet there is little doubt that anyone following Lorayne's advice can improve their performance as he says they will, and do so without an enormous expenditure of effort. It is probably easier to become skilled at such memory feats than it is to become proficient at chess-playing or even driving. In the first part of this chapter I want to consider the methods that have been used over the centuries by stage performers, public-speakers and students cramming for examinations. In recent years many of these techniques have been experimentally analysed by psychologists, and most have been found to live up to the claims of their advocates. I shall try to place them in the context of our knowledge of the workings of the memory system. Then I shall discuss other features of the memory system which may be used to improve remembering. However, towards the end of the chapter I shall have to cast some doubts on the possibility, at least with present knowledge, of developing superpower memories for more than a limited number of situations.

It is a sad comment on the prejudices and interests of psychologists who have studied human learning and memory over the last 90 years that they can offer little practical advice for learning that was not already common knowledge to the ancient Greeks. The experimental study of memory has been too concerned with discovering the basic processes of remembering and too little directed towards answering the request of the man in the street for advice on how he can improve his memory. The theoretical study of the memory processes is a very worthwhile endeavour, but it is a pity that more thought has not been put to the use of this knowledge. However, progress of a sort has been made.

Ten years ago there had been virtually no experimental studies of the memory systems advocated by Lorayne and others. The domination of the behaviourist philosophy, which maintained that statements about mental events were unscientific, discouraged serious study of the mnemonics, which emphasize imagery, mental story-telling and complex mental manipulations. During the last 10 years, however, we have at least come to realize that such systems can exploit important features of the memory system. We may not be able to offer many techniques of memory which have been developed from applications of pure research, but we can offer reliable evidence for the effectiveness of the classical mnemonic methods, which, without such support, may have seemed too bizarre to be worth trying for oneself.

I have just used the term 'mnemonic', which may be unfamiliar to some readers. A mnemonic is a method, device, even trick, for improving memory. This odd word alludes to the Greek goddess of memory Mnemosyne, who in Greek mythology was the mother by Zeus of the nine muses. In the next section I shall describe the more important of the mnemonic techniques. Then in the following section I shall report experimental evidence for their effectiveness.

THE MNEMONIC TECHNIQUES

The Place Method

Most venerable of the mnemonic methods is the *place method* or *method of loci*. This technique was taught to students of rhetoric by Greek and Roman orators such as Cicero so that they could remember the points to be made in long speeches. The method is said to have been invented by a Greek poet named Simonides who lived about 500 BC.

The apocryphal story of the event which led Simonides to invent the place method is as follows (see Yates, 1966, p. 1). Simonides was commissioned to chant a lyric poem at a banquet in praise of the host. In the poem Simonides included several verses to Castor and Pollux, the twin gods. At the end of his performance he was given only half the agreed fee, since the host said that as half the poem was devoted to Castor and Pollux he should go to them for the rest. Shortly afterwards Simonides was called out to see two young men who were asking for him. While he was outside the building collapsed, crushing everyone inside. The two young men were Castor and Pollux, who had saved Simonides from death. The invention of the memory system was the outcome of the problem encountered when clearing up after the tragedy. The relatives of the victims could not recognize the battered-bodies, but Simonides, who knew who had been sitting in each place, was able to identify the remains. This suggested to him the possibility of a memory system in which images of what was to be remembered would be placed in locations in a familiar scene. Later the scene could be mentally scanned and the information retrieved.

Someone wishing to use the place method has first to choose some well-known room or street where there are as many distinctive locations as items to be remembered. If we suppose, for the sake of example, that what is to be remembered is a shopping list of bread, butter, coffee, and so on, then a loaf of bread is imaged as being placed in the first location—on the window ledge, or in the gateway of the first house, or wherever it may be. Then a packet of butter is imaged in the next location, and so on through the list. To recall the list in the appropriate order it is simply necessary, in imagination, to scan round the room or walk down the street, 'reading off' the items as you go.

The place method shares many features with the other mnemonics that have been popular through the ages. First, it appears to make remembering more complicated by requiring whole scenes to be retained. Secondly, it uses imagery as the basis for storage. Thirdly, it draws upon prior knowledge of the room or street to provide an ordered structure in which the items to be learned may be committed to memory.

The evidence to be discussed later does confirm the claim of the Greek teacher of rhetoric that this is a system that will improve recall. However, the place system has limitations. It is necessary to be very well acquainted with a room or street that has a large number of distinctive features. How many of us are sufficiently observant to be ready equipped with such knowledge? If we wished to use the place method we would have to follow the advice of the rhetoric teachers and go out and learn new, well-ordered sets of locations. Even so, I suspect that there are limitations to the number of locations that can be successively examined in memory without oversights occurring. The other limitation is that the method is designed to retain items in order, whereas a system which allowed for recall in any order would be more flexible. A modification of the place system which allowed for such flexibility in the remembering of 50 items was put forward in 1813 by a professional memory expert named Gregor von Feinaigle. His method involved imagining a room in which the walls, the floor and the ceiling were segmented into 50 pieces, each representing a number from 1–50. Each position was made more concrete by imagining some object which permanently occupied the particular place. The item to be remembered in that position was imagined interacting in some way with this object. For recall one simply 'looked' at the appropriate place and saw the familiar object for that place linked with whatever was to be remembered. More rooms could be added to extend the number of locations, but it was initially necessary to spend time memorizing the objects that occupied each location. Presumably because of the time involved in this prior training, Feinaigle's version of the place system has not been experimentally tested.

The Peg or Hook System

The peg or hook method has been central to most memory improvement systems. In it the items to be learned are linked to already known words which are metaphorically imagined as acting as 'pegs' onto which the items to be learned are 'hooked'.

Common peg systems usually provide a concrete noun or peg word which must first be memorized for each of the numbers from, say, 1–100. Once they have been acquired they can be used in a way reminiscent of the place system. Suppose that the peg word for the number 1 is bun, and the first item to be learned is 'dog'. Then an image is formed incorporating the dog and a bun. A dog might be imagined eating a bun. Then, at recall, given the number 1, the memorizer recalls that the peg word for 1 is bun. Recalling bun retrieves the image of the dog eating a bun, and reminds him that the item that went with 1 was 'dog'. Abstract items can be translated into concrete associates so that they can be imaged. For example, an image of a church might be used to remember 'religion'. This system has far greater flexibility than the place method since it is possible to recall the items in any required order, and, while the learning of peg words may be arduous, there is no real limit to the number of pegs that could be used. The learning of the pegs is made easier by their being based on a phonetic alphabet which translates digits into consonant sounds. The exact translations vary from system to system, but a common one is given below.

0	1	2	3	4	5	6	7	8	9
S, Z	T, D	N	M	R	L	J, SH	K, C	F, V	P, B

Peg words to represent numbers are formed by inserting vowel sounds between the appropriate consonants. So, for example, a peg for 32 might be MaN and for 71 might be CaT. Memory improvement systems such as those of Lorayne (1958) and Furst (1957) provide prepared sets of pegs to be memorized.

The consonant–digit translation system, while not as ancient as the place method, is still venerable, having been initially proposed by Winckelman in 1648. Its use is not confined to the generation of memory pegs. It can be used to translate lists of digits that are normally difficult to retain, such as telephone numbers, into meaningful words that are easy to remember. For example, the phone number of the University of Lancaster is Lancaster 65201, which translates to J, L, N, S, T.

With suitable vowels added this becomes JaiL NeST, which might be remembered by an image of a nest inside a prison cell.

One drawback of the peg word system is that even with the aid of the logical structure imposed by the phonetic translation system the initial acquisition of the pegs takes some time and effort. However, for the numbers 1–10, peg words can be quickly learned from the rhyme 'one is a bun, two is a shoe, three is a tree, four is a door, five is a hive, six is sticks, seven is heaven, eight is a gate, nine is a mine, ten is a hen'. This rhyme is learned in one or two recitations and the peg words bun, shoe and so on then used as I described earlier. Consequently, it has been employed by many investigators to teach a short set of peg words and to test the claimed efficiency of the peg system.

Common to both the place method and the peg method is the use of imagery. A third, and simpler, technique which also employs imagery is the link method, which is used to remember a series of items in order. An image is formed linking the first and second items, then one linking the second and third items, and so on for the list. The advocates of the place, peg and link systems say that not only should images be formed, but that they should be vivid, bizarre and active. The justification for this being that, as the author of the *Ad Herrennium* (a text on rhetoric) put it, '. . . ordinary things easily slip from the memory while the striking and the novel stay longer in the mind' (cited by Yates, 1966, p. 9).

Rhymes, First Letters and Sentences

Almost everyone seems to use the 'Thirty days hath September' rhyme for remembering the lengths of the months. In Victorian times, when factual memory was considered more important than it is today, rhymes which listed the kings of England, or geographical details such as names of rivers, were common. In Brayshaw's *Metrical Mnemonics* published in 1849, rhymes were combined with a digit–letter system to help the memorizing of the dates of English royalty.

In many non-literate societies poetic forms have been used to pass on legends, sagas and valuable learning. Indeed, the use of rhythm and rhyme probably predates the place system as a method of improving memory.

The first-letter mnemonic is another in widespread use. The mnemonic has several forms, all based on placing the first letters of the names of the items to be remembered in an easily remembered context. At its simplest, the first letters themselves form real or nonsense words, for example, the name 'ROY G BIV' for the colours of the rainbow and 'CLOD' for the shade of blue of the Oxbridge colours (*Cambridge Light, Oxford Dark.*) To form meaningful words extra letters may be inserted, or each letter may be used as the first letter of a new word, as when 'Richard Of York Gave Battle In Vain' is used to retain the order of the colours of the rainbow. Where there are long lists of names to be remembered in a specific order, several first-letter mnemonics often exist to help the student. There are such mnemonics for the order of the cranial nerves, the colour codes of electrical resistors and for the chemical elements. The reader could probably add several others.

There are other mnemonic devices which are less formal than those so far described. When faced with trying to learn nonsense material, almost everyone attempts to impose meaning and search for meaningful translations into words. Making up stories or placing the things to be remembered in a meaningful sentence is quite a common strategy.

But enough has been said describing the common mnemonic systems. What of their effectiveness?

RESEARCH ON THE EFFECTIVENESS OF THE MNEMONICS

In this section I shall present evidence demonstrating the effectiveness of most of the common mnemonics. Possible explanations of the effectiveness of the mnemonics will be better considered in a later section which examines them in relationship to what has been discovered in research into the properties of the memory system.

The Place System

One of the first investigations of the place system was by Ross and Lawrence (1968), who asked their students to learn many lists of words using the place system, with 40 locations around the college campus as the loci. The lists of 40 nouns were presented once at a rate of about 13 seconds per item. The students were tested immediately, and again after 24 hours. At the immediate test about 38 of the 40 nouns could be recalled in their correct serial position. Even after a day's lapse, recall remained at 34 nouns in their correct order. Unfortunately, Ross and Lawrence did not test a control group who had not been instructed in the mnemonic, so it is difficult to estimate the improvement in memory that occurred. However, performance of their subjects is way above anything that would be expected from subjects unequipped with a mnemonic technique.

Appropriate controls were incorporated by Groninger (1971). One group of subjects first devised their own test of 25 easily ordered locations. The time taken to learn a list of 25 words using the mnemonic was checked and found to be shorter than the time taken by a control group who had not been given mnemonic instructions. Recall was tested after one week and again after five weeks and was found to be superior for the mnemonic group on both occasions. After five weeks the mnemonic group averaged almost 20 words in their correct positions, while the control group averaged less than 10.

It seems, therefore, that the Greek teachers of rhetoric were correct in advocating the place method as a way of considerably improving recall. However, some possible questions are not answered in the experiments described above. What happens if the same places are used repeatedly? Will there be retrieval of inappropriate images or interference preventing retrieval of any image at all? I am not aware of an experiment testing the repeated use of places, but the use of the same peg word for learning several lists has been examined, so some relevant evidence will be discussed in the next section.

An important question unanswered in all these sections is what advantages, or disadvantages, come of frequent practice? Will the skilled memory expert outdo Groninger and Ross and Lawrence's subjects, as a chess expert excels a novice? The answer to that remains open to speculation.

The Peg System

Hunter (1964) in his book *Memory* gives the results of an experiment using the 'one is a bun' mnemonic which shows a dramatic improvement in recall for the group using the mnemonic over subjects not given the technique in learning a list of concrete nouns. Hunter goes on to say that he has tested the mnemonic with over 800 subjects and has almost invariably found an improvement in recall, often to the surprise of the subjects themselves. Bugelski *et al.* (1968) also found improvement in recall, so long as subjects using the mnemonic had longer than two seconds to learn each item. This need for a minimum time is hardly surprising. The subject has to perceive the presented number–noun pair, recall the appropriate peg word for the number, and compose an image linking together the peg and the item he wishes to remember. We have found (Morris and Reid, 1973) that subjects take on average 2.1 seconds to report forming a compound image linking two nouns, so it is not surprising that when a peg word must be recalled the mnemonic method requires more than two seconds per item to be useable.

What happens when the same peg word is used repeatedly? Both Bugelski (1968) and Morris and Reid (1970) required subjects to use the 'one is a bun' mnemonic to learn six successive lists. In our experiment we tried to maximize interlist interference by composing each list of the same 10 nouns, but paired each time with a different number. There are some problems in interpreting the results, since the control groups, who were free to discover better methods of learning the list to those with which they began, gradually improved across the trials, although at no time approached the performance of the mnemonic group. However, the mnemonic groups in both experiments showed no decline in performance, and when questioned afterwards few subjects reported any problems from interfering items. Lorayne, when teaching the peg method as the basis of his memory system, says that there will be no problem caused by competing images. The beauty of using imagery, he says, is that you can forget whenever you wish. This is reminiscent of the solution discovered by Luria's exceptional subject S to his problem of being unable to forget (Luria, 1968). He discovered that he could forget if he wanted to. The wanting was the important factor.

Images

Both the peg system and the place method make use of imagery to link the item to be remembered to the peg or locus. However, some mnemonic methods simply involve the use of mental images to link together the items to be remembered. Serial lists can be learned by imaging successive pairs of items together, or a cue word can be linked with the item to be remembered, as in paired-associate learning. In such situations imagery can produce a very impressive level of recall. For example, Wallace *et al.* (1957) presented very long lists of pairs of concrete nouns to their subjects, who, at their own pace, formed mental images linking the two items together. When presented with the first word from each pair one subject correctly recalled 496 out of 500 of the paired nouns, while the others showed similarly excellent recall. No control subjects were tested, but this was a startlingly good performance by any standards.

A better controlled experiment was reported by Bower (1967). He instructed subjects to learn five successive lists each consisting of 20 pairs of concrete nouns. The average recall of the second word of the pairs, given the first word, was over 60 per cent higher for a group who linked the nouns by mental images than for control subjects who were given ordinary instructions for paired-associate learning.

All the memory experts agree that the images formed should be as unusual and bizarre as possible, but there is little evidence to show that bizarre images lead to better recall. Bower (1970a) reports that in four experiments the subjects who were told to produce bizarre scenes had no better recall than those who were asked to compose familiar, sensible scenes. Delin (1968) also found no improvement when the need for bizarre images was emphasized. However, in Delin's study only 5 seconds were allowed for the formation of an image. It is likely that it takes longer to form a bizarre image than it does to compose a conventional one, so perhaps bizarreness may show its effect when longer time is available at presentation. Bizarreness may also become more important when imagery is frequently used, especially in conjunction with the peg system, where one component of the image appears frequently in other images. Lesgold and Goldman (1973) had subjects form images in which pairs of concrete nouns were linked with cue words. There were six cue words, and 10 pairs were linked to each. Half of the subjects were told to use the same setting for the cue word on each occasion, the others were recommended to use different settings. A description of each image was written, and judged on its uniqueness from other images formed by the same subject. At an unexpected recall test, when given the cue words, the greater the number of unique images formed the better the recall. In addition, the emotional connotations of the images may be important. Sadalla and Loftness (1972) had subjects form images with either positive (pleasant), negative (unpleasant) or neutral emotional contents. They found that there was poorer recall in the neutral image condition than in the other two, which did not differ from one another. It would seem that, as a practical strategy, there is enough evidence to indicate that bizarre images should be formed if possible, but it appears that the main improvement in performance comes from the adoption of an imagery strategy, irrespective of the normality or oddness of the images actually composed.

Stories and Sentences

An alternative to linking unrelated items through images is to compose stories and sentences which supply a meaningful context in which the items can be placed. It is difficult if not impossible to separate the effects of such techniques from those of image formation, since subjects may frequently picture the stories that they compose, while the formation of an integrating image may well presuppose the invention of a suitable story. What can be reported is the success of *instructions* to compose stories or meaningful sentences. For paired-associate learning several studies have demonstrated that sentence mnemonics improve recall compared to a control group who repeat the words by rote (e.g. Aiken, 1971; Paivio and Foth, 1970). Bobrow and Bower (1969) and Bower and Winzenz (1970) compared sentences generated by the subjects to sentences provided by the experimenter. While both conditions led to better recall than that of a control group, in both experiments the performance was higher for subjects who produced their own sentences. However, it would be naive to expect that such a result is independent of the intelligence and age of the subjects, the time available and the quality of the sentences provided by the experimenter.

Perhaps the most impressive of all improvements *via* mnemonic methods was reported by Bower and Clark (1969). They instructed subjects to learn 12 lists of 10 words at their own pace by forming a narrative which incorporated the words. A control subject was paired with each of the experimental subjects and given the same time to learn the lists. At the immediate test, given after each list had been memorized, both groups produced almost complete recall, but at a test after all the lists had been learned, while the subjects who had composed a story could remember 93 per cent of the words in their correct order when given the first word from each list, the control subjects recalled only 14 per cent correctly. Composing a story is therefore an extremely efficient method of learning at list when order must be retained. It is, incidentally, worth noting that here, as in the Wallace *et al.* (1957) experiments, the most impressive effects of mnemonics occur when subjects have been allowed as much time as they require to compose an appropriate mnemonic. In everyday learning situations there is rarely the time stress usually imposed by experimenters investigating memory processes. A true evaluation of the mnemonics is only possible if subjects are allowed sufficient time to carry out the rather demanding instructions involved.

Rhymes and Rhythm

It has been known for many years that poetry is easier to learn than prose (McGeoch and Irion, 1952). However, it is difficult to unravel the possible components of poetry to identify which of them are responsible for this. Rhythm specifies the form of words which will fit into the ongoing recall, and as such will act as both recall cue and post-recall check. Bower and Bolton (1969) looked at the influence of rhymes on recall. They suggested that the rhyming relation between words restricts the range of possible alternatives. They found that paired associates where the words of the pair were related by the first two letters being the same (e.g. hat–ham, bin–bit) were as well recalled as pairs that rhymed as the result of the last two letters being the same (e.g. cat–mat). Both were better recalled than unrelated words. When the number of response alternatives was controlled by using a multiple-choice recognition test there was no better recognition of the rhyming response word than there was of other words.

First-Letter Mnemonics

According to Blick *et al.* (1972), the first-letter mnemonic technique is the one most likely to be adopted by college students who are asked to learn a long, serial list of words, and Gruneberg (1973) found that first-letter mnemonics were the technique most commonly used by students revising for finals. However, unlike the other major mnemonic methods the evidence for the first-letter technique is scanty and unimpressive. Gruneberg (1973), for example, found no relationship between the use of mnemonic techniques and the class of degree obtained. However, while Gruneberg's adoption of degree class as his measure is an admirable attempt to assess the importance of mnemonics in a real-life situation, it does bring with it difficulties in interpretation. Whatever the criteria are that are used by those who mark finals papers, they are unlikely to involve a high weighting to sheer recall. By finals, students are expected to show more creative skills. Those who placed reliance on mnemonics may have put too great an emphasis on factual recall and consequently impaired their overall performance. Another possibility is that it may be the poorer students who adopt mnemonics, especially those designed for the retention of apparently unconnected 'facts'. Better students may see the connections and be concentrating on developing arguments rather than retaining details. At their best, mnemonic techniques may make too small a contribution to performance to be detected by a measure as insensitive as degree classification, where most students fall within two or three categories.

Gruneberg's study examined the use of both types of first-letter mnemonic: those which use the first letters as the first letters of new words which form a meaningful story (the 'Richard of York ...' variety) and those in which words are formed from the first letters (the 'CLOD' variety). All other studies have concentrated on the latter type. Boltwood and Blick (1970) failed to find any improvement over a control group when subjects were instructed to learn a list of 19 unrelated words by generating their own first-letter mnemonics. By contrast, subjects who 'clustered' the words into meaningful categories or subjects who made up a story linking the items performed far better, especially in the late tests after one and eight weeks. Waite *et al.* (1971) also found no improvement in recall by subjects using a first-letter technique, even when the subjects in the group were selected on the basis of their claim that they would ordinarily use the first-letter technique.

The one study which has shown positive results for the first-letter mnemonic is that by Nelson and Archer (1972). They had subjects learn six lists of six words and tested recall after each list had been presented. Half the subjects were given conventional serial learning instructions. Prior to each list, the others were verbally given a word made up of the first letters of the items in the list and were told that the word would aid their recall. At recall, both groups were subdivided, with half of each being given the mnemonic word. Nelson and Archer found that subjects given the mnemonic word recalled more words in their correct order than did other subjects. However, there was a slight, though statistically insignificant, tendency for more words, independent of position, to be recalled by the control subjects. The best recall was by those who only received the mnemonic words at the recall test. If Nelson and Archer's results are reliable, then it would seem that the first-letter mnemonic may aid the ordering of words that are recalled, but does not help to make the individual items easier to recall.

No improvement in ordering of the items was found in a recent experiment at Lancaster University by Neil Cook and myself. Subjects learned six lists of five words and were tested on recall after being shown all the lists; they were tested again a week later. One group of subjects were given a mnemonic word composed from the first letters of the words to be learned, with suitable vowels inserted. A second group were requested to form their own mnemonic word, while a control group were given instructions to simply learn the lists. At both tests there was no sign of either order or item availability being aided by the mnemonics, which seemed rather to inhibit recall.

If it is concluded that first-letter mnemonics do not improve recall in the types of situations tested, why are they so popular and commonly in use? The answer may be that they serve a specific function not yet adequately investigated experimentally. Most of the commonly applied first-letter mnemonics are used where there is no great problem in remembering the names of the items, but there are problems in remembering their order and perhaps their number, which is often arbitrary. This is certainly true of the mnemonics for the colours of the rainbow, the colour codes of electrical resistors, the order of cranial nerves and the musical scales, which are the most popular first-letter mnemonics. It may be that Nelson and Archer are correct when they locate the influence of the first-letter mnemonic as improving the retention of order. The tests of the mnemonics have been concerned so far with the acquisition of new lists. They have shown that in those conditions the first-letter mnemonic is ineffective, but this is not sufficient to imply its uselessness in the situations in which it is most frequently adopted.

PROPERTIES OF THE MEMORY SYSTEM: WHY MNEMONICS ARE EFFECTIVE

At first sight the mnemonics systems can seem rather peculiar. They demand unusual activities such as bizarre imaging or the translation of numbers into words. However, if the major properties of the memory system that have been studied over the past 20 years are considered, it will soon become clear that the mnemonics make use of the strengths of the memory system.

Important factors that influence the efficiency of long-term retention include:
  (a) the extent of organization of the material,
  (b) its meaningfulness and concreteness,
  (c) the presentation at recall of appropriate retrieval cues, and
  (d) the kind of encoding of the material initially undertaken by the subject.

I shall briefly discuss each of these in turn, indicating their place in the functioning of the mnemonic systems.

Organization

Bousfield (1953) demonstrated that subjects tend to recall together items that are members of the same semantic category, even though they were intially separated by unrelated items in the presented list. Since then, the study of organization in both the material presented and the recall produced by the subjects has been an active research area. When, as in Bousfield's experiment, the items can be classified into categories, then these categories are more than simply reflected in the order of recall. Rather, they seem to function as higher-order memory units, and the amount recalled seems to depend on the number of these category unitsrecalled. Evidence for their functioning as higher-order units comes from many studies (e.g. Cohen, 1966; Tulving and Pearlstone, 1966; Tulving and Psotka, 1971), where it was found that if any item from a particular category was recalled, then several would be remembered, and, what is more, about the same number in each category. Kellas *et al.* (1973) measured the intervals between the recall of words from the same and from different categories, and found that on average subjects took five times longer to go from one category to another than from one word to another within a category. Storage on the basis of these higher-order units seems to be a property of the memory system. Tulving and Pearlstone (1966) and Tulving and Psotka (1971) found that if cues to forgotten categories were supplied, recall markedly improved and was independent of interference from other lists that were learned in the same session.

One of the probable factors leading to the success of imagery, sentence and story formation as mnemonics is that they provide a means of organizing apparently unrelated items. For example, the words 'bell', 'dog', 'tie' are not immediately classifiable as related in the way that 'horse', 'cow', 'sheep' would be. However, if an image is formed in which a dog standing on its hind paws is wearing a brightly coloured tie and ringing a large bell with its fore-paws, then the words have been incorporated into one unit. Bower (1970b) demonstrated the importance of such integrating images in paired-associate learning. One group of subjects were told to form images linking together both words in the pair. If, for example, the words were 'cat' and 'table', they might imagine a cat sitting on a table. A second group were told to imagine the two objects separated in their imaginary field of vision, for example a cat on the right and a table on the left. A third group were simply told to repeat the words. Neither recognition of the first word of the pair nor recall of the second differed for the latter two groups, but the recall of the group that had formed integrated images was far superior. With Ralph Stevens, I found similar results for free recall (Morris and Stevens, 1974). Subjects told to link three words together in an image almost invariably recalled the three words together, and had far better recall than subjects told to form an image separately to each word. These latter subjects performed no better than a control group who were given no mnemonic instructions. Both experiments indicate that it is not just the formation of images which is important, but the sort of images formed.

Meaningfulness and Concreteness

When Bartlett (1932) had subjects reproduce stories that they had read, the exact wording of the original was immediately lost, but much of the original theme could be reproduced in precis and paraphrase. The parts of the stories which were most commonly forgotten were those that were unusual and difficult to understand. Other research on long-term memory confirms Bartlett's findings (e.g. Begg, 1971; Baddeley, 1966; Bransford and Franks, 1971). In general, we remember the gist of our experiences rather than their exact details, and we retain best what is most meaningful to us. Noble (1952) demonstrated that the more associations a word or paraword elicits the easier it is to remember. Common words elicit many associations. Paivio (1971) has extensively reviewed the considerable evidence that concrete nouns and phrases are easier to learn than abstract nouns. In summary, something that is concrete and meaningful, with many associations, is much more likely to be remembered than something that is abstract, with little meaning. The conversion from meaningless to the familiar and meaningful is a continually recurring feature of the mnemonic systems. Peg words translate numbers into concrete nouns. The digit–letter system translates phone numbers into common words. The place system uses well-known loci. The sentence–story mnemonics weave a meaningful theme around the unrelated items. The words and sentences of the first-letter mnemonic are usually concrete, familiar and meaningful. Where possible, the mnemonics make use of meaningfulness to aid their effectiveness.

Appropriate Cues

An enormous amount is stored in our memory system. With any information storage system the major problem is that of coding items as they come in so that they can be retrieved when required. One difficulty is that there are limitations to the extent of coding and cross-referencing that can be undertaken. Another is that there is no telling in what circumstances in the future retrieval will be required, so that it is possible that the coding may be inappropriate, as when a book is misshelved in a library, or a file is misplaced. Once 'placed' in the system the piece of information may be available but it is useless if it is not accessible *via* a retrieval search.

An experiment by Tulving and Osler (1968) illustrates the importance of appropriate coding at the time of storage, and the value of a cue at recall. Tulving and Osler showed their subjects lists of words in capitals which for some subjects were paired with another word that is occasionally given as an associate to the first word (e.g. leg–MUTTON; village–CITY). The subjects were told that they would have to recall the capitalized words, but the other words might help. At the recall test, in some conditions the words in lower cases were given to the subjects. Recall was the same both for those who only had these cues at the learning stage and for those who saw them first at recall, but it was 70 per cent better for those who had the cue words at both stages. The words served as cues, but only if they had been stored as such during learning.

One primary function of the place and the peg mnemonics is to provide distinctive retrieval cues where only poor cues would normally exist. Usually, when a list of items is learned the cues may be the position that the items occupied in the list and some incidental associations with adjacent items. The mnemonic methods provide a cue (the loci or peg word) which is specified at the learning stage and which is easily retrieved at the recall stage. There is no problem over the correct way to encode the information, nor over the correct retrieval cue at recall. So long as the places and pegs are well learned, they are available as distinctive bases for storage and retrieval. It can be seen that these mnemonics come to terms with the major problem of the memory system. It is hardly surprising that they can greatly enhance recall.

Encoding Activities

In 1972 Craik and Lockhart proposed a view of the memorizing processes in terms of the 'depths' or 'levels' of analysis through which an item has passed. They argue that an item will initially be encoded at a superficial level, perhaps in terms of its acoustic–articulatory features, and if more time is available or the situation warrants it, it will be more deeply encoded by abstracting relevant semantic information, associations, and so on. Deeper coding takes longer than superficial encoding, and makes more demands on the processing system, but the deeper an item has been encoded, the longer it will be retained. In some situations the subject will only perform superficial encoding. By so doing he will be able to deal more quickly with the items, and hold more of them for a brief period of time, but this extra capacity is gained at the expense of long-term retention, since without the deeper processing the items are soon lost. There is quite a lot of evidence to support this view.

For example, it has often been suggested (e.g. Atkinson and Shiffrin, 1968) that rehearsing items by repeating them over to oneself is one way of entering the items into long-term memory. However, from the depth of coding standpoint such rehearsal requires only superficial encoding—there is no retrieval of the meaning of the words. Therefore, according to Craik and Lockhart rehearsal should be a poor strategy for entering information into long-term memory. This was shown to be the case by Craik (1973). Subjects were told to rehearse aloud the last few words of a list, and were given time for the rehearsal. However, in a later test their recall was no better than that of subjects who had not been given time for the additional rehearsal. The rehearsal only retains information at a superficial level of encoding.

Deeper encoding can be encouraged by setting the subjects a task which requires the use of semantic information. Thus Mazuryk and Lockhart (1974) had one group of their subjects give associates to the words to be learned. On an immediate test these subjects had poorer recall than those allowed to rehearse the words, but on a later test their recall was much superior. Craik (1973) also showed that deciding whether a word fits into a given category or sentence takes longer than saying whether the word is in upper or lower case or whether it rhymes with another word. However, the recall of the words at a later test was superior for the subjects in the former conditions.

The importance of this research for the understanding of the mnemonic techniques is that it shows that the activities of the subject and the encoding of the item that take place are vital factors in retention. The mnemonics encourage the use of semantic information about the items. Such information must be retrieved if the items to be remembered are to be incorporated into a story or an image. The use of the mnemonics therefore demands deep coding of the items. Subjects who do not have the mnemonic strategy to direct their activities may fall into rehearsal, or other methods which do not involve deep coding. However, subjects using the mnemonics go through the processes which will give the greatest probability of long-term retention.

IMPROVING YOUR OWN MEMORY

Applying the Mnemonics

One way to improve your memory is to apply the mnemonic methods in situations where you are likely to forget. The methods can be modified to suit the situation. For example, the following method of learning people's names is recommended by Lorayne (1958). The name is first converted into some concrete substitute. Names like Brown and Cook are easily imaged, but substitutes can be found for all names. For example, Fishter can be made into fish stir, and imagined as a fish stirring; Gorden as a garden; Freedman as a man being fried. Then an outstanding feature of the person's face is chosen and the image of the name is linked to it. So, if Mr. Fishter has deep-set eyes, then you might form an image of a fish stirring his eyes with a large spoon. Another use of imagery is to remember something that you may forget by linking it with an image of the last thing that you are likely to see before you need to remember it. An image of a letter to be posted linked with the front door should remind you of the letter when you see the front door on your way out. There must be many such applications that can be devised to suit your own requirements.

Developing New Mnemonics

Faced with a task which requires considerable memorizing, it may be that none of the currently available mnemonic techniques are suitable. It should, however, be possible to make use of the important features of the memory system discussed earlier. The situation must be carefully examined, by considering the material to be learned, the time available, the circumstances in which recall will be required, whether recall will be cued, whether it must be in order, and so on. Then by imposing as much organization as possible onto the material, by seeing an underlying structure if one exists; by devising cues for the recall stage; by making the material as meaningful and as concrete as possible; and by ensuring that semantic rather than superficial encoding is demanded by your activity, you should be able to minimize the learning time and maximize recall. All this takes time and effort. You may decide that your inefficient memory may be adequate after all.

Practising Remembering

The traditional answer to the question 'Can I improve my memory through practising remembering?' has been 'No', based on studies by William James (1890), who found that practice at learning poetry led to no improvement. However, subjects in memory experiments do tend to get better as they learn more lists. When questioned, they often report changing their methods of learning (Morris and Reid, 1970). The explanation seems to be that sheer practice in the sense of doing the same thing over and over again does not help improve memory, but that the strategy adopted to cope with the learning is very important. Therefore, if through constant practice you test and discover better ways of learning more suited to the particular task, then performance will improve. There need be no fear of overloading the memory. The amount stored in the memory system through intentional memorizing must be an infinitesimally small part of that which is entered without conscious awareness every minute of every day.

Methods of Study

Students are required to learn large amounts of unfamiliar material from books and lectures. I have not dealt with such learning in this chapter, partly because it is considered by Michael Howe in Chapter 8 and by Fitz Taylor in Chapter 6, and partly because it requires a special approach which is well discussed in other texts. Anyone interested is recommended to work through Derek Rowntrees' short programmed text entitled 'Learn how to study' (Rowntree, 1970).

PROBLEMS AND LIMITATIONS IN DEVELOPING A SUPERPOWER MEMORY

I hope that it will be clear from what has gone before that there are opportunities for considerable improvement in the efficiency of memory. This knowledge is not kept secret, and quite a number of people are aware of the potential of the mnemonic systems. Why then do so few individuals have superpower memories? Even those, like myself, who are convinced of the value of the mnemonics make only limited use of them. Why is there this reluctance to enhance recall?

The answer probably has its basis in the effort involved. It is difficult to convert abstract themes to concrete objects, and then to image them in a suitable way. It takes time to learn peg words or develop suitable loci. The time and effort are not so great that I will never make use of the mnemonics.

When my self-esteem is involved, for example as a subject in an experiment, I turn to them to guarantee a good performance. However, in everyday life I do not bother. It would be a mistake to generalize from my own laziness, but the comments of volunteers that I have unsuccessfully tried to train in the peg word system support my view. While they wanted to improve their memories, at the time they were learning they did not feel that the mnemonics were worth the trouble involved. Although they may fully believe that the acquisition of a large number of pegs will provide them with a way of improving their memory, few students are willing to go to the trouble of adequately learning the pegs. As with any skill, it takes time and application to develop a good memory.

Why are we unwilling to make the effort? A full answer, if it could be given, would probably require considering what is meant by 'effort' and what its place is in the cognitive system (see Kahneman, 1973). However, given an everyday understanding of effort, there are at least two factors. One is that we often believe, at the time that we are trying to learn, that we shall not forget. We have too much confidence in our memories. The other factor is that we are aware that the mnemonics can only help us to learn limited types of items. The mnemonics make it possible to learn lists of concrete, unrelated words. However, are our memory problems usually of this sort? If they are not, then the mnemonics will be of little use.

I am not aware of any study which has set out to identify what the ordinary person wants to remember but finds that he cannot. I do not know what makes so many yearn for a better memory. Such ignorance of what should be the aims of a technology of memory needs to be rectified. For the present I can only guess on the basis of my own experience. I think that the most important lapses of memory on my part are when I forget to do some job that I have agreed to do. Common to such situations is a lack of any cue in my daily routine and environment to remind me. Very efficient individuals overcome such problems by noting down what they have to do and regularly consulting their notes. Most of us are either too lazy to do this for other than very important appointments or we think that we shall not forget. The other major failure of memory that I would like to overcome usually involves situations where I want to remember events that at the time they occurred did not seem worthy of special attention. Only at some later time do I want to recall the name of the good hotel, the number of the bus route, how the joke went, and so on.

There are, then, at least two areas where we need techniques for improving memory. We need ways of remembering appointments and commitments, and ways of improving our recall of events which at the time that they occurred did not seem to qualify for the trouble of employing a mnemonic. Until we can successfully do both we shall not possess 'superpower' memories. Yet both will be difficult to improve. In some cases the information will be only superficially encoded, and not stored for long-term retention. When it has been stored, the problem is one of finding or providing a suitable retrieval cue. For appointments, perhaps the right approach is to recognize both the limitations of the memory system and the general unwillingness to organize our lives around an appointments diary. It should be possible to develop techniques which employ notes of appointments, but which involve the maximum accuracy in recall with the minimum need for constant reference to an appointments schedule.

The problem of remembering appointments may be soluble, but more difficult is the development of strategies to improve recall, as opposed to learning. If such techniques could be found they would be valuable to everyone. Yet it is interesting to note that while many different mnemonic techniques for learning have been developed over the years, there is no similar tradition of methods for improving our probing of memory for recall. The problem is to find cues that were encoded at the time of the original entry of the information into memory. When trying to recall, it is therefore a good idea to try to imagine yourself back in the situation again. Events that happened at the same time as the event that you are searching for may serve as retrieval cues, if they can themselves be recalled. The situation resembles that of Tulving and Osler (1968), where cues given at the learning and the recall stages improved recall.

One technique sometimes adopted for remembering the names of people or places is to go through the alphabet to see if one of the letters cues recall. Gruneberg (personal communication) did find that the recall of capital cities was improved in this way. However, the advantage seems to have come from this method keeping subjects working at the task. Control subjects usually give up more quickly, with poorer performance, but if they are induced to keep going they will remember as much as those using the first-letter strategy. I know of no other techniques that have been experimentally investigated. I find it difficult to believe that useful techniques cannot be developed, since Bartlett (1932), Neisser (1967) and others have emphasized the active, problem-solving, reconstructive nature of recall. Surely given this flexibility there is room for improvement through the use of appropriate strategies.

CONCLUSION

I have reviewed the main mnemonic techniques and reported research which indicates that they do, indeed, improve memory. I have tried to identify the properties of the memory system which are employed by the mnemonics to maximize learning. These properties of the memory system could be exploited by other techniques now that many of the general principles of the system are understood. However, towards the end of the chapter I introduced a note of passimism. Even those who know of the mnemonics rarely use them. There are many situations where memory fails us but where mnemonics can offer no help. In particular, there are no techniques for improving recall of those things which did not seem to warrant special mnemonic storage at the time they occurred. It is often our failure to remember these, and appointments and commitments that we have made, that leads us to bemoan our poor memories. Until techniques for improving recall are developed, we shall be only part way towards being able to offer a superpower memory to anyone willing to take the trouble to learn the appropriate methods.

REFERENCES

Aiken, E. G. (1971). 'Linguistic and imaginal mnemonics in paired-associate recall', *Psychonomic Science*, **24**, 91.

Atkinson, R. C., and Shiffrin, R. M. (1968). 'Human memory: A proposed system and its control processes', in K. W. Spence and J. T. Spence (Eds.), *The Psychology of Learning and Motivation: Advances in Research and Theory*, Vol. 2, Academic Press, New York.

Baddeley, A. D. (1966). 'The influence of acoustic and semantic similarity on long term memory for word sequences', *Quarterly Journal of Experimental Psychology*, **18**, 302.

Bartlett, F. C. (1932). *Remembering: A Study in Experimental and Social Psychology*, Cambridge University Press, Cambridge.

Begg, I. (1971). 'Recognition memory for sentence meaning and wording', *Journal of Verbal Learning and Verbal Behavior*, **10**, 114.

Blick, K. A., Buonassissi, J. V., and Boltwood, C. E. (1972). 'Mnemonic techniques used by college students in serial learning', *Psychological Reports*, **31**, 983.

Bobrow, S. A., and Bower, G. H. (1969). 'Comprehension and recall of sentences', *Journal of Experimental Psychology*, **80**, 455.

Boltwood, C. E., and Blick, K. A. (1970). 'The delineation and application of three mnemonic techniques', *Psychonomic Science*, **20**, 339.

Bousfield, W. A. (1953). 'The occurrence of clustering in the recall of randomly arranged associates', *Journal of General Psychology*, **49**, 229.

Bower, G. H. (1967). 'Mental imagery and memory', Colloquium speech to several departments.

Bower, G. H. (1970a). 'Analysis of a mnemonic device', *American Scientist*, **58**, 496.

Bower, G. H. (1970b). 'Imagery as a relational organizer in associative learning', *Journal of Verbal Learning and Verbal Behavior*, **9**, 529.

Bower, G. H., and Bolton, L. S. (1969). 'Why are rhymes easy to learn?', *Journal of Experimental Psychology*, **82**, 453.

Bower, G. H., and Clark, M. C. (1969). 'Narrative stories as mediators for serial learning', *Psychonomic Science*, **14**, 181.

Bower, G. H., and Winzenz, D. (1970). 'Comparison of associative learning strategies', *Psychonomic Science*, **20**, 119.

Bransford, J. D., and Franks, J. J. (1971). 'The abstraction of linguistic ideas', *Cognitive Psychology*, **2**, 331.

Bugelski, B. R. (1968). 'Images as mediators in one trial paired-associate learning—II: Self timing in successive lists', *Journal of Experimental Psychology*, **77**, 328.

Bugelski, B. R., Kidd, E., and Segmen, J. (1968). 'Images as a mediator in one trial paired-associate learning', *Journal of Experimental Psychology*, **76**, 69.

Cohen, B. H. (1966). 'Some-or-none characteristics of coding behavior', *Journal of Verbal Learning and Verbal Behavior*, **5**, 182.

Craik, F. I. M. (1973). 'A "Levels of analysis" view of memory', in P. Pliner, L. Krames and T. M. Alloway (Eds.), *Communication and Affect: Language and Thought*, Academic Press, New York.

Craik, F. I. M., and Lockhart, R. S. (1972). 'Levels of processing: A framework for memory research', *Journal of Verbal Learning and Verbal Behavior*, **11**, 671.

Delin, P. S. (1968). 'Learning and retention of English words with successive approximations to a complex mnemonic instruction', *Psychonomic Science*, **17**, 87.

Feinaigle, G. von (1813). *The New Art of Memory*, Sherwood, Neely and Jones, London.

Furst, B. (1957). *The Practical Way to a Better Memory*, Fawcett World Library, New York.

Groninger, L. D. (1971). 'Mnemonic imagery and forgetting', *Psychonomic Science*, **23**, 161.

Gruneberg, M. (1973). 'The role of memorisation techniques in Finals examination preparation', *Educational Research*, **15**, 134.

Hunter, I. M. L. (1964). *Memory*, Penguin, Harmondsworth.

James, W. (1890). *Principles of Psychology*, Holt, New York.

Kahneman, D. (1973). *Attention and Effort*, Prentice-Hall, Englewood Cliffs, New Jersey.

Kellas, G., Ashcraft, M. H., Johnson, N. S., and Needham, S. (1973). 'Temporal aspects of storage and retrieval in free recall of categorized lists', *Journal of Verbal Learning and Verbal Behavior*, **12**, 499.

Lesgold, A. M., and Goldman, S. R. (1973). 'Encoding uniqueness and the imagery mnemonic in associative learning', *Journal of Verbal Learning and Verbal Behavior*, **12**, 193.

Lorayne, H. (1958). *How to Develop a Super-power Memory*, Thomas, Preston.

Luria, A. R. (1968). *The Mind of a Mnemonist*, Cape, London.

McGeoch, J. A., and Irion, A. L. (1952). *The Psychology of Human Learning*, Longmans, New York.

Mazuryk, G. F., and Lockhart, R. S. (1974). 'Negative recency and levels of processing in free recall', *Canadian Journal of Psychology*, **28**, 114.

Morris, P. E., and Reid, R. L. (1970). 'The repeated use of mnemonic imagery, *Psychonomic Science*, **20**, 337.

Morris, P. E., and Reid, R. L. (1973). 'Recognition and recall: Latency and recurrence of images', *British Journal of Psychology*, **64**, 161.

Morris, P. E., and Stevens, R. S. (1974). 'Linking images and free recall', *Journal of Verbal Learning and Verbal Behavior*, **13**, 310.

Neisser, U. (1967). *Cognitive Psychology*, Appleton-Century-Crofts, New York.

Nelson, D. L., and Archer, C. S. (1972). 'The first letter mnemonic', *Journal of Educational Psychology*, 63, 482.

Noble, C. E. (1952). 'The role of stimulus meaning (m) in serial verbal learning', *Journal of Experimental Psychology*, **43**, 437.

Paivio, A. (1971). *Imagery and Verbal Processes*, Holt, Rinehart & Winston, New York.

Paivio, A., and Foth, O. (1970). 'Imaginal and verbal mediators and noun concreteness in paired-associate learning: the elusive interaction', *Journal of Verbal Learning and Verbal Behavior*, **9**, 384.

Ross, J., and Lawrence, K. A. (1968). 'Some observations on memory artifice', *Psychonomic Seience*, **13**, 107.

Rowntree, D. (1970). *Learn How to Study*, Macdonald, London.

Sadalla, E. K., and Loftness, S. (1972). 'Emotional images as mediators in one-trial paired-associate learning', *Journal of Experimental Psychology*, **95**, 295.

Tulving, E., and Osler, S. (1968). 'Effectiveness of retrieval cues in memory for words', *Journal of Experimental Psychology*, **77**, 593.

Tulving, E., and Pearlstone, Z. (1966). 'Availability versus accessibility of information in memory for words', *Journal of Verbal Learning and Verbal Behavior*, **5**, 381.

Tulving, E., and Psotka, J. (1971). 'Retroactive inhibition in free recall: Inaccessibility of information available in the memory store', *Journal of Experimental Psychology*, **87**, 116.

Waite, C. J., Blick, K. A., and Boltwood, C. E. (1971). 'Prior usage of the first letter technique', *Psychological Reports*, **29**, 630.

Wallace, W. H., Turner, S. H., and Perkins, C. C. (1957). 'Preliminary studies of human information storage', Signal Corps Project No. 1320, Institute for Cooperative Research, University of Pennsylvania.

Yates, F. A. (1966). *The Art of Memory*, University of Chicago Press, Chicago.

8

LEARNING AND THE ACQUISITION OF KNOWLEDGE BY STUDENTS: SOME EXPERIMENTAL INVESTIGATIONS

Michael J. A. Howe

The research described in this chapter was undertaken by myself and some colleagues to investigate the manner in which people acquire knowledge. We have observed learning under circumstances that are comparatively realistic and sufficiently similar in form to those of everyday learning by students for the findings to be of direct applicability to practical questions. We have been particularly interested in learning from materials presented in prose form, and a number of the issues we have found are similar to ones discussed by Fitz Taylor in Chapter 6. Also, some of the learner procedures and strategies described by Peter Morris in Chapter 7 are found to have relevance to prose learning. In the present chapter, rather than providing a broad survey of research, I shall try to illustrate the development of one particular line of research over a period of several years. First, I shall describe an experiment that yielded findings which led us to ask a number of questions concerning learning by mature students. The findings also encouraged us to embark on some studies examining the very practical matter of note-taking, and our investigations are briefly described in a second section. Thirdly, I shall describe experiments which consider the effects of certain presentation variables and learner activities.

AN EXPERIMENT ON LEARNING FROM A SHORT PROSE PASSAGE

In his book *Remembering* (1932), Sir Frederick Bartlett included a large amount of data demonstrating a variety of ways in which the mental processes of individuals who listened to or read information in the form of stories actively contributed to what was remembered. Bartlett's findings made it apparent that when meaningful information is to be remembered the processes that make this possible are by no means restricted to ones of passive storage: on

145

the contrary, with or without his awareness the individual undertakes a range of coding processes through which the received information is acted upon in ways that select, scan, integrate and modify it. This may sometimes result in the individual internalizing a severely distorted version of what was presented to him. The precise form taken by such coding operations depends largely upon the structure of knowledge and the mental processes possessed by the particular individual who attempts to assimilate the material. Although Bartlett's study was entitled 'Remembering', it is possible that some at least of the assimilative processes exert their influence at prior perceptual stages: as William Blake remarked, 'The fool sees not the tree the wise man sees'.

During the past few years there have been a number of attempts to develop Bartlett's insights into the role of individuals' mental processes in cognition, with emphasis on increased precision and further quantification. One such attempt took the form of an experiment published in 1955 by one of Bartlett's students, Harry Kay, the author of Chapter 1 in the present volume. Kay's experiment produced some striking and interesting findings, which led the present author to undertake what was substantially a replication study, with certain modifications. In considering the findings of that experiment (Howe, 1970c) it should be borne in mind that for those aspects of the study which closely parallel the earlier investigation by Kay, the results are remarkably similar.

The chosen learning task was one in which subjects listened to information made available in meaningful prose form and later were asked to attempt to reproduce it. There were two unusual features of the procedure. First, presentation of the material was repeated on a number of separate occasions, generally at weekly intervals. Secondly, the learners made a number of separate recall attempts, again at intervals of one week. To be more precise, on the first session the subjects listened to the prose passage, which was read to them at a rate of 120 words per minute, and approximately two minutes after it had ceased they were told to attempt written recall of it. They were asked to concentrate on reproducing the meaningful contents of the material. Reproduction of the precise form of the passage was to be as accurate as possible, but recalling the substantive content was the major goal. Following the attempt at recall the participants listened once more to the correct version of the passage. A week later there was a second session. This began with the request for recall, following which the subjects listened once more to the original correct version of the passage. There were two further identical sessions, each one week apart, making four sessions in all.

The subjects in the experiment were American postgraduate students enrolled in a course in Education. They averaged 30 years of age. The prose passage used was a short narrative extract, 160 words in length, from the novel *Henderson The Rain King*, by Saul Bellow. This particular passage was chosen because it combined the qualities of high meaningfulness and sufficient unfamiliarity of content to prevent participants from being able to capitalize on previously acquired subject-matter knowledge. The passage is one in which remembering the earlier sentences does not greatly facilitate guessing the remainder.

In order to assess the reliability of meaningful recall scores, two judges assessed the subjects' attempts. For scoring purposes the passage was divided into 20 segments, roughly equal in length, each of which contained information contributing meaningfully to the passage. The important content of each segment was reduced to a two- or three-word phrase, and a judgment of 'correct' was given if the correct items or synonyms of them were provided. To facilitate scoring written guidelines were provided, giving examples of acceptable and unacceptable versions. The achieved level of reliability is indicated by the produce-moment correlation of $+.89$ for scores allotted by the two judges, showing that the measure of meaningful retention was sufficiently reliable for the purposes of the experiment.

The results showing overall accuracy of recall in the successive sessions yield no surprises. On the first session just over eight segments were recalled on average, out of the total 20, and the figure rises gradually but steadily to almost 12 items on the final session. The most striking feature of these particular results is the small size of the week-to-week improvements. One might have anticipated that providing repeated presentations of the correct version of the passage immediately after subjects' attempts to recall the material would give excellent opportunities for individuals to correct themselves, leading to considerable improvements in performance. In the event, the improvements that did occur were very modest.

Of greater interest are the findings that emerge when one compares the detailed contents of each individual's successive recall attempts on the different occasions. It is strikingly apparent that from one week to the next a person's recalled versions of the material are remarkably similar to each other. In other words, each subject reproduces very accurately what he has previously recalled. This is true both in the case of items that are correct and, perhaps less happily, also in the case of incorrect items appearing in attempt to recall the passage. It appears that subjects are unable to profit so much as one might expect them to from the opportunities for improvement and for making corrections that appear to be provided by the repeated presentations of the material. The version that an individual has himself reproduced appears to be particularly stable in his memory, and hence resistant to changes in the direction either of increased accuracy or increased forgetting.

Examination of the detailed results reveals that on average an item recalled correctly on the first recall trial had a 0.7 probability of being recalled again on the succeeding trial. If an item was recalled on each of the first three attempts, the probability of correct recall on the fourth trial was as high as 0.98. However, the probability of an item not recalled on trial 1 being correct on the following attempt was only 0.2, and even when the passage had been presented on as many as three occasions the probability of an item being recalled on the next trial, if it had not previously been recalled, remained at this low level. In short, the probability of an item being correctly recalled on any given trial was only weakly related to the number of times the subject had heard it, as part of the version of the material presented to him, but the probability of recall was very strongly influenced by the contents of the subject's own previous reproductions.

As well as scoring meaningful recall, it is possible to measure verbatim performance, by counting the number of words correctly reproduced. When one scores subjects' recall attempts in this way, the pattern of results in the present study turns out to be very similar to that found for meaningful recall. As it happens, verbatim scoring permits the experimenter to gain an additional measure in the form of a record of the number of items that appear in a subject's attempts at recall but which do not form part of the correct version. It is possible to record how often these incorrect 'additions' are repeated in the subject's succeeding recall attempts, bearing in mind that their absence from the correct original version of the passage, which is always presented between any two recall trials, would appear to facilitate attempts on the part of the subjects to eradicate extraneous items from their memory for the imformation they are trying to remember. In fact, such incorrect additions occurring on the first three recall trials had probabilities of 0.2, 0.3, and 0.4 of appearing again on the respective succeeding trial, and the probability of an addition occurring on both of the first two trials being present again on the third trial was 0.6. It is clear that such incorrect items are by no means easily lost.

It is also apparent that the probabilities of additions which were present on one trial recurring on the next were, in general, considerably higher than the probabilities of successful recall of a correct word if that word had not been reproduced on previous recall trials. For instance, if a word item had been presented to the subject on as many as four occasions in the original passage but not yet recalled by the subject, the probability of it being reproduced correctly on the fourth trial was only 0.1. On the other hand, an incorrect addition that had not appeared at all in the correct version, and which had been produced by the subject on just one occasion, was twice as likely as this to be repeated on the next occasion, the probability being 0.2.

What emerges most clearly from these findings is that what an individual retains is very strongly determined by what he himself has previously done. It is the materials which he himself has already produced or reproduced that will be remembered in the future. Precisely why this should be so is unclear, but presumably some of the coding and processing that the individual must undertake with meaningful verbal materials in order to be able to produce them or to reproduce them on subsequent occasions has the effect of ensuring that those materials have a highly stable place in the cognitive structure of the individual's memory system. Whatever the detailed processes involved, the findings have practical implications, and possibly some broader implications for the matter of deciding upon the most profitable directions of educational research into human learning.

Concerning possible direct implications, it would appear that the not uncommon educational procedure by which a teacher, after providing instruction, administers a test to students and subsequently 'goes over' the test items and provides the correct answers, on the assumption that briefly informing a student what the correct answer should be in instances where he is wrong will help him to subsequently retain the correct version, is not in fact very likely to ensure this. The present experimental findings indicate that in instances where one's own version is incorrect, simply being told the right answer is quite insufficient to ensure its adequate retention and recall in the future. What seems to be needed is a more systematic procedure, whereby the student who has previously been incorrect is required to repeat his steps until he is successful at arriving at the correct answer for himself.

A broader apparent implication of these findings for research into adult learning is that we ought to pay rather more attention to learners' activities— the things they do in the course of learning and the strategies they adopt— and attend less exclusively to instructional variables and matters of presentation—the manner in which materials are made available. The present results are consistent with the view that those variables associated with learner activities are by far the more crucial ones.

FURTHER EXPERIMENTS

The above findings have prompted a number of subsequent experimental developments. First, we have undertaken experiments that examined the effects of repeated presentation and recall under slightly different circumstances. In one such experiment (Howe, 1972a) multiple-choice tests were used to measure recall. It was found that not only were correct test choices repeated from one session to the next, but that the probability of incorrect choices being repeated was also high, being around 0.7, compared with a chance probability of 0.33. This result appears to suggest that the individual coding necessary for stable retention of certain items is by no means entirely due to events taking place at the time of recall. It is more likely that some mental processing at a previous stage is also involved. Howe *et al.* (1974) undertook an experiment to investigate the suggestion that if learners not only listened to the repeated correct items, but also responded in an active manner by making a record in the form either of a dictated copy of the passage or a summary of it, there would be less repetition of errors from one session to the next and greater improvement. The findings were in accord with this suggestion.

The results of the initial experiment have also encouraged us to undertake a number of investigations into the phenomenon of retroactive interference, whereby it has been observed that learning tends to decrease when materials similar to those being acquired are interpolated between the original presentation of the items and subsequent tests assessing the individual's learning and retention. This phenomenon appears to be of some importance for a variety of learning situations, for example in education, where it would appear to indicate a necessity to avoid instructional circumstances in which highly similar materials are presented in close temporal contiguity. Yet the findings

of a number of experimental studies have appeared to suggest that the phenomenon occurs only when the materials to be learned are relatively unstructured
or lacking in meaning, and were this the case the practical significance of
retroactive interference would be relatively trivial.

The findings of our first experiment are consistent with the possibility that
retroactive interference might indeed be a force to be reckoned with in meaningful learning situations, especially in circumstances where material highly
similar to that being learned is not simply presented to the learner between
initial learning and subsequent testing of the original items, but is also actively
produced or reproduced by the learner. Accordingly, a number of experiments
were carried out. In the first one (Howe and Cavicchio, 1971) the original
material and the similar passage concerned alternative life-saving methods
used to induce breathing. No evidence of retroactive interference emerged in
the findings. But a later experiment involving fictional biographies that were
similar in form (Howe and Colley, 1976a) did yield evidence of a retroactive
interference effect, although this was small in magnitude despite a high degree
of similarity in the materials. It is conceivable that retroactive interference
effects, although present, may be insufficiently powerful to be of much practical
importance for learning in the circumstances of everyday life. However,
there might well exist some such effects which are important for certain kinds
of learning but which cannot readily be discerned in the necessarily short
learning sessions to which most controlled experimental research is confined.
This recent experiment yielded some further findings which indicated that what
learners acquired was strongly influenced by their expectancies or mental
sets, an observation which was confirmed and examined in detail in a subsequent study (Howe and Colley, 1976b).

NOTE-TAKING STUDIES

Another outcome of considering the findings of experimental research into
the effects of repeated presentation and recall of porse materials was that
we began to direct our attention to a common student activity, that of taking
notes. The research already described indicated that examining some procedures
and strategies adopted by learners might offer a promising direction for the
study of adult learning. From this point of view the activity of taking notes
seemed especially interesting, since it involved a state of affairs in which individuals were actively engaged not only in receiving information to be learned
but also in recording it. Doing so appeared to require some of the coding
practices in which we were interested. Accordingly we decided to investigate
note-taking activities, and we started by surveying relevant previous research
(Howe, 1972b; 1974; 1975). Since note-taking is an activity that is undertaken
very frequently by large numbers of learners, we were somewhat surprised to
find that previous scientific investigations had been relatively few in number,
and that the results of those that had been undertaken were not particularly
illuminating. Most published studies of note-taking have taken the form of
simple comparison experiments, whereby amount of learning is assessed follow-

ing circumstances that involve note-taking and alternative procedures or methods. Typically, the findings of such studies are that students learn no more and no less under conditions that incorporate the taking of notes than under broadly similar circumstances in which no note-taking is involved.

Studies of this type are probably unlikely to yield much detailed information about the mental processes that are involved in taking notes. One problem is that the assumption that note-taking constitutes a 'method' broadly comparable to alternative educational methods is not entirely correct. Secondly, investigations of this form fail to duplicate adequately closely the everyday circumstances involving note-taking, if only because they neglect to take into account the important fact that students do not merely *take* notes but also make subsequent use of them. The significance of notes to the learner may lie in the combined outcome of both note-taking and note-using activities.

We decided on an approach that involved asking what, if any, are the actual outcomes of taking notes that may have a direct bearing upon learning. A major function of taking notes, and in times prior to the modern introduction of cheap and convenient devices for obtaining copies of the printed word a perfectly sufficient justification for the practice, is simply to provide a record of certain information, albeit not necessarily a very accurate one (Hartley and Cameron, 1967). Apart from this, we considered three additional possibilities. The first is that note-taking contributes to a student's learning by helping him pay attention to the material being studied. This might apply both to lecture and to reading situations. There is little doubt that when individuals give close and sustained attention to what is to be learned, the degree of effectiveness tends to be high. It seemed quite likely that, at least for some people, taking notes would facilitate learning by preventing lapses in attention. Secondly, it appeared possible that the processing and coding required on the part of the learner for taking notes would result in a version of the material to be acquired that was clearer and more meaningful to the individual concerned than material prepared by another person. This suggestion clearly applies only to certain kinds of knowledge. There is little margin for personal interpretations, without introducing actual errors, when one is recording, say, chemical or mathematical formulae. However, at least in some areas of knowledge, the possible advantage of being able to produce a version of the information that makes clear sense within the individual's personal frame of reference appears real enough. The third possibility, closely related to the second, is that the processing on the part of the individual that is necessary in order to produce the notes makes a direct contribution to learning. In practice, evidence for each of the latter two suggestions is hard to disentangle, but the findings of the early experiment on repeated presentation and recall, whereby what learners remembered following each separate presentation was most strongly influenced by their own past performance, would appear to give support to either or both of them.

We have undertaken a number of experiments to investigate note-taking. Some of the findings have merely confirmed what we strongly suspected to be true: for example, that individuals do gain from being able to use their notes for revision purposes (Howe, 1970b). One experiment yielded results which give some support to the suggestion that note-taking does influence attentional behaviours. In this study (Howe, 1970d) the subjects, who were university students, were asked to listen to a prose passage and make notes on it. Subjects were told to keep their notes brief, using relatively few words, but to attempt to retain the important elements of the passage. After this session the participants were required to give their notes to the experimenter, and they had no opportunity to consult the notes during the week between the session and the subsequent recall test, on which occasion they were asked to write down whatever they could remember of the content of the original passage. Subsequently, attempts at recall were scored, the mean score being four meaningful items out of a possible 20. The next step was to compare the contents of each subject's notes with the contents of his own recall attempt. The average number of the meaningful units reproduced in the notes was 10.8, about half the items in the passage. Considering only the items that an individual subject had reproduced in his notes, the probability of any such item being present in his recall attempt one week later was 0.34, whilst the probability of an item that did not appear in his notes being recalled was only 0.05. In short, subjects were around seven times more likely to recall an item if they had previously written it down in their notes than if they had not. This huge difference in learning is most probably due to a number of factors, and the inclusion or exclusion of a particular item at the time of writing the notes may indicate a judgment about the relative importance of item in the passage that might influence the contents of both notes and recall. It does appear highly likely that attentional processes were involved, the contents of both notes and recall reflecting the direction of a subject's attention. It is possible that during the note-taking session, while individuals were taking notes on some items, the activity involved in their doing so prevented them from attending to other material that was currently being presented.

This experiment also yielded some data pertinent to the suggestion that the processing and coding activities that learners must carry out in the course of making notes may lead directly to learning. Inspecting the notes made by different individuals revealed considerable variation in the number of words written down, and the amount of meaningful information reproduced was by no means perfectly related to the number of words. It seemed reasonable to suggest that individual differences in the effectiveness of processing might be examined through computing, for each subject, the ratio obtained by dividing the number of meaningful items recorded in his notes by the number of words appearing in his notes. An individual for whom this ratio was high might be regarded as someone who was successful in conveying a relatively large amount of meaningful information economically, without wasting words. That individual would have needed to undertake certain coding processes in order to transform the information from the form in which it was presented into the version written down by himself.

The next step was to determine whether the values of this ratio achieved by different individuals were related to final recall. Are these note-takers who are 'efficient' in the sense of being economical in their use of words the individuals who also remember most accurately? In fact we did find that there was a positive correlation, modest in size ($+ 0.53$) but statistically significant. Thus it appears quite possible that the mental processes that are involved in note-taking may indeed have some direct influence upon human learning. Of course, the present result does not provide proof that some individuals learn more than others *because* they use a note-taking strategy that involves certain coding processes and economizes on words. Nevertheless, the fact that performance and strategy are correlated indicates a high probability that learning is influenced by the processes involved in note-taking strategies.

Over the past two years Jean Godfrey and myself have been undertaking some further studies of note-taking, financed by the Leverhulme Trust Fund. Our initial studies were prompted by a desire for more knowledge about the kinds of notes students make in everyday circumstances. We asked a number of students, in separate courses, to lend us the notes they had taken from two lectures. We also obtained transcripts of the lectures. A number of detailed analyses of the notes were undertaken, and we encountered considerable variation in the length, form and organization of the notes, and in the use of practices such as making abbreviations. However, we did not find any clear, systematic relationships between length and form of the notes, on the one hand, and, on the other, performance in tests that assessed learning of the lecture contents. (The tests were administered before we asked the students to let us see their notes, so there was no awareness of being in an 'experimental' situation.) Most of the notes we examined did provide a fairly accurate record of the main points of the lecture, but we noticed that particular events in the lecture strongly influenced the notes' contents. For instance, anything at all that was written on the board by the lecturer, however trivial, was likely to appear in most students' notes. Also, it not infrequently happened that a negative statement uttered by the lecturer appeared in a student's notes without the negative.

Our next study was designed to investigate whether there are major differences between notes taken from materials presented by ear, as in lectures, and notes made from printed materials. Investigators in this field have seemed to take it for granted that the two forms are equivalent, in the absence of any real evidence for such an assumption. In fact, our findings did indicate an absence of systematic differences between notes taken under the two kinds of circumstances. Length of notes made, their form and manner of setting out and the use of abbreviations were roughly equivalent, except that the temporal constraints imposed by auditory presentation had some effect in limiting the variability of contents.

In another group of studies we investigated the effects of writing notes under headings. Students listened to 24 sentences relating to a fictional country. Some of them were told to arrange three of the sentences under each of eight categories. All subjects received a revision period, and it was found that those individuals instructed to make use of categories recalled more information than the other subjects. However, it was not clear whether this difference was due to the act of categorizing which took place during note-taking, or to the facility of being able to revise from a categorized form of the material, or to both. The second or third possibilities are indicated by the findings of a further experiment, in which no revision period was allowed. No difference in recall was observed between students who wrote their notes under category headings and those who did not.

Some further studies have involved the manipulation of the number of words written down by note-takers. For example, we found that there were no recall differences between individuals who were required to attempt to write down the whole of a prose passage and subjects who wrote down only the three words in each sentence they considered to be the most important. However, it was observed that those who managed to choose words most appropriate to answering the recall test questions were more successful in the test. We also examined practices such as underlining, and making use of headings. Underlining did not help the students in our study, but the artificially short prose materials we used (250 words) may have been a contributing factor. Crouse and Idstein (1972) found that underlining had an appreciable effect when learners studied a 6,000-word passage.

A final series of note-taking experiments varied both the forms of note-taking activities that students were required to undertake and the kinds of revision facilities that were made available. One interesting finding has been that the effect of allowing subjects to revise from a carefully organized version of the somewhat rambling material to which they had previously listened and taken notes from was related to their previous level of success at recalling the material a few minutes after the original presentation. Students whose recall at this stage was above average were not helped by being given the highly organized version for revision purposes, and they performed just as well at a later test of long-term retention if they had made use of their own notes for revision. However, students who performed poorly at the initial test were considerably aided by being given the opportunity to revise with the organized version, and their level of performance in the long-term recall test was above that attained on the initial test. Contrary to expectations, presentation of the organized version of the material did not interfere with retention, and subjects in the group who were able to revise with this version did not fail to recall in the later test more of the items recalled previously than students who revised from their own notes.

The finding that the effectiveness of a given procedure in a situation involving the measurement of learning following note-taking varies in a manner consistently related to previous learning performance is one which deserves notice in future research. It is always wise to bear in mind the possibility that the effects of any procedure to help learning will depend to a marked extent on the characteristics of the individual learner.

PRESENTATION VARIABLES AND SUBJECT ACTIVITIES

The findings of the experiment on repeated presentation and recall suggested that the form and nature of activities undertaken by the individual in the course of learning were of importance and deserved close attention. In the past few years increased attention has been paid in a number of ways to the effects of several kinds of learner activities. One result of this attention has been the research into mnemonics and related strategies surveyed by Peter Morris in Chapter 7. Another aim of research has been to investigate organizational processes. Research into relatively simple forms of verbal learning, notably by Mandler (e.g. 1968) and Tulving (1966) (reviewed by Howe, 1970a), has led to the investigation of increasingly complex kinds of organizing activities on the part of learners (see Bower, 1970, for a good review).

In our research we decided to start by investigating the effects of some relatively simple learner activities on learning from prose under circumstances that, while adequately controlled for experimental purposes, were also reasonably close to those in which the acquisition of knowledge by students customarily takes place. We commenced with the plausible (but I now think incorrect) assumption that the amount of learning that occurs on a given occasion is directly related to the depth of mental processing that is undertaken by the learner in the course of dealing with the task that confronts him. Some of the findings of the study by Howe et al. (1974) where subjects had to make copies of prose information to which they were listening encouraged us to undertake a further study (Howe and Singer, 1975) comparing the effects of alternative learner activities upon the acquisition of prose knowledge. Eighty-six undergraduates participated as subjects in the first experiment and they all received 10 minutes in which to read a 286-word extract from a New Scientist article concerning the use of cloud-seeding procedures in order to control the weather. This particular choice of materials resulted from the search for learning matter which resembled in difficulty and degree of abstraction the educational materials to which university students are normally exposed, but which was relatively unfamiliar, so that variability between individuals in previous knowledge of the content would be minimal. On the first of two sessions, one week apart, each subject was allocated at random to one of three experimental groups, on the basis of which he was handed a booklet containing instructions appropriate to the group in which he had been placed, containing a typed version of the prose passage, together with the experimental instructions appropriate to his group. One group was instructed merely to read the material, giving any surplus time to rereading. Subjects in the second group were told to use the 10-minute period for copying the passage, word for word. The third group were told to make a summary of each paragraph in the passage. Subjects were warned in advance that they might be asked to recall the material, and in fact two tests were administered, the first of them immediately following the 10-minute study period and the second a week later.

On the basis of previous findings we had fairly confidently predicted that those individuals who were required to undertake the greatest amount of active processing, namely those who made the summaries, would perform best, followed by those who copied, an activity considered to be less demanding of deeper levels of mental activity, with the subjects who merely read the material performing worst. We were somewhat taken aback to discover that our predictions were entirely wrong. The mean number of meaningful segments recalled (out of a possible 25) on the immediate test by the subjects who simply read the passage was 16.3. The group who recorded the passage by copying it averaged 10.3 items, and the mean score obtained by subjects in the group instructed to make summaries was 13.4. Analysis of variance showed the overall condition effect to be statistically significant. The scores of the readers were significantly higher than those of the subjects who made summaries, and these in turn were significantly higher than those obtained by the students who copied. The long-term retention test scores show substantially the same pattern of results. A number of more detailed analyses were undertaken. For example, a check was made to examine the possibility that results were influenced by the fact that some of the subjects who made copies and did not quite finish within the 10 minutes allotted to them might not have been exposed to all the material. Comparison of performance by these individuals in the early and later parts of the passage indicated that the experimental results were not substantially affected by this factor.

Why did the findings of this experiment differ so strikingly from our expectations? When we thought further about the condition in which subjects were required only to read the passage, asking why subjects should perform well under these circumstances, it struck us that this was the condition which allowed learners the greatest amount of freedom of action to pace their learning activities to suit themselves, taking extra time over whatever they found difficult, skipping whatever seemed obvious or unimportant, and generally following the procedures and learning strategies they perferred to use. Subjects in the other two conditions had far less freedom, the task requirements constraining their activities fairly rigidly. It has to be remembered that the undergraduates participating in this experiment form a fairly sophisticated and experienced group insofar as learning or acquiring knowledge presented in prose form is concerned. Perhaps one ought to expect that such students would have acquired considerable expertise in pacing learning effectively and choosing appropriate strategies and procedures. The procedures chosen by these students might well be more appropriate than was the somewhat inflexible regimen of activities prescribed by the experimenter.

We decided to carry out one further experiment. One factor influencing its design was our observation that the recent pattern of results differed rather sharply from that obtained in the experiments by Howe et al. (1974), in which the experimental conditions had seemed to us to be very similar. One difference between the two investigations was that the earlier experiment used auditory presentation, whereas subjects in the study by Howe and Singer (1975) read the material, which was made available to them in written form. We had assumed this procedural difference to be unimportant, but further reflection suggested that possibly we were wrong to do so. When subjects listen to prose materials, a certain degree of constraint is imposed by the pacing of the presentation. Under such circumstances instructions to undertake activities such as copying are unlikely to impose any greatly increased limitations on individuals' freedom of action in dealing with the task material. However, when the materials are presented in printed form, to be read by learners, instructions to copy or to make summaries do clearly impose considerable restrictions upon the participants. Thus the effects of experimenter-imposed activities upon learning might indeed differ according to the mode of presentation being used.

In our next experiment (Howe and Singer, 1975, Experiment Two), we varied both the mode of presentation and the activities that learners were required to undertake. It will be recalled that one of the characteristics of our research was what we considered to be a necessary shift from emphasis upon attending to conditions of presentation, that is the procedures controlled by the experimenter or instructor, towards placing greater emphasis on the activities of the learner. In giving increased attention to the learner's role we had tended to neglect the role of presentation variables. In fact, rather than assuming that one or the other of these two variables is most crucial, it might well be more realistic to expect that their effects will exert an influence in an interactive manner, not entirely discernible from the results of studies in which one of them is varied at a time. The learner activity that is most effective under one condition of presentation may be less effective than alternative procedures when a different kind of presentation is adopted. Therefore we decided to vary both of these two factors in the following experiment.

The experimental subjects were 96 university students, and each was assigned at random to one of six experimental conditions. The material to be learned was the passage used in the previous study. The two independent variables were presentation method and subject activity. Presentation took one of three forms: A, a typed version of the passage, which each subject read on his own; B, auditory presentation at dictation speed; and C, auditory presentation three times at a normal speaking rate. With each form of presentation the total time during which subjects were exposed to the passage was 12 minutes.

The second independent variable, subject activity, took two forms: X, recording the content of the passage by writing down a copy of it, and Y, making no overt response at all. Thus there was in all a total of six conditions, as follows:

AX read and record (copy)
AY read
BX listen to presentation at dictation speed and record
BY listen to presentation at dictation speed
CX listen to presentation at normal speaking rate (three times) and record
CY listen to presentation at normal speaking rate (three times)
All subjects were asked to give close attention to the subject matter, and

they were told that they would later be required to recall the passage contents. Immediately following the presentation period subjects were given a verbal reasoning task, lasting seven minutes. Since it has been shown that tasks of this nature interfere with short-term memory (Howe, 1970a), it is possible to be reasonably sure that recall tests that are attempted subsequently to the administration of such tasks measure relatively stable retention, rather than short-term memory, and provide a reliable indication of the degree of learning that would be retained over longer periods of time.

The main findings are shown below. The scores indicate the number of meaningful units that were correctly reproduced, out of a possible 25.

AX read and record	14.7
AY read	18.5
BX listen at dictation speed and record	13.3
BY listen at dictation speed	12.6
CX listen at normal speaking rate and record	8.7
CY listen at normal speaking rate	17.6

Analysis of variance showed the effects of each of the main variables to be statistically significant. The Neuman–Keuls test was applied to assess the statistical significance of the differences between the individual mean scores. Among the 15 pairs all were significantly different or beyond the 0.05 level except AY and CY, AX and CY, AX and BX, AX and BY, and BX and BY.

Inspection of the mean scores shows that subjects' activities do strongly influence learning but that the manner and extent of their influence depends considerably upon the conditions of presentation. Thus, with written presentation, subjects who simply read the passage performed better than those required to make copies, repeating the finding of the previous experiment. The scores of the readers who made no active response were, indeed, higher than those obtained by subjects allocated to any of the other conditions. However, when presentation was auditory and at dictation speed, subjects who simply listened to the materials performed no better (and non-significantly worse) than those who were required to copy the passage. For the two conditions in which subjects listened to the passage at a normal rate of presentation, those who had to listen gained scores that were as much as twice as high as those obtained by the individuals who had to record the material.

Just as the effects of the alternative subject activities varied according to the form of presentation, it was also found that the effects of the different presentation modes depended upon the activities in which subjects were required to engage. With auditory presentation at dictation speed, for example, recall levels did not differ from those obtained following written presentation, under circumstances where subjects had to copy the information, but written presentation was superior when no copying activity was required. Yet when we compare written presentation with auditory presentation at a normal speaking rate we find that whereas following written presentation subjects required to make copies performed better than the others, no difference in learning was found between these two forms of presentation among the non-copiers.

On the whole, the pattern of results confirmed the suggestion that under conditions of presentation that permit the mature and relatively successful learner considerable latitude to direct his energies in whatever manner he decides will best suit his needs and to engage in those strategies he considers to be most appropriate, subjects tend to learn most when there is no requirement to conform to constraints imposed in an activity directed by the experimenter. But in those circumstances where conditions of presentation do seriously constrain students' strategies, as is most clearly the case with auditory presentation at dictation speed, the additional requirement to copy the passage does not appreciably increase the degree of constraint, and performance does not diminish.

A naive question not infrequently asked is whether students learn more under conditions of written or auditory presentation. In the particular conditions of the present experiment, it is interesting to observe that a difference between the two emerges only in those circumstances where individuals not only had to attend to the material but were also required to engage in copying activities.

One might expect that subjects would perform poorly under those conditions in which the manner of presentation and the required subjects' activities are least compatible. This was indeed the case. The two least compatible combinations, that is, listening without making any response to the passage presented at dictation speed (BY) and attempting to record material presented three times at a normal speaking rate (CX), where the ones in which the lowest average scores were obtained. It can also be noted that this latter condition (CX), which parallels the condition of the Howe et al. (1974) experiment in which the lowest scores were obtained, is the one which most closely approximates the everyday learning conditions in which students take notes as they listen to a lecture. If methods of learning used in higher education were decided upon by the principle of natural selection, it seems dubious whether present lecture methods could long survive. (See Chapter 13 for a fuller discussion of this and related issues.)

The sheer magnitude of the differences found in learning under the varying conditions of the present experiment is worthy of notice. In all conditions subjects were exposed to identical information for an identical total amount of time. Yet retention scores differed very considerably, by a factor of up to two to one. These differences in level performance are by no means trivial, and sufficiently large to merit attention on the part of those who are interested in trying to arrange circumstances under which adult learners can acquire knowledge as efficiently as possible.

In giving this account of a series of experimental studies by one group of researchers, I have attempted to convey something of the continuity that accompanies and guides research endeavours. One thing leads to another. Experimental findings sometimes provide the solutions to problems, but they equally often encourage us to rephrase our questions and reexamine our assumptions. Understanding of the processes of human learning that enter into the acquisition of knowledge is at a relatively crude stage, but, as I believe is indicated by the experimental research described here, we have some awareness of the manner in which individuals' study activities contribute to their performance as learners.

REFERENCES

Bartlett, F. C. (1932). *Remembering*, Cambridge University Press, London.

Bower, G. H. (1970). 'Organizational factors in memory', *Cognitive Psychology*, **1**, 18.

Crouse, J. H., and Idstein, P. (1972). 'Effects of encoding cues on prose learning', *Journal of Educational Psychology*, **63**, 309.

Hartley, J., and Cameron, A. (1967). 'Some observations on the efficacy of lecturing', *Educational Review*, **20**, 30.

Howe, M. J. A. (1970a). *Introduction to Human Memory*, Harper & Row, New York.

Howe, M. J. A. (1970b). 'Note-taking strategy, review, and long-term retention of verbal information', *Journal of Educational Research*, **63**, 100.

Howe, M. J. A. (1970c). 'Repeated presentation and recall of meaningful prose', *Journal of Educational Psychology*, **61**, 214.

Howe, M. J. A. (1970d). 'Using students' notes to examine the role of the individual learner in acquiring meaningful subject matter', *Journal of Educational Research*, **64**, 61.

Howe, M. J. A. (1972a). 'Repeated presentation and retention of meaningful information', *Psychological Reports*, **31**, 840.

Howe, M. J. A. (1972b). *Understanding School Learning: A New Look at Educational Psychology*, Harper & Row, New York.

Howe, M. J. A. (1974). 'The utility of taking notes as an aid to learning', *Educational Research*, **16**, 222.

Howe, M. J. A. (1975). 'Taking notes and human learning', *Bulletin of the British Psychological Society*, **28**, 158.

Howe, M. J. A., and Cavicchio, P. M. (1971). 'Retroactive interference in a meaningful learning task', *Alberta Journal of Educational Research*, **17**, 19.

Howe, M.J.A., and Colley, L. (1976a). 'Retroactive interference in meaningful learning', *British Journal of Educational Psychology*, **46**, 26.

Howe, M. J. A., and Colley, L. (1976b). 'The influence of questions encountered earlier on learning from prose', *British Journal of Educational Psychology*, **46**.

Howe, M. J. A., Ormond, V., and Singer, L. (1974). 'Recording activities and the recall of information', *Perceptual and Motor Skills*, **39**, 309

Howe, M. J. A., and Singer, L. (1975). 'Presentation variables and students' activities in meaningful learning', *British Journal of Educational Psychology*, **45**, 52.

Kay, H. (1955). 'Learning and retaining verbal material', *British Journal of Psychology*, **44**, 81.

Mandler, G. (1968). 'Organization and memory', in K. W. Spence and J. T. Spence (Eds.), *The Psychology of Learning and Motivation*, Vol. II, Academic Press, New York.

Tulving, E. (1966). 'Subjective organization and effects of repetition in multi-trial free-recall learning', *Journal of Verbal Learning and Verbal Behavior*, **5**, 193.

9

PROGRAMMED LEARNING AND EDUCATIONAL TECHNOLOGY

James Hartley and Ivor K. Davies

The aim of this chapter is to give a brief account of the development of self-instructional techniques that are generally classified under the title of programmed learning and educational technology. Our aim is not to talk about machinery and equipment (the usual meaning attached to the term educational technology) but to discuss some underlying questions being asked by researchers in this area.

Two basic questions for the reader to bear in mind throughout this chapter are:

(i) How can instruction be adapted to make it appropriate for each individual learner? and

(ii) How can the quality of instruction be best improved?

It will become apparent that the machinery (and its development) reflect different answers to these questions.

EARLY APPROACHES TO PROGRAMMED LEARNING

S. L. Pressey

Machines and devices to aid teaching and learning have been around for as long as there has been recorded history. The quintain, for instance, was a device used in the Middle Ages to assist knights develop their skills at jousting. It is conventional, nonetheless, to begin a historical discussion of programmed learning with the work of Sydney Pressey in the 1920's. Pressey is accorded first place in the annals of programmed instruction because he was one of the first psychologists to embody the laws of learning—as they were then formulated—into instructional devices. The modern objective test procedure—which was being developed at that time—suggested to Pressey the building of a simple scoring device which could test a learner's achievement after he had been taught something (Pressey, 1926). Pressey, in fact, developed a series of

161

mechanical devices which presented multiple-choice questions to learners and which gave them immediate knowledge about the correctness (or not) of their choice of answer.

These early mechanical devices, which looked rather like crude versions of present-day hand calculators, were later replaced with other more simple devices which basically had the same function (e.g. punch-boards and chemocards). These devices are still in use today. A learner using a punch-board, for instance, studies some material (for e.g. a textbook) in a conventional way; he is then provided with a set of test questions with possible alternative answers for each question, only one of which is correct, and with a board punched with a set of holes to match the choice of alternative answers. For each question the learner responds by pushing a stylus into the hole corresponding to the answer he wishes to choose. A concealed template allows the stylus to pass through only if the right answer is chosen, so the learner knows immediately if his answer is correct or not, and he can try again if he is wrong.

It is important to note here that Pressey's devices are used *after* instruction: that is, they are *testing* rather than teaching devices. Pressey called this 'adjunct programming', by which he meant the use of test questions or programs to test and consolidate achievement *after* conventional instruction. A particualr advantage of adjunct programming is that material can be prepared relatively easily and quickly, and that it can make use of the textbooks and material already available to the student and teacher. Figure 9.1 illustrates an extract from an adjunct program.

---

36. Identical twins are used as subjects in studies of the role of environment in the development of ability because such persons have the same . . . .

A.	environment	C.	development	B
B.	heredity	D.	discernment	

---

37. Newman *et al.* (1937) found that measures of height for identical twins reared together had a correlation coefficient of .98 and identical twins reared separately had a correlation coefficient of .97. Hence the effect on height of being reared apart is . . . .

A.	inverse	C.	significant	B
B.	meaningless	D.	slight	

---

38. Newman also found that the achievement test scores for identical twins reared together showed a correlation of .96: for identical twins reared apart it was .51. The difference is . . . .

A.	inverse	C.	significant	C
B.	meaningless	D.	slight	

---

39. Intelligence test score correlations were found by Newman to be .96 for identical twins reared together, .67 for those reared apart. This tends to emphasise the importance of . . . in the development of intelligence.

A.	weight	C.	heredity	D
B.	height	D.	environment	

Figure 9.1 An extract from an undergraduate adjunct program (Bell *et al.*, 1964) to accompany a chapter on psychological testing in a standard textbook

B. F. Skinner

Professor B. F. Skinner, of Harvard, has often been called 'the father of programmed learning', despite the fact that there were many earlier attempts to automate teaching. The title of 'father' seems to have been accorded to him beacuse of his enormous influence in this field, and possibly because his views are the most widespread (and the most controversial) of all the figures to be discussed. It is interesting to observe at this point that Skinner's interest in education arose because of his frustration with conventional teaching methods (Skinner, 1954).

In 1954 Skinner delivered in Pittsburg a now famous address entitled 'The Science of Learning and the Art of Teaching'. In this paper Skinner analysed what for him were some of the basic limitations of the American educational scene at that time, and his answers to them. He argued that in a conventional classroom situation there were four major limitations.

(i) Educational control was mainly aversive. The student learned in order to escape from negative evaluations, threats and punishments.

(ii) There was a lack of skilful programs which moved the learners forward through a series of progressive or successive approximations to the final complex behaviour required.

(iii) The contingencies of reinforcement were far from optimal. This meant that it was not physically possible for one teacher to reinforce each student in a class of, say, 40 students each time a correct response was made.

(iv) Reinforcement was relatively infrequent. This was seen as the most serious failing of current instruction and of designs for learning. (By reinforcement, Skinner meant providing some event or stimulus that served to strengthen behaviour. In other words, reinforcement makes that behaviour's reoccurrence more probable.)

Skinner's answer to these problems was to set up situations which prevented their occurrence.

The linear teaching program (and the associated linear teaching machine) represent Professor Skinner's solution to the problem of capitalizing on a science of learning. An example from a linear program is shown in Figure 9.2. In it are demonstrated the principles that Skinner was aiming at.

(i) Educational control is not aversive. Learners learn because they want to, under no threat of punishment or failure.

(ii) There is a skilful program which moves the learner one step at a time from simple to more complex behaviour.

(iii) The contingencies of reinforcement are (in Skinner's terms) optimal— learners work at their own pace and receive reinforcement as soon as they make a response.

(iv) The reinforcement for correct responding (in the form of the feedback given for each response made) is frequent.

A further principle, which Skinner did not stress at the time, was that the teaching program itself should have first been tried out and tested, in order to

	A second important condition for efficient learning is the presentation of subject matter in a series of *small logical* steps. The learner must master Step A before he can grasp——B. 20
Step 20	An ancient Greek fable tells us that Milo was able to lift his full-grown bull because he had lifted it daily since it was a calf. Since the animal had *small* increases in weight daily, Milo's weight-lifting 'program' progressed through a series of many——steps. 21
small 21	Unfortunately, under usual classroom conditions it is difficult for the instructor to present subject matter in steps which are sufficiently——in size. 22
small 22	A later item in this program—to which you probably cannot yet respond correctly—reads 'Another condition is that each response is followed by . . .'. That item is a large step beyond the present one. However, after being led through many——steps, you will later be able to—— correctly. 23
small respond 23	This program may seem annoyingly simple. But the merit of a step-by-step presentation of subject matter is shown by the fact that you have made few, if any, incorrect——to the statements or stimuli of this program. 24
responses 24	

Figure 9.2 An extract from *Programmed Instruction: What it is and How it Works*, Milton and West (1961). Copyright © 1961 by Harcourt Brace Jovanovich, Inc., and reproduced with their permission

see if in fact it worked. If it did not do so, it had to be revised until it did.

Several machines have been constructed with the purpose of giving individual learners step-by-step self-paced reinforcement. Inspection of the written material, however, shows that it is the writing of the program rather than the mechanical presentation that provides the difficulties, for the subject matter to be taught requires painstaking analysis. The machines, by contrast, are often little more than boxes containing some form of paper-roll device.

Machines, nonetheless, help control the learning process. Machines ensure that items are presented individually, that the learner cannot move on until he has made a response, that the correct answer is not available until the learner has made his own, and that the learner works through the program in the way intended by the author. Furthermore, a machine format can be intrinsically motivating: most people enjoy pressing buttons, and the bulk of what has to be learned can be hidden so that learners do not feel that the size of the task is beyond them. These advantages of machine-presented programmed learning are not present to the same extent in the (nowadays) more common textbook presentations.

N. Crowder

There have been many objections to linear programs—not least that 'over-programmed' texts provide a boring and a monotonous way of learning—and the principles of programmed learning outlined by Skinner have been subjected to much research and criticism (e.g. see Hartley, 1974).

In the early days Norman Crowder was often presented as a challenger to Skinner's theories—as indeed he was—but it is important to note that originally Crowder's work was being carried out independently of Skinner's. Crowder was not particularly interested in theories of learning: he was interested in whether or not material was communicated successfully (Crowder, 1960). In a Crowder-type program a learner is usually presented with a paragraph of information, and is then asked a question about it. With the question a number of alternative responses or answers are supplied, only one of which is correct. In the machine system the learner is then asked to press a button which indicates which response he has chosen. The program moves on. If the learner is correct, the next item tells why, and then gives fresh information. If, however, an error has been made, the nature of the error is explained, and the learner is directed back to the initial question. If it is a serious error, the learner may be sent along a special remedial subsequence. A machine currently available using this technique is the Autotutor, and, of course, textbook presentations of the same material are also available, although they can be very bulky. A typical item from such a program is shown in Figure 9.3.

This kind of programming is often called the 'branching' system, to contrast it with Skinner's 'linear' one, and its advantages are that it allows more for individual differences in knowledge and compreshension. However, it is important to note that Crowder aims at an 85 per cent correct response rate for his main sequence items; thus, there is less branching for the student than is usually believed. An important theoretical difference between the two systems, however, is that Crowder uses the response to control the behaviour of the teaching machine, rather than to provide reinforcement to the learner. Nevertheless, in practice, there may be less difference in this respect than is generally thought, as the student always receives knowledge of results. The fact that larger items of information are presented at a time, however, makes Crowder-type programs more suitable for older and for more intelligent learners. In many ways, the techniques of branching programs are particularly suitable for dealing with subject material involving complex probelm-solving strategies which can be systematically developed stage by stage.

The 'Late-Developers'

At this point it is convenient to introduce three different approaches to programmed learning, approaches which, although contemporary with Skinner and Crowder, were rather overshadowed by them. These approaches have now blossomed forth, and have more importance today than they had in their formative years.

YOUR ANSWER: 5 amperes.

Correct. With a voltage of 100 and a resistance of 20 ohms we apply Ohm's Law, $I = E/R$, to get a current of $100/20 = 5$ amps.

This is a simple circuit and it can be shown as the diagram at left:

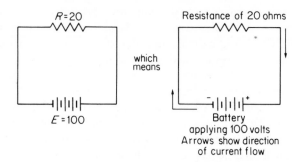

And this should look familiar by now. Remember the formula for calculating watts, $P = EI$? Given any two quantities, you can solve for the unknown.

The same is true for Ohm's Law. If you know voltage and current, you can find resistance. If you know resistance and current, you can find voltage. If you know voltage and resistance, you can find current.

How?

If $I = E/R$, then $E = I/R$ and $R = EI$. page 49
If $I = E/R$, then $E = IR$ and $R = E/I$. page 52
If $I = E/R$, then $E = IR$ and $R = I/E$. page 55
If $I = E/R$, then I don't know what comes next. page 61

Figure 9.3 A typical frame from a branching program on electronics (Hughes and Pipe, 1961). Copyright 1961. Reproduced by permission of The English Universities Press Ltd., and Doubleday & Co.

R. F. Mager

The first of these systems to be discussed is that developed by Robert F. Mager, and is called 'learner-controlled instruction'. Mager, working in the context of industrial training, put forward the novel thesis—in this context— that the learner rather than the instructor should control the sequencing of topics to be learned. Mager let the students know that they could ask any questions they wished about a topic they wished to study (e.g. electronics) and he then let them get on with it, using the instructor as a resource person (Mager, 1961).

In essence, such learner-generated sequences tend to differ from traditional teaching sequences in a number of important ways.

(i) Initial student interest tends to be in the concrete rather than in the abstract, in things rather than in theory, in *how?* rather than in *why?*. For instance, whilst instructor-generated sequences in electronics usually begin with magnetism or electron theory, student-generated sequences typically begin with the vacuum tube.

(ii) Students tend to show interest in function before structure. In electronics, they tend to want explanations of what *happens* to generate a picture on a TV screen before they tackle the question of what *causes* the electron beam to be moved back and forth.

(iii) Students tend to proceed from a simple *whole* to a more complex whole. For instance, they will ask questions about how radio works before asking questions specifically about what makes it work; teachers, on the other hand, tend to proceed from the simple part to the more complex whole.

Mager and his colleagues showed that student-generated sequences were very different from instructor-generated ones, although they can have some commonality. The important thing, however, is to design instructional programs based on *student-* rather than teacher-generated sequences.

T. F. Gilbert

A second system of programming that has developed in potency as the years have passed has been that developed by Thomas Gilbert and his associates, called 'mathetics'. (The word mathetics is not a coined word, but is derived from the Greek word *mathein*, which means to learn.) Gilbert's approach is similar to that of Skinner's in that his programs are linear in format. However, Gilbert focuses more on what program writers do in constructing their programs than the others—who tend to stress more the learner's viewpoint. Gilbert stresses student motivation and the feeling of mastery, or accomplishment, and tends to use much larger steps than Skinner advocated. Also, like Mager, Gilbert first makes clear to the student what is the end goal of the instruction.

The most important difference, however, between mathetics and any of the approaches so far described is, as already noted, that mathetics is a prescriptive rather than a descriptive process. That is, Gilbert not only describes (like Skinner, Crowder and others) principles for producing effective instruction, but he also has produced a prescription—a systematic methodology—which enables people to put these principles into practice (Gilbert, 1962). In theory different individuals attempting to teach a topic using the procedures of mathetics should end up with recognizably similar sequences and materials. This methodology, however, has an extremely complex terminology, and the system is not easy to explain. However, putting it briefly, a matheticist sees the basic problems of program writing as (i) determining what steps a student must take in order to master a subject, (ii) arranging the conditions so as to ensure that the student will take these steps (i.e. how can a student be motivated and reinforced), and (iii) instructing the student in such a way that mastery is achieved as quickly as possible. Davies (1969; 1972) provides more complete and technical accounts, where it will be seen that the whole emphasis of mathetics is based upon the problems of design.

Gordon Pask

It would be invidious, in an article on programmed learning, not to mention the work of Gordon Pask, although it seems a little hard to classify him as a 'late developer'. Pask, working in quite a different tradition and field of expertise, has made a consistently stimulating contribution to the field of programmed learning since the 1950's, and his early papers are now more easily understood than when they were first presented (see Pask, 1960). Initially the contribution of Pask was more applicable to the design of machinery for the teaching of manual skills than to the more verbal areas of learning traditionally associated with programmed materials. In particular his name was associated with the idea of 'adaptive instruction'—speeding the instruction up, or slowing it down in accordance with difficulties experienced by the learner (see Lewis, 1963). Pask's more complex theorizing and his rejection of the Skinnerian paradigm has in fact made his approach more suited to computer-assisted learning, where his major contributions now occur (Pask, 1975a, b). Today Pask is making contributions to the field of task analysis (Pask, 1976a) and to the study of individual differences between learners (Pask, 1976b).

COMPARISON STUDIES

Considerable research effort was spent in the 1950's and 1960's making comparison studies between the different systems of programming discussed above, and, of course, between programmed instruction (of whatever kind) on the one hand and conventional instruction (whatever that is) on the other. Because the results of specific comparisons were not generalizable, Hartley (1966) pooled the results of 112 such studies to see if any generalizations did emerge. The results were as summarized in Table 9.1.

These results speak clearly for themselves: there is evidence that programmed instruction can be as effective as, or better than, conventional instruction in some cases. Perhaps of more interest, however, are the findings of comparison studies in which an instructor with a program has been compared with an instructor alone or a program alone. Of 12 studies known to the writers, 11 have concluded that the instructor plus the program is the better system (Hartley, 1972).

Table 9.1. The results of 112 Students Comparing Programmed with Conventional Instruction

Measures recorded	Number of studies recording these measures	Programmed instruction group		
		Significantly superior	Not significantly different	Significantly worse
Time taken	90	47	37	6
Test results	110	41	54	15
Retest results	33	6	24	3

Note: Figures in the first column differ because not all three measures are recorded for every one of the 112 studies.

Table 9.2. Some Cost Benefits of Programmed Instruction in Industrial Contexts

Investigators	Cost of program	Cost of conventional instruction	Estimated savings
American Bankers Association Ofiesh, 1965	—	—	20%–50% of training time
American Telephone and Telegraph Co. (Ofiesh, 1965)	$218 per student hour	$309 per student hour	29% of instruction 27% of trainee time
Union Carbide Chemicals Co. Ofiesh, 1965	—	—	$90,000 in training to date ($30/man.)
Holme and Mabbs (1967)	£1,500	£1,500	£1,500 per yr.
Hall and Fletcher (1967)	£20,000	—	I week's trainee time Approx. £10,000 per yr.
Oates and Robinson (1968)	£12,500	—	8.2% of training time £24,700 after 2 yrs.
Watson (1968)	—	—	3 hrs per supervisor $90,000 per course
Mills (1968)	£550	—	£1,275 annually
Howe (1969)	£13,500	—	£1,000 for every 3 courses
Jones and Moxham (1969)	—	—	10 weeks' trainee time. Labour turnover reduced from 70% to 30%. Retention of skilled labour

The results described above have been obtained mainly from studies using primary and secondary schoolchildren. A series of industrial studies which used cost-effectiveness as a measure were summarized by Hartley (1972). These results are shown in Table 9.2.

Representative studies which have concentrated specifically on adults and older persons are described by Stewart and Chown (1965), Taylor and Reid (1965), Dodd (1967), Neale et al (1968), Jamieson (1969), Green (1970), Evans (1975) and Mackie (1975). These studies all suggest that there is no simple method which can be called programmed learning which is appropriate for everyone at a given age doing a given task. Two conclusions that can be drawn, though, are that older learners probably like to work with programs for longer sessions than do younger ones, and that the more activity that is built into the program, the better. There is also some avidence that older learners prefer a more discovery-orientated approach than a didactic 'telling' approach (Belbin, 1965). A summary of how some of the difficulties found by older learners

Table 9.3. Problems of Learning for the Adult which Increase with Age, and some Suggested Remedies. Table from Newsham (1969). Reproduced with the Permission of the Controller of Her Majesty's Stationery Office

1. When tasks involve the need for short-term memory
   (a) Avoid verbal learning and the need for conscious memorising. This may often be accomplished by making use of 'cues' which guide the trainee.
   (b) When possible, use a method which involves learning a task as a whole. If it has to be learned in parts, these parts should be learned in cumulative stages ($a, a + b, a + b + c$, and so on).
   (c) Ensure consolidation of learning before passing on to the next task or to the next part of the same task (importance of self-testing and checking).

2. When there is 'interference' from other activities or from other learning
   (a) Restrict the range of activities covered in the course.
   (b) Employ longer learning sessions than is customary for younger trainees (i.e. not necessarily a longer overall time, but longer periods without interruption).
   (c) To provide variety, change the method of teaching rather than the content of the course. A change of subject matter may lead to confusion between the subjects.

3. When there is need to translate information from one medium to another
   (a) Avoid the use of visual aids which necessitate a change of logic or a change in the plane of presentation.
   (b) If simulators or training devices are to be used, then they must be designed to enable learning to be directly related to practice.

4. When learning is abstract or unrelated to realities
   (a) Present new knowledge only as a solution to a problem which is already appreciated.

5. When there is need to 'un-learn' something for which the older learner has a predilection
   (a) Ensure 'correct' learning in the first place. This can be accomplished by designing the training around tasks of graduated difficulty.

6. When tasks are 'paced'
   (a) Allow the older learner to proceed at his own pace.
   (b) Allow him to structure his own programme within certain defined limits.
   (c) Aim at his beating his own targets rather than those of others.

7. As tasks become more complex
   (a) Allow for learning by easy stages of increasing complexity.

8. When the trainee lacks confidence
   (a) Use written instructions.
   (b) Avoid the use of production material too soon in the course.
   (c) Provide longer induction periods. Introduce the trainee very gradually both to new machinery and to new jobs.
   (d) Stagger the intake of trainees.
   (e) If possible, recruit groups of workmates.
   (f) Avoid formal tests.
   (g) Don't give formal time limits for the completion of the course.

9. When learning becomes mentally passive
   (a) Use an open situation which admits discovery learning.
   (b) Employ meaningful material and tasks which are sufficiently challenging to an adult.
   (c) Avoid of blackboard and classroom situation or conditions in which trainees may in earlier years have experienced a sense of failure.

can be overcome is given in Table 9.3. It can be seen that programmed materials can usefully fit into some parts of this table.

In further education, in the military and in industry there have been many applications of programmed learning. In industry, for example, programmed instruction has been used to provide general educational and background courses, as well as training in specific skills. It has been used in small companies, where there are no lasting facilities for instruction, in companies which are characterized by their diversity of location (e.g. banks, building societies, airline and oil companies), and in companies where there is an intermittent supply of trainees (perhaps for seasonal reasons). And, of course, programmed instruction has been widely used in the context of self-instruction and retraining through correspondence courses. At a time when further education is expanding rapidly and we are moving into the era of *education permanente*, we might well expect a proliferation of self-instructional textbooks. Such books, however, are unlikely to look exactly like the ones we have so far described.

COMBINING THE EARLY APPROACHES

In the early days of programmed learning, there was much discussion concerning the relative merits of the different systems outlined above—linear *versus* branching; multiple-choice questions *versus* written response; large steps *versus* small steps; and so on—and compromise solutions appreared. At the University of Sheffield, for example, a system called *skip-branching* was developed (Kay and Sime, 1963). Here the learner tackled a fairly large unit of information first (as in the Crowder system), but made a written response (as in the Skinner system). If the response was correct, the learner moved on to the next major unit of information. If the learner was incorrect, he worked through a linear subsequence of small items (a Skinner-type subprogram) until he eventually arrived at the next main item, where this procedure was then repeated. This approach, like Crowder's, it was argued, was useful where students had wide ranges of initial knowledge and ability and might, for example, wish to revise some material.

What it is important to note here about the early systems and even the compromise skip one, is that in these early days the instructional programs were machine-dominated rather than student-orientated. In other words, if one were producing a linear program, the material had to be arranged in segments in order to fit into a linear machine. Similarly, if one were constructing a branching text, the material had to be written in such a way that a multiple-choice question could be asked at the end of every page. Even in the skip system, constructed response answers were required for main sequence items because the first skip machine built at Sheffield operated on this principle. In later textbook presentations of the skip system there was a tendency to restrict the number of subitems one could use because it was convenient to keep them on the left-hand side of the page with the main sequence items on the right. In other words, in these early days a program's format was more controlled by its method of presentation than by considerations of what it was appropriate for learners to be doing at that particualr moment in time.

More modern approaches to programmed instruction concern themselves with problems raised by this latter question. When is it appropriate to ask a multiple-choice question? When might a careful linear exposition in short steps be most appropriate? Do we need the student to make a response to *every* page? Do we always have to provide a correct answer? Can this point best be made with an appropriate illustration? Is it more appropriate to use lengthy prose passages (with adjunct questions) at certain times? Can learners work in groups on this topic? When is it better for the learner to control his own sequence of questions? And so on. Modern programs are therefore much more flexible than the traditional ones which are so well-known. Readers interested in examining in detail a more flexible approach are advised to consult Susan Markle's (1969) *Good Frames and Bad*—a programmed exemplar of this argument. In this program the reader studies a variety of programming styles, and can skip items whenever necessary. The author always makes clear her opinion, and that she does not always expect the reader to agree.

WIDENING THE CONCEPT OF PROGRAMMED INSTRUCTION

In the middle 1960's the emphasis in programmed learning began to change from examining what the learner did to examining what program writers did in constructing programmed materials (Hartley, 1974). It became clear that the psychology that had sustained programmed learning up to that time was to some extent restrictive (Annett, 1973). Marson (1975) put it thus: 'Programmers, realising the folly of setting out with a medium in search of a message, began to concentrate on what might be learned (the message) before deciding how it should be taught (the medium)'. It thus became clearer that the essence of programmed or systematic instruction lay in working through four inter-retlated steps.

(i) Specifying objectives (knowing where you are going).

(ii) Analysing the learner's task and selecting appropriate teaching methods and media (trying to get there by the best means possible).

(iii) Evaluation (assessing whether you have got there successfully).

(iv) Revision (using the results from the assessment to improve the teaching in stage (ii)).

Now, with this broader approach, programmers began to use a variety of methods (including conventional programs) in stage (ii), *whilst maintaining the other stages*. This wider concept allowed programmers to escape from thinking limited to machines and texts alone, and to think in terms of larger systems—of programmed instructional packages rather than single programmed textbooks: of packages which might contain tapes, slides, visual aids and programmed and conventional instructional materials (see Figure 9.4)— and in terms of whole courses which lasted a complete term or year instead of single lessons. As long as the objectives are clear, the achievement of these

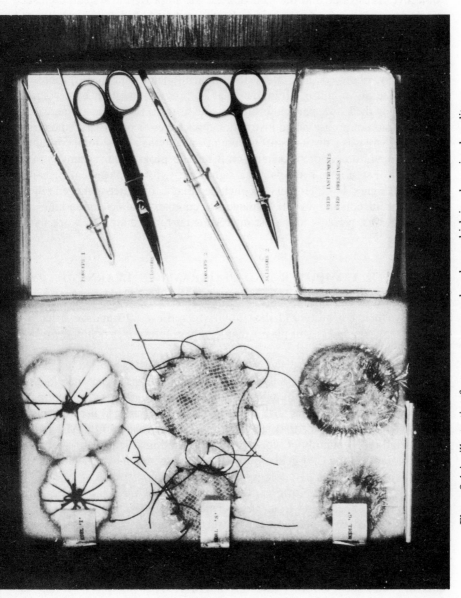

Figure 9.4 An illustration from a programmed package which involves visual, auditory and tactile stimuli, group interaction and practical exercises. Photo by courtesy of Sheila Marson

objectives is assessed and the feedback used to improve the system, then such packages and courses can be said to be programmed. A detailed examination of the role of objectives in such systems is to be found in Davies (1976), and illustrations of more modern approaches in Mackie (1975).

Whitlock (1972), in a survey of changes in the use of programmed instruction in industry, observed three main developments. He found that (i) there was an increase in 'in-house' programs, that is, programs written by certain industries for their own particular and private use; (ii) there was an increase in the provision of programmed instructional packages or prestructured courses; and (iii) there was a distinct shift in emphases from the almost total concentration on operators, apprentices and craftsmen to programs for administrative and clerical staff and, perhaps more significantly, for management personnel up to the highest level. His survey concluded that a computer-managed scheme at ICI for introducing top-line managers to complex financial and administrative skills was, perhaps, the most interesting current example of work in this area.

THE COMPUTER AND PROGRAMMED LEARNING

Three main advantages of computers—their large (but less bulky) storage capacity, their flexibility and their ability to retrieve information speedily—ensure that computers will play a major part in future instructional development.

In this chapter we take the approach that computer-assisted instruction (CAI) can be regarded as a sophisticated extension of the earlier ideas of programmed learning, although many would regard CAI as presenting so many different possibilities that it would be better to regard it as a separate entity. It is true, indeed, that since the 1950's much work on CAI has been conducted independently of work on programmed instruction and that many more workers in the CAI field are likely to come from different fields of enterprise than teaching or psychology—the more common source of research on programmed learning. However, the overall aims of CAI and programmed instruction are the same—to teach efficiently, effectively and economically.

Sophisticated computer-assisted instruction aims to instruct each learner differently. Material for each learner to respond to may be presented not just on the basis of the student's last response (as in Skinner and Crowder systems), but on the basis of his whole history of previous responding, errors made, time taken, routes taken by other students, and indeed, in some cases, on the basis of the student's certainty about the correctness of his response, or even aspects of his personality. Indeed, in one system called TICCIT (Time Shared Interactive Computer Controlled Information Television), learners can select the teaching strategy according to their preferred learning style, for example lots of examples first or parhaps the basic underlying rule (Merrill, 1973). Material may also be paced in CAI systems—speeding up if the student responds quickly, slowing down when he finds the going gets more difficult—or pressure can be adjusted by varying the content of the instructional material and altering the level of difficulty of the items the student is directed to (Pask, 1975a).

The problem for all computer systems, because of their machine-dependence, is how to become cost-effective. This problem is probably best being solved by PLATO (Programmed Logic for Automated Teaching Operation), which is likely to become the first CAI system to achieve costs below $1.00 per student terminal hour. PLATO is solving the problem of cost-effectiveness by developing a widescale use for the system. It is expected that by 1976 there will be some 4,000 terminals connected to the Urbana-Champaign Faculty near Illinois, and that these terminals will be widely dispersed. They are already to be found in Florida as well as in the neighbouring state of Indiana, and there are plans to have some in England.

In considering different computer systems, a distinction has to be borne in mind between hardware, software and courseware. The *hardware* is the physical side of the system, the computer, the terminal, the light pens, etc. The *software* is the operating system which manages the internal operation of the computer and the operation of the *courseware*, which is the instructional materials. It is with the software, the business of managing the instructional materials, that the real advances will be made with CAI—although many would argue that we are still at the Model T stage in CAI development in all three areas. Indeed, a sober assessment would indicate that at present we are at the state of art in all three areas, and all must advance together.

It might be useful at this point to illustrate briefly some of the teaching strategies that have been used in CAI to date.

(i) *Drill and practice* is perhaps the most commonly used form of CAI, and although there is evidence of the effectiveness of CAI at this level (Atkinson, 1974), it is perhaps its least adventurous form of use. At this level the computer is programmed to supply patiently an inexhaustible set of examples, say in arithmetic or algebra, and to administer and to score these exercises. At the same time, students can discover basic rules or strategies for themselves from the flood of examples given. Sudden insights or 'aha's' can be an important part of the process, and are allowed for in many CAI systems. The aim of this approach, of course, is for the student to develop and practice skills under controlled learning conditions. This simple form of drill and practice may be made more complex by arranging the skill into various levels of difficulty. If the student masters one level to a specified criterion (e.g. 100 per cent correct on the last five examples), then the computer will present problems at the next level. Learners in difficulties may have the level of difficulty reduced, and, as noted earlier, one way of increasing or decreasing difficulty is to vary the pace of the instruction.

(ii) *The tutorial* use of the computer is similar to the extended form of drill and practice just discussed, only in this case there is more likely to be a dialogue between the computer and the learner at the teleprinter. Records of how the learner responds to certain questions, how long it takes him to answer and whether or not he appears to have mastered a concept can all determine what

COMPUTER: Before proceeding with the re-examination it might be instructive to pause and consider the diagnostic implications of the information at hand. Perhaps you think it too early to arrive at any definitive conclusion. On the other hand, you may be prepared to make the diagnosis now. Are you?

STUDENT: NO.

C.   Fine. Nevertheless, we've got a fair amount of information—at least enough to raise some, perhaps several, diagnostic possibilities. Have you any in mind?

S.   YES.

C.   Name one.

S.   PNEUMOCOCCAL PNEUMONIA.

C.   Good. The general signs of a pneumonic process are present. Of course, you haven't isolated the bug. Do you think the belly pain and flank pain reinforce the case for pneumococcal pneumonia?

S.   NO.

C.   Right. Though the white count is consistent, isn't it?

S.   YES.

C.   I think so too, but a later reading is indicated to confirm this finding. We've considered one possibility. Do you have another diagnosis in mind?

S.   NO.

C.   In that case I'd like to talk about pulmonary infarction. What I like about that diagnosis is the presence of high fever, rusty sputum, and shaking chills; I don't like the dyspnea, pleural pain, and signs of consolidation—do you agree?

S.   NO.

C.   You're quite correct. I was just trying to see whether or not you were alert—and you were. Now let's see how the patient is today. Begin the physical when you're ready.
(Deleted: requests for general appearance and vital signs.)

S.   PNEUMOCOCCAL PNEUMONIA.

C.   Yes. I remember you liked this diagnosis before. Are you absolutely sure?

S.   NO.

C.   What would help you nail down the diagnosis?

S.   EVIDENCE FROM SPUTUM AND CULTURE.

C.   Good. Anything else?

S.   EVIDENCE FROM X-RAY FINDINGS.

C.   Good. X-ray shows area of consolidation at right lower lobe, consistent with a pneumonic process. Lab reports Grampositive organisms in the sputum smear and the presence of pneumococci in the culture. Had you thought to rule out things like appendicitis and acute pyelonephritis? Apparently you weren't thrown off by the referred abdominal pain. In any case, you've made the correct diagnosis.

Figure 9.5 Extract from a medical diagnosis computer printout, from Swets and Feurzieg (1965). © 1965, by the American Association for the Advancement of Science, and reproduced with permission

material is next presented to him. Figure 9.5 provides an example of the kind of printout that emerges from a computer and a student in a limited tutorial mode.

It is possible to classify 'learner-controlled instruction' by CAI under this *tutorial* heading, although in this case the sequence is determined more by learner requests to the computer than by more conventional instructional methods (e.g. see Grubb, 1968).

(iii) *Laboratory tests, simulations and gaming.* In this situation computers are used to simulate some of the activities of, for example, chemical laboratories, management decision-making or medical diagnosis, the idea being that skills can be acquired in less time and with none of the dangers inherent in normal real-life activities. In some situations, for example, the learners might do a 'dry run' with the computer before trying the real thing. To take one of the examples listed above, in a simulated production process, learners might be assigned the problem of coordinating a number of assembly lines: they could order any number of checks to be run, and the computer would display the outcomes. Thus computers can be used to assess the implications of a present decision for a future state by, as it were, running the program forward to see what would happen if. . . . In brief, with this form of CAI the learner can *play* about a great deal with the computer and *learn* in the process. In a statistics package being developed at the University of Leeds, for example, the student can order different size samples, samples of different abilities, different statistical tests, and can see (and learn) the implications of all these facts in working out the probabilities of events occurring by chance (Hartley and Sleeman, 1971). The visual display capabilities of some CAI systems like PLATO have an important part to play in this context, for they have great value in simulated work.

(iv) *Using students to write programs.* One of the most exciting uses of CAI is that where the learners themselves write the program. One investigator with young children in this area, Seymour Papert, argues that children learn by doing, and by thinking about what they do—and that children can be given an unprecedented power to invent and to carry out exciting projects by providing them with access to computers with a suitable, clear and intelligible programming language. Papert particularly argues for this view in the area of mathematics teaching (Papert, 1972). An increasing number of computer programs like 'course-writer' are now becoming available, which enable the learner to be prompted by the computer in the steps involved. Writing one's own program, it is argued, helps develop logical thinking skills, and with a computer it is possible to do this without fear of failure. Somehow it seems much less disturbing to correct errors in your program than it is to correct errors in your thinking.

(v) *Computer-managed instruction.* A different use of the computer, rather than employing it for teaching, is to use it to aid the management of teaching by others. Using computers to help organize the college timetable, to score objective tests, to diagnose learning difficulties and to recommend specific prescriptions are all examples of this kind of approach. There is a wide scope for this form of use of computers in our educational system (Sime, 1968), although, interestingly enough (except for some rather mundane instances), the potential has nowhere been exploited.

Illustrative examples of British work in the areas just described are provided by Hooper and Toye (1975).

The advantages of CAI

Because it combines large storage capacity with flexibility and rapid retrieval, CAI clearly offers a great deal to an education system, as well as posing great difficulties and challenges. There are many situations where CAI would be an expensive and an inappropriate method of approach, but nevertheless there are circumstances where it seems possibly to be the best approach. When a learner's response has to be instantly measured, evaluated and the results of this evaluation transmitted to the learner or the teaching program *before* the next response can be made, then the speed of CAI makes this form of instruction almost mandatory. Training in high-speed motor skills provides a case in point, as well as training students to solve problems.

Secondly, when it is necessary to deal with wide individual differences in learners, then CAI seems appropriate. A word of caution, however, is perhaps necessary at this point. It seems to be a popular assumption that a system that caters for individuals is in itself a good thing. There are, however, instances of where this may be just an expensive luxury. To handle such complexity requires incredibly sophisticated soft and courseware. Smallwood's study—to be cited below—suggests in effect that a computer can be used to develop an effective sequence for all students taking a particular topic.

Thirdly, when diagnosis and prescriptions are required, it is suggested that a computer can act as a better record-keeper and decision-maker than can an overloaded teacher. Diagnosis is sometimes so complicated that probably only a computer can handle all the relevant domains and apply them all systematically.

Finally, the more adventurous educational uses of computers, such as those described by Papert, seem to indicate great possibilities, particularly for the development of thinking itself.

CAI and the Early programming systems

In drawing this section to a close it seems important not only to reiterate the two questions which the reader was asked to bear in mind throughout the chapter, but also to point out some of the crucial differences between CAI and the earlier systems that have been discussed.

The early programming systems ran into two types of problem which are important to bear in mind when considering CAI. An anecdote concerning Norman Crowder illustrates both points. When Crowder was first developing his branching system he worked initially with book formats. His first main program (a one-year course on the principles of electronics) filled 14 volumes of branching text—making a pile some 15 in high which weighed approximately 30lb! Such problems of bulk suggested to Crowder the desirability of putting all of this material onto film; in addition, with film, more sophisticated branching techniques could be used. The Autotutor Mark I which Crowder developed was a complex teaching machine with sophisticated branching, film and sound. Unfortunately, however, it was both expensive and unreliable, so a simpler device (the Autotutor Mark II—the present-day machine) was devised. In short, teaching sophistication was sacrificed for engineering reliability, a point that CAI systems are now beginning to redeem.

This tale suggests two morals: (i) non-computer systems tend, if used on a large scale, to produce bulky text or film materials whose management is complex; (ii) sophisticated instructional techniques, however desirable, may founder on the rocks of unreliable machinery. PLATO, the CAI system described earlier, is in fact a success because of its reliable engineering. SOCRATES (System for Organising Content to Review and Teach Educational Subjects) developed by Stolurow at the University of Illinois, which was more sophisticated in terms of instructional design, was unfortunately not so sophisticated in terms of its engineering. SOCRATES is no longer operational. In terms of these two tales, then, what can we expect for the future? As indicated in this chapter, we may expect (i) more reliable and (relatively) inexpensive hardware; (ii) the development of better software systems which will permit easy lesson construction and will increase reliability; and (iii) an increasing use of more sophisticated learning designs for CAI such as those suggested by Papert and the simulation and game environment typical of PLATO.

The two questions asked at the beginning of this chapter were (i) how can we adapt instruction to make it appropriate for each individual learner? and (ii) how can we improve the quality of the instruction? The answers to these questions in terms of CAI are interrelated. It is clear from the discussion that, in principle, CAI allows programmers to deal with individual differences in learners more effectively than did the previous systems. Sequencing is determined by a variety of factors, not just by the previous response. When, in the early days, it was stated that programmed learning provided individualized instruction, this was not true—at least not in the sense that it is with CAI. Early programs were predetermined sequences which were developed from empirical tryouts with samples of student members of the target population for whom the programs were hopefully intended. The instructor wrote the program, and successive evaluations refined it. In some CAI systems, however, the material can be stored in the computer and may be retrieved (by random access) in any sequence or combination—depending on the learner's wishes. Indeed, the computer is capable of monitoring the sequences chosen, and the errors made, and in itself 'learning' from the experiences of working with particular learners.

Smallwood, as early as 1962, described a CAI program that 'homed down', as it were, from presenting different sequences to individual students to eventually presenting just one or two sequences which were equally effective for larger numbers of students. In other words, the computer had 'learned' from its teaching of the initial students taking the program. Smallwood's approach used sophisticated software to optimize courseware. So, for CAI, evaluation

180

and improvement of the quality of the instruction can be continuously on-going activities (rather than retrospective ones) and can take into account *all* the learners who have used the program (rather than a sample). If the early programmers aimed at producing *satisfactory* solutions (they seem to work for a group), the later CAI ones are aiming at producing *optimal* solutions (i.e. the the best solution for an individual). The true significance of CAI lies in the fact that a student may be given a unique sequence of materials, challenging him in a way probably unforeseen by the original programmer.

REFERENCES

Annett, J. (1973). 'Psychological bases of educational technology', in R. Budgett and J. Leedham (Eds.), *Aspects of Educational Technology VII*, Pitman, London.

Atkinson, R. C. (1974). 'Teaching children to read using a computer', *American Psychologist*, **29**, 169.

Belbin, E. (1965). 'Problems of learning for the over 40's', *Gerontologia*, **7**, 61.

Bell, N. T., Feldhusen, J.F., and Starks, D. O. (1964). *Adjunct Programs and Individual Quizzes to Accompany a Course in Educational Technology*, Purdue University, Lafayette, USA.

Crowder, N.A. (1960). 'Automatic tutoring by intrinsic programming', in A. A. Lumsdaine and R. Glaser (Eds.), *Teaching Machines and Programmed Instruction*, NEA, Washington.

Davies, I. K. (1969). 'Mathetics: an experimental study of the relationship between ability and practice in the acquisition of basic concepts in science', Unpublished Ph.D. thesis, University of Nottingham.

Davies, I. K. (1972). 'Presentation strategies', in J. Hartley (Ed.), *Strategies for Programmed Instruction: An Educational Technology*, Butterworths, London.

Davies, I. K. (1976). *Objectives In Curriculum Design*, McGraw-Hill, London and New York.

Dodd, B. T. (1967). 'A study in adult retraining: the gas man', *Occupational Psychology*, **41**, 143.

Evans, L. F. (1975). 'Unconventional aspects of educational technology in an adult education program', in L. F. Evans and J. Leedham (Eds.), *Aspects of Educational Technology IX*, Kogan Page, London.

Gilbert, T. F. (1962). 'Mathetics—the technology of education', In M. D. Merrill (Ed.) 1971), *Instructional Design: Readings*, Prentice-Hall, New York.

Green, A. J. T. (1970). 'Programmed learning in the heavy chemical industry: operator training', in A. C. Bajpai and J. F. Leedham (Eds.), *Aspects of Educational Technology IV*, Pitman, London.

Grubb, R. E. (1968). 'Learner controlled statistics', *Programmed Learning and Educational Technology* **5**, 1, 38.

Hall, C., and Fletcher, R. N. (1967). 'Programmed techniques in the G.P.O.', *Programmed Instruction in Industry I*, Pergamon, London.

Hartley, J. (1966). 'Research report', *New Education*, **2**, 1, 29.

Hartley, J. (Ed.) (1972). *Strategies for Programmed Instruction*, Butterworths, London.

Hartley, J. (1974). 'Programmed instruction 1954–1974: a review, *Programmed Learning and Educational Technology*, **11**, 278.

Hartley, J. R., and Sleeman, D. H. (1971). 'A computer-based statistical laboratory: some views and experiences', in D. Packham *et al.* (Eds.), *Aspects of Educational Technology V*, Pitman, London.

Holme, K., and Mabbs, D. (1967). 'Programmed learning—an expanding discipline', In M. Tobin (Ed.), *Problems and Methods in Programmed Learning*, Part 4, National Centre for Programmed Learning, University of Birmingham.

Hooper, R., and Toye, I. (Eds.), (1975). *Computer Assisted Learning in the United Kingdom*, Council for Educational Technology, London.

Howe, R. C. (1969). 'Programmed learning—a programmed initial installation training course', *Post Office Electrical Engineers Journal* (January).

Hughes, R. J., and Pipe, P. (1961). *Introduction to Electronics*, Hodder & Stoughton, London.

Jamieson, G. H. (1969). Learning by programmed and guided discovery methods at different age levels', *Programmed Learning & Educational Technology*, **6**, 26.

Jones, A., and Moxham, J. (1969). 'Costing the benefits of training', *Personal Management*, **1**, 4, 22.

Kay, H., and Sime, M. E. (1963). 'Survey of teaching machines', in M. Goldsmith (Ed.), *Mechanisation in the Glassroom*, Souvenir Press, London.

Lewis, B. N. (1963). 'The rationale of adaptive teaching machines', in M. Goldsmith (Eds.), *Mechanisation in the Classroom*, Souvenir Press, London.

Mackie, A. (1975). 'Consumer-oriented programmed learning in adult education, in L. F. Evans and J. Leedham (Eds.), *Aspects of Educational Technology IX*, Kogan Page, London.

Mager, R. (1961). 'On the sequencing of instructional content', in I. K. Davies and J. Hartley (Eds.) (1972), *Contributions to an Educational Technology*, Butterworths, London.

Markle, S. (1969). *Good Frames and Bad*, 2nd edn, Wiley, New York.

Marson, S. (1975). 'What happened to programmed learning?', *Nursing Times*, 1425 (September).

Merrill, M. D. (1973). 'Premises, propositions and research underlying the design of a learner controlled computer-assisted instruction system: a summary for the TICCIT system', Paper available from the author, Division of Instructional Services, Brigham Young University, Provo, Utah, 84502.

Mills, D. (1968). 'Clerical training in the quality department of Bryce Berger Ltd.', *Programmed Instruction in Industry* **2**, No. 11, Pergamon, London.

Milton, O., and West, L. J. (1961). *Programmed Instruction: What it is and How it Works*, Harcourt Brace Jovanovich, New York.

Neale, J. G., Toye, M. H., and Belbin, E. (1968). 'Adult training: the use of programmed instruction', *Occupational Psychology*, **42**, 23.

Newsham, D. B. (1969). 'The challenge of change to the adult trainee', *Training Information Paper 3*, Department of Employment and Productivity, HMSO, London.

Oates, A. A., and Robinson, C. F. (1968). 'Programmed learning for clerical work in the G.P.O.', *Programmed Instruction in Industry 2*, 2, Pergamon, London.

Ofiesh, G. D. (1965). *Programed Instruction*, American Management Association, New York.

Papert, S. (1972). *New Educational Technology: Six Reprints*, Turtle Publications, P. O. Box 33, Cambridge, Massachusetts 02138, USA.

Pask, G. (1960). 'Adaptive teaching with adaptive machines', in A. A. Lumsdaine and R. Glaser (Eds.), *Teaching Machines and Programmed Learning*, National Educational Association, Washington.

Pask, G. (1975a). *The Cybernetics of Human Learning and Performance*, Hutchinson, London.

Pask, G. (1975b). *Conversation, Cognitive and Learning*, Elsevier, Amsterdam.

Pask, G. (1976a). 'Conversational techniques in the study and practice of education', *British Journal of Educational Psychology*, **46**, 1, 12.

Pask, G. (1976b). 'Styles and strategies of learning', *British Journal of Educational Psychology*, **46**, 2, 128.

Pressey, S. L., (1926). 'A simple apparatus which gives tests and scores—and teaches', in A. A. Lumsdaine and R. Glaser (Eds.) (1960), *Teaching Machines and Programmed Learning*, NEA Washington.

Sime, M. E. (1968). 'Computers as test beds for teaching systems', in I. K. Davies and J. Hartley (Eds.) (1972), *Contributions to an Educational Technology*, Butterworths, London.

Skinner, B. F. (1954). 'The science of learning and the art of teaching', In A. A. Lumsdaine and R. Glaser (Eds.) (1960), *Teaching Machines and Programmed Learning*, NEA, Washington.

Smallwood, R. D. (1962). *A Decision Structure for Teaching Machines*, MIT Press, Cambridge.

Stewart, D., and Chown, S. (1965). 'A comparison of the effects of a continuous and a linear programmed text on adult pupils', *Occupational Psychology*, **39**, 135

Swets, J., and Feurzieg. W. (1965). 'Computer-aided instruction', *Science*, **150**, 572.

Taylor, J., and Reid, R. L. (1965). 'Programmed training in a London Store', in I. K. Davies and J. Hartley (Eds.) (1972), *Contributions to an Educational Technology*, Butterworths, London.

Watson, P. G. (1968). 'An industrial evaluation of four strategies of instruction', *Audio-Visual Instruction*, **13**, 2, 156.

Whitlock, Q. A., (1972). 'Programmed learning and educational technology in industry, in A. J. Romiszowski (Ed.). *APLET Yearbook of Educational and Instructional Technology 1972/73*, Kogan Page, London.

PART THREE

LEARNING AND MODERN SOCIETY

INTRODUCTION TO PART THREE

The diverse chapters in this final section share a common concern with the acquisition of relatively specific varieties of learning in particular circumstances that have emerged in the highly sophisticated cultures of advanced modern societies. The title of Chapter 10, Adult Learning and Industrial Training, by Mike Smith, is self-explanatory. Smith considers the varied circumstances in which industrial training is required, and he outlines several general requirements. He examines problems relating to selection for training and surveys some of the kinds of training that are encountered. Finally, recent developments in industrial training are outlined, and Smith provides an interesting discussion of some matters that are of common concern to training and to wider aspects of social psychology.

Chapter 11, Learning to Cope with Atypical Force Environments, by James Reason, is about the problems encountered by man when he puts himself into situations, typically involving motion at considerable speed, which are strikingly different from those encountered in human environments during the lengthy period of man's evolution. Reason outlines some of the circumstances whereby people today are placed in such 'unnatural' environments and describes the effects of these circumstances upon the human system. He describes the adaptive processes that occur as humans become able to cope with the changes incurred by, for instance, unusual movement or space travel. Reason also contributes an explanatory model that attempts to explain both the effects of atypical force environments and the forms of adaptation that can take place.

The twelfth chapter, by James Hartley and Peter Burnhill, concerns Understanding Instructional Text: Typography, Layout and Design. The authors point out that although typographical characteristics influence and place limitations upon the use of text as a medium for learning, we have remained remarkably ignorant until recently about the manner in which typographical factors actually influence understanding. Hartley and Burnhill survey recent research into the effects of factors such as page—size, organization of items and layout, and show that items such as these can exert a large influence upon the ease with which we can understand and learn from printed information.

185

In Chapter 13, Are Teaching Innovations in Post-Secondary Education Irrelevant?, Donald Bligh makes some provocative observations and raises interesting questions about the effectiveness of accepted practices in adult education. He argues that we cannot solve the practical problems of post-secondary learning without considering basic values, and he points out that, for many purposes, what educators consider to be the most important objectives are less crucial than some other factors. Bligh draws attention to a number of mistakes and misapplications that have frequently been made, and argues that several methods and procedures have been widely introduced and accepted in the absence of any clear evidence regarding their effectiveness. Bligh considers that educators have been concerned with the presentation of information at the expense of some social processes which may prove to be of greater real importance to the learner.

The subject of the final chapter (Chapter 14), The Open University as a Forum for the Implementation of New Approaches To Learning, might be considered as forming a wholehearted attempt to come to grips with some of the problems raised in Bligh's chapter. Peter Morris describes some of the innovations introduced at the Open University, and demonstrates that careful thought and imagination have been applied to a range of problems encountered in the attempt—one which many people agree has on the whole been remarkably successful—to bring advanced learning in a number of fields to large numbers of people who vary very considerably in aptitudes, qualifications and in previous experience. The Open University does appear to have been successful in aiding many people to acquire intellectual skills, and it seems to achieve its ends much more economically than existing alternative institutions for higher education. Morris's fascinating description of the ways in which this newly conceived and developed organization for encouraging advanced adult learning on a wide scale makes use of the resources available to it, showing clear strengths and some weaknesses, provides a fitting conclusion to the book.

10

ADULT LEARNING AND INDUSTRIAL TRAINING

J. Mike Smith

THE CONTEXT OF INDUSTRIAL TRAINING

In theory at least, the *sine qua non* of adult learning in industry is the contribution it can make towards increasing the efficiency of the workforce. In practice, the situation is not so clear. One of the complicating factors is that training is only one of a whole variety of interchangeable ways of achieving this objective of increasing the efficiency and range of a workforce. Industrial trainers are sometimes apt to forget that improved selection, improved equipment design and even judicious poaching of the more able employee of a competitor may be solutions which are more cost-effective than increased training. In a nutshell, the point is that training must be kept in its context as *one* management tool. Another complicating factor is the complexity of organizational goals. These goals will have a crucial bearing on the amount of adult learning which is planned and carried out. Traditionally, the only goal of industry is considered to be the maximization of shareholders' profit. In today's conditions this view may be naive: in certain situations social and political objectives can be more important. Training may, for example, be politically expedient in times of unemployment because it is one easy action which politicians can be seen to be taking. In other situations, perhaps in a small family firm, or in certain departments of larger firms, the overriding organizational goal may not be efficiency but to provide a pleasant and congenial pastime for the proprietor and long-serving employees during their declining years. In such situations, the quantity and quality of adult learning required may be somewhat circumscribed.

In spite of these necessary qualifications, it would be difficult to underestimate the amount of industrial training which is undertaken by a multiplicity of different bodies. Most obviously, training is undertaken by the organizations themselves. The organizations need not be industrial organizations in the strict sense. The police force, health authorities, the armed forces and large catering organizations are good examples of non-industrial concerns which have to make a substantial training effort. If there is a geographical concentration of firms with similar training interests, they may pool their training effort in some form of group training scheme. These group schemes are particularly suitable where the individual firms are too small to justify their own training facilities, or where the training need is very specialized. Other types of training may be organized at the level of a whole industry, by the appropriate Industrial Training Board or the appropriate trade association. Still other types of training may be organized at national level by the government agencies such as the Training Services Agency, whose own Skill Centres aim to provide occupational training in basic skills such as bricklaying, computer programming or typing. Or the resources of the educational system may be used to provide day-release courses, block release courses or evening classes.

A GENERAL TRAINING PARADIGM?

In a field as complex as industrial training, where the 'special' situation is the rule rather than the exception, it is impossible to outline an approach which has universal generality. However, probably most industrial training specialists would accept an idealized paradigm containing six steps, which could be adopted as a basic model that could be modified to suit particular situations. The six steps are: identifying objectives, analysing training needs, analysing tasks, preparing training, conducting training and finally, evaluation and modification of training.

Step 1: Identifying Objectives and Requirements

The initial stage of identifying objectives is often overlooked in the haste of getting a training course off the ground. This first stage requires close and clear communication between the policy-making bodies and the training department. The training department needs to know both the organization's immediate plans for the next year and the longer-term plans. It will need to know whether the organization is to expand, contract or change its 'product' or location in any significant way. It will also need to know if there is impending legislation, such as metrication or decimalization, which might affect the operation of the company and its workforce.

Step 2: Identifying Training Tasks

The second stage is to identify those objectives and requirements which are best met by training techniques rather than other management techniques. If the tasks which are identified are very complex, it may be necessary to formalize this stage into a coherent plan whereby the tasks are broken down into smaller units and time-scheduled in the best sequence.

Step 3: Task Analysis

Once the objectives have been operationalized into training tasks, some form of task analysis will usually be undertaken. The exact form of task analysis will depend entirely on the parameters of the actual situation. Blum and Naylor (1968) offer a relatively comprehensive overview of the methods available, while Annett and Duncan (1967) and Duncan (1974) discuss some of the basic issues involved. A practical example of the role of task analysis in the adult retraining of gasmen is described by Dodd (1967).

Probably the most widely used techniques of task analysis are the critical incident approach pioneered by Flanagan (1954) and the skills analysis propounded by Seymour (1968). In essence, the critical incident approach adopts the view that while a job requires many activities such as memo-writing, clocking in, form-filling, only a few activities have a critical impact insofar that a substandard performance of these activities will be reflected in a substandard outcome. Identifying these critical incidents and specifying how they should be performed can be highly technical, but in a practical setting they will often be determined by systematically asking groups of competent and skilled workers or their supervisors. Once the critical tasks have been established, methods of performing them are devised after observation, analysis and interpretation of the way they are performed by a skilled worker.

Seymour's approach is directly relevant to this latter stage. The skills analysis propounded by Seymour (1968) divides job content into two main areas, *knowledge* content and *skill* content. The *knowledge* content may be further subdivided into (1) workplace knowledge—the knowledge of the workplace that the worker needs to have in order to get to his workbench and be ready and able to perform his work, the names of machines, tools, materials and processes, and (2) quality knowledge—the tolerances and production standards to be met. The *skills* content focuses on *how* a worker *does* his job. By observation, analysis of videotapes or slow-motion cine film, each action will be broken down into the actions of the right hand and those of the left hand. In addition, the visual cues, the tactile and kinesthetic cues and unusual or difficult movements or sensory discrimination will be identified. Seymour's approach was developed for operatives, largely in the knitwear industry, but it is surprising to see how, with some modification, it may be applied to more recent concerns such as social skills training.

Step 4: Preparing Instruction Schedules

Once the tasks to be learned have been identified and adequately described, the next step is to prepare instruction schedules which will efficiently impart knowledge and skill to the trainees. Only at this step are the range of learning factors encountered, including knowledge of results, massed *vs* distributed practice, sequence of learning and motivation. A good review of these factors in learning efficiency is offered by Gagné and Bolles (1959), and Glaser's

(1965) approach adds emphasis on 'entering behaviour', i.e. the state of the trainee when he starts training. This emphasis is a welcome reminder that trainees are individuals who vary according to their abilities, knowledge and skills. Often, choosing the right 'learning method' is difficult.

One of the most useful guides is the CRAMP training design algorithm (Pearn, 1975). The acronym CRAMP was developed by R. M. Belbin (1969) as a mnemonic for *five major types of learning* commonly encountered in adult learning situations:

*C*omprehension-type learning or understanding theoretical subject matter;

*R*eflex-skills learning of skilled movements such as sewing machining;

*A*ttitude development, say, towards the public whom the trainees have to encounter;

*M*emorization; and

*P*rocedural-type learning of a series of simple instructions.

The algorithm incorporates the advantages and disadvantages of about *20 different training techniques*, ranging from the magnification method, cueing and fading, to the progressive part method or the cumulative part method of learning.

The two major elements, the types of learning and the training techniques, can be connected by a flow diagram which starts with the different types of learning, and, taking into account other task characteristics and characteristics of the trainees, traces a path to the most appropriate training technique for the circumstances. For example, if training is essentially a substantial memory task and the trainees are aged over 30, the path might lead to the cumulative part method. On the other hand, a substantial memory task involving trainees under the age of 30 might lead to the progressive part method. In still different situations, discovery learning or case studies, or role-playing or T-groups, might be recommended.

Granted that any algorithm designed to assist the identification of the most suitable training method must have its limitations, it is unfortunate that the CRAMP training design algorithm pays scant attention to the social behaviour of trainees during training. Indeed, it is probably symptomatic of a more general neglect of social factors, which is surprising since the attitudes of the trainee, the interpersonal relations in the training situation and inter-group relations between trainees, experienced workers and management can nullify courses of action which appear to be perfect as far as the learning factors are concerned.

Step 5: Conducting Training

Discussions of training design often take for granted the obvious step of conducting the training. Indeed, in practice the training itself sometimes seems to get lost among the administrative chores of arranging instruction, timetabling and record-keeping. At this stage the skills of the instructor, the efficiency of equipment and the adequacy of accommodation are crucial.

For example, problems arise concerning selection and training of instructors availability of accommodation and adapting it to provide a suitable training environment, and providing sufficient learning aids in the right place at the right time.

Step 6: Evaluation

The final stage in the generalized training paradigm is evaluation to check if the training has achieved its objective. At operative level, this stage is relatively simple. The performance of trainees in terms of quantity and quality is measured and compared to experienced worker standard—which will have been previously established by pragmatic procedures. Evaluation of other levels of training presents more problems. In management training in particular, where timespan of discretion—the time-lag between a decision and its consequences—may be many years, evaluation is very difficult.

In other cases, where the primary aim of training is a change of attitude, a variety of attitude measurement techniques may be required. One promising technique for use in this area is the repertory grid, based on Kelly's personal construct theory (Kelly, 1955). The repertory grid method is statistically very complex, but it has the advantage of allowing each individual to construct a measuring instrument which is uniquely relevant to himself. In essence, the trainee is asked to name the elements (usually the people such as 'my boss', 'a subordinate', 'a colleague') which are relevant to him. He is then presented with random triads of the elements he has nominated and asked to say which of the three is the odd man out, and why. In this way the constructs (that is, the way the elements are thought about, for example, old fashioned, good, ambitious) are elicited. The elements and constructs are cast in a grid, with the elements along the top and the constructs down the side. The subject is then asked to rate each of the elements on each of the constructs. A thorough analysis of the resulting data inevitably requires the use of one of the computer packages such as the INGRID package developed by Slater (1972). From the results, however, it is possible to gauge a subject's cognitive complexity in a given area and to build a model of his construct system and one of the relationships between the different elements.

To measure the attitudinal learning resulting from training, the models obtained before and after training can be contrasted and, if possible, compared with the models obtained from the grids of control groups. Unfortunately, promising though it is, the technique has a number of limitations: it is time-consuming and sometimes difficult to use in a group-testing situation and, because the initial stages are very unstructured, it may place a strain on the rapport between the trainer and the trainee. One good example of the use of repertory grids in the evaluation of management training is given by Smith and Ashton (1975).

Evaluation of some kind is an essential step in developing a system for adult learning in industry which is both relevant and effective. Ideally, evaluation and the development of criterion measures should be considered as soon as the training objectives have been defined. In practice, however, training evaluation is a hard row to hoe. In an industrial setting, where production is paramount, evaluation may give rise to pressures on staff, time and resources, and it is often difficult to obtain adequate control groups, or to set aside 10 per cent of the training budget for evaluation programs.

Selection for Training

An element which is so far missing from the generalized training paradigm is the selection of trainees. There are, of course, situations where selection is either unnecessary or impractical. If the skills are simple and can be learned by the vast majority of people, the interposition of a selection procedure for trainees merely represents an additional cost with a very small yield. Similarly, in a period of labour shortage and of buoyant demand, employers may be happy to engage anyone who in the words of some employers 'is still warm and has the strength to work the doorbell'. In most situations, however, the cost of trainees who either leave before the end of training or fail to reach experienced worker standard is sufficiently high to justify a selection procedure designed to detect and eliminate the most likely of these cases.

The array of procedures used to select trainees is vast and ranges from the humble five-minute interview to careful psychometric testing or the use of special tests to measure trainability *per se*. Psychometric tests of personality such as Cattell's 16 P.F. test or the Guilford—Zimmerman test are most useful at the level of management training. Multiple regression equations exist which attempt to predict characteristics such as the ability to 'grow' into a new job, scholastic aptitude or likely professionalism (Cattell *et al.* 1970). Attainment tests can be used at the level of technician training to establish if intending trainees have the background knowledge necessary in order to benefit from further training. At operative level, tests of practical abilities such as manual dexterity have been found useful. For example, the Purdue pegboard, a test which requires pins to be placed in holes using a pair of tweezers, has been used in the knitwear industry to select trainees for delicate jobs such as 'linking' where the stitches from the neck of the garment have to be picked up and matched with the stitches of the collar.

In recent years there have been attempts to measure training *per se*, and a number of these trainability tests have been developed at the Industrial Training Research Unit, Cambridge (Downs, 1970). The essence of 'trainability tests' is that the potential trainee is shown how to perform a typical sample of the job she will have to learn. This job sample is chosen according to three main parameters: (1) is it based on the key elements in the job, (2) it involves only those elements which can be imparted in the short learning period of the test, i.e. under 30 minutes, and (3) it is difficult enough to discriminate between capable and incompetent applicants. The instructors then demonstrate the task to the trainees and after a short practice the trainees are asked to produce

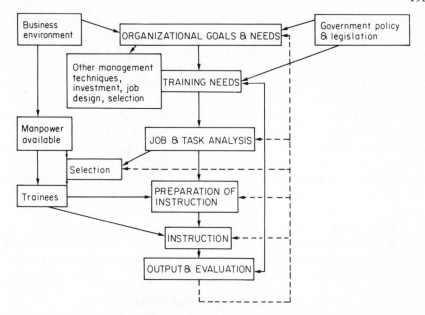

Figure 10.1 A generalized training paradigm

the item by themselves. The amount they have learnt is gauged by checking off the mistakes they make against a checklist of errors. On the basis of this 'score' and other observations, the instructor comes to a conclusion regarding the trainees' trainability potential.

When all the steps of the generalized training paradigm are considered as a whole, they can be taken to form a training subsystem which resides within the wider system of an industrial organization. An overall appreciation of this subsystem is more easy to obtain when it is stated in diagrammatic form. With systems diagrams such as Figure 10.1 or similar diagrams produced by Eckstrand (1964), Tilley (1968) and Dodd (1967), the causal relationships between the interlocking parts can be made explicit. The timing and nature of the consequences of disturbances in various parts of the system can be predicted with greater ease and precision.

One final point to consider before leaving the topic of the generalized training paradigm is the assumptions it makes about organizational structure. Generally it assumes that business is organized according to the Weberian bureaucratic model, with considerable role specification and clear lines of authority based on logic and rational 'laws'. This type of organizational structure, epitomized by the organizational chart that pervades many companies in both the industrial and service sectors of the economy, was perhaps a reasonably good approximation to large business organizations in the first half of this century. But it has been increasingly criticized by organizational theorists. Merton (1952) and Argyris (1974), for example, claim that this type of organization leads to dysfunctions. Furthermore, Toffler (1972) suggests that an accelerating rate of change will be *the* characteristic of the future. Business organizations will need to adapt to new problems by quickly forming '*ad hoc*' groups of individuals whose pooled experience and knowledge would seem likely to find a solution. Once the particular problem has been solved the group would be dissolved. Thus Weber's bureaucracy will be replaced by forms of '*ad hocracy*'. If this development occurs, it will clearly have great implications for the organization of adult learning in industry. Learning in the form of training for the performance of clearly prescribed roles will be useless. By the time all the stages of the generalized training paradigm have been followed, and some allowance made for evaluation and feedback, the situation may have changed and the training been abandoned. The problem of replacing the generalized training paradigm with another that can cope with these stresses is difficult to solve. Presumably, some form of generalized training to produce quick and accurate perceptions of situations and the ability to cope with rapid change could be devised. Since these are more the aims of education, the overdrawn distinctions between education, training and learning could well disappear.

VARIETIES OF TRAINING

The types of training undertaken in industry may be listed, though the following list is by no means exhaustive.

Induction training	Technician training
Operative training	Instructor training
Supervisory training	Booster training
Clerical and commercial training	Versatility training
Management training	Retraining
	Pre-retirement training

Most of these categories are fairly self-explanatory and simple take their name from the category of personnel involved, shedding little light on the actual training undertaken.

Induction training is a fairly familiar concept inspired by the need to reduce the high rates of labour turnover which are commonly experienced among new recruits. Usually, it consists of two main elements: providing essential information such as the location of the wages office, lavatories and canteen, and instructing in essential procedures such as safety routines or how to make out a work docket; in addition, as Morea (1972) points out, induction training can help the socialization of the trainee into a new workgroup.

Booster training and versatility training are less common. *Booster* training is used when the level of operative performance has fallen below some acceptable limit. The operatives are then given some extra training designed to improve either the quality or the quantity of output. Usually the emphasis is on improving the speed of performance while still maintaining quality standards. One useful device involved in booster training is the pacing machine (Toye, 1973). The operative's task will be broken down into its constituent segments. The operative will then sit at the machine for short periods of about

30 minutes each day and, while she is performing her job, auditory signals will be given to mark the point when she should have completed each particular segment of her task. Initially the timing of the signals will be generous, so that she can easily complete each segment in time. On subsequent days the timing will be gradually speeded up until the required speed of performance is obtained. Various types of pacing machine are available. Some merely give a signal at the end of each segment, while others give continuous information by using a signal of increasing pitch or volume during each segment.

Versatility training simply involves learning to do more than one job. It is particularly important in small firms who employ only a few workers on each process. Eventualities such as absence and illness of staff happen infrequently, but when they do arise the absence of one person can create a bottleneck in the production process, because that one worker may represent 50 per cent of productive capacity at that point. Few small firms can afford either supernumaries to give cover in these situations or the alternative of holding large stocks. The most practical answer is to train a few workers up to an acceptable standard in several skills so that they can be redeployed to avoid bottlenecks buidling up. Both versatility training and booster training are distinctive in that the trainees are almost invariably long-term employees who have a great deal of background knowledge about the firm, its products and its methods.

Another dimension to the training process is the place where training is carried out. Here, the main alternatives can be listed as:

on-the-job training (the sit-by-Nellie method)
vestibule training
training centres
training in educational centres.

On-the-job training has been the backbone of apprenticeships since before mediaeval days. On starting work the recruit is told to 'sit by Nellie' and watch what she does. Sit-by-Nellie training has the advantage of being realistic, and is widely accepted as the 'proper' method of training. Unfortunately, it has a number of powerful disadvantages. The success of 'sit-by-Nellie' training depends largely on the characteristics of Nellie herself. She may pass on inefficient working methods and restrictive attitudes. Furthermore, Nellie has her own job to do. Even though she may be paid a small premium for taking a trainee under her wing, it may not be considered adequate compensation for the trouble of having the trainee under her feet, and she may not be prepared or able to devote time and thought to the learning processes of the trainee. The selection of Nellie as the trainee's mentor raises other issues. In all probability, Nellie will not have been trained in the essential skills of job analysis and communication. Indeed, she may have been chosen because she is the 'best' or fastest worker, but it is risky to assume that the fastest worker is the best instructor. The consequence of these disadvantages is that on-the-job training usually takes a long time. Contrary to first impressions, when the trainee's wages, Nellie's wages and factory overheads are included, on-the-job training can prove very costly indeed.

In an attempt to overcome these drawbacks, the Government's TWI (*Train*-ing *W*ithin *I*ndustry) scheme includes Job Instruction in one of its modules. The course takes about 10 hours and is usually split into two five-hour sessions. It is given to Nellie within the factory itself by qualified training officers. The aim of the courses is to impart the basic skills of operative training which can then be used in the on-the-job, sit-by-Nellie situation.

Vestibule training, which takes place in a special area—either a training school or area of the workshop that has been set aside—is generally more efficient at getting trainees up to experienced worker standard in a short time. It may even be possible to arrange an ideal learning environment. There may, however, be acute problems at the end of training when the trainee is moved from the seclusion of the training school to the rigours of the factory floor.

In principle, *training in training centres* such as the Government Skill Centres is much the same as vestibule training but with the disadvantages writ large. Because training centres may have to cater for the needs of several firms, the training has to be more general, so that the specific modes of working have to be gained after starting work with a specific employer. This, and other consider-ations, can make the transition from the training centre to the factory floor quite traumatic.

It is perhaps at the level of technical training and clerical training that *training in educational establishments* is most important. Evening classes are almost universally accepted as the means by which employees can better themselves. Indeed, among the older generation of supervisors and lower management, evening classes were probably the main and perhaps the only form of formal training they received, and they usually look back on their recollections with great affection. After 20 or 30 years of technical change, it is doubtful if the night school system is, on its own, an adequate means of transmitting the complex or involved and intricate technological skills needed today. Other trainees may be fortunate enough to be granted day releases for one day a week from their firm in order to attend the local 'technical college'. A slightly different pattern, useful in cases where the daily journey from work to technical college is too long, is the block release system where trainees will go to college, perhaps having accommodation found for them, for a two-or three-week concentrated course. Unfortunately, block release courses are sometimes unpopular because it can place a great strain on the factory floor if one individual is absent for prolonged periods. Another disadvantage is that some trainees have difficulty in assimilating such concentrated instruction.

TWO RECENT DEVELOPMENTS IN INDUSTRIAL TRAINING

The earlier parts of this chapter set out to give an overall appreciation of the variety and problems of adult learning in industry. Many of the topics which have been touched on deserve a chapter in their own right. To illustrate some of the deeper issues involved in adult learning in industry, a rather more extended consideration will be given to two areas within the field of industrial training which have recently come to the fore.

RETRAINING OLDER WORKERS

The reasons why the retraining of older workers has come into prominence in recent years are pretty obvious. The medical and social advances of the last century have enabled a larger proportion of people to live on into their 50's, 60's and 70's. In addition, the rate of technological change has accelerated so that it is no longer likely that a worker can start at the age of 15 and remain in the same type of job until he retires. Indeed, it could be argued that we have already moved into the two-or three-skill society, where it is the accepted pattern for workers to have to change their type of employment during their 30's and their 50's. This development is not limited to employees in operative grades. Robbins (1972) has noted that many graduates in industry are now facing mid-career problems.

Seymour (1966) wrote 'In the future the training given to a worker under twenty-one will be largely outdated by the time he is thirty-one', and identifies two main causes of a man having to change his job as market changes and technological changes. After an economic analysis of the problem, Sokel (1970) concludes: 'Older workers suffer certain disadvantages in responding to the newer patterns of human resource utilization necessitated by both changes in technology and in tastes and preferences. These changes have brought about a significantly different occupational distribution from that which prevailed at the time when the present day over 45's entered the world of work or made educational and training decisions in their career choices. In the main these changes have been towards occupations and activities requiring higher levels of skill, greater amounts of education and training and have frequently embodied knowledge and methods unknown a few decades ago'.

Other methods of identifying the occupations of workers who are likely to need retraining have been attempted. Smith (1973b; 1974; 1975), for example, has shown that an occupation's age structure may be a good index of its suitability for older workers, and the age structures of all British occupations have been worked out. However, one of the major problems facing any retraining programme is the reluctance of older workers to enrol. Studies by Smith (1973a) and Newsham (1975) suggest that those older workers who are willing to retrain tend to be those who have had a more varied employment history in the past, who have home circumstances which would allow them to obtain the maximum retraining grants, who score more highly on tests of mental ability and who have had some previous experience of adult education in some form or another.

The use of 'trainability tests' to assess suitability for retraining has been mentioned above. Other approaches have produced some contradictory results. Belbin and Belbin (1969) consider the importance of previous experience, and they report: 'The value of "experience" now becomes much more questionable. For example, in one establishment where tuition was being given in television repairs, trainees who had some previous experience in electronics were found to be less successful than a group of ex-coalminers who were being retrained for the new job. Those with previous related experience were inclined to use their knowledge to pinpoint probable causes of faults in the television sets; this resulted in an unsystematic and time consuming approach. The coalminers, lacking this knowledge, took more readily to the use of the approved strategy in tracing faults'. Similarly, Good (1967), investigating trainee computer programmers, found that it was the graduates entering training straight from university who proved more successful in training than those trainees who had had industrial experience or immediate experience in computer programming. Attempts have also been made to predict how well older trainees would succeed in training from various aspects of biographical data. One of the few positive findings is that older trainees who have 'active' rather than 'passive' sparetime interests tend to be more successful (Mottram, 1970).

It is still common to hear the old adage 'You can't teach an old dog new tricks' as a rationalization for not attempting to train employees over the age of about 35. To some extent there may be some justification. Various authors have found that older trainees have less confidence, take longer to learn and find it difficult to eliminate mistakes they are making. This justification is, however, only part of the story. The main point is that the *method* of training is much more important for older trainees. In particular, older trainees seem to be handicapped by traditional 'chalk-and-talk' teaching methods which place emphasis on memorization. A number of causes have been suggested. It may be that memory processes deteriorate with age or it may simply be that older trainees are unused to this type of learning because of the long intervening period since they left school. In addition, the older trainee may be unduly quality-conscious, which inhibits the building of skills that depend on speed of action (Belbin and Toye, 1970). Another difficulty observed in older trainees is the persistence of mistakes. In an experimental situation, for example, Kay (1951) found that once older subjects had for some reason 'learned' the wrong response, they found it difficult to modify their errors and built up a pattern which persisted even in the face of evidence that it was wrong.

This dismal catalogue presents only one side of the picture. There are many examples where older trainees have been as successful as younger trainees provided that appropriate training methods were adopted. Jamieson (1966a) was able to train subjects as old as 44 to use a sewing machine, when according to conventional factory wisdom applicants over the age of 21 were considered to be too old. Jamieson's method involved a series of exercises which had to be performed at full speed, but as they progressed, the standards became more exacting. Unfortunately, not all new methods seem to work to the advantage of the older learner, Chown *et al.* (1972) ran a comparison of a programmed instruction method and a discovery method of learning and found that whereas the 'discovery method' of instruction benefitted the older trainees, the programmed instruction method seemed to offer very little advantage.

The discovery method is now probably the most recommended training method for use with older trainees (R. M. Belbin, 1969). During experiments on training sorting-office personnel at the GPO Dr E. Belbin (1958) tried various methods which were thought to be suitable to older trainees. Initially, cards bearing coloured dots were to be posted as quickly as possible into the appropriate letterboxes, which bore numbers. The task was to learn the relationship between the colour codes and the numbers. The learning method could be either memorizing a chart showing the relationships between colour and number, or the activity method, in which the cards bore the number as well as the colour code and the trainee had to post the cards into the boxes bearing the same numbers. In the test 'run' the list giving the relationship between colour and number was removed from the first group, and both groups sorted cards which only bore the colour code. The results showed that the older groups performed best with the activity method of learning. In general terms, the same finding emerged from subsequent experiments both in the GPO sorting office and in a 'mending' task drawn from the textile industry. From their results, Belbin was able to conclude, 'Not only were the older people able to learn an industrial task reasonably well by this "activity" type of method, but their performance compared very favourably with that of younger trainees. The comparison of this method with other methods in our former experiments with young trainees ... showed that it yielded somewhat better results than the traditional method, which makes considerable demands on memorization'. Further experiments (E. Belbin and Downs, 1964) confirmed this view and the finding later became a cornerstone of the discovery method outlined in a Training Information Paper (R. M. Belbin, 1969). In essence, the discovery method is a style of teaching which structures a situation so that the trainee learns by actively finding out the principles and relationships himself. Thus, for example, instead of a trainee being shown a diagram of a piece of equipment and given a lecture on how it works, the trainee would be given the actual piece of equipment with the parts clearly labelled. Provided that safety considerations are taken into account, the trainee learns the functions of each part and how the equipment works by operating it himself. In itself this idea is simple and was propounded centuries earlier by Rousseau in his book on the education of Émile. What is new is the application to adult learning in industry and the scientific vigour of its evaluation.

SOCIAL PSYCHOLOGY AND ADULT LEARNING IN INDUSTRY

Finally, it would be wrong to conclude a chapter on adult learning and industrial training without drawing attention to the growing relevance of the tools of social psychology to the issues of industrial training. It has already been noted that social psychological phenomena such as attitudes, interpersonal perceptions and intergroup behaviour are as important in determining the success of training programs as the correct analysis of the task and the proper preparation of instruction. Social psychological techniques are also relevant to the evaluation of many training courses. However, the real impetus for the greater involvement of social psychology in training matters is the growing awareness that a modern service economy makes great demands on the social skills that a person may have. There is also the growing realization that these skills can be improved by training. To give an ordinary humdrum example, attendants and waitresses in motorway service areas constantly draw upon their social skills when dealing with clients, and these skills can be improved by various types of training (Cooper and Oddie, 1973). Social skills training of this kind—which has applications in a wide range of practical industrial situations—draws upon some very basic aspects of social psychological research such as the psychology of non-verbal communication or interactive process analysis of meetings (Bales, 1950).

Already, a number of training courses in industrial relations include an element of the interactive process analysis pioneered by Bales. Usually his initial categories of behaviour are modified slightly to meet the peculiarities of an industrial setting (for example Rackham, 1971). The trainees working in syndicates may be given a case study and asked to arrive at a solution. Their behaviour while they are solving the problem will be observed and scored. At the end of the exercise the subject's own behaviour profile and the group profile are discussed. The cycle may be repeated several times so the trainees can experiment and see the consequences of their own behaviour, and it is hoped that behaviour will change in a way that will help the group meet its objectives. In an industrial relations course, for example, it would be hoped that such a procedure would reduce friction-producing behaviour such as 'shutting out' or the development of a 'defend–attack spiral' while increasing behaviours such as 'bringing in' and 'consensus seeking' which may assist the discovery of acceptable solutions. At present, such developments in social skills training are only in their infancy but as the economy develops as a service economy, social psychological aspects may become one of the growth areas of industrial training and adult learning in industry.

REFERENCES

Annett, J., and Duncan, K. (1967). 'Task analysis and training design', *Occupational Psychology*, **41**, 211.
Argryris, C. (1974). *Applicability of Organizational Sociology*, Cambridge University Press.
Bales, R. F. (1950). 'A set of categories for the analysis of small group interaction', *American Sociological Review*, **15**, 146.
Belbin, E. (1958). 'Methods of training older workers', *Ergonomics*, **1**, 207.
Belbin, E. (1969). 'Older adults in training', Conference Proceedings of the Association of Technical Institutions, June, 1969.
Belbin, E., and Belbin, R. M. (1969). 'Selecting and training adults for new rork', *Interdisciplinary Topics in Gerontology*, **4**, 66.
Belbin, E., and Downs, S. M. (1964). 'Activity learning and the older worker', *Ergonomics*, **7**, 429.
Belbin, E., and Toye, M. (1970). 'Adult training: forcing the pace', *Gerontology*, 33 (April).
Belbin, R. M. (1969). *The discovery Method in Training*, HMSO, London.
Blum, M. L., and Naylor, J. C. (1968). *Industrial Psychology*, Harper & Row, New York.

Cattell, R. B., Eber, H. W., and Tatsuoka, M. M. (1970). *Handbook for the 16PF*, NFER, Windsor, Berks.

Chown, S., Belbin, E., and Downs, S. (1972). 'Programmed instruction as a method of teaching paired associates to older learners', *Journal of Gerontology*, **22**, 212.

Cooper, C. L., and Oddie, H. (1973). 'Group training in a service industry: improving social skills in motorway service area restaurants', in C. L. Cooper (Ed.), *Group Training for Individual and Organizational Development*, Karger, Basle.

Dodd, B. (1967). 'A study in adult retraining: the gas man', *Occupational Psychology*, **41**, 143.

Downs, S. (1970). 'Predicting training potential', *Personnel Management*, 26 (September).

Duncan, K. (1974). 'Analytical techniques in training design', in E. Edwards and F. P. Lees (Eds.), *The Human Operator in Process Control*, Taylor & Francis, London.

Eckstrand, G. A. (1964). 'Current status of the technology of training', *AMRL Document Technical Report*, **64**, 86 (September).

Flanagan, J. C. (1954). 'The critical incident technique', *Psychological Bulletin*, **51**, 327.

Gagné, R. M., and Bolles, R. C. (1959). 'A review of factors in learning efficiency', in E. Galanter (Ed.), *Automatic Teaching: The State of the Art*, Wiley, New York, pp. 21–48.

Glaser, R. (1965). 'Psychology and instructional technology', in R. Glaser (Ed.), *Training Research and Education*, Wiley, New York.

Good, R. (1967). 'Study of Predictors and Criteria in the Selection of Data Processing Personnel', Unpublished M. A. Thesis, Birkbeck College, London.

Jamieson, G. H. (1966a). 'Age, speed and accuracy: a study in industrial retraining', *Occupational Psychology*, **40**, 237.

Jamieson, G. H. (1966b). 'A pilot study of recruitment and training', *Occupational Psychology*, **40**, 167.

Kay, H. (1951). 'Learning of a serial task by different age groups', *Quarterly Journal of Experimental Psychology*, **3**, 166.

Kelly, G. A. (1955). *The Psychology of Personal Constructs*, Norton, New York.

Merton, R. K. (Ed.) (1952). *Reader in Bureaucracy*, Free Press, New York.

Morea, P. C. (1972). *Guidance, Selection and Training*, Routledge & Kegan Paul, London.

Mottram, R. D. (1970). 'Adults changing jobs. Predicting trainability using biographical data', *Gerontology*, 4 (April).

Newsham, D. B. (1975). *The Will to Retrain*, ITRU Research Paper SY1, Industrial Training Research Unit, Cambridge.

Pearn, M. (1975). *CRAMP A Guide to Training Decision: A Users Manual*, ITRU Research Paper, Industrial Training Research Unit, Cambridge.

Rackham, N. (1971). *Developing Interactive Skills*. Wellan.

Robbins, W. G. H. (1972). 'Mid-career problems of graduates in industry', in G. Williams, and H. Greenway (Eds.), *Patterns of Change in Graduate Employment*. Society for Research into Higher Education, London.

Seymour, W. D. (1966). 'Retaining for Technological Change', Paper read to National Conference of Institute of Personal Management.

Seymour, D. W. (1968). *Skills Analysis Training*, Pitman, London.

Slater, P. (1972). *Mimeographed Notes on Ingrid 72*. Medical Research Council, London.

Smith, J. M. (1973a). 'Age and retraining: a study of characteristics of older workers who volunteer for retraining', *Occupational Psychology*, **47**, 141.

Smith, J. M. (1973b). 'Age and occupation: the determinants of male occupational age structures—Hypothesis H and Hypothesis A', *Journal of Gerontology*, **28**, 4, 484.

Smith, J. M. (1974). 'Age and occupation: a review of the use of occupational age structures in industrial gerontology', *Industrial Gerontology*, **1**, 2, 42.

Smith, J. M. (1975). 'Occupations classified by their age structure', *Industrial Gerontology*, **209** (Summer).

Smith, M., and Ashton, D. (1975). 'Using repertory grid technique to evaluate management training', *Personal Review*, **4**, 15.

Sokel, I. (1970). 'Economic changes and older worker utilization patterns', *Interdisciplinary Topics in Gerontology*, **6**, 43.

Tilley, K. (1968). 'A technology of training', in D. Pym (Ed.), *Industrial Society*, Penguin, Harmondsworth.

Toffler, A. (1972). *Future Shock*, Pan Books.

Toye, M. (1973). '*Pacing and Pacing Machines: an Evaluation*', ITRU Research Paper TR4, Industrial Training Research Unit, Cambridge.

11

LEARNING TO COPE WITH ATYPICAL FORCE ENVIRONMENTS

James T. Reason

INTRODUCTION

A consideration of the process whereby we adapt to unusual and initially disturbing force environments does not usually find its way into texts on learning, so perhaps its presence here deserves some preliminary word of explanation. The case for dealing with such a topic in the present book rests on two points. The first is that the phenomenon discussed in this chapter shares most if not all of the essential attributes normally ascribed to the learning process. It would, for example, fall comfortably within the definition offered by Hilgard and Bower (1966): 'Learning is the process by which an activity originates or is changed through reacting to an encountered situation, provided that the characteristics of the change in activity cannot be explained on the basis of native response tendencies, maturation or temporary state of the organism (e.g. fatigue, drugs, etc.)'. It would also fulfill the condition emphasized by Gagné (1967) that this change should be one that is retained in some degree with the passage of time. The second point is a more practical one. Our increasing reliance on various modes of transportation exposes us to more and more atypical force environments, so that our well-being and perhaps even our lives—in the more exotic vehicles—depend upon a better understanding of the adaptive processes that come to protect us against the ravages of these biologically alien conditions.

The chapter is in three parts. The first is concerned with explaining more precisely what is meant by the term 'atypical force environment', and with classifying the various types of *sensory rearrangement* that result from exposure to different force environments. The second part reviews the principal experimental findings with regard to the adaptation process. In effect, it poses the questions that need to be answered by any adequate theory of the underlying mechanisms. In the final part, a *neural mismatch* model is presented which seeks to explain, in information-processing terms, the acquisition and retention of 'protective adaptation' to atypical force environments in particular, and to conditions of sensory rearrangement in general.

WHAT IS AN ATYPICAL FORCE ENVIRONMENT?

To answer this question, it is best to begin with some appreciation of what constitutes a 'typical' force environment, where the term 'typical' refers to what is biologically typical rather than that which now characterizes our present artifact-dominated lifestyle.

After the first few months of life, human beings were designed to be actively self-propelled animals, moving at around 3–4 mph over a primarily two-dimensional world under conditions of normal terrestrial gravity. It is *only* under these conditions that our position and motion senses—the eyes, the vestibular receptors and the non-vestibular proprioceptors—function in harmony to provide us with functionally corelated information concerning our orientation in space. In other words, all the spatial senses normally tell the brain the same story. But when we allow ourselves to be transported passively in any one of the wide variety of vehicles at our disposal, or when we are spun, rolled, pitched or rocked in laboratory and fairground devices, this delicate harmony is disrupted to produce a mismatch between the signals communicated by these usually synergistic receptors.

For our present purposes, therefore, we may define an atypical force environment as one that is created primarily (though not exclusively) through the agency of real or illusory (i.e. visually-induced) passive motion, and which produces the condition that Held (1961) termed *sensory rearrangement*. That is, when the information arriving at one set of receptors is artificially distorted to render it incompatible with the pattern of sensory inputs arriving at functionally related receptors. A crucial consequence of this distortion is that, during the early preadapted stages of rearrangement, there is a conflict between the current sensory influx and the pattern of inputs expected on the basis of past experience, or what Held called 'exposure-history'.

Sensory rearrangement can take many different forms depending on the prevailing circumstances and which senses are party to the conflict, but for convenience they can be subsumed under two general headings:

(1) *visual–inertial rearrangements* (where the term 'inertial' includes both the vestibular and non-vestibular proprioceptors)—here the conflict is *between* sense modalities; and

(2) *canal–otolith rearrangements*—here there is an intramodality conflict between the two sets of receptors *within* the vestibular system, the semicircular canals (acting as the head's angular speedometers) and the otolith system (acting as multidirectional linear accelerometers).

For each category of sensory rearrangement, we can logically distinguish three types of conflict. If A and B represent portions of normally correlated receptor systems—visual–inertial or canal–otolith—then these three types of conflict can be represented as follows: *type 1*—when A and B *simultaneously* signal

Table 11.1. Some Laboratory and Everyday Examples of the Six Categories of Sensory Rearrangement

---

A. Visual-inertial rearrangements

Type 1: when the eyes and the inertial receptors simultaneously signal contradictory motion information, e.g. watching waves over the side of a ship, making head movements while wearing some optical device that distorts vision.

Type 2: when the eyes signal bodily motion in the absence of corroborating information from the inertial senses, e.g. watching a large-angle moving picture shot from a vehicle that is subjected to linear and/or angular accelerations, operating a fixed-base car or aircraft simulator equipped with a dynamic visual display.

Type 3: when the vestibular system and other proprioceptors signal motion in the absence of visual corroboration, e.g. reading a map in a moving vehicle, riding in a vehicle without external visual reference.

B. Canal-otolith rearrangements

Type 1: when the canals and the otoliths simultaneously signal contradictory information concerning the position and motion of the head, e.g. when the head is tilted in a rotating environment (i.e. when exposed to cross-coupled angular accelerations—see text).

Type 2: when the canals signal head motion in the absence of otolithic corroboration, e.g. during zero-gravity space flight, or during caloric stimulation of the outer ear.

Type 3: when the otoliths signal head motion in the absence of corroboration from the semicircular canals, e.g. during steady-state rotation about an earth-horizontal axis, or about any off-vertical axis.

---

contradictory or uncorrelated information; *type 2*—when A signals in the absence of an *expected* B signal; and *type 3*—when B signals in the absence of an *expected* A signal. On the basis of these classifications, we can distinguish six distinct categories of sensory rearrangement, examples of which are given in Table 11.1.

Three points need to be made about this classification scheme. First, visual–inertial and canal—otolith rearrangements can and frequently do coexist in many force environments. Thus, canal–otolith conflicts are often exacerbated by concurrent visual–inertial conflicts, depending on the extent and the nature of the visual reference. Second, it must be stressed that no fundamental distinction is made between actual bodily motion and apparent bodily motion which is induced by viewing a scene that, under real-life circumstances, would be accompanied by vestibular stimulation. In other words, viewing a Cinerama picture shot from a moving rollercoaster car is just as much an atypical force environment for the spectator sitting perfectly still in his cinema seat as the experience of actually riding in the rollercoaster was for the cameraman; the only difference lies in the precise nature of the sensory rearrangement. Third, all of the situations cited in Table 11.1 are known to produce *motion sickness:* a fact that tells us something very important about the nature of the provocative stimulus—namely, that it always involves a condition of sensory rearrangement in which the vestibular system is either directly or indirectly implicated. It is this fact, in particular, that has been largely responsible for the considerable attention given to the mechanisms of adaptation, since it offers the most satisfactory means of reducing motion sickness susceptibility (see Reason and Brand, 1975).

THE PRINCIPAL RESEARCH FINDINGS

Since many of the findings to be discussed below were derived from studies of adaptation in a rotating environment—or, more specifically, to cross-coupled angular stimulation—it would be helpful to preface this section with a brief description of the both the stimulus and the basic experimental procedure.

As indicated in Table 11.1, exposure to cross-coupled angular accelerations (sometimes called Coriolis stimulation) produces a type 1, canal–otolith rearrangement in which these two normally synergistic receptors simultaneously signal contradictory position and motion information. This occurs whenever the head is tilted about some axis other than the axis of platform rotation. During and immediately following the head motion, the subject experiences a sensation of apparent rotation about an axis that is orthogonal to both the head-tilt and platform axes. This arises because semicircular canals, previously unstimulated by the platform rotation, are brought into the plane of this rotation by the head tilt, causing an accelerative cross-coupled stimulus to be delivered to the cupula–endolymph systems of these canals. Meanwhile, the otoliths continue to signal the head tilt accurately. The strength of this cross-coupled stimulus is determined by the angular velocity of the platform and the angle through which the head is moved. More detailed accounts of the mechanics of this stimulus have been given elsewhere (Guedry and Montague, 1961; Weaver, 1965; Melvill Jones, 1970). This phenomenon has been extensively studied over the past two decades, largely because of its implications for life aboard projected manned space vehicles that rotate to provide artificial gravity.

Many of the studies designed to assess adaptation to this stimulus have required subjects to make a series of controlled head and body movements. At the end of each movement, they are asked to indicate whether or not they experienced any unusual sensations due to the cross-coupled stimulus. For any particular angular velocity, the rate of adaptation is indicated by the number of head movements executed prior to an operationally defined adaptation criterion where a predetermined number of consecutive head movements each elicited a negative response, that is, a response indicating that the sensations accompanying the head movements were indistinguishable from those produced by identical movements in a stationary environment. The usual practice is to increase the angular velocity in a series of 1-rpm steps up to some terminal velocity, where the subject is required to attain the adaptation criterion prior to the next velocity increment. This stepwise exposure allows the investigator to measure the amount of stimulation required to normalize the illusory sensations at each velocity level and, at the same time, it reduces the risk of motion sickness occurring *en route*.

Aside from its implications for rotating spacecraft, however, the chief advantage of the rotating environment is that it permits a degree of stimulus control not usually found in other force environments. In addition, there are firm grounds for believing that the adaptive processes observed in the rotating environment hold true for a wide range of atypical force environments.

1. The Temporal Pattern of Adaptation and its Aftereffects

Observations derived from a number of different force environments (Groen, 1960; Guedry, 1965; Reason, 1969) indicate that there are three distinct stages in the adaptive process: (a) an *initial exposure phase* in which illusions of apparent motion, various psychomotor disturbances and motion sickness make their appearance with latencies ranging from milliseconds to hours, depending upon the nature of the sensory rearrangement and its severity; (b) a *continued exposure phase* in which perceptions gradually return to the veridical and the various adverse reactions (which the possible exception of drowsiness) diminish and eventually disappear through continued interaction with the rearranged environment; and (c) an *aftereffect phase* following the return to the previously typical environment in which the reactions characteristic of the initial exposure phase are temporarily reinstated. Where these reactions have a directional sign, as in the illusions of apparent motion, this is reversed with respect to the initial exposure phase. With further exposure to the typical environment, these reactions disappear until—by all outward and subjective appearances, at least—the individual is restored to his original state. It is noticeable that the rate of 'readaptation' to the typical environment is considerably more rapid than the initial rate of adaptation to the atypical environment (Reason and Graybiel, 1970). But reactions such as motion sickness may be as severe in the early part of the aftereffect phase as they are during the initial exposure phase.

These three phases are readily apparent during and immediately after continued exposure to a rotating environment. Initially, the head movements provoke visual and somatic illusions of apparent motion. In addition, as the subject endeavours to bring his head down to one of the pads situated around his chair, he feels himself being deflected to one side so that he may even miss the pad (the 'giant hand' effect). He may also experience a gradual increase in epigastric awareness leading to acute nausea and perhaps vomiting. But with continued head movements, these reactions diminish in intensity until, eventually, they are indistinguishable from those evoked by the same head movement in a stationary environment. On stopping the rotation, no aftereffects are experienced so long as the subject keeps his head perfectly still. But should he attempt to make head movements identical to those executed during the perrotational phase, he will experience the same illusory sensations (but opposite in direction to those provoked by perrotational head motions) and motion sickness reactions as were encountered during the initial exposure to the cross-coupled stimulus. With continued head movements, these after-effects will rapidly subside until perception is restored to its original prerotational state.

2. The Long-term Retention of Adaptation

What happens when a previously adapted individual returns to the same force environment for a second time? To what extent does the protection gained on the first exposure reveal itself on subsequent occasions? Are there substantial 'savings' of adaptation, or is it dissipated during the intervening period in the typical environment? Some answers to these important practical questions have been provided by two recent experiments, once again using cross-coupled stimulation (Reason and Brand, 1975).

The first experiment was designed to assess the retention of adaptation to repeated exposures of graded cross-coupled stimuli. Eight young men received eight adaptation sessions in alternate directions of rotation over a total period of 24 weeks. The first four sessions were each separated by an interval of one week, then there was an interval of six weeks followed by two more sessions at one-week intervals. Then came a gap of 12 weeks followed by the two final sessions, again separated by an interval of one week. The results indicated a steady build-up of 'savings' of protective adaptation as reflected by the progressive reduction in stimulation required to achieve the adaptation criterion. There was a corresponding decline over sessions in motion sickness symptomatology and loss of well-being. Table 11.2 shows the percentage 'savings' in the mean total number of head movements required to attain the adaptation criterion on sessions 2–8 as compared with session 1.

The second experiment examined the relationship between the 'savings' of adaptation on the second of two exposures to graded cross-coupled stimulation and the time interval between them. Twenty-five young men were assigned to five equal groups matched for motion sickness susceptibility: the 1-day, 2-day, 7-day, 14-day and 21-day groups, where these times refer to the interval

Table 11.2. Percentage 'Savings' in Stimulus Exposure to Adaptation over Session 2–8

Session no.	Time after first exposure (weeks)	Percentage 'savings' in no. of head movements required to neutralize illusory sensations
2	1	30
3	2	43
4	3	55
5	9	60
6	10	63
7	22	70
8	23	69

between the first and second exposures to the same graded cross-coupled stimulus. The results revealed no decline in savings with increasing time intervals. The mean savings on session 2 fluctuated around a value slightly in excess of 50 per cent, irrespective of the time elapsed since session 1. In other words, the subjects required, on average, approximately half the number of head movements to neutralize the illusory sensations on session 2 than they did on session 1. Although slightly less consistent, the same pattern of reduction in the second session also held for motion sickness susceptibility as indicated by the well-being ratings and symptom scores. From these data, it is clear that a substantial proportion of the protective adaptation acquired on the first session was still intact during the second.

Taken together, these two studies indicate that adaptation to an atypical force environment is retained in some degree for long periods of time. The results of the second study further show that whatever loss of adaptation there is occurs fairly rapidly after the end of the adapting session, and that thereafter the level of protective adaptation remains relatively stable. This suggests an exponential pattern of adaptation decay, and the findings of the first study indicate that the time-constant of this decay curve increases as a function of the number of adapting sessions that preceded it. In other words, the greater the number of preceding adapting sessions, the slower will be the rate of adaptation decay following the last of them and the higher will be the relatively stable level of retained adaptation. This argument is shown diagrammatically in Figure 11.1. Although there is as yet only slight evidence to support it, we may speculate further and hypothesize that the time-constant of adaptation decay increases in a negatively accelerating fashion with repeated exposures, as shown in Figure 11.2. This means that although the amount of protective adaptation measured at some point following the last exposure increases with the number of preceding exposures, it is unlikely that it will ever remain permanently at the 100 per cent level. In other words, there is always likely to be some loss of adaptation, albeit very small, no matter how many times an individual has been exposed to the adapting stimulus.

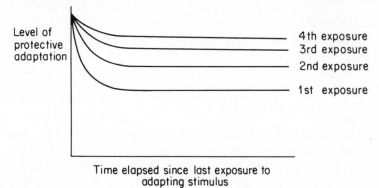

Figure 11.1 Some speculations regarding the rate of decay of protective adaptation following repeated exposures to the adapting situation

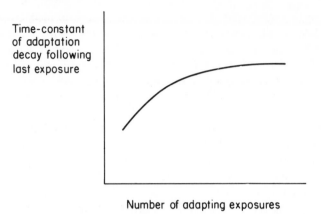

Number of adapting exposures

Figure 11.2 Further speculations regarding the relationship between the time-constant of adaptation decay and the number of previous exposures to the adapting stimulus

3. Active Versus Passive Interaction with the Atypical Force Environment

Several studies by Held and his collaborators have shown that active movements are superior to passive movements in acquiring adaptation to visual distortion involving the displacement, curvature or tilt of the seen environment (Held and Hein, 1958; Held and Bossom, 1961; Held and Mikaelian, 1964; Mikaelian and Held, 1964). Although several other investigators (Wallach *et al.*, 1963; Weinstein *et al.*, 1964; Howard *et al.*, 1965; Howard, 1970) deny the *essential* role of self-produced motion in adaptation to optical distortion—having shown that adaptation can occur with passive motion under certain conditions—the present consensus is that active movements by the subject facilitate the process of adaptation, although they are clearly not, as Held originally suggested, a necessary condition for its occurrence.

Held (1965) argued that it was the efferent components of the active movement which made it superior to passive movement. Its importance derives from the fact that 'only an organism that can take account of the output signals to its own musculature is in a position to detect and factor out the decorrelating effects of both moving objects and externally imposed body movement'. In Held's opinion, the key to the adaptation process lies in the availability of 'reafference'—a term coined by von Holst (1954) to describe the sensory feedback that arises from self-induced movement. We shall return to this notion at a later point.

So far, little or no evidence has been obtained regarding the relative effectiveness of active or passive motion in acquiring adaptation to inertial rearrangements such as weightlessness and cross-coupled accelerations. Nearly all the work to date has involved active, self-induced movements on the part of the subjects. However, the expectation, based on the optical distortion work, would be that adaptation can occur with passively induced head motions, but that it will be acquired far more effectively as the result of voluntary activity. Some evidence to support this notion within a rotating environment has been obtained by Oosterveld (1970).

4. The Extent of the Sensory Rearrangement

There is considerable evidence to show that the rate of adaptation to an atypical force environment depends to a large degree upon the extent of the prevailing rearrangement between the spatial senses. The smaller the extent of the rearrangement, the more rapid is the rate of adaptation—or, to be more precise, the smaller is the exposure required to neutralize the initial reactions (Reason and Brand, 1975). In any atypical force environment, the extent of the rearrangement depends upon two factors: (a) the *number of* discrepant sensory channels, and (b) the *magnitude* of the discrepancy within any one sensory channel. In a rotating environment, for example, the first factor depends largely on the nature and the extent of the visual reference available to the subject. The adverse consequences of the cross-coupled stimulus are reduced if the subject is permitted a clear view of the earth-stable environment surrounding the rotating platform (external visual reference), or if his eyes are closed (vision-absent). By contrast, the ill-effects of this stimulus are enhanced if the subject is allowed a full view of the illuminated interior of the rotating device with no external visual reference (internal visual reference). A study designed to compare rates of adaptation to identical cross-coupled angular stimulation under three conditions of visual reference—external, internal and vision-absent—revealed that it required approximately 30 per cent more head movements to neutralize the illusory sensations in the internal visual reference condition than it did in either of the other two (Reason and Diaz, 1970). This was the condition in which there was the greatest number of discrepant sensory channels.

A recent study carried out in zero-gravity during the Skylab missions provided further support for this conclusion (Graybiel et al., 1975). Astronauts were required to execute standardized head movements (front, back, left and right) in a chair that could be rotated at angular velocities up to 30 rpm. The inflight tests were carried out on and after mission day eight, by which time all the astronauts were adapted to working in weightless conditions. In all the rotation tests aloft, the eight astronauts tested were virtually symptom-free, in marked contrast to their reactions to the same rotational stimulus during pre- and post-flight tests on the ground. These investigators concluded: 'Inasmuch as the eyes were covered and the canalicular stimuli were the same aloft as on the ground, it would appear that lifting the normal gravitational stimulus to the otolith organs was an important factor in reducing susceptibility to motion sickness even though the transient linear and Coriolis accelerations generated under the test conditions were substantial and abnormal in pattern'. Thus, when the conflicting visual and otolithic inputs were effectively removed, as they were in the adapted astronauts during the inflight tests, the cross-coupled stimulus was robbed of its usually considerable nauseogenic potency.

5. The Specificity and Transfer of Adaptation

The bulk of the research evidence indicates that adaptation is normally highly specific to the particular stimulus conditions under which it was acquired: this is revealed in two ways. First, by the reinstatement of the nausea syndrome and allied disturbances when the conditions of rearrangement are changed even slightly after adaptation to the original conditions has been acquired. Second, there is a good deal of evidence to show that adaptation acquired in one situation fails to confer protection to any but the original circumstances, or at least to circumstances which contain the important nauseogenic ingredient of the original situation. Thus, sailors who have adjusted to the fairly vigorous motion of, say, a frigate or a fishing trawler, find that they have little or no protection against seasickness when they come to transfer to a vessel with different motion characteristics, even one in which the motion is comparatively sedate such as that of an aircraft carrier or ocean-going liner.

The classic experiments on the specificity of adaptation to cross-coupled stimulation were carried out by Guedry and his co-workers at Pensacola (Guedry *et al.*, 1962; 1964). In one study, subjects were required to make controlled head motions in one quadrant of the frontal plane. For half the subjects, this movement consisted of a 45° tilt towards the right shoulder; in the other half the same degree of tilt was made to the left shoulder. During the test session, the strength of the nystagmic and illusory reactions in the practised quadrant declined steadily over a period of hours. Towards the end of the run, subjects were required to make head motions in the unpractised quadrant as well. It was found that the strength of the illusory reactions produced by this quantitatively similar stimulus was only slightly less than that evoked by the initial motions in the practised quadrant. This clearly demonstrated that little or no adaptation had transferred from the practised to the unpractised quadrant, a conclusion that was further endorsed by the postrotatory after-effects: none were detected in the unpractised (unadapted) quadrant, but strong aftereffects were elicited by head movements in the practised (adapted) quadrant.

A later study (Reason and Graybiel, 1969) demonstrated that adaptation to cross-coupled stimulation was temporally as well as directionally specific. Three subjects were required to make approximately 8,000 head movements at 1-rpm step increases in angular velocity up to a terminal velocity of 10-rpm over a period of three days. These head and body flexions were carried out at 3-sec intervals for the greater part of the session. But when, on the third day, the subjects had achieved adaptation to criterion, this rate was altered so that the movements occurred at 6-sec intervals in the same directions as before. Immediately, the new temporal pattern evoked the reinstatement of illusory sensations which then took in the region of 100–160 head movements to neutralize.

Paradoxically, however, this same study also revealed that the protective adaptation acquired to precisely controlled 90° head movements in four quadrants—front, back, left and right—could generalize to much more extensive multidirectional movements. At two points in the head movement schedule, at 6 and at 10-rpm, stressor tests were given to assess the limits of the protective adaptation so far acquired. These involved the execution of large and rapid head movements in all directions, which would undoubtedly have had devastating effects on unadapted subjects. But in neither test did these stressful motions provoke more than a mild stomach awareness, suggesting that some degree of generalized protection had been achieved. It seems likely that this was a function of 'overadaptation'; that is, of the very large number of adapting head movements previously executed by the subjects.

To summarize: it seems that when the adapting exposure is of short to moderate duration, the adaptation so acquired is highly specific to the prevailing stimulus. But when the adapting session is extended well beyond the point of adaptation—the point at which the illusory sensations are no longer detectable by the subject—some degree of generalization does occur, although its extent has not yet been fully determined.

THEORETICAL CONSIDERATIONS

It should be made clear at the outset that the model of adaptation proposed below, the *neural mismatch hypothesis*, makes little claim to originality, except perhaps in its specific application to atypical force environments. Its origins can be traced directly to von Holst's (1954) 'reafference hypothesis', and to the later modifications of this notion made by Groen (1960) and Held (1961). In addition, this model shares with a number of other theories (Sokolov, 1960; Rock, 1966) the central assumption that the adaptive process involves two distinct stages. In the first, the current sensory inputs are matched to a neural record of previous stimulation. The second stage depends upon the results of this matching process. If there is a discrepancy between the present and stored information, a mismatch signal is generated which sets in train a number of physiological and behavioural events whose precise nature depends upon the receptors involved and the strength of the signal. Essentially, the process of adaptation is due to the information contained in the neural store being progressively updated and consolidated so that, eventually, it approximates to the current sensory influx. When this match is achieved, the second stage is not activated and the individual is considered to have adapted (or readapted) to his force environment.

1. Components of the Neural Mismatch Model

The basic structural components of the model and their interrelationships are illustrated in Figure 11.3. The key component for adaptation is the one labelled *neural store*. Following Held (1961), it is proposed that this '... acts as a kind of memory which retains traces of previous combinations of concurrent efferent and reafferent signals. The currently monitored efferent signal is presumed to select the trace combinations containing the identical efferent part and to reactivate the reafferent trace combined with it'. A schematic

214

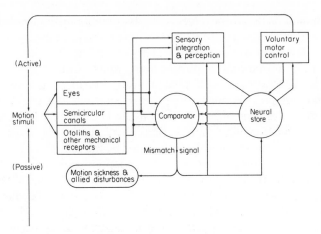

Figure 11.3 Principal components of the neural mismatch
model of adaptation

representation of one of these stored trace combinations, or *spatial engram*, is shown in Figure 11.4. It can be seen that the engram consists of two distinct elements: (1) a copy of the efference, or command signal, and (2) the reafferent trace combinations previously associated with this particular efference—of which two are shown in Figure 11.4. Let us imagine, for example, that this particular efference was 'Tilt the head 45° to the right shoulder'. The presence of two different reafferent trace combinations indicates that this command has been executed under two different sets of environmental conditions. The left-hand trace combination is strongly defined and linked to the efference trace by a well-established associative bond. This represents the reafferent trace combination provoked by the head tilt in the typical environment. The right-hand trace, containing different visual, canal and otolith stimulus traces, is much less consolidated and more weakly associated with the efference trace. Let us assume that this reafferent trace combination is one that has been stored as the result of a relatively brief exposure to cross-coupled angular stimulation. The purpose of Figure 11.4 is merely to illustrate that the same efference trace can be associated with two quite disparate reafferent traces of differing degrees of consolidation, and the foregoing example of a right head tilt in stationary and rotating conditions is given to indicate how this could occur. This point is emphasized since it is crucial to subsequent arguments as to the functioning of the model.

The other structural components of importance are (a) *the comparator unit* that compares the currently signalled reafferent inputs with reafferent trace combinations selected by the storage unit; (b) a *voluntary motor control unit* that initiates self-produced movements by sending appropriate efferent signals to the effector organs (muscles, joints, etc.); and (c) *a sensory integration and perception unit* that serves the dual function of integrating the inputs from the various spatial senses prior to the storage or comparison activities and also

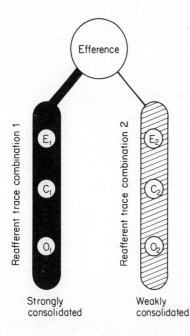

Figure 11.4 Schematic representation of spatial engram. E, visual input; C, canal input; O, otolith, etc., inputs

of originating the perceptions that are contingent upon the matching process carried out by the comparator. In addition, there are also the various neuro-humoral mechanisms responsible for the production of motion sickness and allied distrubances. These, like the illusory perceptions, are activated by the mismatch signal emitted by the comparator. And, as we shall see later, this mismatch signal also controls the adaptation process. But before considering this, let us state some of the assumptions that govern the strength of the mis-match signal.

2. Assumptions Governing the Strength of the Mismatch Signal

Three assumptions govern the strength of the mismatch signal. These are derived from the empirical observations stated in the previous section.

(1) The mismatch signal increases as a function of the extent of the discrepancy present in any one sensory channel. For example, in the case of a rotating environment it would increase as a function of the angular velocity and the angle through which the head was tilted.

(2) The mismatch signal increases as a function of the number of discrepant sensory channels contributing to the rearrangement. Thus, the mismatch signal is greater when a visual discrepancy is superimposed upon a canal–otolith conflict than when vision is absent—other factors being equal.

(3) The mismatch signal diminishes as a function of the strength or degree of consolidation of the stored trace combination. This assumption means that even when all other conditions are met for a match between the current sensory inputs and the stored trace combination, a mismatch signal will still

be generated if the latter has not reached a sufficient degree of consolidation, where this is acquired through the repeated laying down within the store of the same reafferent combination.

3. How the Model Works: A. The Self-produced Motion Case

When the transaction with the atypical force environment is through the agency of self-produced movements, as in a rotating environment when the subject moves his head voluntarily, the presumed sequence of events underlying the acquisition of protective adaptation is summarized in the flow diagram shown in Figure 11.5. Let us concentrate on the events specifically concerned with adaptation.

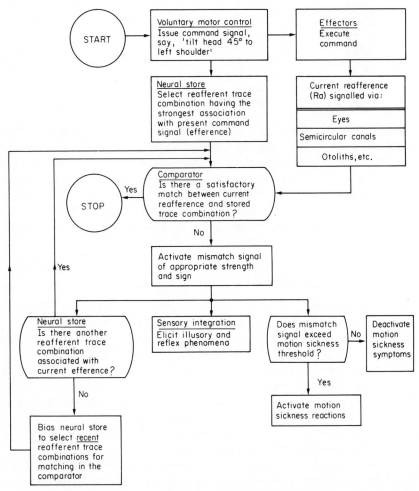

Figure 11.5 Flow diagram showing the functioning of the model in the case of self-produced movements

The sequence begins with the efference ('tilt head 45° to left shoulder'). This is communicated simultaneously to the effector organs and the neural store. It is postulated that the first instruction given to the neural store is to select the reafferent trace combination which has the *strongest* associative bond with the current efference. To find it, the neural store first seeks a match between the current efference and the efferent component of a spatial engram. Having done this, it checks the attached reafferent trace combinations for strength and selects the strongest. It is the rapidity of this information-retrieval process which is presumed to confer such advantage to the active as opposed to the passive motion situation. The reafferent trace combinations are 'addressed' by their associated efferent components, and are hence readily accessed.

Having been selected by the neural store, the appropriate reafferent trace combination is delivered to the comparator where it is matched to the current reafference generated by the effector activity. If the match is satisfactory, the adaptive sequence stops. But if there is a discrepancy between the stored and current information, a mismatch signal is generated which goes to at least three destinations: the sensory integration and perception unit, the mechanisms responsible for the production of motion sickness and allied disorders and—most importantly for the adaptation process—back to the neural store.

On receipt of the mismatch signal, the neural store selects the next strongest reafferent trace combination for matching in the comparator. If this also produces a mismatch signal, the cycle repeats itself until all the reafferent trace combinations associated with the efference have been exhausted, or until an appropriate reafferent trace has been found and consolidated to a sufficient degree so that the comparator accepts a match. If, however, there are no other traces associated with the efference, the neural store operates on the third instruction in this interative process: it becomes biased to select recent reafferent trace combinations for matching in the comparator. In other words, it selects those trace combinations guaranteed to achieve a match once sufficiently consolidated, namely, those generated by the existing rearranged force environment. The remainder of the adaptation process is then one of consolidation until the comparator accepts them as a satisfactory match with the current reafference. It is presumed that recently acquired reafferent traces are too fragile or ephemeral to satisfy the matching criteria adopted by the comparator. To achieve a sufficient degree of strength and permanence, they need to be reinforced many times by repetitions of the same reafferent combination. That is, in the case of cross-coupled stimulation, for example, they need to be consolidated by repeated head movements producing the same combination of visual, canal and otolith reafferent inputs. When this point is reached, the comparator accepts the match and the adaptation process is terminated so long as the same stimulus conditions prevail.

When the adapted individual is returned to his typical force environment, a process of readaptation ensues which is similar in most respects to that described above. However, there are two important points of difference. First, the appropriate reafferent trace combination is likely to be more highly consolidated than any other associated with the efference. Consequently it will be accessed very rapidly and will be of sufficient strength to satisfy the matching criteria. Hence, the readaptation process is achieved very quickly in comparison to adapting to a novel force environment. Second, the sign of the mismatch signal emitted by the comparator will be reversed with respect to that provoked during the preceding period of maladaptation. As a result, illusory phenomena elicited during this aftereffect phase will be opposite in direction to those experienced in the preceding phase.

4. How the Model Works: B. The Passive Motion Case

When the subject is moved passively by some external agency (as in a rotating room, when he is seated in a chair that is tilted mechanically by means outside his direct or indirect control), no efference signal is generated and so the rapid accessing of the appropriate stimulus traces provided by the efferent trace component is unavailable. As a result, the process of selecting appropriate stored traces for matching with the current afferent inputs is a very lengthy and inefficient one. Lacking the convenient 'cueing' of traces present in the self-produced motion case, it is possible that the neural store has to seek out

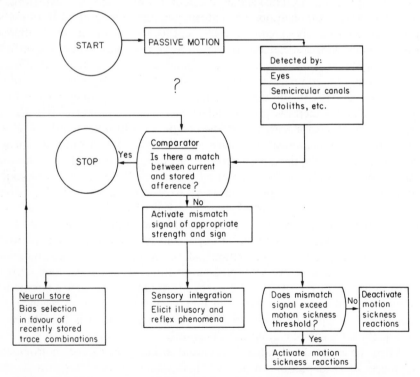

Figure 11.6 Flow diagram showing the functioning of the model in the case of passive movements

individual visual or vestibular traces for matching in the comparator; a procedure not unlike that of finding a book in a library that has no catalogue or perhaps one that merely directs the reader to search in a particular set of stacks. A speculative account of how the neural mismatch model works under passive motion conditions is shown in Figure 11.6.

5. Some Concluding Comments on the Neural Mismatch Model

It is believed that the model outlined above accounts for most of the principal empirical findings concerning adaptation to atypical force environments. In addition, it provides some explanation of the mechanisms underlying the production of motion sickness, which has been defined elsewhere as 'a self-inflicted maladaptation phenomenon characterised primarily by the presence of pollor, cold sweating, nausea and vomiting, which occurs at the onset and cessation of conditions of sensory rearrangement when the pattern of inputs from the vestibular system, other proprioceptors and vision is at variance with the stored patterns derived from recent transactions with the spatial environment' (Reason and Brand, 1975, p. 275). However, there remains the question of how protective adaptation can generalize to stimulus conditions other those which specifically induced it. It will be remembered from our earlier discussion of the specificity of adaptation that even small alterations in the stimulus conditions were sufficient to reinstate the various maladaptation phenomena. Yet when subjects were 'overadapted' to limited quadrantal head movements in a rotating room, they somehow acquired protection against far more stressful and extensive movements. How could this be explained by the model?

One possibility is that the comparator adjusts its matching criteria according to the degree of consolidation of the reafferent trace combination. That is, with only moderately consolidated traces it adopts fairly strict criteria; but when the trace is highly consolidated by repeated exposures to the rearranged conditions, it relaxes these criteria so that it disregards even quite considerable discrepancies between the trace and the current reafference as long as they were characteristic of the same rearranged conditions. In other words, it accepts what the Americans call a 'ball park' solution (Arbib, 1972).

Finally, there remains another research question of considerable interest. To date we have only considered extreme cases along the active–passive continuum. But what of intermediate situations where the subject—like the vehicle operator—retains some degree of *indirect* control over his own movements? How would this affect the adaptation process? Observations of car drivers and pilots indicates that they enjoy considerable immunity to motion sickness. The controller of a vehicle is being transported passively, yet being an integral part of a closed-loop control system where the consequences of his volitional adjustments of the controls are fed back to him either directly or *via* instruments, he shares many of the important characteristics of an actively self-propelled individual. Would these shared characteristics allow him to adapt nearly as rapidly as the actively moving individual? Such a question is open to empirical investigation, and the answers obtained would have important implications for our understanding of the mechanisms underlying the acquisition of adaptation to all rearranged environments.

REFERENCES

Arbib, M. A. (1972). *The Metaphorical Brain*, Wiley, New York.

Gagné, R. M. (1967). *The Conditions of Learning*, Holt, Rinchart & Winston, New York.

Graybiel, A., Miller, E. F., and Homick, J. L. (1975). 'Individual differences in susceptibility to motion sickness among six Skylab astronauts', *Acta Astronautica*, **2**, 155.

Groen, J. J. (1960). 'Problems of the semicircular canal from a mechanico-physiological point of view', *Acta oto-larying.*, *Stockholm*, Suppl. 163, 59.

Guedry, F. E. (1965). 'Habituation to complex vestibular stimulation in man: transfer and retention of effects from twelve days of rotation at 10 rpm', *Percept. mot. Skills*, **21**, 459.

Guedry, F. E., Graybiel, A., and Collins, W. E. (1962). 'Reduction of nystagmus and disorientation in human subjects, *Aerospace Medicine*, **33**, 1356.

Guedry, F. E., Kennedy, R. S., Harris, C. S., and Graybiel, A. (1964). 'Human performance during 2 weeks in a room rotating at 3 rpm', *Aerospace Medicine*, **35**, 1071.

Held, R. (1961). 'Exposure history as a factor in maintaining stability of perception and coordination', *J. Nerv. Ment. Dis.*, **132**, 26.

Held, R. (1965). 'Plasticity in sensory-motor systems', *Sci. Amer.*, **213**, 84.

Held, R., and Bossom, J. (1961). 'Neonatal deprivation and adult rearrangement: complementary techniques for analysing sensory-motor coordinations', *J. Comp. Physiol. Psychol.*, **54**, 33.

Held, R., and Hein, A. (1958). 'Adaptation of disarranged hand–eye coordination contingent upon reafferent stimulation', *Percept. Mot. Skills.*, **8**, 87.

Held, R., and Mikaelian, H. (1964). 'Motor-sensory feedback versus need in adaptation to rearrangement', *Percept. Mot. Skills*, **18**, 685.

Hilgard, E. R., and Bower, G. H. (1966). *Theories of Learning*, Appleton. Century, Crofts, New York.

Howard, I. P. (1970). 'The adaptability of the visual-motor system', in K. J. Connolly (Ed.), *Mechanisms of Motor Skill Development*, Academic Press, London.

Howard, I. P., Craske, B., and Templeton, W. B. (1965). 'Visuomotor adaptation to discordant exafferent stimulation', *J. exp. Psychol.*, **70**, 189.

Melvill Jones, G. (1970). 'Origin, significance and amelioration of Coriolis illusions from the semicircular canals: a non-mathematical appraisal', *Aerospace Medicine*, **35**, 984.

Mikaelian, H., and Held, R. (1964). 'Two types of adaptation to an optically-rotated visual field', *Amer. J. Psychol.*, **77**, 257.

Oosterveld W. (1970). Personal communication.

Reason, J. T. (1969). 'Motion sickness—some theoretical considerations', *Int. J. Man–Machine Studies*, **1**, 21.

Reason, J. T., and Brand, J. J. (1975). *Motion Sickness*, Academic Press, London.

Reason, J. T., and Diaz, E. (1970). 'The effects of visual reference on adaptation to Coriolis accelerations', *Flying Personal Research Committee Report No. 1303*, Ministry of Defence (Air), London.

Reason, J. T., and Graybiel, A. (1969). 'Adaptation to Coriolis accelerations: its transfer to the opposite direction of rotation as a function of intervening activity at zero-velocity', NAMI-1086, NASA Order R-93, Naval Aerospace Medical Institute, Pensacola, Fla.

Reason, J. T., and Graybiel, A. (1970). 'Progressive adaptation to Coriolis accelerations associated with 1 rpm increments in the velocity of the Slow Rotation Room', *Aerospace Medicine*, **41**, 73.

Rock, I. (1966). *The Nature of Perceptual Adaptation*, Basic Books, New York.

Sokolov, E. N. (1960). 'Neuronal models and the orienting reflex', in M. A. Brazien (Ed.), *The Central Nervous System and Behaviour*, J. Macy, New York.

von Holst, E. (1954). 'Relations between the central nervous system and the peripheral organs', *Brit. J. Anim. Behav.*, **2**, 89.

Wallach, H., Kravitz, J. H., and Lindauer, J. A. (1963). 'A passive condition for rapid adaptation to displaced visual direction', *Amer. J. Psychol.*, **76**, 568.

Weaver, R. S. (1965). 'Theoretical aspects of the role of angular acceleration in vestibular stimulation', *Acta Oto-Laryngol.*, Suppl. **205**, 1.

Weinstein, S., Sersen, E. A., Fisher, L., and Weisinger, M. (1964). 'Is reafference necessary for visual adaptation?', *Percept. Mot. Skills*, **18**, 641.

12

UNDERSTANDING INSTRUCTIONAL TEXT: TYPOGRAPHY, LAYOUT AND DESIGN

James Hartley and Peter Burnhill

The history of typographic research is a lengthy one, going back into the 1880's, and probably before. The research has been ably summarized by several workers, notably Tinker (1965), Spencer (1969) and Watts and Nisbet (1974). Useful bibliographies are also available (e.g. see Macdonald-Ross and Smith, 1973; Hartley *et al.*, 1974). From this research, together with that carried out in other related fields, it is possible to draw up a list of guidelines which may be useful to authors and printers designing instructional materials. In fact at the end of this chapter we present such a list, containing nearly 50 entries.

The guidelines are useful, but they are by no means sacrosanct. It will be obvious to the reader (as it is to the authors) that thev have not been slavishly obeyed in the writing of this chapter. Guidelines make general statements which must be treated with caution when applied to specific problems. The observant reader will also notice that, despite the long history of typographic research, the typographic contributions to the guidelines are relatively modern. Until recently, it would seem, typographical research has not had a great deal of relevance to authors and designers, to printers and to publishers.

WHY SHOULD THIS BE SO?

Why *is* the early research of little practical value? There seem to be several reasons. Firstly, the classical research literature on typography has concerned itself with molecular issues (i.e. with tiny details) rather than with molar ones (i.e. with broad-scale issues). Much research in typography has focused on problems of legibility at the levels of typefaces, typesizes, individual letters and words, and all in relation to relatively unstructured text such as prose. Researchers have tended to ignore higher-level organizational problems (which in practice determine decisions made at lower levels).

Secondly, work on the legibility of typefaces, for example, has tended to be oversimplified and divorced from the questions which are actually asked by practitioners when a choice of typeface has to be made. For instance, a typographer does not ask: is typeface A more legible than B?, but can A be reduced in size satisfactorily? What happens to the characters when a text, printed in typeface A, is copied on an office machine? And so on. Past research on the legibility of reading matter at the level of characters and words has not provided practitioners with a checklist of the performance characteristics of typefaces.

Thirdly, a more specific complaint about the traditional research in this field is that there has been an uncritical acceptance of conventional typographic practices. We shall argue and illustrate below that many typographic practices hinder rather than help the reader, and that fundamental rethinking is needed here. In passing, we may note here that we think that existing typographic practices have not been challenged because most of the research has been conducted by psychologists working in isolation from practising typographic designers.

Fourthly, but relatedly, much of this research is of an experimental nature, using materials which are simplified and divorced from their real-life context. Indeed, many of the guidelines which we have culled from the legibility research have not been tested in the natural context of a full page of meaningful print. Printers and typographers recognize the oversimplification inherent in such research, and thus, quite rightly, tend to regard it with suspicion.

Finally, we would maintain, most typographical research has no theoretical base; that is, experimental work has been conducted without reference to a coherent view of the principles entailed in typographical decision-making. Such an approach may be of value for decision-making in a specific context, but it permits no generality.

WHAT IS THE APPROACH TODAY?

This gloomy picture of the value of typographic research is, fortunately, now changing. The interest among psychologists (who are largely responsible for typographic research) has been broadening, and more complex problems, particularly those that arise in the context of education and learning, are now being examined. In addition, and more important, psychologists have begun to collaborate with typographic designers on the design and layout of instructional materials, and to evaluate the results of their joint endeavours. Over half the papers in the March 1975 issue of *Programmed Learning and Educational Technology* (an issue devoted to typographic research) were joint publications by psychologists and typographers.

Hartley and Burnhill (1975) and Macdonald-Ross and Waller (1975a) have argued independently that there is now a modern consensus between researchers and typographers: both groups have come to see the defects of the older literature and both would like to remedy them in a joint effort. Both groups are agreed, too, that research should and can be of value to practical designers, to authors and printers. Macdonald-Ross and Waller (1975a) suggest in their article a possible way of making typographic research more relevant. They argue that the first things to be acknowledged are (i) that the purpose of typographic research should be to help with practical decision-making, and (ii) that typographers have a great deal of implicit knowhow which should not be ignored. Next, they advance a three-stage practical research program which involves (i) the criticism of existing solutions; (ii) the production of alternatives; and (iii) the testing or evaluating of these alternatives in a real-life situation, with all the complexity that this entails. The research thus starts with a practical problem and finishes with a decision. The approach is illustrated in their article by a critical analysis of materials from Open University course texts.

In our own research (which is the joint product of a typographer and a psychologist) we are concerned to stress the importance of preplanning and a rational approach to the design of instructional materials. Such an approach, we maintain, is necessary if there is to be a proper concern for clarity and cost-effectiveness. Three aspects of this approach which we would like to discuss here in detail are (i) the need for standard page-sizes, (ii) the value of preplanning and (iii) the rational use of space too convey structure.

WHY DO WE NEED STANDARD PAGE-SIZES?

If the reader examines instructional materials he will no doubt find that they come in many shapes and sizes. Until recently there have been no specific rules or guidelines which would suggest to authors, designers or printers the reason for choosing one page-size in preference to another. The research literature on textbook design offers no assistance, for page-size is not an issue that features in any major textbook on typographic research. Why, then, do we consider page-size so important?

The size of the page determines the size of the overall visual display to the reader. The reader needs to be able to scan and read this display easily, be it large (e.g. an atlas) or small (e.g. a pocket dictionary). Readers need to be able to read, to scan and to focus on both gross and fine details. The size of the page determines the decisions the designer must make to convey these details to the reader.

Decisions about page-size are crucial because they form the baseline from which the remaining typographic decisions are made. Once the size of the page is determined it is possible to decide upon the layout of the page, the interline spacing and line-lengths of the text. Following these decisions come ones about the positioning of illustrations and so on. In other words, page-size is to typographic planning as site-size is to the design of buildings: it constrains what can be done.

The dimensions of a page are normally a function of the size of the initial manufactured sheet of printing paper from which the pages are made (by folding economically). The present-day variety in page-sizes reflects an equally unprincipled variety in the current manufacture of printing paper sheet sizes. Such an approach, of course, is quite uneconomical, and requires simplification.

The need to rationalize paper sizes is scarcely a new issue in the history of information printing. In 1798, for example, the French Government prescribed a standard based on the proportion of 1 : 1.41 with a basic sheet size of one square metre in area. In 1911, Wilhelm Oswald proposed a 'world format' of 1 : 1.414 based on sheet sizes measured in multiples of 10 × 14.1 mm. In 1922 the German standard, DIN 476, was published. This standard combined the previous suggestions: the ratio of 1 : 1.414 was retained with a basic sheet of one square metre. This standard, together with the A, B and C series of sizes, was adopted in 1958 by the International Organisation for Standardisation (ISO) and is now recommended by most of the 50 or more national standards organizations which comprise membership of ISO. The dimensions of the A and the B series of sizes are set out below. The C series relates to envelope sizes for use with standard-size documents and does not concern us here.

ISO series of trimmed paper sizes

A series		B series	
Designation	Size (mm)	Designation	Size (mm)
AO	841 × 1189	BO	1000 × 1414
A1	594 × 841	B1	707 × 1000
A2	420 × 594	B2	500 × 707
A3	297 × 420	B3	353 × 500
A4	210 × 297	B4	250 × 353
A5	148 × 210	B5	176 × 250
A6	105 × 148	B6	125 × 176
A7	74 × 105	B7	88 × 125
A8	52 × 74	B8	62 × 88
A9	37 × 52	B9	44 × 62
A10	26 × 37	B10	31 × 44

The unifying principle of the ISO recommended range of sizes is that a rectangle with sides in the ratio of 1 : 1.414 $(1 : \sqrt{2})$ can be halved or doubled to produce a series of rectangles, each member of which retains the proportions of the original. For example: A4 folds in half to form A5. A rectangle of any other proportion will generate geometrically similar rectangles only at every other point in the process of halving or doubling.

It is this unique characteristic of the ISO range of page-sizes which is so valuable in the day-to-day work of typographic designing. Geometrical similarity of format means, amongst other things, that typeset information which has been prepared for standard-size pages need not necessarily be reset, but simply enlarged or reduced photographically, when it is required for use with any other format which complies with the ratio of 1:1.414. Similarly, artwork for diagrams and illustrations, and the blocks or negatives made from such artwork, need not be remade when used in differing contexts, such as the design of wall charts, work cards, or overhead projector transparencies, where the format also complies with the standard width-to-depth ratio. In other words, looking to the future, the use of standard formats will ease the interchange of information as between information carriers of differing kinds, and may, indeed, help us change our current notions concerning the idea and function of textbooks.

The rationalization of book sizes also has other wide implications. These concern not only the economics of paper manufacture and its use, but also the whole process of book design, specification, manufacture, packaging, storage and transportation. Although a concern for the textbook as an industrial product may seem somewhat remote from the subject matter of this chapter, the rationalization of textbook sizes has important economic implications.

A further comment can be made here about the value to research in this area of the rationalization of page-sizes. This concerns work on the relationships between how a text is intended to be used and the way in which its component parts might be arranged on the page. If, as up to now, every research problem is unconstrained by any concern for the page-size on which the matter is to be arranged, then every problem must be regarded as a new one. Such a situation prevents systematic research and evaluation. It also limits the accumulation of knowledge through 'on-the-job' practice. In our view, therefore, the recognition of standard page-sizes by research workers is a necessary condition for further development in the design and evaluation of instructional materials.

WHAT IS THE VALUE OF PREPLANNING?

A glance at the pages of instructional materials will show that the component parts of the information are highly differentiated and varied in character. Unlike story books, which may consist of little more than lines of text set in paragraph form with an occasional heading, instructional materials normally contain a wide variety of components—such as listed information, programmatically developed statements, numbered items, diagrammatic presentations, explanatory notes and pictorial features of many kinds.

Furthermore, many of these materials are not intended for continuous reading. In the instructional situation the learner's focus of attention is constantly ranging from his place on the page to somewhere else: to the instructor, to responses made by other learners, to a practical task, and, of course, back again to his place on the page. From this point of view, instructional materials are tools used in a highly interactive and relatively unpredictable sequence of events.

The spatial organization of the text must reflect this situation, not by being as unpredictable as the events of the learning process or practical task, but by providing a consistent and trustworthy frame of reference from which the learner can move to and from without confusion. The typography must be as consistent as regards the position of the component parts of the information as are the walls and ceillings of the instructional setting.

The principal weakness in the typographical architecture of materials we have examined is a lack of consistency in the positioning of functionally related parts. For example, the relative positions of tables and illustrations and of text which refers to them frequently change both within a page and from page to page. As the text is being used, the reader must constantly be asking 'Where am I supposed to go from here?'.

This kind of muddle in linear organization and spatial grouping provides evidence not only of a lack of rigour in the initial planning of the page, but also of a weakness in the communication bridge between design and production. in short, the absence of consistency in the positioning of related parts indicates that layout decisions have been made *during the process* of physically assembling the image (type and illustrations) prior to the process of its multiplication by printing.

In the world of building, this would be equivalent to erecting a house without reference to a formal specification or plan. When it is considered that the cost of producing a handbook may be equivalent to that of erecting a building, then some idea may be gained of the wastage and cost of muddling through in this way. As is well known, the cost of making corrections in relatively simple text is far more than the cost of assembling the type in the first place. The cost of constantly making changes in the process of assembling complex textual arrangements is, of course, higher still. The cost to the student in terms of learning is something which, at present, we do not have the means to measure.

The Reference Grid

If confusion and waste are to be minimized in the planning and production of instructional text then the arrangement of the parts must be decided on in detail before the steps are taken to set in motion the setting of the type and the making of the illustrations. If decisions and changes as regards the size and position of the component parts of the page are made *during* the process of production, than confusion and waste are bound to occur. One essential element in planning in the communication to the printer of design requirements and in the ultimate use of the material is the typographic reference grid. This element has clearly been absent from the design and specification of most instructional materials we have examined.

In a less disciplined approach to print design than that required for instructional materials, a sketch is sometimes drawn showing rectangles to indicate blocks of 'text' and the position of illustrations. Strictly speaking, such a drawing is not a reference grid. As can be seen from Figure 12.1 (a), the basic reference grid is a system of coordinates which maps out the information area of the page in identically dimensioned modules of space. This basic grid is the foundation for the drawing of a master reference grid, or set of grids, to be used in specifying the linear and spatial requirements of the work in hand (see Figures 12.1 (a), 12.1 (b), 12.1 (c) and 12.1 (d).

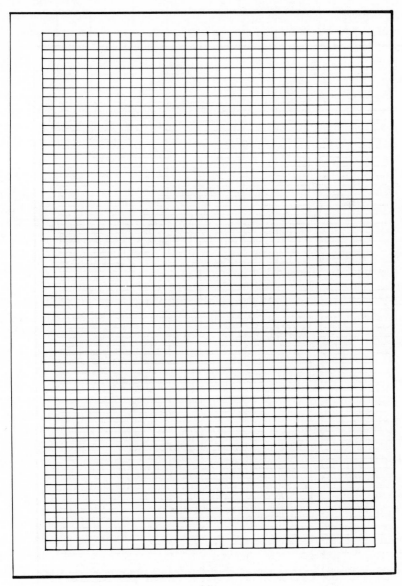

(a)

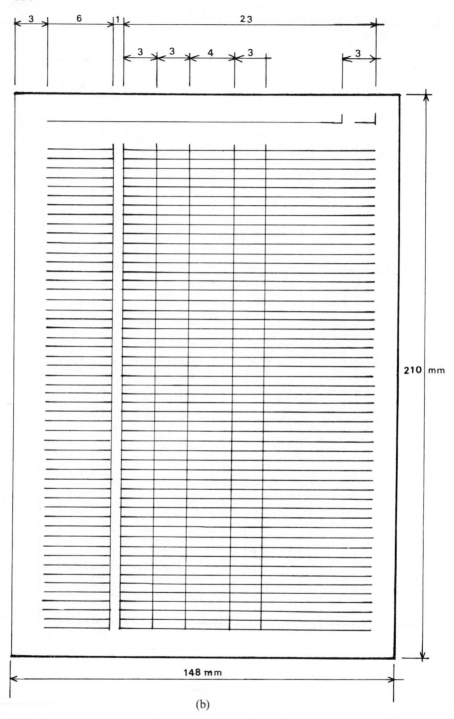

(b)

Part-time Vocational Courses

City and Guilds Creative Studies Courses

The undermentioned courses have been designed mainly for those mature students who wish to follow a course of vocational and personal reasons. The Courses are made up of two parts: Part 1, involving 2 years' study and Part 2, involving 1 years' study. External examinations for both Parts involve written papers and coursework assessment.

■ Fashion CGLI 780

Part 1
1st & 2nd years

The aim is to develop an awareness of fashion as a whole in addition to a high standard of Craftsmanship using modern methods of making up.

Part 2
3rd year

A more advanced study of the items in the Fashion Part 1 syllabus.

Day Course

Course symbol: DF1   Course tutor: Miss M Jeavons

class	day	time	room	subject
71004	Tues	$9\frac{1}{2}$-$12\frac{1}{2}$	Ov20	Practical
71014	Tues	$1\frac{1}{2}$-4	Ov15	Common Core/Millinery
71024	Thurs	$9\frac{1}{2}$-$12\frac{1}{2}$	Ov20	Design and Pattern Cutting
71034	Thurs	$1\frac{1}{2}$-4	Ov20	Theory and Textiles

Evening Course

Course symbol: EF1   Course tutor: Mrs H E C Keeling

class	day	time	room	subject
71064	Mon	$6\frac{1}{2}$-$9\frac{1}{2}$	Ov20	Practical
71074	Thurs	$6\frac{1}{2}$-$9\frac{1}{2}$	Ov15	Common Core/Theory

■ Embroidery CGLI 782

Part 1
1st & 2nd years

Students will be trained to develop a creative approach to the Craft, design being an integral part of the study. A knowledge of traditional techniques will form a background to contemporary developments.

Part 2
3rd year

The subject is studied in greater depth with emphasis laid upon advanced techniques and historic research.

Day Course

Course symbol: DE1   Course tutor: Mrs M P Archer

class	day	time	room	subject
71104	Tues	$9\frac{1}{2}$-$12\frac{1}{2}$	Ov17	Design and Experimental Work
71114	Tues	$1\frac{1}{2}$-4	Ov17	Common Core/Practical
71124	Thurs	$9\frac{1}{2}$-$12\frac{1}{2}$	Ov17	Drawing
71134	Thurs	$1\frac{1}{2}$-4	Ov17	Practical

(c)

Part-time Vocational Courses

City and Guilds Creative Studies Courses

The undermentioned courses have been designed mainly for those mature students who wish to follow a course of vocational and personal reasons. The Courses are made up of two parts: Part 1, involving 2 years' study and Part 2, involving 1 years' study. External examinations for both Parts involve written papers and coursework assessment.

■ **Fashion** CGLI 780

Part 1
1st & 2nd years

The aim is to develop an awareness of fashion as a whole in addition to a high standard of Craftsmanship using modern methods of making up.

Part 2
3rd year

A more advanced study of the items in the Fashion Part 1 syllabus.

Day Course

Course symbol: DF1   Course tutor: Miss M Jeavons

class	day	time	room	subject
71004	Tues	$9\frac{1}{4}$-$12\frac{1}{4}$	Ov20	Practical
71014	Tues	$1\frac{1}{2}$-4	Ov15	Common Core/Millinery
71024	Thurs	$9\frac{1}{4}$-$12\frac{1}{4}$	Ov20	Design and Pattern Cutting
71034	Thurs	$1\frac{1}{2}$-4	Ov20	Theory and Textiles

Evening Course

Course symbol: EF1   Course tutor: Mrs H E C Keeling

class	day	time	room	subject
71064	Mon	$6\frac{1}{2}$-$9\frac{1}{2}$	Ov20	Practical
71074	Thurs	$6\frac{1}{2}$-$9\frac{1}{2}$	Ov15	Common Core/Theory

■ **Embroidery** CGLI 782

Part 1
1st & 2nd years

Students will be trained to develop a creative approach to the Craft, design being an integral part of the study. A knowledge of traditional techniques will form a background to contemporary developments.

Part 2
3rd year

The subject is studied in greater depth with emphasis laid upon advanced techniques and historic research.

Day Course

Course symbol: DE1   Course tutor: Mrs M P Archer

class	day	time	room	subject
71104	Tues	$9\frac{1}{4}$-$12\frac{1}{4}$	Ov17	Design and Experimental Work
71114	Tues	$1\frac{1}{2}$-4	Ov17	Common Core/Practical
71124	Thurs	$9\frac{1}{4}$-$12\frac{1}{4}$	Ov17	Drawing
71134	Thurs	$1\frac{1}{2}$-4	Ov17	Practical

(d)

Figure 12.1 (a) A basic reference grid. This grid maps out the information area of the page. (b) A master reference grid. This grid specifies the particular design requirements of the work in hand. (c) Text and grid combined. This figure shows how the grid and the text relate. (d) The final printed page. This page provides a reliable frame of reference for the reader which is consistent throughout the book

Summary

In this section, we have argued (i) that the printed page must provide a reliable frame of reference from which the learner can move away and to which he can return without confusion; (ii) that for economic and functional reasons planning the pages to this end should be completed before work is begun on the setting of the text or the making of the artwork; and (iii) that the typographic reference grid is an essential tool in the process of such planning. A more detailed discussion of typographic reference grids can be found in Froshaug (1967), Macdonald-Ross and Waller (1975b) and Hartley and Burnhill (1976). Parallel and closely related concepts can be found in the field of modular coordination in architecture.

HOW CAN SPACE BE USED TO CONVEY STRUCTURE?

Unlike the prose of a novel, much information printing (i.e. the printing of technical journals, conference proceedings, instructional leaflets, bibliographies, college prospectuses, textbooks, etc.) contains material that has a clearly defined hierarchical structure: that is, paragraphs or items that can be conceived of as having different levels of rank. Often, in Government Reports for example, these levels are explicitly made clear by the use of a numbering system (e.g. 1.0, 1.1, 1.2, 1.2(i), 2.0, 2.1, etc.). We would wish to maintain that the nature of this hierarchical structure can also—and perhaps more clearly—be conveyed to the reader by a systematic use of space.

Figure 12.2(a) shows an extract from a complex piece of prose whose clarity is not helped by its original typography. The total four-page document, in fact, contained seven levels of text. On page one alone there are six levels: there is a main item of business; special resolution A is part of this; statute 4 is a part of resolution A; statute 4 has three parts; part 2 has subsections (a) and (b); and subsection (a) has parts (i), (ii) and (iii). Such a text is difficult— if not impossible—to read, especially when, as in Figure 12.2(a), the spatial organization of the text is at variance with the sense. Figure 12.2(b) shows a respaced typed equivalent (reduced to A5) where the hierarchical structure of the document has been clarified by the use of rational vertical and horizontal spacing.

In order to evaluate the effectiveness of the revised layout (Figure 12.2(b), an experimental comparison was made. Workbooks were constructed which asked subjects to find information in one or other of the two documents, both of which were typed out in full—one with the original and one with the revised spacing—and both reduced to A5. The subjects (undergraduate psychology students) were asked to do three things: to find and circle (i) the main items of business, (ii) the four special resolution, A, B, C and D, and (iii) a particular sentence in the document, which in the original seemed somewhat bizarrely placed. (It told the reader *after* he had struggled through the materials that the decisions had already been agreed upon at a previous

THE BRITISH PSYCHOLOGICAL SOCIETY

(Incorporated by Royal Charter)

NOTICE IS HEREBY GIVEN that a Special General Meeting of the Society with be held in the Small Meeting House, Friends House, Euston Road, London NW1 on Saturday 26 October 1974 at 10.30 o'clock in the forenoon, when the following business will be transacted.

(1) To consider, and if thought fit, to approve the following SPECIAL RESOLUTIONS subject to obtaining the formal approval of the Privy Council:

A. That the Statutes of the Society be amended in the manner following, namely, by deleting the existing Statutes 4 and 8 and substituting the following new Statutes:

4. GRADUATE MEMBERS

(1) All persons who were elected Graduate Members of the old Institution and all persons who are elected as hereinafter provided shall be Graduate Members.

(2) A candidate for election as a Graduate Memeber:

  (a) shall satisfy the Council that he has one of the following qualifications and such higher qualifications as may be provided in the Rules: —

   (i) a university degree for which psychology has been taken as a main subject;

     or

   (ii) a postgraduate qualification in psychology awarded by an authority recognised by the Council;

     or

   (iii) such other qualification in psychology as the Council shall accept as not less than the foregoing;

     or

  (b) shall pass to the satisfaction of the Council such of the Society's examinations as may be required by the Rules.

(3) The Council may elect such eligible candidates to be Graduate Members as it thinks fit.

8. SUBSCRIBERS

(1) All persons who were elected Subscribers of the old Institution and who are elected as hereinafter provided shall be Subscribers.

(2) No technical qualification shall be required of a candidate for election as a Subscriber.

(3) A Subscriber shall be proposed in accordance with the provisions of the Rules.

(a)

The British Psychological Society

(Incorporated by Royal Charter)

Notice is hereby given that a Special General Meeting of the Society will be held in the Small Meeting House, Friends House, Euston Road, London NW1 on Saturday 26 October 1974 at 10.30 o'clock in the forenoon, when the following business will be transacted.

1st item of business

To consider, if thought fit, to approve the following Special Resolutions subject to obtaining the formal approval of the Privy Council: (These Special Resolutions are identical with those approved in principle at the Society's Annual General Meeting held in Bangor on 6 April 1974, with the exception of Statute 15 (see below) in which maximum permitted subscriptions have been reduced.)

Resolution A

That the Statutes of the Society be amended in the manner following, namely, by deleting the existing Statutes 4 and 8 and substituting the following new Statutes:

Statute 4: Graduate Members

(1) All persons who were elected Graduate Members of the old Institution and all persons who are elected as hereinafter provided shall be Graduate Members.

(2) A candidate for election as a Graduate Member:

(a) shall satisfy the Council that he has one of the following qualifications and such higher qualifications as may be provided in the rules:-

(i) a university degree for which psychology has been taken as a main subject;

or

(ii) a postgraduate qualification in psychology awarded by an authority recognised by Council;

(b)

Figure 12.2 (a) Extract from a complex document whose clarity is not aided by its typography. (Figure slightly reduced in size.) (b) A spaced typescript version of (a) to show how the structure is aided by the layout. (Figure slightly reduced in size: the original page size was A5.) (Reproduced with permission of the British Psychological Society)

Table 12.1. Error Rates in Retrieval of Information from the Original and the Revised Layout of the BPS Document

	Original version	Revised version
Question 1	$12/23 = 52\%$	$1/21 = 5\%$
Question 2	$17/23 = 74\%$	$3/21 = 14\%$
Question 3	$1/23 = 4\%$	$1/21 = 5\%$

Table 12.2. The Times Taken to Answer the Questions by Students *who were Correct*

		Original version	Revised version	Significance
	Median	1.09″	37.5″	
Question 1	Range	29″–5′26″	8″–2′57″	$p < 0.01$
	N	11	20	
	Median	21.5″	30.5″	
Question 2	Range	15″–1′14″	8″–1′05″	—
	N	6	18	
	Median	37.0″	14.5″	
Question 3	Range	13″–2′54″	5″–1′25″	$p < 0.001$
	N	22	20	

meeting.) The students were asked to time themselves, and to record in the workbook the times it took them to do these three things. The results are shown in Table 12.1 and 12.2.

These results show that when the students used the typed equivalent of the original pamphlet over half of them could not find the main items of business, and that three-quarters of them could not find all the four special resolutions. (With the revised version, however, students performed significantly better.) The results also showed that those students using the original version who could find these items (and the third one) took significantly longer with the original than with the revised version.

A point worth raising here is that it may appear to the reader that manipulating space in this way is likely to add to the number of pages used in a text and thus to the costs of production. Our answer to this is twofold: (i) if comprehension is important, then skimping on paper is in fact costly (in another sense); (ii) by using a preplanned rational approach production costs in themselves may be reduced. (An example of this latter point was provided in our study describing the redesign of a college prospectus: the number of pages used was increased from 208 to 232, but the cost was reduced from £1,470, which did not include extra charges for author's corrections, to £1,180, with no charges for corrections; see Burnhill *et al.*, 1975.)

SOME FURTHER CONSIDERATIONS

A particular feature of our approach is that, by its very nature, it is critical of some of the long-standing and persistent practices in page layout and display. Amongst these are: the centring of headings and other textual components; the practice of changing arbitrarily the internal spacing of the material in order to force the text to fill out a fixed width and depth ('justification'); inconsistency in the sequencing of the grouping of parts; excessive use of indention in texts which do not consist simply of pages of information arranged in paragraph form; and an excessive variety in the sizes, styles and weights of typeface chosen to code heading levels.

These and other commonly seen features of printed and typewritten information stem from the tendency to apply the bilateral mode of symmetry to layout: that is, to 'balance' the parts about the central axis of the page. This approach tends to divorce the abstract and the visible characteristics of the language from the syntactic structure of the message. It could justifiably be termed 'illiterate' for, clearly, the component parts of a text are not mere objects of varying shapes and sizes to be displayed like ornaments on a mantleshelf or pictures on a wall. In addition, this approach is uneconomical from the point of view of print production.

Such a traditional approach to the spatial organization of a text may not lead to confusion for the reader when the text has a relatively simple structure, with, like this chapter, an occasional heading between strings of information set in paragraph form. However, when the text contains a number of differing components operating at numerous levels in the structure of the whole document, then the use of bilateral symmetry as an organizing method can produce an image on the page which is at variance with the ergonomics of reading. Figure 12.2(a) has illustrated this. Figure 12.3 provides a further illustration: the reader cannot maintain his focus on the sense whilst at the same time having to sort out the arrangement of the material.

Finally, we may note here that this traditional approach sometimes can be positively dangerous. Dennis (1975), for example, showed that such an approach to the design of drug labels led to errors by nurses in the selection of drugs—errors which were reduced by the use of a rational approach to typography of the kind described in this chapter.

Summary

Our approach treats the internal intervals of space not only as means for separating parts, but also as a way of grouping them functionally. This requires, firstly, that the intervals are determined by reference to the position of parts as members of a hierarchical structured system; and, secondly, that the dimensions of the intervals are changed systematically and specified in advance of production by reference to multiples of a fixed unit of measurement. To do this requires the use of a specially designed planning grid.

WHAT ABOUT CONTENT?

So far it may appear to the reader that in this chapter we have been more concerned with layout than with content. We would maintain, however, that

Table 4. *The use of constructs on photographs*

Type of construct	Mean for Group I	Mean for Group II	Z*	P
Psychological	2·3	4·4	−3·7	< 0·0001
Physical	2·7	2·5	1·1	n.s.
Social	2·2	2·7	−1·5	n.s.
Activity	3·1	3·7	−2·6	< 0·004
Non-human	2·7	2·4	1·4	n.s.

* Mann–Whitney *U* test (one-tailed).

Table 5. *Clinical ratings and use of constructs: product-moment correlations*

Type of construct	Stimulus material Photographs	People
Psychological	−0·74**	−0·33*
Physical	0·08	0·00
Social	−0·22	0·01
Activity	−0·14	−0·07
Non-human	0·01	0·31

* *P* < 0·05.   ** *P* < 0·01.

Table 6. *Mean number and type of constructs used by Groups I and II on photographs and people*

Type of construct	Group I Photos	Group I People	Group II Photos	Group II People
Psychological	2·3	2·7	4·4	4·2
Physical	2·7	1·7	2·5	1·8
Social	2·2	2·0	2·7	2·0
Activity	3·1	1·7	3·7	2·2
Non-human	2·7	0·3	2·4	0·0

affective flattening and withdrawal for the whole group (Table 8).

Psychological constructs and social withdrawal

Correlations between the number of psychological constructs used by patients, and the scores on the Venables scales are shown in Table 9. The results indicate that the more sociable patients use more psychological con-

Table 7. *Flattening of affect and social withdrawal*

Venables scale	Mean for Group I	Mean for Group II
Total activity	25·0	30·0
Activity–Passivity	7·9	8·6
Sociability–Withdrawal	17·3	22·0

Low scores indicate withdrawal.

Table 8

	Total withdrawal	Activity	Sociability
Flattening of affect	−0·32	−0·04	−0·38*

*P < 0·05.

Table 9. *Psychological constructs and social withdrawal: product-moment correlations*

Venables scale	Photographs	People
Total withdrawal	+0·18	+0·19
Activity	+0·08	+0·03
Sociability	+0·26	+0·24

structs, although the correlations are not statistically significant, unlike in the study by Williams & Quirke (1972).

Verbal ability, flattening of affect and the use of psychological constructs

Verbal ability correlated negatively with flatness of affect ($r = −0·38$; $P < 0·05$) and positively with the number of psychological constructs used in differentiating between photographs ($r = +0·41$; $P < 0·05$). This

Figure 12.3 An example of how a bilaterally symetrical approach to typography can produce results which are at variance with the ergonomics of reading. (Figure slightly reduced in size; reproduced with permission of the authors, the British Psychological Society and Cambridge University Press)

form and function go hand in hand. Whenever we have come to revise the layout of an instructional document, we have almost invariably found that we have wanted to edit the text too. Whilst revising the instructions for the use of a particular brand of weedkiller, for example, we found that our revised spatial arrangement indicated that the original instructions did not make sense. If writers and printers of instructional materials think about the spatial arrangement of their text then, we argue, content will be improved. Clarity in layout leads to clarity in content because it requires clarity of thought.

ARE THERE ANY GUIDELINES FOR IMPROVING INSTRUCTIONAL TEXT?

A number of guidelines can be culled from the work of typographers and from research literature to help improve the clarity of instructional text. Such guidelines are summaries of complex issues, and thus to some extent they are oversimplifications. Guidelines are of most use if examples can be provided to illustrate the points being made. This, of course, is impracticable in a chapter of this length, so we have listed authors who provide examples and readers may consult them for further details if necessary. Readers are reminded at this point, however, that guidelines are not dogma to be followed, but rather ideas to think about when preparing instructional text.

We have divided the guidelines into four overlapping areas: typographical features; prose materials; grammatical features; and the layout of tables, graphs and illustrations.

1. Typographic Features

As we have argued in this chapter, the International Standard page-sizes are preferable to non-standard ones on economic and technical grounds. The sizes A4 (210×297 mm) and A5 (148×210 mm) are the ones most commonly used.

Again as we have argued in this chapter, the layout of text should be planned in detail in advance of production. To be effective, planning implies a method for telling the printer what to do and for pinpointing the required position on the page of every item of information to be typeset and printed. An essential item in such a specification system is the typographic reference grid.

For straightforward prose printed on an A4 page a two-column structure is probably better than a single-column structure. A single-column structure is probably better than two columns for complex text which includes large tables, diagrams, graphs, etc., provided that the paragraphs are separated by a line space (Burnhill et al., 1976).

The space between words should be consistent (i.e. unjustified). Unjustified text (standardized word spacing) is no more difficult to read than justified text (variable word spacing), and indeed some research suggests that it is easier for older and for less able readers (Zachrisson, 1965; Gregory and Poulton,

1970). Unjustified text should be less costly to set than justified text. Making corrections in unjustified text is also less costly.

The breaking and the hyphenating of words at line-ends becomes unnecessary with unjustified text. Starting a sentence with the last word of a line can also be eliminated. These requirements should be stated in the typographic specification if poor typographic practice is to be avoided.

The space used to separate items (such as paragraphs) should be a fixed unit of measurement, or, in the case of syntactic grouping, multiples of a fixed unit developed in binary series (1, 2, 4, 8, etc.) (see Figure 12.2 (b)). Normally, the dimension of the unit should be that of the baseline to baseline dimension (line feed) which has been specified for setting the text. This dimension in turn should be greater than the typesize by an amount which is not less than the dimension specified for the word spacing of the text. The norm for word spacing is about 0.25 of the typesize; that is, the space allocated to the lower-case letter i.

Once decided upon, the spacing should not be changed arbitrarily from page to page. Consistency in the internal spacing of the information should take precedence over the renaissance fashion for setting text to a fixed line-width and page-depth. It also costs less to set type with a consistent and rationally determined interval spacing system than it does to change the spacing for formalistic reasons after the matter has been typeset.

Different typesizes affect the horizontal dimension of the text as well as the vertical. The larger the typesize the fewer the number of words per given line-length. It is possible, therefore, that large typesizes (and/or short line-lengths) may irritate some readers. This point is illustrated in *Getting Started* (Hawkins *et al.*, 1975), where the examples are printed in a smaller typesize than the main text. We would maintain that the examples are easier to read.

The most suitable typefaces to use are those which will withstand degradation when processing and printing is less than perfect and when the page is likely to be copied. Typefaces to avoid are those that contain fine lines which may break down, small internal spaces which may fill in, and letters which appear to touch one another when slightly over-inked. Typefaces with idiosyncratic design features should also be avoided (Spencer *et al.*, 1975).

It is difficult to recommend particular typesizes without referring to specific typefaces because the different measurement systems used in typography conflict, and the designated typesize of a particular typeface does not specify the actual size of the printed image (Hartley *et al.*, 1975a) In general, however, a good all-purpose size is 10 point type on a 12 point line to line feed; 8 point on 10 point is possibly about as small as one would want to go in the design of instructional materials.

Lower-case letters (set in bold face if necessary) are better for headings and subheadings than are long strings of capital letters or italics. Information set in lower-case letters is easier to read than when printed in upper-case characters (Tinker, 1965).

Key terms, new vocabulary and phrases can be printed in italics or bold type, or underlined (in typescript). However, as might be expected, the research on such typographic cueing suggests that this often has little effect unless the reader knows in advance what the cues mean (Christensen and Stordahl, 1955; Coles and Foster, 1975; Rickards and August, 1975).

Using colour as a typographic cue is often unnecessary and if it is overdone it can cause problems for the reader. There is no need to use colour on every page simply because it is technically possible to do so. Colour should be used sparingly, and its function explained to the learner.

A number of non-optimum factors combined, though not strictly cumulative, may drastically reduce reading efficiency (Spencer, 1969).

2. Prose Materials

Summaries at the beginning of chapters can help a learner to organize his thoughts about what is to follow (Hartley and Davies, 1976).

Summaries at the end of a passage are also often useful for revision purposes, especially if the main points made in the chapter are listed.

There are a number of ways of asking readers to do things *before* they start to read a text which help their subsequent understanding of the material. Summaries, overviews, pre-tests and advance organizers are examples of such different pre-instructional techniques. The similarity of and the differences between these different approaches have been compared by Hartley and Davies (1976).

A clear, concise title at the beginning of a article helps the reader to orientate himself, and so aids subsequent recall (Dooling and Lachman, 1971).

Headings and subheadings (ranged from the left), togehter with a systematic use of space, can be used to convey the structure of complex text. This point has been argued in this chapter and illustrated in Figure 12.2 (b).

Excessively long paragraphs should be avoided.

When scanning text rapidly it is easier to see paragraphs separated by a line space than paragraphs denoted by indention.

If indention is used to convey grouping and substructure (as in Figure 12.2 (b) in this chapter) then confusion can arise for the reader if indention is also used to denote a new paragraph. This is particularly so when the paragraphs are very short. In this situation it is better to use a line space to separate paragraphs, and multiples of line space and possibly indention to convey structure (as in Figure 12.2(b)).

3. Grammatical Features

Short, simple sentences are often easier to understand than long ones. This self-evident proposition is too often forgotten.

Few sentences should have more than one subordinate clause. The more subordinate clauses there are, the more difficult it is to understand a sentence (Miller, 1964; Wright and Barnard, 1975).

Indeed, each grammatical complication added to a sentence causes an increment of difficulty in comprehension (Davies, 1972; Wright and Barnard, 1975).

If possible, write sentences in the active voice and avoid connections such as 'except', 'or', 'if' and 'unless' (Davies, 1972; Wright and Barnard, 1975).

In general, avoid the use of negatives, particularly double ones (Wason, 1965; Davies, 1972). Negative qualifications *can* be used, however, for making a particular emphasis, and for correcting misconceptions. Double negatives in imperatives (e.g. Do not ... unless ...) are actually easier than single negatives (Wright and Barnard, 1975).

When two (or more) points are to be discussed, it is best to discuss them in the order in which they are initially presented. (For example, avoid saying 'Taking the last point first ...'.)

Readers remember more from discursive text when headings and subheadings are written in the form of questions rather than in the form of statements (Robinson, 1961). Questions encourage people to examine what they are reading and to look for related facts and ideas.

Questions influence the depth of processing. Specific questions help people to remember specific cases; higher-order questions lead to remembering generalizations which include specific cases (Rickards and DiVesta, 1974).

A question put at the start of a discourse often leads to specific learning. A question embedded in the text, but given after the relevant content, sometimes leads to more general learning (Boyd, 1973; Bull, 1973; Ladas, 1973). Test questions placed at the end of chapters are often ignored by readers.

It is best to ask questions about one thing at a time. Wright and Barnard (1975) reported that questions such as 'Are you over 21 and under 65?' caused difficulties for some people over 65 who answered each part of the question in turn.

Requirements should be put positively. For example: 'We suggest you summarize the main points of this chapter' might be better written 'What are the main points of this chapter?' (Macdonald-Ross, 1975).

Familiar words are easier to understand than are technical terms or complex words which mean the same thing. For example, the earlier sentence 'Indeed, each grammatical complication added to a simple sentence causes an increment of difficulty in comprehension' could probably have been better written as 'The more grammatical complications you add to a sentence the harder it is to understand it'. Authors should try to see if there are simpler ways of expressing their ideas.

When presenting data, prose descriptions often seem less offputting than actual numbers. Everyday words which act as rough quantifiers, for example 'nearly half the group', are adequate for most purposes and seem to be handled reasonably consistently by different people.

Hammerton (1976) suggests phrases which can be used with confidence as follows:

Numerical value to be conveyed	Suitable form of words
> 3/4	Almost all of ...

60%–70%	More than half of ...
50%–60%	Rather more than half of ...
40%–50%	Nearly half of ...
20%–40%	Part of ...
< 1/4	A very small part of ...

However, the effects of age and context may be important. In tests of children's behaviour (for example, 'Take a few/a lot of beads from this tray') effects were found which were due to age and to the total number of beads available (Cohen, 1960).

Similarly, verbal descriptions of probabilities are less offputting for many people than actual figures. However, the interpretation of a verbal description of probability seems to be less consistent than that of quantity. Cohen (1960) again showed age and context effects in studies of children's behaviour. In a study of 125 adults he found the 'average chances out of 100' assigned to probability expressions in a political and in a meteorological context were as follows:

	Chances out of 100	
	Political context	Meteorological context
is certain to	73	70
is likely to	63	56
probably will	55	54
may	52	48
it is most imporbable that ... will ...	33	37

If precision is required, then actual quantities may be given with the verbal quantifier. For example, one can say 'Nearly half the group—43 per cent—said ...' or 'There was a distinct chance ($p < 0.06$) that ...'.

Complex instructions, legal documents or 'government prose' are difficult to understand when set out in prose form. Flow charts or decision tables may be more effective, but the optimal format depends upon the topic and the conditions of use. It has been suggested that flow charts are perhaps best for sorting out complex information, tables when presenting complex information, but that linked statements are best if the material has to be remembered (Davies, 1972; Wright and Reid, 1973). Of course, the reader must know in advance how to read a flow chart or table. Many do not.

The readability of text can be assessed by various readability formulae. Good accounts of the strengths and weaknesses of different readability formulae can be found in Klare (1974–75; 1976). The simplest formula for use with technical text is that discussed in detail by Sticht (1973), and outlined by Klare (1974–75, p. 84).

4. Tables, Graphs and Illustrations

Tables vary in complexity and function (for example from a calendar to a logarithm table). In the presentation of a complex table there needs to be a full and direct display of all the information a user will need. The reader should not have to work out an answer from the figures provided (Wright and Fox, 1972).

Tables can be designed to present information clearly without the need for printers' 'rules'. Horizontal rules can be used to help group information, but should be employed sparingly (Burnhill *et al.*, 1975).

With complex tables it is helpful to have:

(i) items arranged so that they are scanned vertically rather than horizontally;

(ii) appropriate spacing within and between columns (i.e. with related pairs closer than unrelated ones) (Wright, 1968; Wright and Fox, 1972).

If the columns in a table are lengthy, then use regular line spacing (about every five items) as this helps retrieval (Wright, 1968; Wright and Fox, 1972).

If the table is wide and contains many columns, then row headings can be placed both to the left and to the right to help comprehension (Wright, 1968; Wright and Fox, 1972).

If there are many rows and columns, then the headings can be numbered or lettered. However, the use of numerous columns and rows and consequent footnotes should be avoided if possible (Wright, 1968; Wright and Fox, 1972).

Left-ranging tables (i.e. tables in which items are not centred over one another but range from the left-hand margin) are easier to construct, quicker to type and to typeset, and are no less comprehensible than tables arranged in the centred style (Burnhill *et al.*, 1975; Hartley *et al.*, 1975b).

Tables which cut across two-column formats and tables which are divorced from associated textual reference may cause the reader to lose track of an argument. The same is probably true for graphs and illustrations (Whalley and Fleming, 1975; Burnhill *et al.*, 1976).

If the author knows in advance the page-size of the final product then this can help him in the choice of suitably sized illustrations and graphic materials.

Graphs, like tables, have many different functions. The simplest kinds of graph, and the easiest to understand are line graphs and bar-charts (Schutz, 1961; Feliciano *et al.*, 1963).

If the aim of a graph is to compare different conditions, then several lines can be plotted on the same graph. However, a large number of lines can be confusing, and it is probably best to separate them by typographic cues (for example different symbols) or to use separate graphs (Schutz, 1961).

Bar-charts can be subdivided (for example a total score can be shown as a composite of a number of different subscores) but such compound bar-charts can be confusing (Croxton and Stryker, 1929; Hawkins *et al.*, 1975).

Pie-charts are said to be easy to understand but they can be misleading (Croxton and Stryker, 1929). It is difficult to judge proportions accurately when segments are small and it is also difficult to put in the lettering. Pie-charts give a general impression of quantitative relationships but subtle differences are difficult to detect compared with bar-charts, which are based on multiples of a square module or a regular unit of two-dimensional space. Pie-charts are also difficult to understand if charts with different diameters are being compared (Hawkins *et al.*, 1975).

Bar-charts are a better method of presentation than are cross-sectional drawings of three-dimensional objects such as spheres, cubes and blocks of columns, when the task of the reader is to estimate percentages and quantities (Dickinson, 1973; Hartley and Burnhill, 1976).

Factors which inhibit the legibility of graphical aids are:

(i) reversed lettering (i.e. white letters on a black, or dark, background);

(ii) show-through (i.e. the appearance on the page of the image of lines or drawings printed on the reverse side);

(iii) words set at an angle to the horizontal;

(iv) haphazardly arranged lines connecting labels to reference points;

(v) unprincipled variety of typesizes and styles; and

(vi) functionless use of colour.

Finally, there is one overall guideline which is applicable to *all* instructional text. This is that initial layouts need to be tried out with samples of the target population for whom they are intended and then revised on the basis of the results obtained. This should be done before designs are finally committed to publication. One cannot assume just because one has, for example, constructed a graph, that the point being made is now automatically understood by the learner. The effectiveness of a graph—and anything else—needs to be tested.

ACKNOWLEDGMENTS

The research descorbed in this chapter is supported by the Social Science Research Council to whom we are indebted.

REFERENCES

Boyd, W. M. (1973). 'Repeating questions in prose learning', *Journal of Educational Psychology*, **64**, 1, 31.

Bull, S. (1973). 'The role of questions in maintaining attention to textual material', *Review of Educational Research*, **43**, 1, 83.

Burnhill, P., Hartley, J., and Young, M. (1976). 'Tables in text', *Applied Ergonomics*, in press.

Burnhill, P., Hartley, J., Young, M., and Fraser, S. (1975). 'The typography of college prospectuses: a critique and a case history', in L. Evans and J. C. Leedham (Eds.), *Aspects of Educational Technology IX*, Kogan Page, London.

Christensen, C. M., and Stordahl, K. E. (1955); 'The effect of organisational aids on comprehension and retention', *Journal of Educational Psychology*, **46**, 2, 65.

Cohen, J. (1960). *Chance, Skill and Luck*, Penguin, Harmondsworth.

Coles, P., and Foster, J. J. (1975). 'Typographic cueing as an aid to learning from type-written text', *Programmed Learning & Educational Technology*, **12**, 2, 102.

Croxton, F., and Stryker, R. E. (1929). 'Barcharts versus circle diagrams', *Journal of the American Statistical Association*, **22**, 473.

Davies, I. K. (1972). 'Presentation strategies', in J. Hartley (Ed.), *Strategies for Programmed Instruction*, Butterworths, London.

Dennis, I. (1975). 'The design and experimental testing of a hospital drug labelling system', *Programmed Learning & Educational Technology*, **12**, 2, 88.

Dickinson, G. C. (1973). *Statistical Mapping and the Presentation of Statistics*, Arnold, London.

Dooling, D. J., and Lachman, R. (1971). 'Effects of comprehension on the retention of prose', *Journal of Experimental Psychology*, **88**, 216.

Dwyer, F. (1972). *A Guide for Improving Visualised Instruction*, State College Pa. Learning Services.

Feliciano, G. D., Powers, R. D., and Kearl, B. E. (1963). 'The presentation of statistical information', *Audio-Visual Communication Review*, *II*, 3, 32.

Froshaug, A. (1967). 'Typography is a grid', *The Designer*.

Gregory, M., and Poulton, E. C. (1970). 'Even versus uneven right-hand margins and rate of comprehension in reading', *Ergonomics* **13**, 4, 427.

Hammerton, M. (1976). 'How much is a large part?', *Applied Ergonomics*, **7**, 1, 10.

Hartley, J., and Burnhill, P. (1975). 'Contemporary issues in typographic research', *Programmed Learning & Educational Technology*, **12**, 2, 73.

Hartley, J., and Burnhill, P. (1976). *Textbook Design: A Practical Guide*, Unesco, Paris in press.

Hartley, J., and Davies, I. K. (1976). 'Pre-instructional strategies: the role of pre-tests, behavioral objectives, over-views and advance-organisers', *Review of Educational Research*, **46**, 2, 239.

Hartley, J., Fraser, S., and Burnhill, P. (1974). 'A selected bibliography of typographic research relevant to the production of instructional materials', *Audio-Visual Communication Review*, **22**, 2, 181.

Hartley, J., Young, M., and Burnhill, P. (1975a). 'The effects of interline space on judgements of typesize', *Programmed Learning & Educational Technology*, **12**, 2, 115.

Hartley, J., Young, M., and Burnhill, P. (1975b). 'On the typing of tables', *Applied Ergonomics*, **6**, 1, 39.

Hawkins, S., Davies, I. K., Majer, K., and Hartley, J. (1975). *Getting Started: Guides for Beginning Teachers*, Blackwell, Oxford.

Klare, G. R. (1974–75). 'Assessing readability', *Reading Research Quarterly*, X, 1, 62.

Klare, G. R. (1976). 'Judging readability', *Instructional Science*, **5**, 1, 55.

Ladas, H. (1973). 'The mathemagenic effects of factual review, questions on the learning of incidental information: a critical review', *Review of Educational Research*, **143**, 1, 71.

Macdonald-Ross, M. (1975). 'Questions', Internal document, Institute of Educational Technology, Open University.

Macdonald-Ross, M., and Smith, E. B. (1973). *Bibliography for Textual Communication*, Institute of Educational Technology, Open University.

Macdonald-Ross, M., and Waller, R. (1975a). 'Criticism, alternatives and tests: a conceptual framework for improving typography', *Programmed Learning & Educational Technology*, **12**, 2, 75.

Macdonald-Ross M., and Waller, R. (1975b). *Open University Texts: Criticism and Alternatives*, Institute of Educational Technology, Open University.

Miller, G. A. (1964). 'The psycholinguists', *Encounter*, **23**, 1, 29.

Poulton, E. C. (1969). 'How efficient is print?', in I. K. Davies and J. Hartley (Eds.) (1972), *Contributions to an Educational Technology*, Butterworths, London.

Rickards, J. P., and August, G. J. (1975). 'Generative underlining strategies in prose recall', *Journal of Educational Psychology*, **67**, 6, 860.

Rickards, J. P., and DiVesta, F. J. (1974). 'Type and frequency of questions in processing textual material', *Journal of Educational Psychology*, **66**, 354.

Robinson, F. (1961). *Effective Study*, Harper & Row, New York.

Schutz, H. G. (1961). 'An evaluation of formats for graphic trend displays', *Human Factors*, 99 and 108.

Spencer, H. (1969). *The Visible Word*, Lund Humphries, London.

Spencer, H., Reynolds, L., and Coe, B. (1975). 'The effects of image degradation and background noise on the legibility of text and numerals in four different typefaces',

Report available from the Readability of Print Research Unit, Royal College of Art, 6a Cromwell Place, London.

Sticht, T. G. (1973). 'Research towards the design, development and evaluation of a job functional literacy training program for the United States Army', *Literary Discussion*, *IV*, 3, 339.

Tinker, M. A. (1965). *Legibility of Print*, Iowa State University Press, Ames.

Vernon, M. (1953). 'Presenting information in diagrams', *Audio-Visual Communication Review*, **1**, 147.

Wason, P. (1965). 'The contexts of plausible denial', *Journal of Verbal Learning & Verbal Behaviour*, **4**, 7.

Watts, L., and Nisbet, J. (1974). *Legibility in Children's Textbooks*, National Foundation for Educational Research, London.

Whalley, P., and Fleming, R. (1975). 'An experiment with a simple reading recorder', *Programmed Learning & Educational Technology*, **12**, 2, 120.

Wright, P. (1968). 'Using tabulated information', *Ergonomics*, **11**, 331.

Wright, P., and Barnard, P. (1975). 'Just fill in this form: a review for designers', *Applied Ergonomics*, **6**, 4, 213.

Wright, P., and Fox, K. (1972). 'Explicit and implicit tabulation formats', *Ergonomics*, **15**, 175.

Wright, P., and Reid, F. (1973). 'Written information: some alternatives to prose for expressing the outcomes of complex contingencies', *Journal of Applied Psychology*, **57**, 2, 160.

Zachrisson, B. (1965). *Legibility of Printed Text*, Almqvist & Wiksell, Stockholm.

13

ARE TEACHING INNOVATIONS IN POST-SECONDARY EDUCATION IRRELEVANT?

Donald M. Bligh

INTRODUCTION

Obviously innovations in teaching *can* be relevant to the major purposes of education, but the question is whether in practice they usually are. In this chapter I shall consider the effects of innovations, basing my exposition on the following three general statements.

The first point is that the major objectives of post-secondary education are not primarily concerned with the acquisition of information, but with the development of patterns of thought, attitudes and motivation. Secondly, innovations in teaching have not, in general, improved its effectiveness because they have overemphasized the acquisition of information. Thirdly, innovations in the socio-emotional methods and contexts of teaching have been neglected.

1. THE MAJOR PURPOSES OF POST-SECONDARY EDUCATION ARE THE DEVELOPMENT OF THOUGHT, ATTITUDES AND MOTIVATION

This proposition may be widely accepted by people with different philosophies and from different sectors of post-secondary education, but, being a statement of values, it cannot be proved without prior agreement on basic values. The present section will therefore be concerned largely with reasoned descriptions of common beliefs about the aims of post-secondary education, rather than final justification of them. It may be objected that a book with a psychological emphasis should not be concerned with values, but the application of any science begs value questions. 'Education' is a value-laden concept (cf. Peters, 1966) and the criterion of relevance must relate to the bearing of methods and content upon the achievement of its purposes.

Vocational Courses

The majority of students in post-secondary education study essentially vocational courses. From the point of view of employers the purpose of such courses is to fit students to do their intended jobs better. Most students have this purpose too, but they also want to obtain formal qualifications. This objective is more immediate and usually takes precedence.

It must be admitted that there are some jobs which are purely mechanical and require no thought. Insofar as students in post-secondary education are given training for such work, the vocational part of my argument is false. But most jobs for which an education is given require some kind of problem-solving because they include meeting new situations which demand the selection of different responses. Problem-solving is a thought process, and therefore the training for such work includes teaching students to think. This is certainly so for courses in the fields of engineering, agriculture, medicine, law and commerce. Where a student only aims to obtain a formal qualification, the method of assessment will either require him to demonstrate such thought or it will not. If it does, the student will aim to develop his powers of thought and the conclusion holds good. If it does not, it is at once apparent that a much-needed innovation is to reform the method of assessment, and without this other innovations have in practice been irrelevant.

People do their work better if they are well motivated. (This statement is difficult to deny because it is virtually a truism.) If it is the purpose of vocational courses to help students to do their work better (also virtually a truism) it follows that the increase in certain kinds of motivation is part of the purpose of vocational courses.

There are few kinds of work that do not include relationships with other people. There is reason to think that people work better when they have certain attitudes towards other. For example, harmonious relationships seem to be related to high productivity. Although it is possible that only students with these qualities will be selected, it is likely that the enhancement of these attitudes and interpersonal relationships will be part of the purpose of vocational courses.

However, because these arguments depend upon general characteristics of working situations, they will be inapplicable to non-vocational courses.

Non-vocational Courses

Some courses are non-vocational in the sense that they do not train students for any specific profession, but they are vocational in the sense that they purport to teach certain generalizable skills. This controversy has an ancient history. In the past it was claimed that the patterns of thought required in Latin and Greek could usefully be transferred to work in the British Civil Service. More recently writers as diverse as Bloom (1956) and Hirst (1965) have assumed the transferability of certain thought patterns almost independently of content. The extent to which transfer takes place is matter which I will not pursue. It is sufficient for my argument that some transfer of attitudes and thought processes occurs and that teachers intend it to do so.

Non-vocational courses are sometimes justified on the grounds that some knowledge is intrinsically valuable. Knowledge of a subject is said to be an end in itself. Firstly, any argument for the intrinsic value of factual knowledge could probably be applied to the value of thought (cf. Bligh *et al.*, 1975). Secondly, if the knowledge is not to be the object of some emotion or affect, it is not obvious what this could mean. Values are ascribed by people; they do not exist as independent essences. It may make sense to claim that 'education is essentially valuable' (Peters, 1966), but not the courses that only partly constitute it.

Thirdly, as applied to factual knowledge, the belief seems implausible. Either the study of the subject is the only thing that is an end in itself, or it is not. If it is, it is the ultimate value to which all actions in a person's life should be directed. Even the choice of 'puffed wheat' or 'cornflakes' for breakfast should ultimately be resolved in terms of the one thing that is valuable in itself. This seems absurd. If there are one or more other activities believed to be ends in themselves, there is a possible conflict between them. For example, if the satisfaction from playing golf and the study of a subject are both ends in themselves, a decision to study the subject on some occasion can only be justified in terms of a higher-order principle of value; and in this case the course of study is not an end in itself.

Fourthly, if items of knowledge are to be learned in isolation, why should one item be deemed more valuable than another? How is the knowledge selected? The answer is almost invariably that knowledge is not learned in isolation, but *related* in a mesh of various ways. The knowledge is also selected so that it can be *applied* to wider issues not considered in the course. Its understanding can give some basic *satisfaction;* and it is not the knowledge that is valuable, but the process of learning it—a way of *thinking*. As soon as this reply is made, the italicized words show that non-vocational education is also concerned with developing patterns of thought and attitudes.

Other Aims

There is, of course, an infinity of other aims in post-secondary education. Different people will emphasize the need to 'pass on our culture' or to revolutionize it; to be independent, creative and tolerant; to foster 'excellence'; to help students seek their 'identity'; to experience enjoyment; to develop powers of reasoning, criticism, judgment; and so on. Although it is not at all clear what some of these aims mean, they are clear enough not to be a challenge to my first proposition. Most support it. Consequently, although they are important viewpoints, they will not be considered further here. Because it is always possible that the reader has other counterarguments, this account cannot be conclusive.

It is *not* being argued here that the acquisition of information has no function in post-secondary education. It is, of course, a necessary part of the study of most disciplines, but it is not sufficient. If students are to learn to think, they will need some information to think about. Much of this they usually know already, but some may have to be taught. Thus innovations in teaching have not been irrelevant *because* they taught facts. They are not *necessarily* irrelevant. It is a matter of emphasis. The relevance of fact-teaching innovations *is* necessarily indirect and has in practice been very restricted because few significant advantages have been consistently demonstrated. The merit of certain *techniques* of teaching when using particualr methods seems to be more demonstrable. Some of these techniques may be innovatory, but most have been known for centuries. These points form the theme of the next section.

2. TEACHING INNOVATIONS HAVE NOT USUALLY IMPROVED THE EFFECTIVENESS OF TEACHING

Until recently innovations in teaching have concentrated on teaching facts, rather than thought or enthusiasm. This may be because teaching has been conceived as a process of presentation, rather than a variety of social techniques to generate mental activities. Furthermore, innovations do not seem to have taught facts demonstrably better or worse than traditional methods. This is not to say that they do not; there are fundamental difficulties in this kind of research.

As in the first section of this chapter, these assertions are not amenable to deductive proof. They may be illustrated historically.

The Craze for Visual Aids Lacked Experimental Support

During the Second World War it became necessary to retain large numbers of people with no previous post-secondary education. At school level the distinction between verbal and spatial abilities was confused with levels of ability and made to support a 'grammar' school and 'technical school distinction. Both the ability level of the population to be retrained and the increasing by technical nature of the war effort seemed to require spatial teaching methods —extensive use of visual aids. After the war, when many of the training personnel took jobs in education and industrial training, the use of visual aids was naively associated with 'good' teaching.

Even supposing this association was valid for the war effort, the purpose of that training was quite different from much of post-secondary education. Instant obedience and conformity were needed by the military; routine unthinking behaviour was acceptable in the mass production of munitions; but we have seen in the first section that the objectives of adult and higher education include critical enquiry, independence of mind, contemplative reflection, appreciating both sides of an argument and breadth of understanding.

I am not claiming that visual aids are *necessarily* irrelevant when teaching these, or other, important objectives. It is quite obvious that they can convey concepts and experience which words alone cannot. The quantity of information contained in some simple diagrams could take many pages to express in words, and they may be continuously presented in a way that speech cannot. For this reason they have a place in teaching such subjects as philosophy, where they are often scorned. But, in practice, they have been used inappropriately, with blind faith rather than careful consideration of their effects in particular educational contexts.

Perhaps it was for this reason that after the war M.D. Vernon and others began to study the effectiveness of visual aids. In a series of experiments she presented demographic statistics and data on the war effort graphically, pictorially, verbally and numerically in various combinations to people with wide ranges of intelligence, age and educational level (1946; 1954). Verbal material, such as a coherent argument, seemed to enhance the memory of graphic illustrations, but not the other way round (1952). She concluded that graphs and charts had little advantage over verbal and numerical presentations. In some cases visual aids even caused confusion. They seemed to involve a language of their own which had to be learned before they could be understood.

Her findings, have been interpreted as favouring the argument that innovations in visual aids were irrelevant, or at least irrelevant without some training in their use. However, it is not so simple. Her criteria are always verbal and sometimes numerical, but rarely graphic and pictorial. Some questions required simple recall and numerical responses; others demanded oral descriptions and verbal responses to general questions. With these criteria it is hardly surprising that scores appeared to depend on 'ability to understand and use language', 'to interpret graphic material' (in language?), 'to generalise from particular instances' and to think relevantly without preconceived ideas (M.D. Vernon, 1946).

Yet this may not be a matter for criticism. If the highly verbal emphasis of most educational criteria is accepted, Vernon may have been right to use the criteria she did. Innovations may be irrelevant because they are ineffective, or because they are effective at doing something irrelevant. Hence if the craze for visual aids was not irrelevant on the first account, it was irrelevant on the second. They may need to be coupled with innovations in methods of assessment.

Teaching at a Distance Neglects Social Motivation

The Second World War accelerated a social revolution. Working adults aspired to social advancement through radio and correspondence courses. A characteristic of both these methods is that they teach at a distance and social interaction is minimized. They both suffer from high dropout rates, except in countries where group activity is organized. Repeatedly it has been found that the *social* organization of these courses is the main determinant of motivation (see Bligh *et al.*, 1975).

Belson (1952) has shown that comprehension from radio instruction is much less than has commonly been supposed and P.E. Vernon (1963) found that comprehension decreased sharply when more than half a dozen points were made, although there could be some improvement when the style was more conversational than literary. Schneider (1954) reported difficulties with attention span, and whilst the increasing availability of tape-recorders has eased his problem, many experimenters have shown that innovations using tape-recorders are no more effective than traditional teaching for the acquisition of information, and are ineffective for other objectives (e.g. Frank and Lesher, 1971; Snyder et al., 1968; Popham, 1961; Bligh, 1974).

The success of teaching by correspondence and radio varies with the amount of involvement and activity by the students. In short, their success depends, not upon their presentational element, but upon the extent to which other aspects of the course require thought, motivation and social interaction.

Film was Continually Misused

In the same way that the war gave an impetus to the use of static visual aids, so the power of the prosperous film industry to entertain led to unrealistic estimates of the power of film to educate. Film has advantages, but its limitations were not recognized and the medium was misused. Consequently, as an innovation its relevance to the purpose of post-secondary education was small unless coupled with discussion or other active methods.

Innovations using film are not always or necessarily irrelevant. Film has obvious advantages. It can show movement and colour. It may provide realistic experience of events otherwise inaccessible through distance (e.g. tribal customs in Samoa), time (e.g. a Nazi rally), temperature (e.g. flows of molten steel), pressure (e.g. the behaviour of weightless astronauts), danger (e.g. defusing a bomb) or expense (e.g. industrial fire-fighting). Processes such as the wing movements of birds in flight or the growth of a cell may be slowed down or speeded up. Perfected demonstrations may be magnified, repeatedly shown, and observed by large classes. There is also reason to believe that practical skills are learned more quickly when film loops are available (Goodhue, 1969; Weiss et al., 1971).

Nevertheless, there are limitations which restrict its relevance. Films are expensive to produce and difficult to edit. Commentaries provided cannot be appropriate to more than a narrow range of students or courses. For example, Craig (1956) has shown that silent film with the teacher's own commentary achieved significantly higher test scores on both immediate and delayed recall than a sound version used alone. The rapidity of movement and changing shots can be overcome if film is supplemented with 'stills' of other teaching (Pirkheim, 1961). Bacquet showed that only when combined with discussion were films more effective in helping young people to choose a career than traditional teaching or the provision of a booklet. Postlethwait, Novak and

Murray (1964) has made great claims for his 'audio-tutorial' system, which provides a self-service for films in combination with other media), but he provides little compelling evidence.

While colour may entertain and give aesthetic appeal, it does not increase learning unless it is part of the teaching technique as distinct from its style. It needs to be related to the content. Colour has often been irrelevant because it has been used for realism rather than clarity. Just as realistic photographs have been shown to be less effective than schematized line drawings (Dwyer, 1971), so Laner (1954) showed that the provision of a realistic experience was less effective as a demonstration than a series of still line drawings. Thus, the arguments in favour of film in terms of movement, colour and 'realistic' still lack empirical support. What is important for learning is clarity.

In one enquiry Peters and Scheffer (1961) found there were all kinds of administrative difficulties with the use of films. Films often arrived too late and could not be kept long enough for teachers to prepare. Information given by distributors was inadequate. Many rooms were not equipped for their use. The loss in time through disruptive room changes outweighed their benefits. Few teachers knew how to use projection equipment. Most teachers were not sufficiently aware of the educational qualities of films to know how to use them. Most films are too long and fact-packed to sustain attention. Partly for these reasons, a Government working party on the use of film (Francis, 1963) concluded that universities should be encouraged to form libraries of short sigle-concept films. For many students they are too closely associated with entertainment to provoke habitual concentration for learning unless their teachers adopt techniques which demand it.

The case for film remains unproven. The point is not that film is necessarily irrelevant but that it has been continually irrelevant because it has been misapplied. It is continually used on its own with inappropriate commentaries in long presentations which overrate fidelity at the expense of clarity.

Leaving aside the numerous studies of the emotional effects of film on young people during and immediately following presentation, there is little evidence on the effects of film on adults. It is probably most effective if used as a stimulus to other activity, not as a self-sufficient method. In an experiment with children, Simon (1961) showed that films can stimulate creative writing, but that this is strongly influenced by the social and motivational context in which they are used.

Only in rapid reading has the use of film with adults been at all closely studied, and here the results have been repeatedly contested or ignored. Even allowing for the exaggerated claims of commercial companies, considerable regression following immediate increases in reading speed and wide individual differences, there are appreciable improvements which make this innovation relevant to post-secondary education. But even here, the charge of irrelevance is not far away. It is arguable that post-secondary students do not need to increase reading speeds so much as to improve their reading techniques such as skipping, skimming, summarizing and making flexible use of appropriate strategies.

The Misapplication of Television

My argument with reference to television is similar to that for film, but not so strong. Television has been misapplied as a substitute for traditional teaching rather than a supplement to it. Television has features which give it a clear advantage over films. It may teach at a distance and be relayed to more than one place at a time. Its definition and colour are not so good, but editing is easier and cheaper. Because erasure is possible and replay is immediately available without film-processing, it is more congenial to the amateur, and this includes most teachers.

As with film, the trouble with television is that it is associated with a passive role outside the educational context. This passivity is strikingly illustrated in a series of observations by Belson (1959). Viewers' other pursuits and interests, as measured both by their active pursuit of them and expressions of feeling, were markedly reduced in the years immediately after acquiring a television set and only recovered after five or six years. Even television programmes on topics of former interest had little effect in reviving former activity. Belson's findings hardly imply that television stimulates much thought. This conclusion is reinforced by a series of experiments by Daines and Neilson (1962, 1963a, b; Daines, 1962). They speak of a 'telehypnosis' in which a considerable amount of factual material was absorbed at a superficial level, but they repeatedly report that there was little understanding of 'the deeper significance' or 'the underlying principles', even by the more intelligent viewers.

If we accept that television is capable of teaching information, it could be a justifiable innovation if it did so more effectively. Yet of 202 studies at college level reported by Chu and Schramm (1967), 152 found no significant difference in effectiveness compared with traditional methods. Traditional methods were superior in 28 and less effective in 22. Comparisons at school level also showed predominantly insignificant differences, but a slight majority of those that were significant favoured television. Chu and Schramm do not report the precise criteria in each case, but as they stand, the figures lend weight to the view that the effort and expense of television teaching may be irrelevant to the main purpose of college education when traditional methods can be used. Educational television has been most successful when used in conjunction with complementary social methods of teaching (e.g. by the Open University and in East Germany).

Where there is no alternative, television may be a worthwhile innovation. In particular the microteaching technique, in which student-teachers view their own teaching and repeat it with different classes until faults are corrected, has proved more effective than the traditional alternatives using supervisors' opinions (Perrott, 1975). Television can be used in innovatory ways to good purpose, but usually it is not.

The Principles of Programmed Learning are not Universal

Another innovation expected to change the face of post-secondary education was programmed learning. It is based on important principles which have been much neglected in education. Yet while they were not irrelevant, they were soon found not to be universal, and to apply less generally with adult students (Leith, 1969).

The principles of 'active learning', 'small steps' and 'frequent feedback on performance' seemed to imply breaking a subject into small units and testing the learning on one unit before proceeding to the next. Yet students at post-school level find frequent tests irritating. They appear to work faster and longer with better understanding if material is presented in units large enough to interrelate a number of concepts within them. This interrelation implies an element of thought. Older students do not feel encouraged by positive feedback when the small step size suggest minimal achievement (Wright, 1967; Gessner, 1974), and overt activity seems to be less important when students have background knowledge (Leith and Buckle, 1965). Many adults who prefer to skip, skim or obtain an overview of a topic become annoyed when forced to proceed slowly upon a predetermined linear path. Their imagination is stifled by convergent questions apparently requiring 'right' answers which do not allow them to relate the subject to their own experience, which may be considerable. While we may expect that many adults prefer to work at their own pace, the principle of 'self-pacing' has been challenged by Moore (1967), who found no difference between students forced to work at the same speed as others in a group and those who could work individually. Similarly, experiments by Stones (1967) and Gallegos (1968) showed that students can go a little faster than their inclination without appreciable loss in learning. Teaching machines seem to be more expensive and less flexible than printed texts without increasing effectiveness. Branching programmes have been criticized on the grounds that they are not fundamentally different from linear ones (Stones, 1967), that only a small proportion of the branches are ever used (Senter et al., 1966), that they do not contain significantly more remedial material (Kaufman, 1964), and that when explanations are substituted for remedial loops students learn as much in less time (Biran, 1966; Biran and Pickering, 1968). Most of all, although programmes could be used to teach complex problem-solving, the commendable desire to make a topic easy to understand frequently led to a purely expository approach. In particular, originality and powers of criticism are objectives that are not easily achieved by programmed learning; yet these are major objectives of post-secondary education.

The Social Element in PSI Provides an Exception

The relevance of programmed learning to the major purposes of post-secondary education lies in its spin-off innovations. The most popular of these is the 'Keller plan' of 'PSI' (a 'Personalized System of Instruction'). In this method the course is split into units of roughly one week's duration, students are given assignments which may include reading, problem-solving, laboratory work or any other activity, and they then report to a senior student (a 'proctor') for a test which usually contains about 10 questions, including one requiring a discursive answer. Each student discusses his answers with the proctor. This is like a tutorial in which they are both learning. Students whose answers attain a satisfactory level are given the next assignment and may at times be permitted to attend lectures. Those whose performance is below this level are given advice and may retake the test after further study. Members of the teaching staff are available for consultation, and they monitor students' progress.

The Keller plan contains elements of self-pacing, rewards following testing, active learning and frequent feedback. The steps are smaller than in typical university courses examined once a year, but students have the freedom to work through their assignments using skipping, skimming or any other style they choose. Testing is not so frequent as to be irritating. More important, there are opportunities for social contact with other students in discussion of work, problem-solving and critical enquiry. All kinds of thought may be taught and the method is generally popular. Furthermore, compared with traditional methods, the Keller method is at least as effective, if not more so (Sherman, 1974). It is therefore a major exception ot the generalization heading this section. Yet it is important to note that it is an exception precisely because of its social, interactive element, and that this consists of thoughtful discussion focused on problem-solving.

The Unproven Value of Tape-slide Teaching

There has been remarkably little research on the effectiveness of tape-slide programmes. Pullon and Miller (1972) reported that it was slightly more effective than traditional teaching in a biological laboratory. Goodhue (1969) and others have shown that laboratory work can be completed in less time with fewer errors when tape-slides are used as reference material. At Harvard students of haematology welcomed the method when it included multiple-choice questions.

The method has all the advantages of other self-pacing techniques, and tapes can easily be modified and brought up to date. They could release staff from formal teaching and increase their contact with students. It is likely that this is crucial to their effectiveness.

The Relevance of Computers is an Unfulfilled Promise

So far computer-assisted instruction (CAI) has been a disappointment. The term 'CAI' is vague. The 'assistance' may consist of the presentation of questions and information, the provision of immediate knowledge of students' perform-ance, carrying out routine calculations, bibliographic searches and demonstra-tions, the production of complex data for use as examples, and the conduct of games or simulations. The largest of the Carnegie Reports on Higher Education is on 'the instructional uses of the computer' (Levien, 1972), but it concentrates more on costs than effectiveness.

McKeachie (1969) quotes five studies giving apparently favourable evidence for CAI compared with traditional methods of teaching. (Unfortunately, all the references were omitted from his bibliography.) In Britain £2 million has been spent on CAI, and although there has been much talk of evaluation, no tangible results have yet been published. It seems unlikely that CAI adopting linear or branching programmed learning techniques will be any more successful than programmed learning itself. Indeed, it is hard to see any psychological reason why CAI should be more *effective* than other methods, but it could be more efficient, particularly when there are large numbers of students, unchanging courses and other favourable conditions. It is too early to say that CAI is irrelevant, but it can be said that its relevance has not yet been demonstrated.

Some Reservations

However, it must be said in defence of innovations in teaching that even if it was true that they have not been successful in the past, this says nothing about the future. The failure of previous innovations does not constitute an argument against new methods in teaching. It is possible that innovations lead to an all-round improvement in teaching because of the thought and effort they generate. In any case, it has only been argued that the greater effectiveness of innovations has not been *demonstrated*. The reasons may lie partly in the difficulty of demonstration rather than the merits or demerits of the methods compared. For example, experimental comparisons of teaching methods are impossible to control (Bligh, 1974; Beard *et al.*, 1976). The proportion of variance attributable to teaching methods may be very small. Reliable and valid tests are extremely difficult to construct. Furthermore, experimental measures frequently assume that students' test scores will increase in a linear fashion with improvement, whereas a threshold model may be more appropriate. At either side of certain critical levels of difficulty, test questions may be too easy or too difficult to show difference between teaching methods. Scores on these questions may cloud genuine differences which would be statistically significant if only questions between these levels were considered. As in medical practice and musical performance, where there are large numbers of interacting variables and individual differences, teaching is an art which may be informed rather than governed by scientific demonstration.

Conclusion

Within the scope of this section only a limited number of teaching 'innovations' can be briefly considered. We have concentrated on a few methods that make presentations. It is, of course, logically possible that there are presentational innovations not considered here which, in addition to the Keller plan, do achieve the major purposes of post-secondary education. If so I am unaware of them. The possibility is unlikely, because all that presentation methods can present is information (including, perhaps, the information that someone else has certain attitudes, motives or thoughts) and all students can acquire is that information. Their own thoughts, feelings and motives are processes or dispositions internal to them. I have argued elsewhere (Bligh, 1972) that changes in these things require active methods of learning such as discussion, not passive reception as in lectures or other presentational methods.

Innovations relevant to the major objectives of post-secondary education are social, not informational, in character. There have been few innovations of this kind. It is part of the argument of the next section that education has too often been conceived as a process of presentation and communication rather than a social process of elicitation.

3. INNOVATIONS IN THE SOCIO-EMOTIONAL METHODS AND CONTEXTS OF TEACHING HAVE BEEN NEGLECTED

This section argues that the objectives achieved by post-secondary education depend primarily upon the social experiences of its students. Students' dropout and degree of success depend primarily on social factors in their college experience. Consequently, the most relevant innovations involve the use of small groups.

Social Innovations are Relevant to Student Dropout and Success

In most countries students enter post-secondary education with the intention of completing a degree or diploma course. (In the USA this is frequently not true, but research quoted from that country in this section includes only students who had this intention.) If students drop out, they fail to achieve their aim. The theme here is that the causes of dropout are primarily social and that some innovations relevant to achievement of students' initial aims are therefore social in nature as distinct from being narrowly academic. They are concerned with the relation of students to other people and their self-adjustment, rather than their relation to academic subject matter.

It is, of course, true that academic difficulties and failure are common causes of student dropout, but they are not the most common causes and they are frequently only the symptoms of underlying social problems. A recent report by Astin (1975) shows 'poor grades' as only the fourth most commonly cited cause, boredom, financial difficulties and family problems being more frequent. The poor correlation between students' failure and their intelligence, scholastic aptitude and other measures of ability has suggested (Miller, 1970) that other factors influence academic performance, so that grades are easily overrated as a primary cause of student dropout and even this fourth ranking may flatter their importance, Clearly students need some ability to succeed, but the level required is not as high as is commonly believed. Miller has reported that students with IQs as low as 105 gained degrees, and some university scientists have surprisingly low IQ scores. It has been found repeated by that academic success is not very closely related to intelligence test scores (e.g. Entwistle, 1974; Schwartzman et al., 1961; Vernon, 1963).

Factors mentioned by students as sources of difficulties at college include 'social isolation', inadequacy or remoteness of teaching staff, difficulty in budgeting between work and social interests, too much travelling time, financial problems and living at home with parents (Malleson, 1959). Study difficulties included poor concentration, and one may suspect that the causes of this frequently lie in anxiety over personal relationships (see Blaine and McArthur, 1961). Difficulties in settling down to work and doubts about vocational choice were important findings by other researchers (see, for example, Miller, 1970; Astin, 1975). Miller has reported a study by Merrill (1964) showing that students who drop out come from relatively less harmonious families with less stable relationships. They were less flexible in their patterns of study and less likely to seek academic help from tutors or other teaching staff. Students from rural backgrounds find the adjustment to university life in urban areas more difficult than other students (Janzen and Hallworth, 1973). It is a fairly general finding that students from lower socio-economic groups have a higher rate of dropout. (See, for example, Brockington and Stein, 1963; Furneaux, 1963; Feldman and Newcomb, 1973; and a review of research in Miller, 1970.) The central point here is that certain social factors are necessary to ensure that students complete their courses. The major purposes of post-secondary education cannot be completely achieved if they do not. This is not to say that the degree of success with which these purposes are achieved varies with the social factors. The factors are necessary but not sufficient conditions. The purposes are not achieved for over 10 per cent of students. Relevant innovations will achieve them.

The point is an educational counterpart of Herzberg's two-factor theory. The causes of student failure are not the reverse of the determinants of success. The former are social factors, the latter cognitive. The most important variables related to academic success are motivational. Even some of these, such as the desire for recognition and prestige within a college value system, are social in origin; but not all. A student's interest in his subject could be pursued at the expense of satisying social desires, but even here his interest is most reliably initiated and cultivated through personal interaction. As will be argued in the next section, the innovations required to give students recognition and to generate their enthusiasm in a subject have an interpersonal element in a way that visual aids, programmed learning, computer aided learning and so on do not. Similarly, there is reason to believe (Entwistle, 1974) that the degree of academic success is related to how students organize their work. There is no one right way to do this. They need advice individually or in small groups. Thus, innovations to raise the level of success, require changes in the social organization of post-secondary education, and it is to some of these we should now turn.

The Most Relevant Innovations Involve Small Groups

So far in this section it has been argued that the factors affecting dropout from post-secondary education are mostly related to the students' social conditions, particularly personal relationships. The extent to which students succeed is related to their motivation. Thus it is the socio-emotional context of their lives which appears to be most influential.

Insofar as the major purposes of post-secondary education are to do with the students' thinking, it seems reasonable to suppose that the most relevant influences, and hence the most relevant innovations, will relate to cognitive factors. There is no conflict here.

The innovations most needed in post-secondary education are those which require students to think and learn, and which provide the socio-emotional support for them to do so.

It has been argued elsewhere (e.g. Bligh, 1972; Bligh *et al.*, 1975) that teaching methods involving discussion in small groups are the most effective for developing patterns of thought, attitudes and motivation. To psychologists this is not news; and the mass of evidence need not be repeated here. The literature on psychotherapy is a testimony to the influence of discussion on attitudes, emotions, motivation and other aspects of personality. Gestalt psychologists emphasized the importance of perceiving relations between ideas; discussion can provide this. Post-war experiments on attitudes have shown the power of groups (see, for example, Hovland *et al.*, 1953). Carl Rogers, Asch (1951), Abercrombie (1965), Klein (1961; 1965) and many others have described student-centred groups and their effects on thinking. The effect of groups has been described by anthropologists. A large part of sociology would not exist if members of groups did not come to share common beliefs and attitudes. Hence the power of group methods to achieve the major objectives of post-secondary education described in section 1 does not need to be re-argued here. What are required are innovations in its use. One recent book describes the use of buzz groups, brainstorming, horseshoe groups, case-study method, syndicate method, group tutorials, seminars, free group discussion, group counselling, sensitivity groups and other methods (Bligh *et al.*, 1975), but these are only a fraction of many potential methods.

Groups may be organized, composed and motivated in various ways. The tasks they are given may be infinitely varied. There is a need for much greater enterprise in varying these characteristics.

It is not the purpose of this chapter to propound new methods of group teaching, but it may relate common practice to our present knowledge. Learning groups in post-secondary education frequently (1) consist of students all at the same stage (2) in the same subject who (3) meet with a tutor (4) at a predetermined hour (5) for a fixed length of time (6) to discuss a prearranged imposed topic (7) prepared individually (8) from the same sources and (9) with the dominant motive of fear—fear of being judged. Of course, the organizational and historical reasons for this are fairly clear, but current ideas in psychology and sociology might lead us to encourage diversity in group composition (1)(2)(8), spontaneous expression of thoughts and feelings (9), a mutually supportive group climate (7)(8)(9), and the evolution of group norms by consensus (4)(5)(6), groups small enough to enjoy personal interactions (1) (e.g. by eye contact) and democratic styles of leadership (3). In short, innovations relevant to the major purposes of post-secondary education lie in the way people meet and talk to each other. They require a change in attitudes, away from an authoritarian paternalism and towards the relaxed laughter that comes when people work together on a common task.

CONCLUSION

This chapter is an appeal to remember that education should be a humane process. The modern pressures of economics, institutional size, student competition and teacher publications can squeeze out the human touch, and make interpersonal innovations desirable.

The essential point is that the deficiencies in post-secondary education will not be remedied by television and computers. Nor will such deficiencies be greatly affected by curriculum reform; student representation on academic committees will have little effect; and they are even less likely to be overcome by amalgamating geographically separated colleges to form vast polytechnic or multiversity institutions. The solutions are simpler, cheaper, more human and, usually, very local in character. Their local nature makes them impossible to detail. The most relevant innovations in teaching lie in the development of new forms of group work. But some of the most pertinent innovations do not lie in teaching *methods* at all. They consist of thoughtful techniques such as rearranging chairs in a classroom to form a circle; the provision of coffee at suitable times where staff and students can meet spontaneously; giving students praise, recognition and reassurance when due; being willing to admit ignorance; but, most of all, a change in the attitude of many teachers.

Here they face a dilemma. They cannot teach students to be self-motivated and to think independently without questioning authority. If students are to question authority, this will include the authority of teachers. This is distasteful to teachers, first because it undermines their academic prestige, position and power, and second because they feel they need these things for classroom management. This requires a degree of honesty and openness between teachers and students which only interaction can bring.

REFERENCES

Abercrombie, M. L. J. (1965). *The Anatomy of Judgement*, Hutchinson, London.

Asch, M. J. (1951). 'Non-directive teaching in psychology; an experimental study', *Psychological Monographs*, **45**, 1.

Astin, A. W. (1975). *Preventing Students from Dropping Out*, Jossey Bass, New York.

Beard, R. M., Bligh, D. A., and Harding, A. G. (1976). *Research into Teaching Methods in Higher Education*, 4th edn., Society for Research into Higher Education.

Belson, W. A. (1952). 'An enquiry into the comprehensibility of "topic for tonight",' BBC Audience Research Department, Report No. LR/5 1080. 56pp. Cited in *Council for Cultural Co-operation 1966, European Research in Audio-Visual Aids, Part 2 Abstracts*, published by Council for Europe.

Belson, W. A. (1959). 'The effects of television upon the interests and initiative of adult viewers', BBC. 11pp. Cited in *Council for Cultural Co-operation 1966, European Research in Audio-Visual Aids, Part 2 Abstracts*, published by Council for Europe.

Biran, L. A. (1966). 'A comparison of a scrambled sequential presentation of a branching programme', Research Report on Programmed Learning No. 9, National Council for Programmed Learning, University of Birmingham, England.

Biran, L. A., and Pickering, E. (1968). 'Unscrambling a herring bone: an experimental evaluation of branching programming', British Journal of Medical Education, 2, 213.

Blaine, G. B., and McArthur, C. C. (Eds.) (1961). Emotional Problems of the Student, Appleton-Century-Crofts, New York.

Bligh, D. A. (1972). What's the Use of Lectures?, 3rd edn, Penguin, Harmondsworth.

Bligh, D. A. (1974). 'Are varied teaching methods more effective?', Ph.D. Thesis, University of London.

Bligh, D. A., Ebrahim, G. J., Jaques, D., and Piper, D. W. (1975). Teaching Students, Exeter University Teaching Services.

Bloom, B. S. (1956). Taxonomy of Educational Objectives: Cognitive Domain, Longmans.

Brockington, F., and Stein, Z. (1963). 'Admission, achievement and social class', University Quarterly, 18, 52.

Chu, G. H., and Schramm, W. (1967). Learning from Television: What the Research Says, Stanford Institute for Communication Research.

Craig, G. D. (1956). 'A comparison between silent and sound films in teaching', British Journal of Educational Psychology, 26, 202.

Daines, J. W. (1962). 'Report of an investigation into the Associated Rediffusion Series entitled "The Story of Medicine", 1960–1961', University of Nottingham Institute of Education. Cited in Council for Cultural Co-operation 1966, European Research in Audio-Visual Aids, Part 2 Abstracts, Published by Council for Europe.

Daines, J. W., and Neilson, J. B. (1962). 'Discovering Science' (a report on an investigation into the BBC series), Nottingham Institute of Education.

Daines, J. W., and Neilson, J. B. (1963 a). 'Report of an investigation into the Associated Television series "Theatres and Temples of the Greeks"',' Nottingham Institute of Education. Cited in Council for Cultural Co-operation 1966, European Research in Audio-Visual Aids, Part 2 Abstracts, Published by Council for Europe.

Daines, J. W., and Neilson, J. B. (1963 b) 'Report on a television investigation "Romeo and Juliet" Associated Television', Nottingham Institute of Education. Cited by Council for Cultural Co-operation 1966, European Research in Audio-Visual Aids, Part 2 Abstracts, Published by Council for Europe.

Dwyer, F. M. (1971). 'An experimental evaluation of the instructional effectiveness of black and white and coloured illustrations', Didakta Medica, The Pennsylvania State University, Philadelphia.

Entwistle, N. J. (1974). 'Sylbs, Sylfs and Ambiverts; labelling and libelling students', Inaugural lecture, University of Lancaster.

Feldman, K. A., and Newcomb, T. M. (1973). The Impact of College on Students (two volumes), Jossey-Bass, San Fransisco.

Francis, W. L. (Chairman) (1963). 'Report of a working party', Department of Scientific and Industrial Research, HMSO, London.

Frank, R. E., and Lesher, R. E. (1971). 'An evaluation of the effectiveness of taped lectures-in a community college setting', Scientia Paedagogica Experimentalis, 8, No. 1, 16.

Furneaux, W. D. (1963). 'The too few chosen and the many that could be called', in P. Halmos (Ed.), Sociological Studies in British University Education, Sociological Review Monograph No. 7, University of Keele.

Gallegos, A. M. (1968). 'Experimental pacing and student pacing of programmed Instruction', Journal of Educational Research, 61, 339.

Gessner, F. B. (1974). 'An experiment in modified self-paced learning', Engineering Education, 64, No. 5, 368.

Goodhue, D. (1969). 'Tape-recorded lectures with slide synchronisation. A description of the method', Journal of Biological Education, 3, No. 4, 311.

Hirst, P. H. (1965). 'The logical and psychological aspects of teaching', in R. S. Peters (Ed.), The Concept of Education, Routledge & Kegan Paul, London, pp. 40–60.

Hovland, C. I., Janis, I. L., and Kelley, H. H. (1953). *Communication and Persuasion*, Yale University Press.

Janzen, H. L., and Hallworth, H. J. (1973). 'Demographic and biographic predictors of writing ability', *The Journal of Experimental Education*, **41**, No. 4, 43.

Kaufman, R. A. (1964). 'The systems approach to programming', in G. D. Ofiesh and W. C. Meierhenry (Eds.), *Trends in Programmed Instruction*, Papers from the National Society for Programmed Instruction and the Department of Audio-Visual Instruction Conference, 1963.

Klein, J. (1961). *Working with Group*, Hutchinson, London.

Klein, J. (1965). *The Study of Groups*, Routledge & Kegan Paul, London.

Laner, S. (1954). 'The impact of visual aid displays showing a manipulative task', *The Quarterly Journal of Experimental Psychology*, **6**, No. 3, 95.

Leith, G. O. M. (1969). 'Programmed learning in higher education', in D. Unwin (Ed.), *Media and Methods*, McGraw-Hill, New York.

Leith, G. O. M., and Buckle, C. F. (1965). 'Mode of response and non-specific background knowledge, Interim technical report, National Centre for Programmed Learning, School of Education, Birmingham.

Levien, R. E. (Ed.) (1972). 'The emerging technology: instructional uses of the computer in higher education, A Carnegie Commission on Higher Education and Rand Corporation Study. McGraw-Hill, New York.

McKeachie, W. J. (1969). *Teaching Tips: A Guidebook for the Beginning College Teacher*, D. C. Heath and Co., Lexington, Mass.

Malleson, N. B. (1959). 'University student, I Profile 1953, A study of one year's entry to university College London', *Universities Quarterly*, **13**, No. 3.

Merrill, K. E. (1964). 'The relationship of certain non-intellective factors to lack of persistence in higher ability students and persistence of lower ability students', University of California, Berkeley. Ph.D. thesis University of California, cited in *Dissertation Abstracts* No. 25, 3939, and in G. W. Miller (1970), *Success, Failure and Wastage in Higher Education*, Harrap.

Miller, G. W. (1970). *Success, Failure and Wastage in Higher Education*, Harrap.

Moore, D. (1967). 'Group teaching by programmed instruction', *Programmed Learning and Educational Technology*, **4**, No. 1, 37.

Perrott, E. (1975). *Microteaching*, Society for Research into Higher Education.

Peters, J. M. L., and Scheffer, M. C. J. (1961). 'Onderzoek naar het gebruik van audio-visuele hulpmiddelen buj het technisch onderwijs' (Research into the use of audio-visual aids in technical education), Den Haag.

Peters, R. S. (1966). *Ethics and Education*, Unwin University Books.

Pirkheim, F. (1961). 'Preparing a classroom film by showing of wall charts', SHB Film-Post Wein No. 89, 12 pp. Cited in *Council for Cultural Co-operation 1966 European Research in Audio-Visual Aids, Part 2 Abstracts*, Published by Council for Europe.

Popham, W. (1961). 'Tape-recorded lectures in the college classroom', *Audio-Visual Communication Review*, **9**, 119–128

Postlethwait, S. N., Novak, J., and Murray, H. T. (1964). *An Integrated Experience Approach to Learning*, Burgess, Minneapolis.

Pullon, P. A., and Miller, A. S. (1972). 'Evaluation of method of self-teaching laboratory Portion of pathology', *Journal of Dental Education*, **36**, No. 11, 20, cited in *Society for Research into Higher Education Abstracts*.

Schneider, W. (1954). 'Horerlebnis und akutstische Anschauung' (Listening and auditory attention), Film Bild Ton, IV, Munchen, 5 pp., in *Council for Cultural Co-operation 1966 European Research in Audio-Visual Aids, Part 2 Abstracts*, Published by Council for Europe.

Schwartzman, A. E., Hunter, R. C. A., and Prince, R. H. (1961). 'Intellectual factors and academic performance in medical undergraduates', *Journal of Medical Education*, **36**, 353.

Senter, R. J., *et al.* (1966). 'An experimental, comparison of an intrinsically programmed text and a narrative test', Final Report No. AMRL-TR-65-227, Aerospace Medical Research Labs., Wright-Patterson, AFB Ohio, USA, cited by C. J. Lawless (1969), 'Programmed learning in the developing countries of Africa', *Programmed Learning and Educational Technology*, **6**, 189.

Sherman, E. (Ed.) (1974). *PSI: 41 Germinal Papers: a Selection of Readings on the Keller Plan*, W. A. Benjamin, California.

Simon, J. (1961). 'Apport de la prjection animee a l'expression ecrite de l'enfant (Contributions of annimated films to written expression of the child)', *Bulletin du Centre Audio-Visual*, R. 18.

Snyder, W. V., Greer, A. M., and Snyder, J. (1968). 'An experiment with radio instruction in an introductory psychology course', *Journal of Educational Research*, **61**, No. 7, 291.

Stones, E. (1967). 'Strategies and tactics in programmed instruction', In M. J. Tobin (Ed.), *Problems and Methods in Programmed Learning*, The Proceedings of the 1967 Association for Programmed Learning and the National Centre for Programmed Learning Birmingham Conference.

Vernon, M. D. (1946). 'Learning from graphical material', *British Journal of Psychology*, **36**, Part 3, 145.

Vernon, M. D. (1952). 'The use and value of graphical methods of presenting quantitative data', *Occupational Psychology*, **26**, 22 and 96.

Vernon, M. D. (1954). 'The instruction of children by pictorial illustration', *British Journal of Educational Psychology*, **24**, 171.

Vernon, P. E. (1963). 'The pool of ability', in P. Halmos (Ed.), *The Sociological Review Monograph No.* 7, University of Keele.

Weiss, M. B., Berg, C. R., and Probst, C. O. (1971). 'Programmed self-instruction of dental techniques; a pilot study', *Journal of Dental Education*, **35**, 455, cited in *Society for Research into Higher Education Abstracts*.

Wright, P. (1961). 'The use of questions in programmed learning', *Programmed Learning and Educational Psychology*, **4**, 103–107.

14

THE OPEN UNIVERSITY AS A FORUM FOR THE IMPLEMENTATION OF NEW APPROACHES TO LEARNING

Peter Morris

What follows is a personal evaluation of the Open University's teaching system. The Open University has an excellent Institute of Educational Technology whose staff are concerned with providing advice on educational techniques. They know far more than I do about the technical innovations that have been and will be attempted by the course teams of the University. However, my main intention is not to catalogue new teaching methods, nor to either advertise or denigrate the Open University teaching system. Rather, I want to present the thoughts of someone who has prepared courses both in the Open University and in conventional universities. I want to describe both the problems involved in teaching several thousand students whom you will never meet, and the advantages produced.

THE OPEN UNIVERSITY SYSTEM

By now, so many people have studied an Open University course that it is probable that the reader knows someone who is or has been an Open University student. Few can by now have failed to see an Open University TV programme and there must be many who, like me, are every so often annoyed by having to change from VHF to medium wave when Open University radio programmes come on the air. However, unless you have yourself been a student or a member of the Open University full-time or part-time staff you may well be ignorant of the full range of teaching media that are used by almost every Open University course. A brief review may therefore be helpful.

Each Open University course is taught over a period of almost a year, beginning in February and ending with examinations in November. A course which in theory requires 10–12 hours work per week by the average student leads to a full credit, while one requiring half as much work leads to a half credit. Students must accumulate six credits for an ordinary degree and eight for an honours degree.

A full credit course is usually divided into 30+ units, each unit a week's work. As part of each unit there will be a correspondence text, probably a radio programme and possibly a TV programme. Frequently the course is divided into blocks containing several units and the correspondence texts for the block are published together in one volume. For example, in the *Introduction to Psychology* course (a half credit course with 16 units) there are five blocks, two example titles being 'Approaches and Methods' and 'Psychometrics'. Within the Psychometrics block there are three units titled 'The construction of tests', 'The use of tests' and 'A theory of personality'.

For each block there will probably be a separately published Study Guide with notes on the TV and radio programmes and continuous assessment questions. There are two sorts of continuous assessment. One sort, known as Tutor Marked Assignments (TMAs), which are usually in the form of an essay, are marked by the student's part-time course tutor. The other, which are multiple choice in nature, are known as Computer Marked Assignments (CMAs) and are, as the name implies, marked by computer.

The number of assignments varies from course to course, but a full credit course will commonly have 8 TMAs and 8 or more CMAs. Common, but nor universal, are specially published readers to accompany the course, Home Experimental Kits for science subjects, and gramophone records. Students are also expected to attend several tutorials during the year in the local Study Centre with their part-time tutor. Finally, for some courses, there are week-long Summer Schools held on university campuses where, in an intensive programme of events, an effort is made to provide teaching situations that are impossible in other circumstances.

THE COURSE TEAM

Each course is prepared by a course team. The idea of a team rather than an individual preparing and being responsible for a course is one of the unusual features of the Open University system. If you were to enter a well-attended course team meeting you might be surprised by the number of people there. There would be the chairman and several other academics, whose job is to write the correspondence texts and present the TV and radio programmes. However, the academics whose names appear as authors might be a minority of those present. Several other academics would be there in an advisory capacity, as representatives from related course teams. There would almost certainly be a staff tutor. He or she supervises the activities of part-time course tutors in one of the 13 regions into which the country is divided. Staff tutors provide the course team with vital first-hand information on what part-time tutors can or cannot do, and, more importantly, what students want and think. The meeting would also include a representative of the Institute of Educational Technology who can advise on teaching techniques. Already it will be clear that many people are involved in the course production, but those so far mentioned may account for only half of the full course team. The complete team might also include two or three BBC producers, one or two course or research assistants with the arduous job of administering the day-to-day assembling of the course, a designer to advise on illustrations and layout, and an editor. While it would be rare for everyone to be present at any one meeting, most meetings would include a majority of those mentioned above.

PROBLEMS IN DESIGNING AN OPEN UNIVERSITY COURSE

So far I have described the Open University teaching media and the people responsible for preparing courses. It will be clear already that the organization and teaching methods of the Open University differ in several ways from those of a conventional university. The reasons for the differences are the problems involved in teaching at a distance.

The essential problem facing the Open University course team is how to write a course which will accomplish what is normally achieved through lectures, seminars, tutorials and practicals as well as through directed reading. But what is normally achieved.? At a conventional university students arrive with some or no prior knowledge of the subject which they are to study. After three or four years they are tested by examinations on a variety of skills and their knowledge about the subject that they have acquired during those years. Some of their activities during the time have led to them acquiring the knowledge. However, it is very unlikely that anyone has tried to describe in detail the skills that should be acquired for any particular academic discipline. This is partly because of the rapid changes that take place in each discipline, and partly because for teaching purposes in a conventional university it is not necessary to specifically state what these skills are, so long as the staff can recognize instances of them, and know what activities will teach them to their students. However, since the Open University must use different methods, it is more important that the skills to be taught should be clearly defined so that alternative teaching techniques can be developed. But specifying these skills is difficult. For most disciplines it is probably fairly easy for an academic to define the pieces of factual information that a student should know. In setting and marking examination papers the teacher draws on his intuitions concerning this pool of knowledge and the range of skills. However, while factual knowledge may be easy to specify, few would place factual knowledge as the most important possession of the successful finals students. They most certainly need to know many facts and theories, but they must be able to go beyond rote retention and demonstrate higher-order skills. They must be proficient in the analysing and synthesizing skills of the discipline. It is for these skills that examiners search the scripts of examinees.

There is no doubt that students learn these skills through the teaching techniques and in the educational environment of the conventional university. Are they acquired by listening to lectures, by taking part in seminars, or by interchange and discussion with other students? Probably in all these and many other different ways. The Open University student can easily be provided with the equivalent of lectures, but seminar situations are not so easy to simulate, and the debate over coffee that may be a common feature of a keen student's life at a conventional university can occur only infrequently for the Open University student.

The Open University course team, therefore, has to tackle the preparation of the courses with little help from knowledge of what and how to teach acquired at other universities. Yet, this may not be so great a disadvantage as it might seem. To a considerable extent the skills to be taught will depend on the purpose for which the course exists, while the teaching methods are determined by the situation. It may be an advantage to be able to start uninhibited by earlier analyses and ask just what an Open University student doing such and such a course ought to know. We do know something about the variables that influence learning. Perhaps the Open University can use its resources to teach at least as well, or better, than the conventional university.

THE DESIGN OF A SPECIFIC COURSE

There are all rather abstract considerations. More will be gained if we examine the planning of an actual course. The Open University system of course team planning encourages a questioning of what should be taught. Each course team will set about its planning in its own way, and, although I have had experience of several course teams at work, most of my time was occupied with preparation of the *Introduction to Psychology*, half credit course. This particular team had the benefit of John Annett's experience with planning programmed instruction. I do not want to claim that the course is especially good. The very limited time available for preparing this particular course meant that much of the actual writing was hurried, and the individual unit planning may not be too pleasing in retrospect. However, a good deal of serious thought concerning what students ought to know and be able to do by the final examination went into the design of the course.

We began by asking ourselves about the purpose and place of the course. At the most general level, what could students hope to gain from studying it, and what could we hope to achieve? Clearly we could provide only an introduction in a half credit course. For some students the course had to serve as a basis for future higher-level study in psychology, whilst for others it provided a single experience of psychology, perhaps a twelfth or less of the total work in their degree, which might range across many of the disciplines represented at the Open University. The course needed both to convey to one group of the students what psychology is about and to make a start in training another group of the students to be psychologists. When the dual needs of the course had been recognized, other decisions about the nature of what was to be taught followed. If it was necessary to give students who may take no more psychology courses a flavour of the subject, then neither an historical nor a very wide-ranging but low-level course would be suitable. The student would want to know what psychologists do *now* and why, rather than what they did once. The implication of this is that certain topics needed to be tackled in detail, while the reasons for the differing approaches of qualified psychologists should be explained.

Since the decision on the nature of the course lay with the course team rather than one individual as is commonly the case in conventional universities, it is likely that more thought than is usual was put into the overall framework of the course. At times grandiose designs were mooted. My mental picture of the development of psychology resembles the graphs of evolutionary development of the different divisions of the animal kingdom, which expand and contract across time as they map the development and decline of trilobites, dinosaurs and so on. Similar graphs can be drawn for psychology, with introspectionism, behaviourism, information processing and so on beginning with small numbers, expanding to their heydays, and then contracting. Such graphs were drawn in that planning stage as the possibilities for the course were mulled over. Could a course be designed around common recurrent questions such as the heredity/environment debate? Eventually the present structure was adopted. It consists of an introductory block describing the range of psychology and some early approaches; a block on psychometrics which concludes with a fairly detailed examination of Eysenck's personality theory; a block on behaviourism which sketches its development, the findings of research on learning, and applications in behaviour therapy and programmed instruction; a block on human information processing dealing with perception, memory and skills; and a final block in which intelligence and accidents are considered from the three standpoints that were described earlier.

The course as it finally appeared had several features which distinguish it from of introductory course. Much has been left out or dealt with only in a peripheral way, but the student is taken in detail into some of the important issues and areas of psychology. What is of interest here is that the design of the course emerged as a result of considerable discussion and consultation between the members of the course team and that it was planned 'from the top downwards', beginning with the central purposes of the course and developing from there.

There can, of course, be disadvantages in having several individuals involved in course planning. Progress can be delayed if personalities clash or if there is basic disagreement about the purpose of the course and the material that is relevant, and this has happened in some Open University courses. Clearly, much depends on the skill of the chairman and the good nature of the team members. The major advantage is that the skills, experience and viewpoints of several people can be drawn on to mould the course.

CONSTRUCTING THE CORRESPONDENCE TEXTS TO ENCOURAGE LEARNING

The actual writing of the correspondence texts and the radio and TV scripts is, and probably must be, an individual affair. A committee can help by commenting, suggesting, criticizing, but the production of the drafts of the teaching texts must obviously be the work of individuals, usually writing in their own homes. Of course, the quality of the course will depend not only upon the written texts, but also upon the BBC programmes and the activities of the students in response to them.

The greatest difficulty facing an Open University student is his isolation from others studying the same course. There is no one to discuss with, no one to ask questions of, no one to see when further explanation is required. As I said earlier, exactly when and how learning takes place in the conventional university setting is not well understood, but enough is known about the memory processes to suggest strategies in organizing teaching material. Considerable research (see Tulving and Donaldson, 1972, for a review) has demonstrated the importance of organization in learning. Where subjects are presented with information to be learned which is organized so that it exploits their previous knowledge, then their recall far exceeds that of subjects who are shown the same material but randomly arranged (Bower, 1970). Where subjects can find a way of organizing apparently random information their learning is much improved (Morris and Stevens, 1974). Therefore one of the objectives in designing teaching material must be to provide a clear organization which can be used by the student.

In recent years there has come a realization that the activity of the subject in a memory experiment has considerable consequences for the amount that he or she will remember later. In my earlier chapter on learnings strategies (chapter 7) I dealt in greater detail with this issue. Several experiments (e.g. Mazuryk and Lockhart, 1974; Craik, 1973) have demonstrated that when subjects actively attempt to use the information that they are given meaningfully, although over a short period they may remember slightly less than a subject who has simply rote-repeated what he has to learn, at later tests they will retain far more. For long-term retention it is necessary for subjects to draw upon past knowledge and semantically encode what they experience. To achieve for maximum degree of learning it is necessary to actively involve the learner in the material. Such active involvement is one of the fundamental functions of seminars and tutorials, but these are the teaching media which are least available to an Open University student. However, as I shall shortly describe, it is possible through the style of the correspondence text to encourage active involvement.

In fact, the lack of contact with teachers and other students can be counterbalanced in a variety of ways. First, the success of the learning process depends upon the activity of the students themselves. Whilst situations can be devised to increase the likelihood of active mental manipulation of the material to be learned, nothing within the teacher's command can be guaranteed to motivate an apathetic student. But few if any Open University students are apathetic. They are all highly motivated, otherwise they would not be paying hundreds of pounds of their own money to obtain a degree, nor spending most of their spare time over several years in studying. There is the potential already available for active learning. Secondly, the author of an Open University correspondence text has some control over the behaviour of the student. At a conventional university the staff have little certainty of the appropriateness of the lecture notes taken by their students. They can recommend reading, but cannot be sure whether it will be read, let alone in what order and what detail. Only in seminars can they make students fully aware of what they do not know or have failed to learn. Further, there are always problems in finding suitable readings to recommend. In contrast, the Open University author is preparing his own reading for the student. He can tell the student in advance his aims and object-ives, and in the text he can direct the student to read from the set books, perhaps only a page or two, before returning to the text. Since the student can be assumed to own the set books, it is possible to direct his thinking and reading far more sensitively than in the conventional situation.

When one begins to write correspondence texts there is a tendency to produce booklike, continuous, scripts, and some texts are of this form. However, the opportunity exists for writing a text fitted to the special readership. For example, a unit from a correspondence text for the *Introduction to Psychology* course contained the following which distinguish it from an ordinary textbook: (a) a list of important terms and concepts used in the unit; (b) a brief study guide; (c) a list of the set book readings that would be required as part of the unit work; (d) a list of objectives, 15 in number, which define what the student should be able to do having completed the unit; (e) wide margins for notes; (f) questions with 'student stoppers' between question and answer; (g) side-headings identifying paragraphs in which important terms are defined; (h) mini-experi-ments and examples to be carried out; (i) an end-of-unit set of self-assessment questions on the main points covered in the unit.

An examination of this list makes the general philosophy apparent. First, the object is to make as clear as possible to the student what is expected of him and to help him to concentrate on the learning without unnecessary distractions. An active approach to the text is encouraged and a means of evaluating per-formance is provided. Finally, an attempt is made to make revision as straight-forward as it can be. Through these techniques it is hoped that some of the disadvantages related to the lack of direct contact with teaching staff can be overcome.

Especially important are (d), (f) and (i). Let us consider each in turn a little more deeply.

First (d). In few conventional universities are students clearly told what they should be able to do and at what level. Open University students are informed that by the end of the unit they should be able to 'discuss' some topics, 'describe' others and merely 'illustrate' some others. Here help is being given to answer the question 'What should I know?' or 'What should I revise?' Such statements of objectives would probably benefit all learner's, but the Open University student is at an especial disadvantage to the ordinary student. It is normally a good policy to take lecture topics as defining a course. Further more, the manner in which he treats each topic may give hints about what the lecturer considers important. Such hints are lacking at the Open University, where the correspondence texts resemble a combination of lecture, seminars and readings, with TV and radio programmes providing supplementary teaching. A clear statement of objectives is necessary to replace the lecturer's tone of voice!

Next (f). Questions during the text should encourage the student to use the new information that has just been acquired. Hopefully, this will lead to deeper coding and longer retention. However, the momentum and inertia of reading is such that given a question it is tempting to skip on immediately to the answer, and it is impossible to prevent this, but it is possible to make it less easy. This is done by breaking the text between question and answer with some horizontal pattern that arrests the eye and reminds the student that he should think before jumping on. In the *Introduction to Psychology* course the 'student stopper' was two horizontal coloured lines, but some other courses have used more elaborate and wider patterns.

Finally (i). Having read a long text it is difficult to know what you have gained from it unless there is a chance to test yourself. Many students fool themselves that they know all about a course because they have passively read through their notes once or twice and recognized the material. Recall is almost always more difficult than recognition. The provision of questions at the end of the unit text also allows the student to check whether he has fulfilled the objectives given at the beginning. For example, an objective of the unit on memory is: 'Describe how research on free recall of categorized material demonstrates the importance of organization in the long term memory'. One self-assessment question is: 'How would you arrange the following list of words to improve their recall? ash, dove, tree, lawyer, sparrow, profession, elm, doctor, oak, skylark, architect, beech, bird'. In answering that question the student will make use of knowledge about experiments on organization that he has read earlier, and will go a long way towards satisfying himself that he can meet the objectives that have been set. It is just as important to boost the student's confidence that he is achieving what is required as it is to draw his attention to limitations in what he has learned from his earlier studies. Self-assessment questions are also useful at revision time, when they allow the student to test his memory of the unit without having to read through the text, and avoiding the recognition-but-not-recall trap mentioned earlier. With the approach of the examination it is especially important to give the student confidence in his learning and abilities.

SET BOOKS AND READING TIME

As he works through the correspondence text the student will sometimes be directed to read a section from one of the set books. These books have been chosen because they can be purchased for a reasonable price, and because they provide material suitable for the course. Often publishers recognize the Open University set book status with special notices on the cover. There is a danger that the unsuspecting bookshop browser will assume that an Open University set book has received some sort of seal of approval, but this is not always the case. A book may be recommended because it puts forward a point of view that will be critically examined in the correspondence text. It might not be recommended to be read on its own.

The officially recommended reading from the set books may often be quite limited in length. This is because the amount of reading involved per unit is calculated and usually controlled. Since it is assumed that the student will work for 10–12 hours on each unit, only a limited amount of reading can be set. The suggested basis for estimating the amount of time that the average student will spend reading is to presume that they will work at a rate of 50 words per minute. This sounds a very slow rate to those who recall that the common reading rate is several hundred words a minute. However, the low figure takes into account time for more than one reading, time for answering questions, and so on.

On this basis it would appear that students should be able to read 30,000 words in each unit. However, this is still an overestimate, since within the 10–12 hours for study have to be included time for listening to radio programmes, watching TV programmes and completing course-work assignments. Having reduced the time available to allow for these, there is probably little time for more than 20,000 words of prescribed reading.

Although we are probably only too well aware of the limited amount of time that we have ourselves for reading, I am not sure that the average university and college teacher is as sympathetic to the time limitations on his students as he is to those on himself! It is easy when teaching a course to recommend a vast quantity of reading which you believe to be necessary for a proper grasp of a subject. However, a few calculations might help to modify this enthusiasm. For example, a student taking the second-year psychology course at Lancaster University spends two-thirds of his time studying the psychology components of the course. If we expect the average student to work for 39 hours a week, then 26 of these will be given to psychology. Of these, almost 10 hours a week will be taken up by direct teaching, leaving four hours a week to spend in preparation for each of the four main courses. Even if there are no essays to be prepared during that week, it is unreasonable, on the basis of the Open University estimate of reading speed, to expect more than 12,000 words to be read if the material is at all challenging. While this figure may be lower than necessary, since the student will find fewer exercises and questions in the reading than the Open University student will find in a correspondence text, it is probably not far out. The student will probably have to read some parts more than once, and should be taking notes. With 500 words to a page in a normal-sized text this comes to just 24 pages! Of course diligent students will read more, and lazy students will claim that they do not have time to read even this much. However, I suggest that courses should be planned with the average student in mind, with plenty of provisions made for the keener student.

The Open University system is convenient in being such that realism about how much students can read is made more acceptable by the flexibility of the correspondence text. It is possible to say 'Now read pages 1 and 2 of X' and then continue, assuming that the student has done so. Set books and correspondence texts can be integrated in a way that is impossible in the normal lecture—seminar system.

ASSESSMENT

Few things concentrate the student's mind like the threat of an impending examination, but examinations are terrifying to some. The trend towards more continuous assessment during courses has therefore been to the advantage of both staff and students, since it carries into the teaching year some of the motivation of assessment, while allowing the student to build up a good record to have behind him when he enters the examination. The Open University divides assessment equally between continuous assessment and examination.

As mentioned earlier, the continuous assessment takes two general forms. One is tutor marked, the other marked by computer. The TMA offers the flexibility of a human marker and it is possible to vary the activity required of the student. Sometimes the TMA may require a straight-forward essay, but at other times the student might be asked to summarize the results of a home experiment. Less conventional are the Computer Marked Assignments, CMAs. The student is provided with a set of multiple-choice questions and answers and records his choice on a computer card by pencilling in a circle representing the chosen answer. Batches of the cards can be rapidly marked by the University's computer, so that Computer Marked Assignments are far cheaper than those marked by tutors.

Considerable flexibility in the marking schemes for CMAs have been developed, and some academics have become adept at exploiting the multiple-choice format. For example, by asking 'Which of the following was *not* given as a criticism by X?' the student is required to find out all the criticisms that X did give. Multiple-choice assessment is, however, arduous for the person preparing the questions, and there are problems in identifying the difficulty of any question. This is just one of the feedback problems that I shall consider in more detail later.

For the student, the CMA offers the opportunity to consult with others, and such consultation is encouraged by the University. Although at first some students feel that they are cheating by talking over the questions with fellow students, it is just this sort of discussion which is so valuable for learning and so difficult to arrange within the Open University system. I have a strong impression that Open University students are far more cooperative in their learning than are students at conventional universities. Where possible, self-help groups form and several students gather together to talk over their current difficulties and ideas. I have rarely met such cooperation at ordinary universities. The disadvantages of isolation plus the feeling that in such a big organization one is not in competition with one's neighbour seem to help the Open University students to become academically cooperative.

The Open University examinations are often like those of any other university. However, the concentration upon objectives at the design stage of the course should have implications for this final assessment stage. The objectives should include a summary of the skills expected of students, and these skills should be evaluated in the examination. The conventional essay has its place, but there are additional ways of testing the skills of the examinees. For the *Introduction to Psychology* course we had decided at an early stage that one of the higher-level objectives was that the student should acquire the ability to criticize a badly designed and badly interpreted experiment. During the examination, therefore, one part of the paper required criticism of a brief report of an imaginary experiment in which mistakes of various sorts had been made in the selection of subjects, experimental material, interpretation of graphs, and so on. Different levels of sophistication in criticism can be catered for if the report of the imaginary experiment is carefully constructed. Such a direct test of the analytic abilities of the student provides evidence which is easily compared from one candidate to the next and which does not rely on such abilities showing themselves voluntarily in the answers to less specific questions.

TELEVISION AND RADIO

I have said little so far about the television and radio components of the courses. This may seem strange, since at one time the Open University was to be 'The University of the Air'. While the TV and radio programmes are the Open University activities which most frequently catch the public attention, for the Open University student they are a valuable but supplementary part of the course. It is not possible to assume that all students will be able to see or hear the programmes, and it would therefore be unfair to examine material only presented on radio or TV. Although an Open University course would survive the removal of its BBC programmes, much would be lost. The Open University student would otherwise have little opportunity to see expensive experimental equipment, experiments with animals, and other demonstrations which can easily be mounted in an ordinary university. Thanks to TV the student can discover what the authors of the correspondence texts look like. Because radio programmes are relatively easy to produce, one way of making the course more human, while helping with unforeseen difficulties, is to include programmes made as late as possible. These late-made radio programmes allow a few students to question the lecturers directly on parts of the course which they found confusing or controversial. The answers are probably useful to most of those taking the course. The TV makes possible home experiments which could not otherwise be performed. For example, in part of one programme for the *Introduction to Psychology* the TV is used as a pursuit rotor. A circle of light is tracked around the screen with a photoelectric cell which records time on target on the counter-timer with which every student is supplied in the Home Experimental Kit. The resources of radio and television also make stimulating experiences possible for the Open University student which are not available in the conventional course. There can be lectures and discussions by famous experts and films of situations unobservable by a class of students. I will give just two examples of the latter from the *Introduction to Psychology* course. One involved using an outside broadcast unit which made it possible to film the everyday goings on in a token economy ward of a mental hospital. The second used careful film editing to illustrate vividly the separate ballistic and controlled components of movement when pegs are transferred from one hole to another. The dramatic effect of seeing these things for oneself cannot be acquired from a verbal discription, or any graph.

THE PROBLEM OF LACK OF FEEDBACK ON COURSE CONTENTS

In what has gone before I have concentrated upon the advantages provided by the Open University system. Where problems have been considered, they have been the problems of the student trying to understand the course in isolation from the teaching staff and other students. However, an account of the Open University teaching system would be incomplete if the major problem facing the academic preparing an Open University course was not discussed. This problem is one of feedback upon the course that he is giving.

In conventional universities many lecturers complain that they get little to guide them from the faces and behaviour of their lecture classes. However, given the opportunity there are usually students who will demand further clarification of difficult points. It is possible to find out a lot that is wrong and sometimes a little that is right in discussions with tutorial groups or student representatives. Once problems have been recognized steps can be taken to put them right and to compensate in later teaching. There is a feedback loop, with information on the teaching being used to modify later teaching.

At the Open University such modification in the light of the problems of students taking the course is rarely possible, because the course is almost completely written before the first parts are received by the students. Some adjustments can be made, but only of a crude sort. Parts of the course can be made optional, and special radio programmes may be provided to help clarify difficult sections, but such options are only open on a few occasions. There is no chance for fine tuning, as there is when a lecturer stops to explain a confusing concept. At first sight it may come as a surprise that courses are produced so far in advance, but there are two simple reasons. First, every word of the course has to be written, rather than spoken from notes, and every word must then be printed. As anyone who has tried it knows, writing a chapter on some topic takes far longer than it takes to prepare a lecture on the same topic. It takes several weeks to prepare the first draft of a unit, and many more before the final revisions have been made and the editor can take over. Then printing takes considerable time, and the printed texts must be ready well in advance of the mailing day so that they can be collated with the other material to be sent to the student. There are not only correspondence texts to be written, but TV and radio programmes to be planned and made, study guides to be written,

CMAs and TMAs to be set, Summer Schools to be designed, home experiments to be tested, and so on. It is impossible for course writing and course presentation to overlap to any extent.

For the unit author this is a severe problem, and especially so for those preparing their first course. A student may fail to understand a crucial passage in the text. If so, there may be no alternative to which he can turn. On the other hand, if every point is spelt out in elaborate detail many readers will soon be bored. Three sources of advice are available to the author. One is the other members of the course team, the second is the external academic assessors who review each text, the third is a small sample of prospective students who read and comment up on each unit. Each member of the course team receives a copy of each draft of the correspondence text, which they read, comment upon and return to the author. Similar comments come from the academic and the student assessors, so that when the time comes to revise the draft the author will have comments, often in detail, from 10 to 20 different people. In the light of these he can rewrite the manuscript. Since the academic assessors are usually well-known experts in the field covered by the text, the accuracy of the material is safeguarded. However, it is difficult to be sure that the comments of the course team and student assessors fully sample the behaviour of prospective students. The student assessors who attempt each unit are usually busy on other courses and financial limitations restrict their numbers to a handful. Course team members may be too familiar with what is being taught to spot potential problem passages for naive learners. Once a test has been printed it is expensive to revise, and is intended to last for four years. Oversights that do slip through the initial assessment may be perpetuated. Students and tutors often inform the central staff of mistakes, but rectifying these is difficult and expensive where not impossible. For example, The *Introduction to Psychology* course has 1,500 students, so that the cost in postage alone of a notification of an error sent to each student would be £100. That is before taking the cost of paper, printing and envelopes into account, let alone the staff to supervise the addressing, printing and mailing. It is much cheaper to avoid such difficulties when writing the initial text.

It is a feature of the Open University that mistakes, when they occur, are much more likely to be noticed than are mistakes made by lecturers who have no permanent record taken of their teaching. The Open University course texts are marketed and the TV and radio programmes can be seen or heard by anyone. The Open University is open in more senses than just its freedom from entrance requirements.

DEGREE STRUCTURE AND COUNSELLORS

In 1975 the Open University was offering over 70 courses. To study some of the higher-level courses it was necessary to have completed lower-level prerequisite courses, but, even with this limitation, the range of options open to the Open University student is enormous. Students must complete the required number of courses, but which courses are chosen depends upon them. It is therefore possible to specialize in some discipline (although there may never be enough courses to provide the specialization of a single honours degree at a conventional university) or to select courses which interest the particular individual. Courses are written at different levels, foundation level, second level, third level, and possibly, in the future, fourth level. The course credits required for a degree must come in part from the higher-level courses to ensure that the student develops academic skills. He cannot obtain a degree by merely dabbling at a low, introductory level in a lot of areas. The hope is that graduates of the Open University will have received a higher education, in a wide range of topics, which may be more appropriate to later employment than the specialized degrees normally obtained at conventional universities. It is also possible that out of combinations of courses may come experts on the integration of the findings and techniques of several disciplines.

This optimism may be well founded, but I must admit to a lingering suspicion that there are some important academic skills which cannot be taught until the student is brought to the 'growing edge' of the discipline and must himself face the problems of the researcher on whose efforts the contents of the discipline are based. Some Open University courses achieve this level of sophistication, but with limitations on the numbers of courses in any particular discipline there will always be a conflict between depth and breadth of coverage. Adequate breadth of cover may preclude study in depth.

Each student is faced with the complex network of choices all leading to a degree. To aid in the choice of appropriate schemes of study the Open University has employed several full-time and many part-time counsellors to advise students on courses that will suit their particular interests, abilities and aspirations. The counsellors will also advise on methods of study as well as helping students faced with non-academic problems which may interfere with their study. The Open University Courses Handbook describes the role of Counsellor at the University as unique and says that it should not be compared with counsellors in other fields of education. Certainly, given the complexity of course choice and the problems of part-time adult education, the Open University counsellor has an important, valuable role to play.

EVALUATION OF THE OPEN UNIVERSITY SYSTEM

I have described some of the distinctive features of an average Open University course. In this final section I shall consider some possible criticisms of the Open University mehtods.

Central to the Open University system is the extensive course planning that takes place, partly necessitated by the need to teach so many students at a distance. As I said earlier, a lecture may take only hours to produce, but a correspondence text takes several months. However, even if the amount of planning at the Open University is initiated by the problems of the teaching situation, it is maintained and extended beyond the minimum set by these constraints by a real belief that carefully constructed courses are worthwhile. Is this true?

I hesitate to involve myself in the debate between those educational technologists who firmly believe in the desirability of specifying what is to be taught and those teachers who feel that their activities are directed towards some open-ended goal that cannot be captured in a list of objectives. I will, however, risk the following comments. First, teachers must have some principles for selecting course contents and some idea of what a good student should be able to do. There is nothing to be lost in trying to identify what these principles are, since only those that are recognized can be evaluated by the teachers themselves. Secondly, since few would deny that teaching involves the development of skills over and above the acquisition of 'facts', the clear definition of these skills is at least a first step towards the development of methods for teaching them more successfully. Thirdly, it does not necessarily follow that the recognition of an explicit statement of those objectives will lead to poorer development of those undefined skills dear to the hearts of the opponents of directed teaching. Unforeseen beneficial results are just as likely as 'spin off' from teaching designed to fulfil specified objectives as they are from less directed teaching. Finally, some people may worry about the degree of control, and the implication that the writers of objectives think they know what is 'good' knowledge. Should not students be allowed the freedom to select, and browse and discover for themselves? Yes, those that want to should. But where students want to learn about a subject in the quickest and most direct way, planned courses should be provided. For most Open University students there is no opportunity for self-tuition since they do not have access to a sufficiently well-stocked library. Nor have they opted into the Open University system to be told to teach themselves. Many feel that they have lost several years and now want to learn the facts and skills of their chosen courses as quickly as possible.

Another contentious feature of the Open University system is the basis of course preparation. It is debatable whether the advantages of several persons collaborating on a course outweigh the loss of academic freedom involved for the teacher who no longer has the right to teach just what he wishes. The Open University system could not function otherwise, but perhaps with the greater ease of course preparation and presentation in conventional universities one individual may be able to present a more integrated course.

There is no simple answer, since so much depends on the nature of the particular course and the personalities of the collaborators. A course with wide coverage beyond the expertise of one individual obviously needs a team effort. However, a series of lectures or an Open University correspondence text may be best planned by one person who can know his own overall plan without having to state it explicitly or argue each stage.

What can conventional higher education establishments gain from the experience of the Open University? For one thing, a recognition of the wide range of methods available for encouraging learning. Secondly, an incentive to ask what they are teaching, and why. The Open University system has developed to deal with the difficult problem of teaching at a distance, and many of its solutions may not be relevant to the conventional teaching situation. However, some may be. That is for the teaching staff in the more traditional establishments to evaluate for themselves.

REFERENCES

Bower, G. H. (1970). 'Organizational factors in memory', *Cognitive Psychology*, **1**, 18.

Craik, F. I. M. (1973). 'A "Levels of Analysis" view of memory', in P. Pliner, L. Krames and T. M. Alloway (Eds.), *Communication and Affect: Language and Thought*, Academic Press, New York.

Mazuryk, G. F., and Lockhart, R. S. (1974). 'Negative recency and levels of processing in free recall', *Canadian Journal of Psychology*, **28**, 114.

Morris, P. E., and Stevens, R. (1974). 'Linking images and free recall', *Journal of Verbal Learning and Verbal Behavior*, **13**, 310.

Tulving, E., and Donaldson, W. (1972). *Organization of Memory*, Academic Press, New York.

AUTHOR INDEX

283

288

SUBJECT INDEX